Guitar for Songwriters

Leo Cavanagh

Cengage Learning PTR

CENGAGE Learning
Professional • Technical • Reference

Australia • Brazil • Japan • Korea • Mexico • Singapore • Spain • United Kingdom • United States

Guitar for Songwriters
Leo Cavanagh

**Publisher and General Manager,
Cengage Learning PTR:** Stacy L. Hiquet

Associate Director of Marketing:
Sarah Panella

Manager of Editorial Services:
Heather Talbot

Senior Marketing Manager: Mark Hughes

Product Manager: Orren Merton

Project/Copy Editor: Cathleen D. Small

Technical Reviewer: Greg Utzig

Interior Layout Tech: MPS Limited

Cover Designer: Mike Tanamachi

Indexer: Sharon Shock

Proofreader: Gene Redding

© 2015 Leo Cavanagh.

CENGAGE and CENGAGE LEARNING are registered trademarks of Cengage Learning, Inc., within the United States and certain other jurisdictions.

ALL RIGHTS RESERVED. No part of this work covered by the copyright herein may be reproduced, transmitted, stored, or used in any form or by any means graphic, electronic, or mechanical, including but not limited to photocopying, recording, scanning, digitizing, taping, Web distribution, information networks, or information storage and retrieval systems, except as permitted under Section 107 or 108 of the 1976 United States Copyright Act, without the prior written permission of the publisher.

> For product information and technology assistance, contact us at
> **Cengage Learning Customer & Sales Support, 1-800-354-9706.**
>
> For permission to use material from this text or product,
> submit all requests online at **cengage.com/permissions**.
>
> Further permissions questions can be emailed to
> **permissionrequest@cengage.com**.

All trademarks are the property of their respective owners.

Cover images © lem/Shutterstock.com and © YKh/Shutterstock.com.

All other images © Leo Cavanagh unless otherwise noted.

Library of Congress Control Number: 2014937103

ISBN-13: 978-1-305-11670-2

ISBN-10: 1-305-11670-4

Cengage Learning PTR
20 Channel Center Street
Boston, MA 02210
USA

Cengage Learning is a leading provider of customized learning solutions with office locations around the globe, including Singapore, the United Kingdom, Australia, Mexico, Brazil, and Japan. Locate your local office at: **international.cengage.com/region**.

Cengage Learning products are represented in Canada by Nelson Education, Ltd.

For your lifelong learning solutions, visit **cengageptr.com**.

Visit our corporate website at **cengage.com**.

Printed in the United States of America
1 2 3 4 5 6 7 16 15 14

I am most fortunate in having Paul and Elizabeth Cavanagh as my parents. They were always supportive and encouraged curiosity and hard work. This book is dedicated to them and to all who have shared their time, knowledge, and love.

Acknowledgments

I have been extremely fortunate to have had many great teachers in my life, both in and out of music. They include Joe Wagner, my first guitar teacher, who was the best inspiration a young guitarist could have. There are also Dave Froehlich, who made theory come alive, and George Barnes and Jackie King, who were so generous in sharing their knowledge from years of playing experience.

About the Author

Leo Cavanagh is a guitarist and teacher living in the San Francisco Bay Area. Besides leading a jazz quintet performing his original compositions, he has composed and performed music for the Napa Valley Shakespeare Festival and transcribed the music for the songbooks of former Monkee Michael Nesmith and bluegrass musician Peter Rowan. He appeared at the Healdsburg Guitar Festival and with Arthur Fiedler and the San Francisco Pops Symphony. He is the author of *Beyond Power Chords*. He recently released *Leo Cavanagh and the Ellington Project*, a recording of his arrangements of the music of Duke Ellington for acoustic jazz trio.

Contents

Introduction xii

Chapter 1 The Basic Chords: Major, Minor, and Seventh   1

The Basic Major Chords for Guitar 2
The Basic Minor Chords for Guitar 4
The Basic Seventh Chords for Guitar 6
Exercises Mixing Major, Minor, and Seventh Chords 8

Chapter 2 I, IV, and V   11

Exercises with I, IV, and V Major Chords. 13
    I-IV-V-IV 13
    I-IV-I-V 14
    I-V-IV-V 15
I, IV, and V in Minor 16
    Im-IVm-Vm-IVm 16
    Im-IVm-Im-Vm 17
    Im-Vm-IVm-Vm 18
I, IV, and V with Seventh Chords 19
    I7-IV7-V7-IV7 20
    I7-IV7-I7-V7 20
    I7-V7-IV7-V7 21
I, IV, and V with Mixed Chord Types 22

Chapter 3 The Harmonized Scale   25

Some Common Progressions Using the Harmonized Scale 28
    I-IIm-IIIm-IV 28
    I-VIm-IIm-V7 29
    I-IIIm-IV-V7 30
    I-I7-IV-IVm 31
The Harmonized Scale in Minor Keys. 33
Some Common Progressions in Minor Keys 34
    Im-IVm-♭VI-V7 34
    Im-♭III-IVm-V7 34
    Im-♭VII-♭VI-V7 35
    Im-IVm-IIm7(♭5)-V7 36

Contents

Chapter 4 Power Chords   37

Chapter 5 Accompaniment Styles   43
Strumming 43
Muting and Accents 44
Bass Notes 46
Descending Bass Lines 47
Fingerpicking 48
     Fingerpicking Exercises: Pattern 1 48
     Fingerpicking Exercises: Pattern 2 50
     Fingerpicking Exercises: Pattern 3 52
Common Fingerpicking Patterns 53
Styles 55
     Rock. 56
     Swing 56
     Reggae/Ska 56
     Country 57
     Latin 57
     Blues 57

Chapter 6 Bar Chords Part I: The Basics—Major, Minor, and Seventh Chords in All Keys   59
Form 1 Bar Chords with the Root on the Sixth String 60
     Major 61
     Minor 61
     Dominant Seventh. 61
Form 1 Bar Chord Diagrams 62
     Major 62
     Minor 62
     Dominant Seventh. 63
Getting Comfortable with Bar Chords 63
Form 1 Bar Chord Exercises 64
Muting 67
Form 2 Bar Chords with the Root on the Fifth String. 68
     Major 68
     Minor 69
     Dominant Seventh. 69
Form 2 Bar Chord Diagrams 70
     Major 70
     Minor 70
     Dominant Seventh. 71
Form 2 Bar Chord Exercises 71

Contents

Form 3 Bar Chords	74
Major	74
Major	74
Minor	75
Dominant Seventh	75
Form 3 Bar Chord Diagrams	76
Major	76
Minor	76
Dominant Seventh	77
Form 3 Bar Chord Exercises	77

Chapter 7 Bar Chords Part II: Putting Them Together   81

Bar Chord Diagrams, All Forms	82
Form 1	82
Form 2	82
Form 3	82
Using Bar Chords to Transpose	82
Bar Chord Exercises Using All Forms	83
Harmonized Scale Progressions Using Form 1 and 2 Bar Chords	85
I-IIm-IIIm-IV	85
I-VIm-IIm-V7	86
Finding I, IV, and V Quickly with Bar Chords	87
Exercises with I, IV, and V7 Bar Chords in All Keys	88
I-IV-V7-IV	89
I-IV-I-V7	90
I-V7-IV-V7	91

Chapter 8 Chord Construction: How to Build Chords and Find Good Voicings   93

How Chords Are Built	93
Major Chords	94
Some Voicings of Major Chords	95
Form 1 Variations	96
Form 2 Variations	96
Form 3 Variations	96
G Form Variations	96
Minor Chords	97
Some Voicings of Minor Chords	98
Form 1 Variations	98
Form 2 Variations	98
Form 3 Variations	99
G Form Variations	99
Dominant Seventh Chords	99

Contents

Some Voicings of Dominant Seventh Chords 100
    Form 1 Variations 101
    Form 2 Variations 101
    Form 3 Variations 101
    G Form Variations 101
    Other Dominant Seventh Forms 102
Chord Voicings 102
Notes to Omit 103
I-IV Examples with Different Voicings 103
Ways to Play I-IV-V7-IV Up the Neck 106
Playing I, IV, and V in Minor Keys 109
    Im-IVm Examples 110
Ways to Play Im-IVm-V7-IVm Up the Neck 112

Chapter 9 More Chord Formulas   115

About Chord Formulas 115
Major-Type Chord Formulas 115
Major-Type Chords 116
    Major 6th (R,3,5,6) 117
    Major 7th (R,3,5,7) 117
    Major 9th (R,3,5,7,9) 117
    6/9 (R,3,5,6,9) 118
    Major 13th (R,3,5,7,9,13) 118
    Major 7th(♯11) (R,3,5,7,♯11) 118
    Major 9th(♯11) (R,3,5,7,9,♯11) 119
    Add 9 (or Add 2) (R,3,5,9) 119
Minor-Type Chord Formulas 119
Minor-Type Chords 120
    Minor 7th (R,♭3,5,♭7) 120
    Minor 6th (R,♭3,5,6) 121
    Minor 6/9 (R,♭3,5,6,9) 122
    Minor 9th (R,♭3,5,♭7,9) 122
    Minor 7th (♭5) (R,♭3,♭5,♭7) 123
    Minor 11th (R,♭3,5,♭7,9,11) 123
    Minor (Major 7th) (R,♭3,5,7) 123
    Minor 6th (Major 7th) (R,♭3,5,6,7) 124
    Minor 9th (Major 7th) (R,♭3,5,7,9) 124
Dominant Chord Formulas 124
Dominant-Type Chords 126
    9th (R,3,5,♭7,9) 126
    11th (R,3,5,♭7,9,11) 127
    13th (R,3,5,♭7,9,13) 127
    7(♭5) (R,3,♭5,♭7) 127

ix

Contents

9(♭5) (R,3,♭5,♭7,9) 128
7(♯5) (R,3,♯5,♭7) 128
9(♯5) (R,3,♯5,♭7,9) 128
7(♭9) (R,3,5,♭7,♭9) 129
7(♯9) (R,3,5,♭7,♯9) 129
7(♭5♭9) (R,3,♭5,♭7,♭9) 129
7(♭5♯9) (R,3,♭5,♭7,♯9) 130
7(♯5♭9) (R,3,♯5,♭7,♭9) 130
7(♯5♯9) (R,3,♯5,♭7,♯9) 130
7(♯11) (R,3,5,♭7,♯11) 130
9(♯11) (R,3,5,♭7,9,♯11) 130
7(♭9♯11) (R,3,5,♭7,♭9,♯11) 131
7(♯9♯11) (R,3,5,♭7,♯9,♯11) 131
13(♭5) (R,3,♭5,♭7,9,13) 131
13(♯11) (R,3,5,♭7,9,♯11,13) 131
13(♭9) (R,3,5,♭7,♭9,13) 131
7(♭13) (R,3,5,♭7,9,♭13) 131
7sus4 (R,4,5,♭7) 131
7sus4(♭9) (R,4,5,♭7,♭9) 132
13sus4(♭9) (R,4,5,♭7,♭9,13) 132
7(alt) (R,3,♭5 or ♯5,♭7,♭9 or ♯9) 132

Chapter 10 Jazz Chords and Progressions: Adding Some Spice 133
II-V-I 133
The Circle of Fifths 133
IIm7-V7 Progressions 137
IIm7-V7-IMaj7 Exercises 139
Embellishing and Substituting Chords 141
IIm7-V7-IMaj7 Substitutions 142
II-V-I in Minor Keys 146
IIm7(♭5)-V7-Im7 Progressions and Substitutions 147

Chapter 11 More Chords, Progressions, and Ideas 151
Diminished Chords 151
    Diminished Chords as Passing Chords 154
    The ♯IV Diminished Chord 155
    The Diminished Chord in Place of 7(♭9) 156
Augmented Chords 158
    Augmented Chords as Dominant Seventh Chords in a Minor Key 158
    Augmented Chords as Passing Chords 159
Embellishing or Simplifying 160
    When You Don't Know That Chord, Simplify 160
    Major-Type Chords 161

Minor-Type Chords	161
Dominant Seventh-Type Chords	161
Chords with ♯5 or ♭5	161
Suspended Chords (7sus4)	161
m7(♭5)	161
Extensions and Alterations	162
Too Many Changes	162
Moving Voices within Chords	162
Minor Chords with Moving Voices	163

Chapter 12 The Blues — 167

The Basic Blues Progression	167
Blues #1, Using Form 1 Bar Chords	168
Blues #2, Using Form 1 and 2 Bar Chords	169
Blues #3, with a Triplet Feel	170
Blues #4, with Power Chords	171
A Blues Progression with More Changes	172
Blues #5, with More Chords	172
Blues #6, with the Form 3 F Chord	173
The Blues with Dominant Seventh Chords	173
Blues #7, with Seventh Chords	174
Blues #8, with Bass Notes	175
The Blues in Minor Keys	175
Blues #9, in A Minor	176
The Minor Blues with More Changes	176
Blues #10, in D Minor	177
Another Version of the Minor Blues	177
Blues #11, in F Minor	178
Playing the Blues with Three- and Four-String Chords	179
Blues #12, with Smaller Chords	179
Blues #13, with Three-String Chords	180
Blues #14, with Four-String Chords	181
Blues #15, with Two-String Chords	182
Blues #16, with Sliding, Muting, and Bass Notes	183
The Blues and Tenth Chords	184
Blues #17, with Tenth Chords	185
Jazz Changes for the Blues	186
Blues #18, with Jazz Changes	186
Blues #19, with Anticipations	188
Another Set of Jazz Changes for the Blues	189
Blues #20, with More Jazz Changes	190

Index — 191

Introduction

The guitar has long been a favorite instrument for songwriters—portable, easy to get started on, not too loud for late-night composing, and of course great-sounding. It sounds intimate and personal accompanying a singer by itself, or it can scream and really kick a band into high gear. But the guitar can also severely limit your songwriting if you don't truly explore what it has to offer. This book is intended to help you expand your use of the guitar as a songwriter.

The basic chords—major, minor, and seventh in good guitar keys—are the first thing you'll want to learn. Before playing up the neck and playing in more difficult keys, get solid with the basics. Chapter 1 starts with the basics.

Groups of chords often appear together in many different songs. If you are aware of how chords are related to each other, you can practice those common chord changes and be more prepared for them in pieces you are playing. A large part of this book is dedicated to chord progressions—chord patterns that go together in different keys and specific forms that work well on the guitar. There is a logic to chord progressions, and knowing that logic can make it easier to come up with the sound you want. You can get a book with 57 ways to play a C chord, but it will do you a lot more good to know what chords are related to C and which version of the C chord is best to use when going to a certain version of that related chord.

The I, IV, and V chords are the most common chords in any key, and they enable you to play thousands of songs. This concept, with lots of examples, is covered in Chapter 2.

The harmonized scale is the next step in learning chord progressions. Once past I, IV, and V, the harmonized scale explores additional related chords in any key. This is the topic of Chapter 3.

Power chords (Chapter 4) have a distinctive sound that can allow you to play in many keys. Popular in a lot of rock styles, particularly with electric guitar, they are limited but easy to learn.

If you are accompanying yourself, you want to know different accompaniment styles—strumming, fingerpicking, bass notes, and more. Your left hand holds the notes, but your right hand adds the personality—loud, soft, peaceful, driving… This is the topic of Chapter 5.

Beginning guitarists usually learn "folksinger" chords—about a dozen or so chords at the end of the neck that enable you to play in a few keys. There is a limited number of these chords. To play chords such as E♭, B, F♯, or Cm, you need to use bar chords. Bar chords have no open strings, so they are movable—they can be played anywhere on the neck of the guitar. They enable you to play in any key or to insert distinctive sounds into a song already in a comfortable key. As a person who has played guitar in a lot of bands over a lot of years, I can tell you that playing in a variety of keys and chords is essential to keeping things interesting. Bar chords are introduced in Chapter 6 and studied in more depth in Chapter 7.

A songwriter should use a chord because it's exactly right, not because it's where his or her fingers are used to going. As you learn more about chord construction (Chapter 8), you can find the chord you need almost anywhere on the neck. This topic includes the notes that go into any given chord and how to find those chords all over the neck.

Chapter 9 covers more chord formulas—how to build more complex chords heard in jazz and other styles of music. Sometimes a chord may have a complex name but may not be all that difficult to hold. This chapter gets into a lot of chords with fancy names.

Jazz chords can really add some zing to your sound. These are chords that have an additional note or more in the harmony. It's like adding chocolate syrup, whipped cream, nuts, and a cherry to your ice cream. Chapter 10 puts the chords from the previous chapters into practice, applying them to common jazz progressions. It takes those progressions and looks at ways to embellish or substitute the chords to get a great jazz sound.

Chapter 11 looks at diminished and augmented chords, at how to simplify or embellish chords, and at moving voices within chords and how they can add spice to your songs.

The blues is a classic American form that has been adapted to many styles of music. The blues is not just B.B. King—it's played by Chuck Berry, the Beatles, Willie Nelson, and bands that don't even know they are playing the blues. Variations on the blues, with different chords or different beats, permeate much of American music.

Because the blues form is so adaptable, I use it in Chapter 12 to tie everything together. There are 20 examples of the blues, using different chords, keys, beats, and accompaniment styles. If you can play these, you will get ideas to apply to your own songs, even if you don't use a blues progression.

> Many of the examples in this book can be heard on the website for this book (http://cengageptr.com/guitarforsongwriters), especially accompaniment styles and the blues. The guitar icon indicates an example that has an audio file on the website.

When writing a song, there are no "rules"—you can do anything you want. However, knowing about music can help you familiarize yourself with the styles of your favorite performers. You don't have to sound like any of them, but you have a path to follow that will help you find that sound you want or a path to avoid if you want something else. A teacher of mine used to say, "Control is freedom." He meant that the more control you have, the more you can do. Master your instrument, and doors will open. Don't limit your playing or your songwriting because you only know a few chords. Explore the beauty of chords, keys, and rhythms, and your songwriting capabilities will expand.

Companion Website Downloads

You may download the companion website files from http://cengageptr.com/guitarforsongwriters.

The Basic Chords: Major, Minor, and Seventh

THE MAIN TYPES OF CHORDS ARE MAJOR, MINOR, AND SEVENTH. If you become comfortable with these, it's fairly easy to go to fancier chords. A *major chord* can be indicated with a letter: C stands for the C major chord. E♭ indicates the E flat major chord. Sometimes a major chord is indicated with "Maj" or an upper case "M" after the letter. C, CMaj, and CM all mean the C major chord.

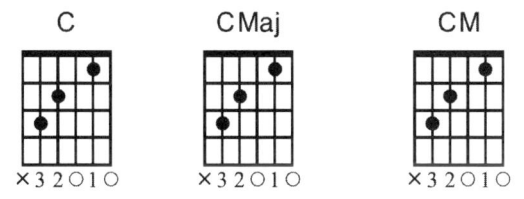

```
    C           CMaj          CM
  ┌┬┬┬┬┐      ┌┬┬┬┬┐       ┌┬┬┬┬┐
  ├┼┼┼●┤      ├┼┼┼●┤       ├┼┼┼●┤
  ├●┼┼┼┤      ├●┼┼┼┤       ├●┼┼┼┤
  ├┼●┼┼┤      ├┼●┼┼┤       ├┼●┼┼┤
  └┴┴┴┴┘      └┴┴┴┴┘       └┴┴┴┴┘
  × 3 2 0 1 0  × 3 2 0 1 0  × 3 2 0 1 0
```
Three ways of indicating the same chord.

A *minor chord* is indicated with "min" or a lower case "m" after the letter. Cmin or Cm indicates the C minor chord.

The *seventh chord* is written with a 7 after the letter. Technically speaking, it stands for the Dominant 7th chord, but most people just say "seven," unless you're a music major in college. It is written as C7. (This chord is different from the major seventh chord, written CMaj7.)

The differences between the types of chords will be explained later in this book, as well as how to find them on your own all over the neck.

Following are the easiest major, minor, and seventh chords on the guitar and some exercises to go with them. After that, we will examine which ones go together best.

Reading the Chord Diagrams:

1,2,3,4	The fingers of your left hand, starting with your index finger.
×	Try not to play this string.
o	Play this string open (no fingers).
⌒	Bar—lay your first finger flat to cover all of the indicated strings.

Guitar for Songwriters

The Basic Major Chords for Guitar

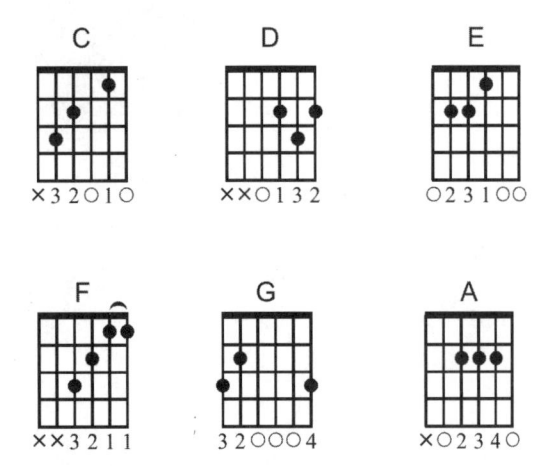

C
x 3 2 0 1 0

D
x x 0 1 3 2

E
0 2 3 1 0 0

F
x x 3 2 1 1

G
3 2 0 0 0 4

A
x 0 2 3 4 0

These are the easiest major chords to hold on the guitar. Below are some exercises using these chords. Later, we'll look at which ones are more closely related.

You can hear the next example by downloading the audio file Example01 from http://cengageptr.com/guitarforsongwriters.

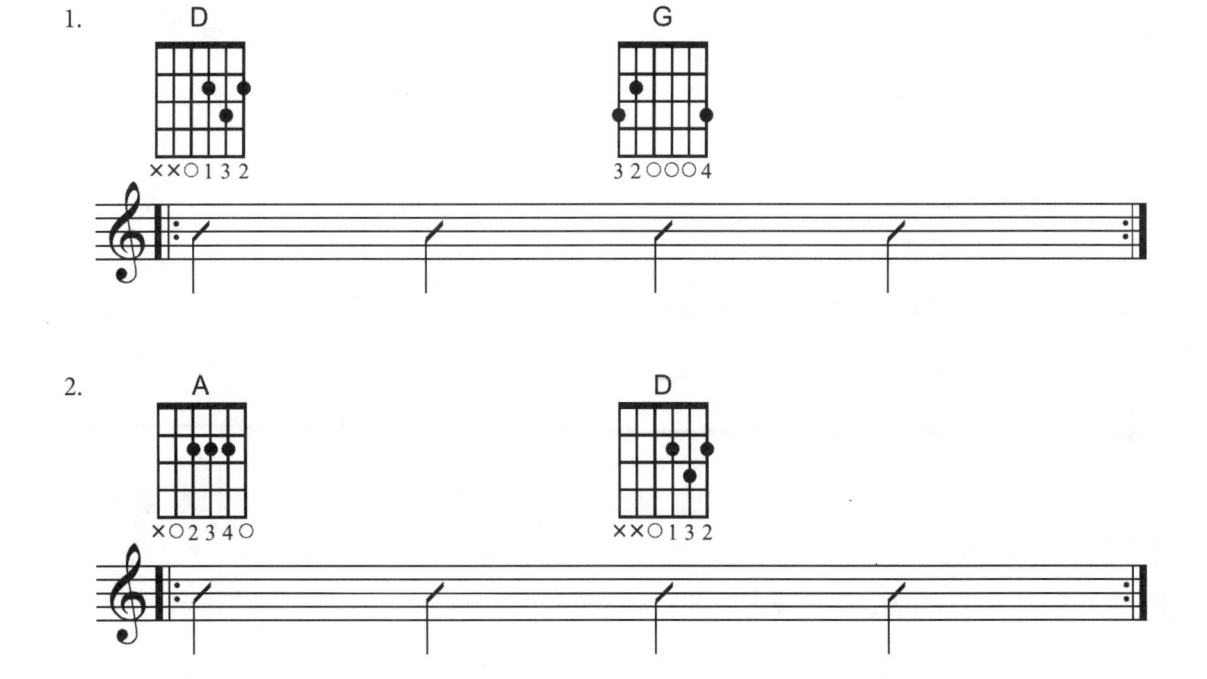

1. D
    x x 0 1 3 2

    G
    3 2 0 0 0 4

2. A
    x 0 2 3 4 0

    D
    x x 0 1 3 2

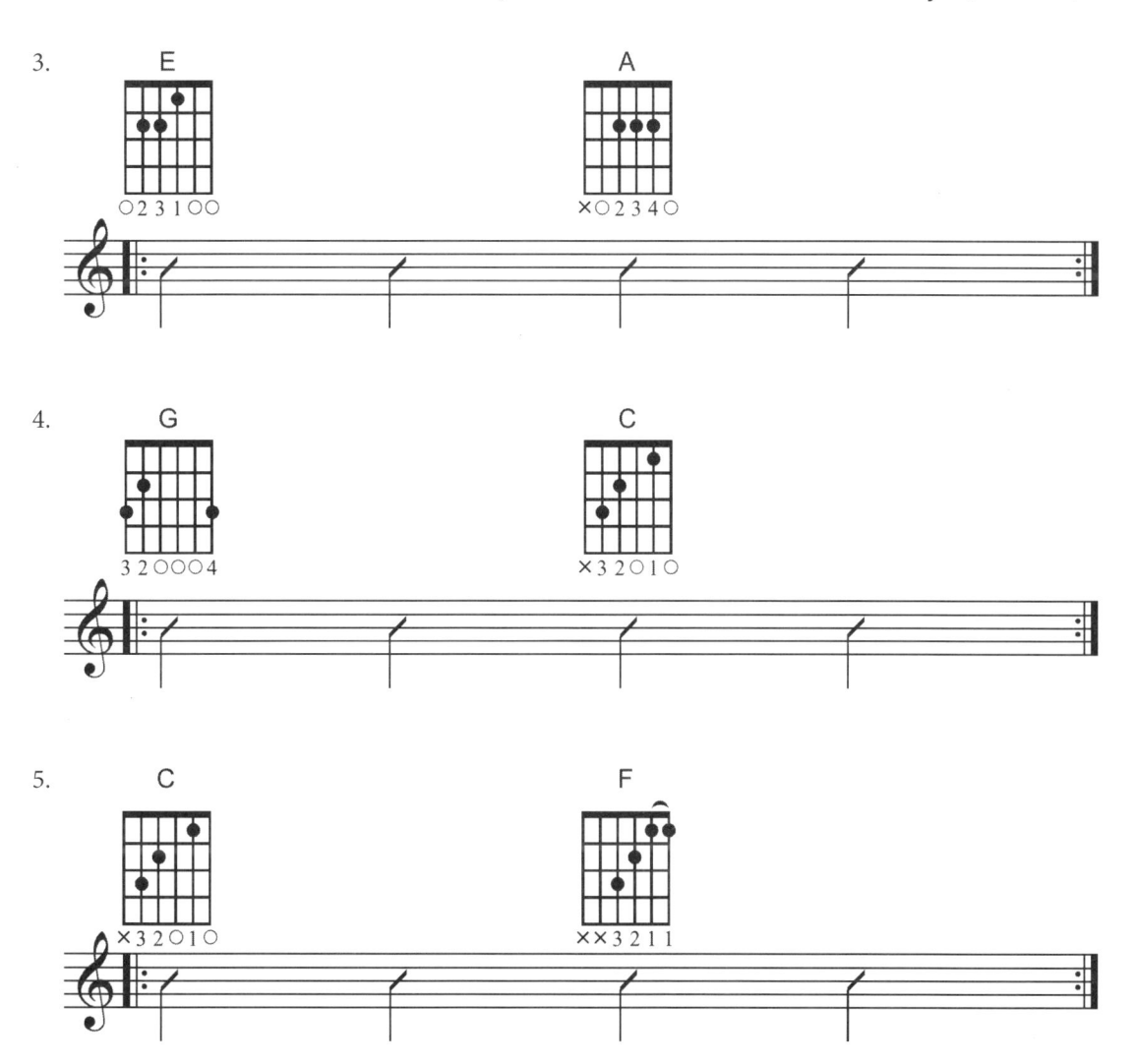

Chapter 1 The Basic Chords: Major, Minor, and Seventh

3. E   A

4. G   C

5. C   F

If the F major chord is new to you, it may take some time before it sounds good. Keep practicing it!

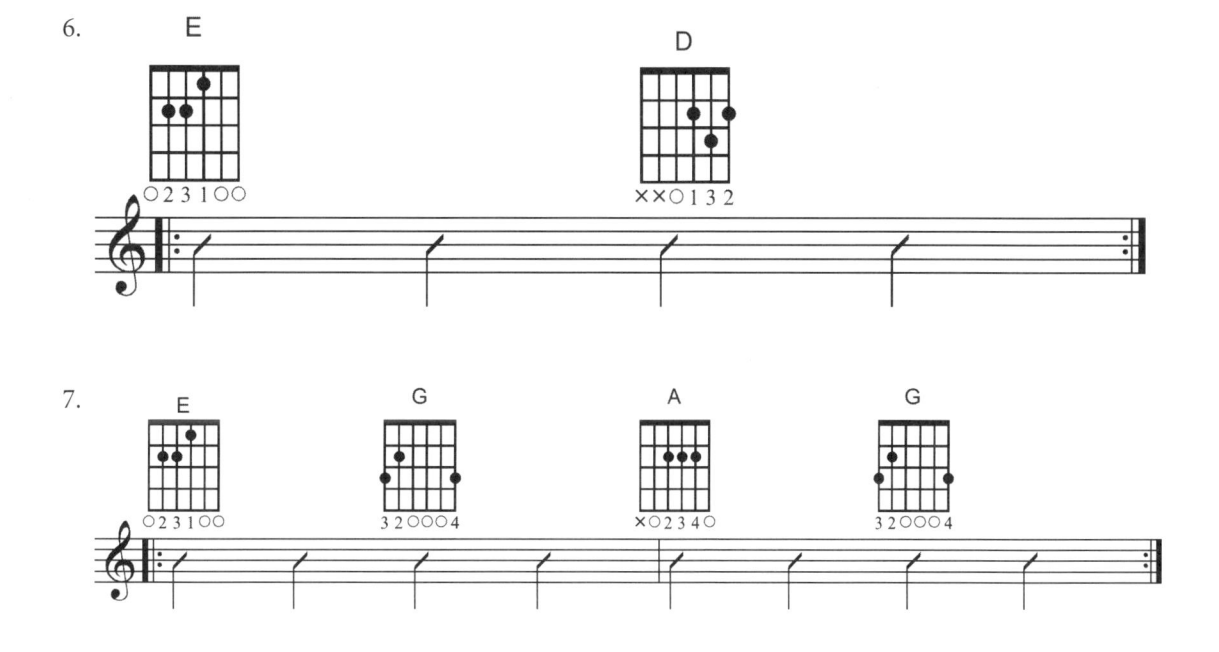

6. E   D

7. E   G   A   G

Guitar for Songwriters

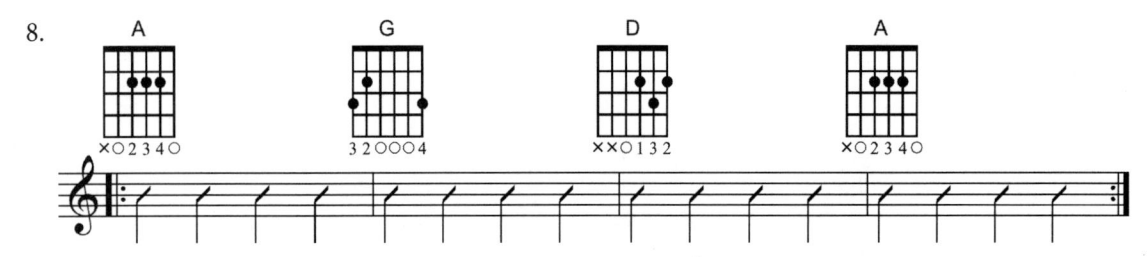

8. A   G   D   A

Played at the right tempo, this should sound like the end of "Hey Jude."

The Basic Minor Chords for Guitar

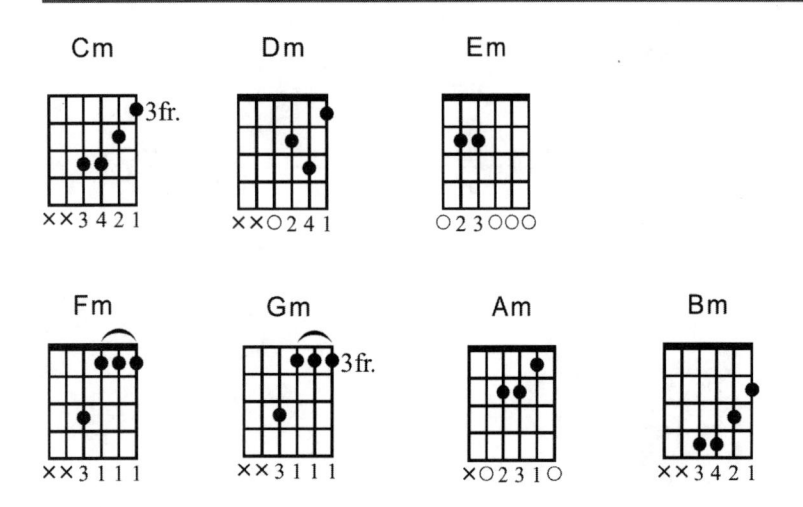

Cm   Dm   Em

Fm   Gm   Am   Bm

The following exercises use only these minor chords.

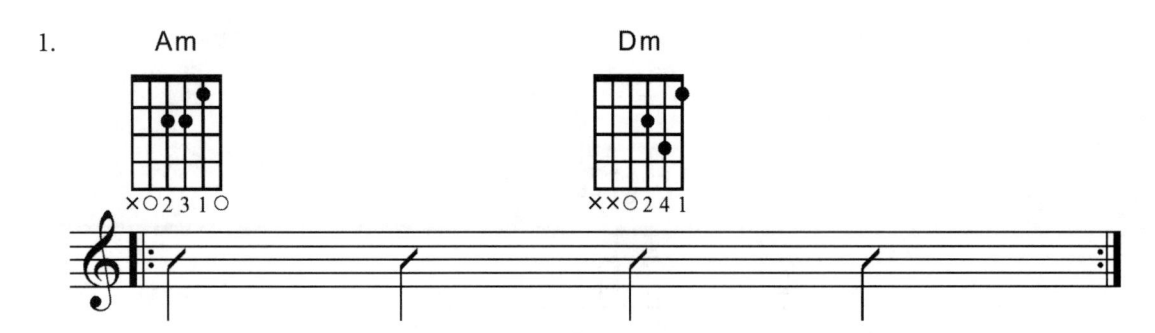

1. Am   Dm

Chapter 1 The Basic Chords: Major, Minor, and Seventh

2. Em   Am
   0 2 3 0 0 0   x 0 2 3 1 0

3. Gm 3fr.   Cm 3fr.
   x x 3 1 1 1   x x 3 4 2 1

4. Am   Bm
   x 0 2 3 1 0   x x 3 4 2 1

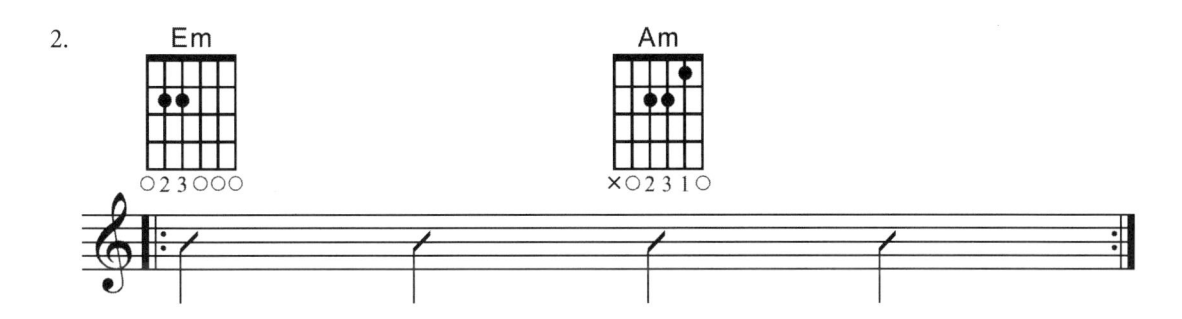

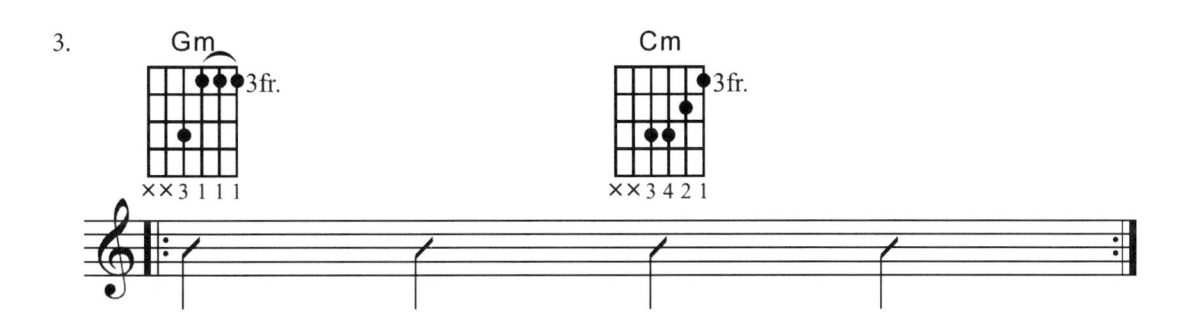

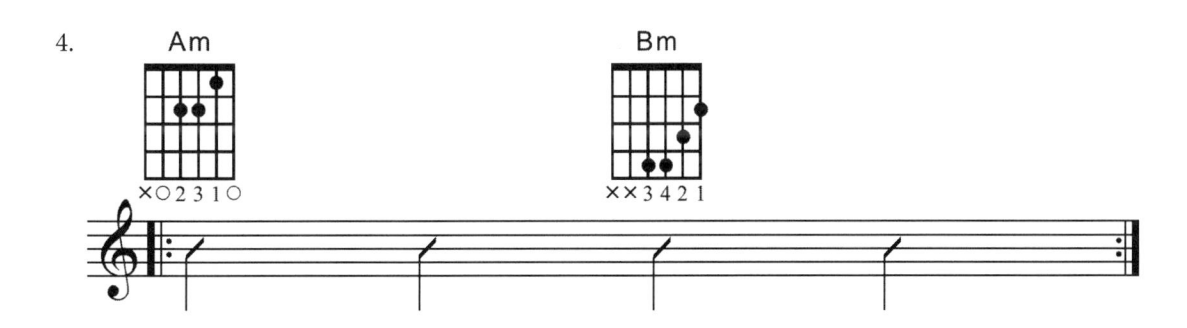

Special Guitar Tip: In a situation like exercise #4, if you hold the Am with your second, third, and fourth fingers instead of the usual fingers, you can slide them when switching to Bm.

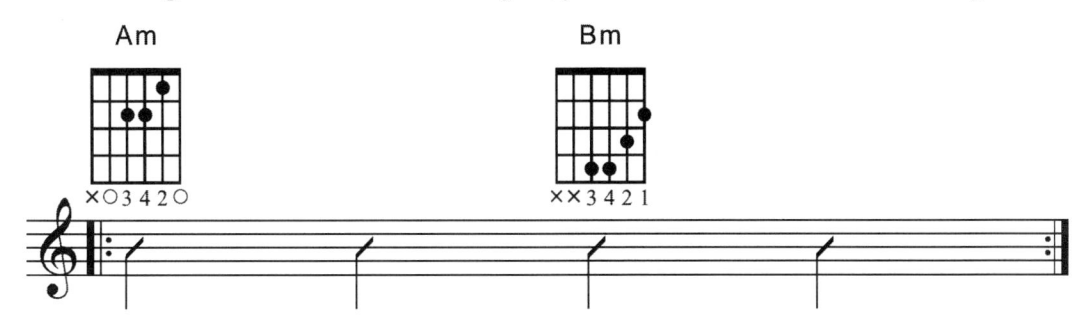

Am   Bm
x 0 3 4 2 0   x x 3 4 2 1

Slide your fingers along the neck and add or remove your first finger only.

Guitar for Songwriters

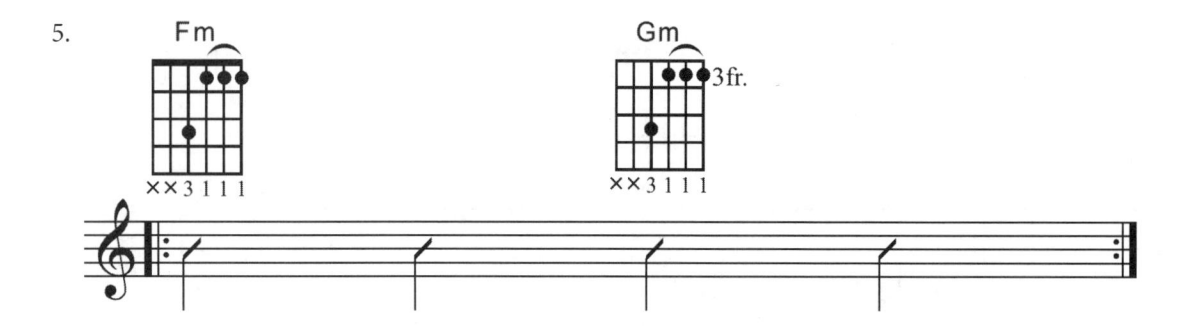

5. Fm   Gm 3fr.
   ××3111   ××3111

Release the pressure but keep your fingers lightly on the strings as you slide between Fm and Gm.

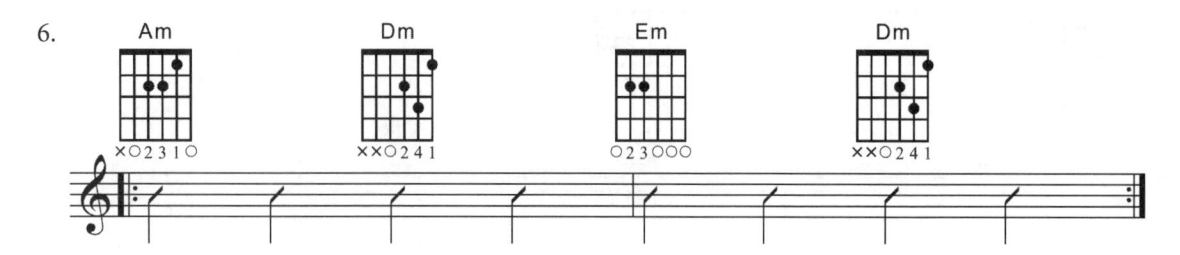

6. Am   Dm   Em   Dm
   ×02310   ××0241   023000   ××0241

The Basic Seventh Chords for Guitar

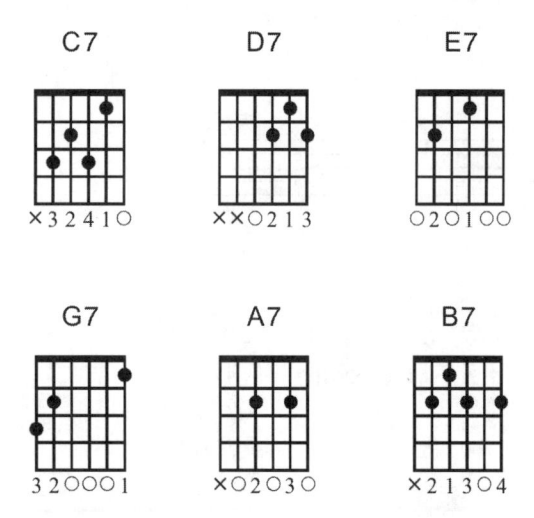

C7   D7   E7
×32410   ××0213   020100

G7   A7   B7
320001   ×02030   ×21304

The exercises with seventh chords can have a more "bluesy" sound.

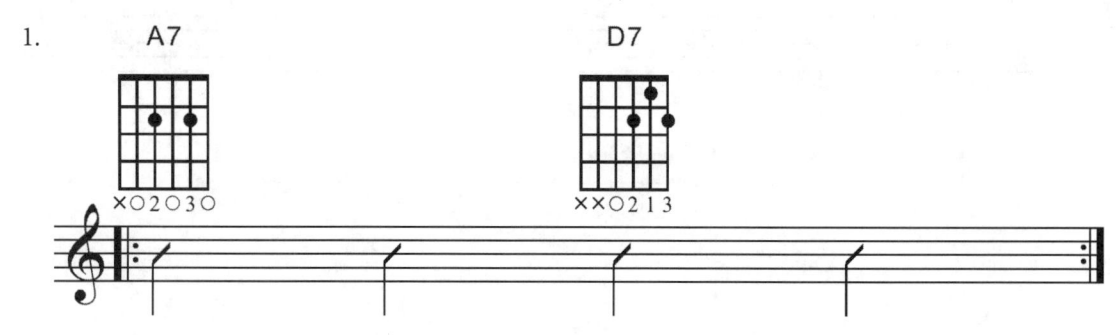

1. A7   D7
   ×02030   ××0213

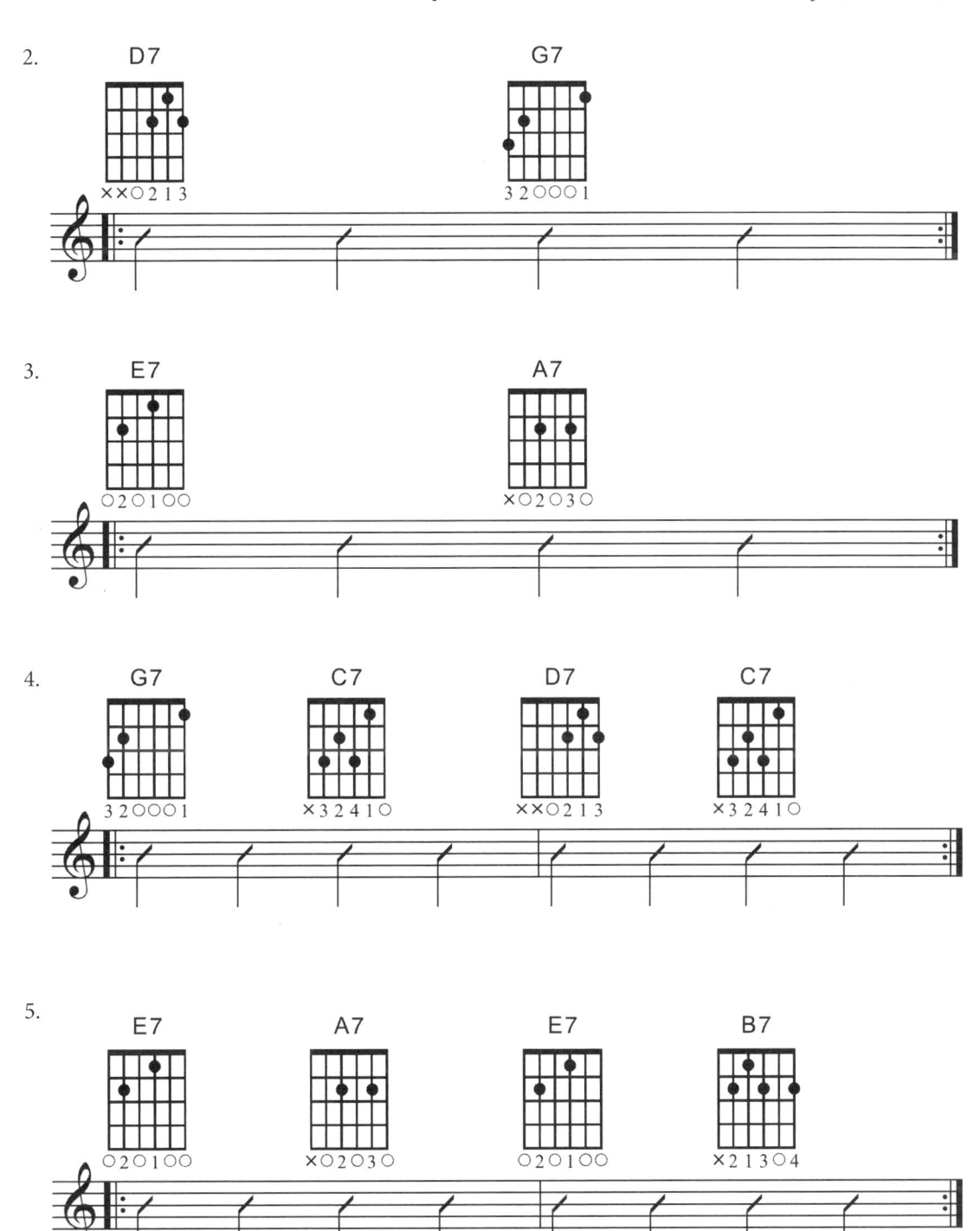

Chapter 1 The Basic Chords: Major, Minor, and Seventh

Guitar for Songwriters

Exercises Mixing Major, Minor, and Seventh Chords

Here are some exercises using common chord progressions in the easy guitar keys. In the next chapter, we will examine these progressions more closely and play them in different keys.

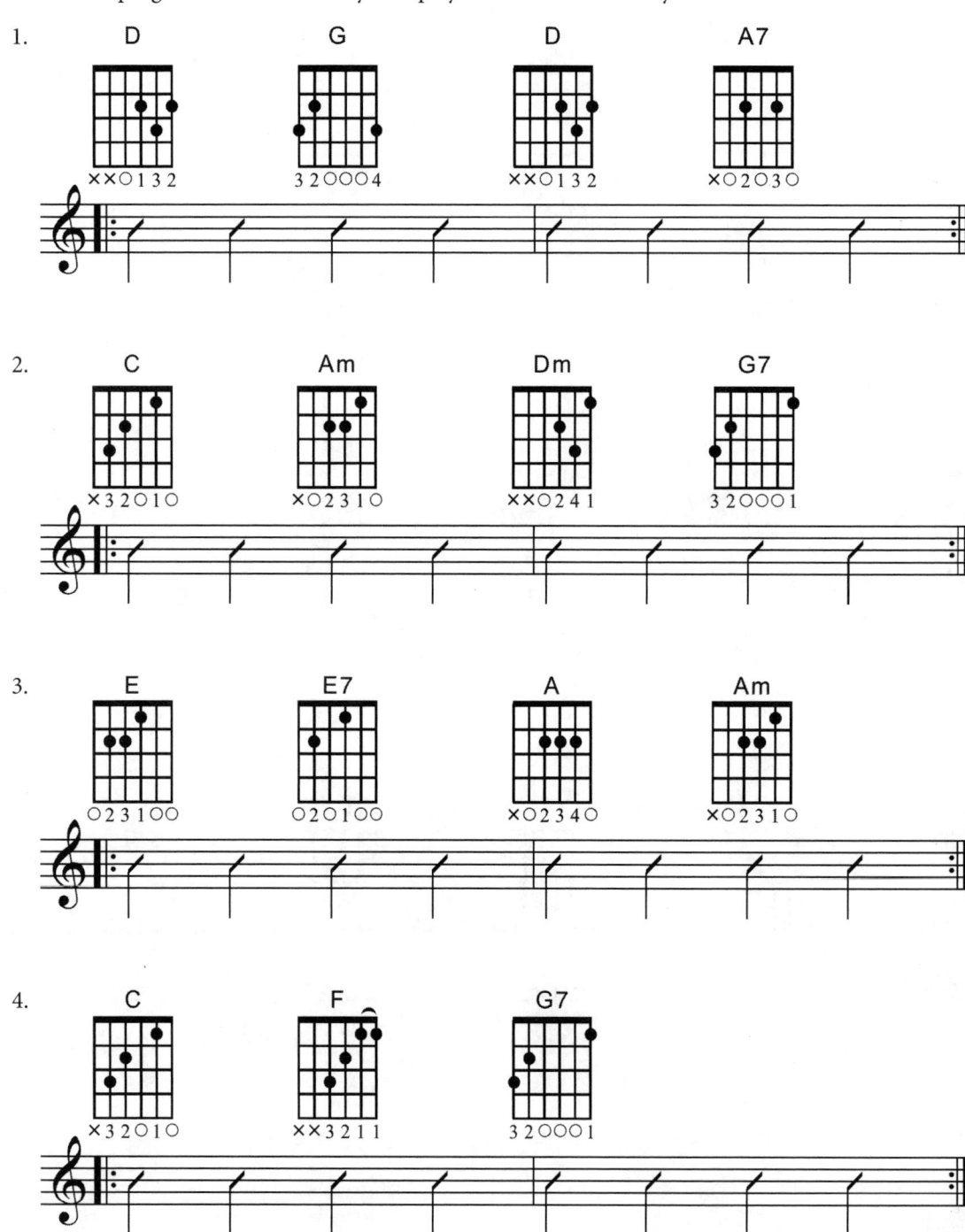

1. D — G — D — A7

2. C — Am — Dm — G7

3. E — E7 — A — Am

4. C — F — G7

Chapter 1 The Basic Chords: Major, Minor, and Seventh

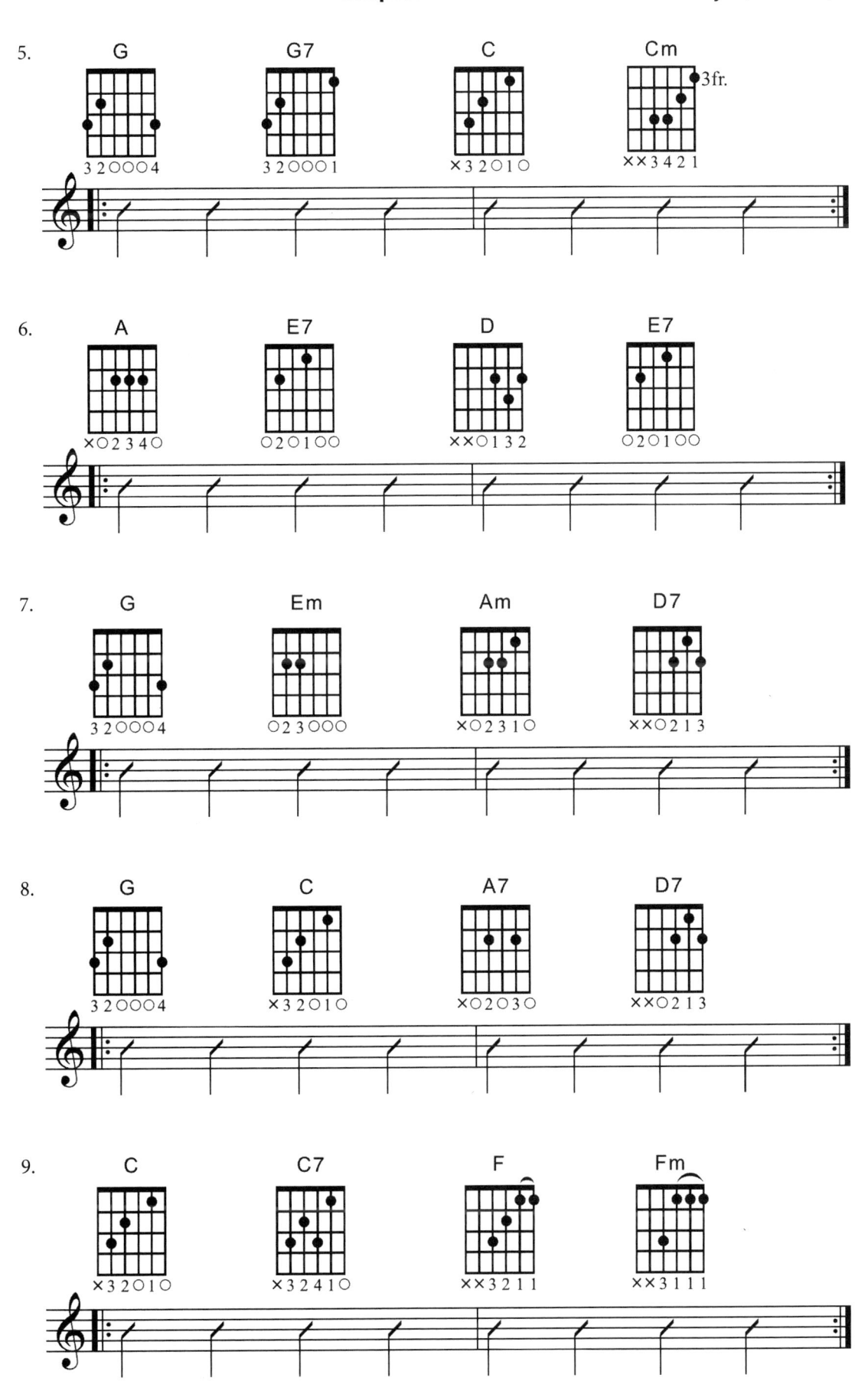

Guitar for Songwriters

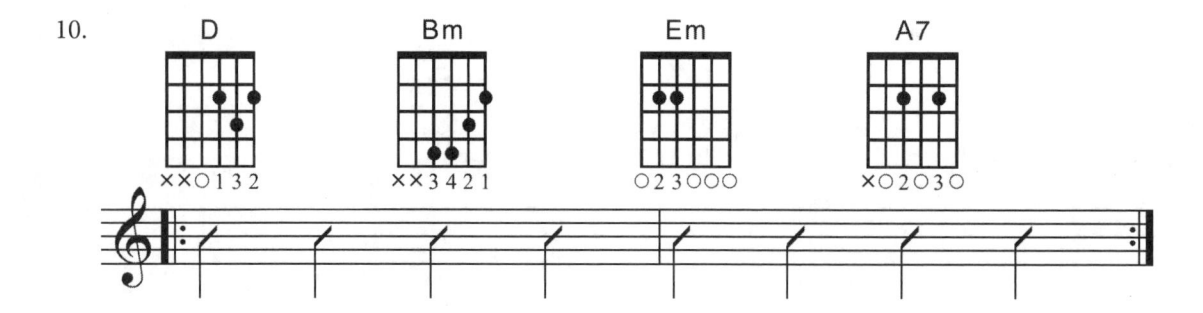

10.

2

I, IV, and V

YOU CAN PLAY THOUSANDS OF SONGS WITH JUST THREE CHORDS. In this chapter, we'll examine these chords in the easy guitar keys, and later in all keys. Familiarity with playing the three main chords in all keys is a major step in getting comfortable with chords.

Musicians often refer to chords by numbers rather than by their letter names. You may hear someone say, "It goes one, four, one, five." The person is referring to the relationship of the chords to the key of the song. The "one" chord in the key of C is C major; the "one" chord in the key of D is D major.

These numbers are often written in Roman numerals. "One, four, five" would be written I, IV, V. Music-theory students often refer to them as *tonic, subdominant,* and *dominant.*

The most common chords in any key are the I, IV, and V chords—the chords built on the first, fourth, and fifth notes of that key's major scale. In the key of C major, C is the first note of the scale, F is the fourth, and G is the fifth. That means that the C, F, and G major chords are the ones you are most likely to see in the key of C. If you're comfortable with these chords, you can easily play many songs in the key of C.

> *The most common chords in any key are the I, IV, and V chords—the chords built on the first, fourth, and fifth notes of that key's major scale.*

The key of C: The most important chords in this key are C, F, and G.

To find the most common chords in other keys, find the first, fourth, and fifth notes of that major scale. For instance, in the key of D, the first, fourth, and fifth notes are D, G, and A. The most common chords in the key of D, therefore, are D major, G major, and A major.

The key of D: The most important chords in this key are D, G, and A.

When you count up a scale, you must take into account any sharps or flats in that key. In the key of F, the fourth note is a B♭. The most common chords in the key of F are F, B♭, and C. In the key of B, the fifth note is an F♯. The most common chords in the key of B are B, E, and F♯.

Guitar for Songwriters

F G A B♭ C D E F

The key of F: The most important chords are F, B♭, and C.

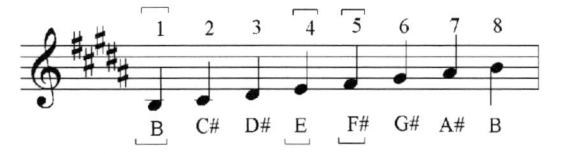

B C# D# E F# G# A# B

The key of B: The most important chords are B, E, and F♯.

This doesn't mean that you must use the I, IV, and V chords in a song you write. You can use any chords you wish. However, these are the most commonly heard ones. Thousands of folk songs, country songs, and the blues use only the I, IV, and V chords. Analyze some folk songs to see whether they use these chords. You'll see that they occur quite frequently, in many variations.

The chord built on the fifth of the scale can be played as a dominant 7th chord. The V7 chord in the key of C is G7. In the following examples, try switching between V and V7 and listening for the difference.

> *Thousands of folk songs, country songs, and the blues use only the I, IV, and V chords.*

The easiest keys on the guitar are probably C, D, E, G, and A. If you play with trumpets or saxophones, you'll find yourself playing in F, B♭, E♭, and A♭ frequently. Whatever keys you focus on, practice changing between the I, IV, and V chords in different orders. Those are the chord changes you're most likely to come across in any key.

Table 2.1 shows the progressions in the keys that are easiest on the guitar. Later in this book, after I introduce bar chords, I'll explain keys in more detail and give you exercises in all 12 keys.

Table 2.1 I, IV, and V in the Easy Guitar Keys

Key	I	IV	V
C	C	F	G
D	D	G	A
E	E	A	B
G	G	C	D
A	A	D	E

Chapter 2 I, IV, and V

Exercises with I, IV, and V Major Chords

Thousands of songs use just the I, IV, and V chords. Play them in a different order, with a different number of beats and in different styles, and you may recognize some familiar songs.

I-IV-V-IV

The progression is used in many old rock tunes. Change the beat, and you'll hear "Louie, Louie" or "Wild Thing."

1. The key of C major:

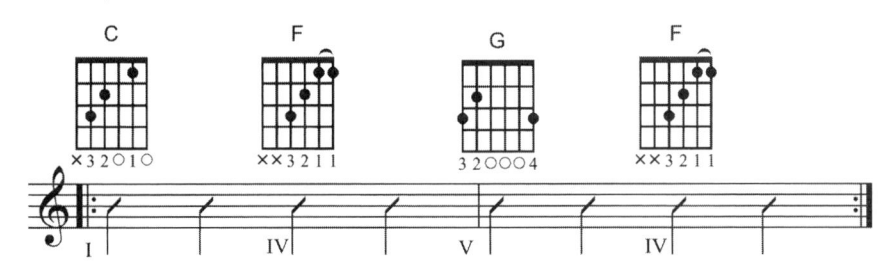

   C (x32010) — F (xx3211) — G (320004) — F (xx3211)
   I — IV — V — IV

2. The key of D major:

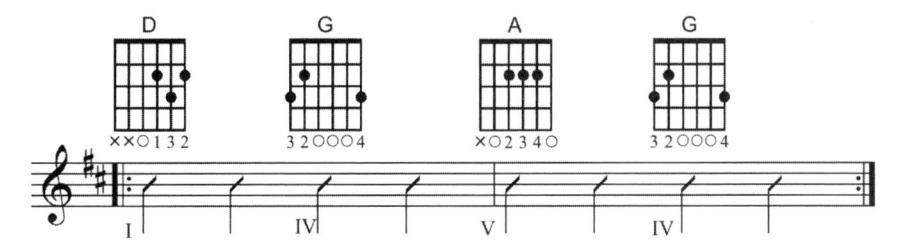

   D (xx0132) — G (320004) — A (x02340) — G (320004)
   I — IV — V — IV

3. The key of E major, using the V7 chord:

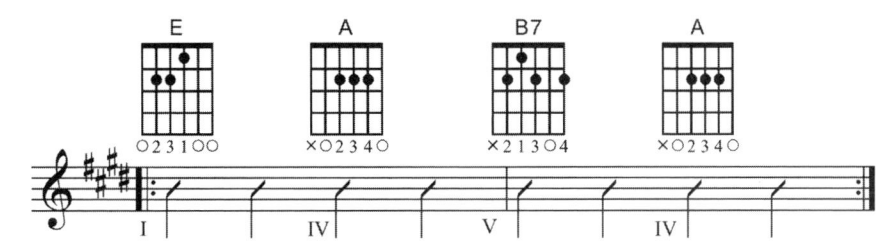

   E (023100) — A (x02340) — B7 (x21304) — A (x02340)
   I — IV — V — IV

4. The key of G major:

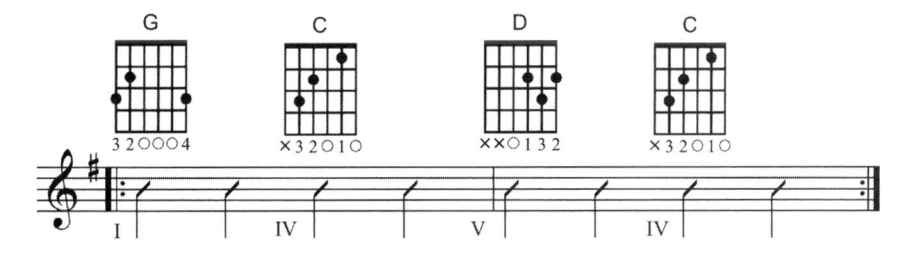

   G (320004) — C (x32010) — D (xx0132) — C (x32010)
   I — IV — V — IV

13

Guitar for Songwriters

5. The key of A major:

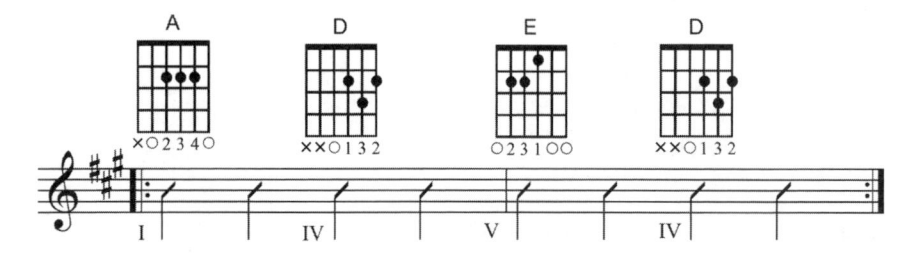

I-IV-I-V

Here is another combination of I, IV, and V chords, in the same keys. Give the chords four beats each, and they fit part of Van Morrison's "Brown-Eyed Girl."

1. The key of C major:

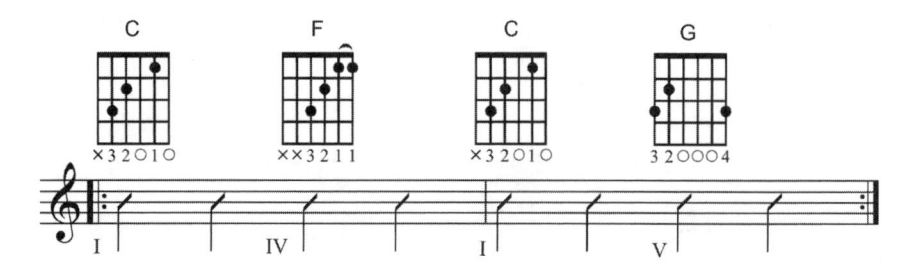

2. The key of D major:

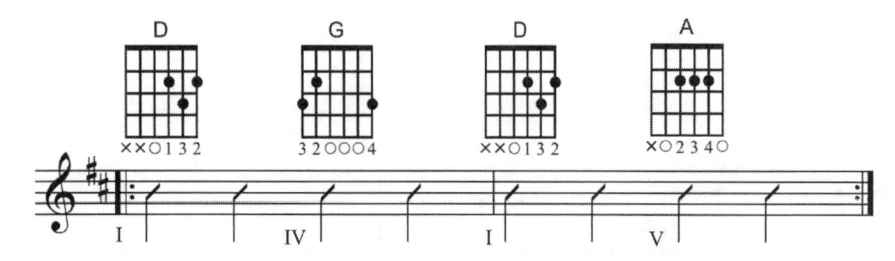

3. The key of E major:

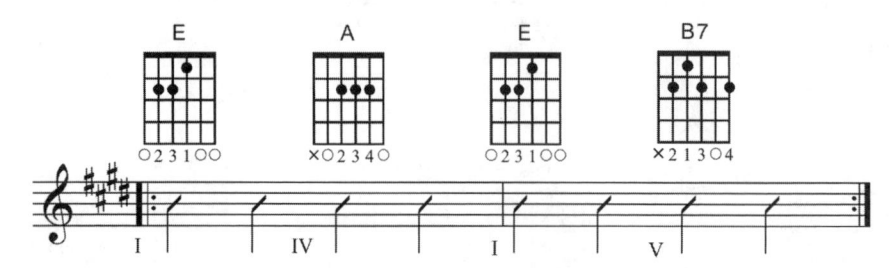

Chapter 2 I, IV, and V

4. The key of G major:

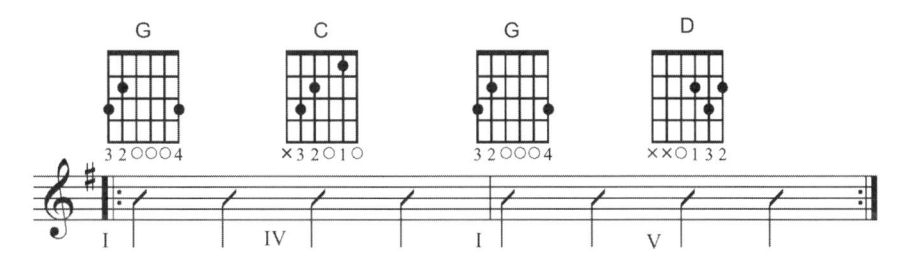

[G chord — 3 2 0 0 0 4] [C chord — ×3 2 0 1 0] [G chord — 3 2 0 0 0 4] [D chord — ×× 0 1 3 2]

I   IV   I   V

5. The key of A major:

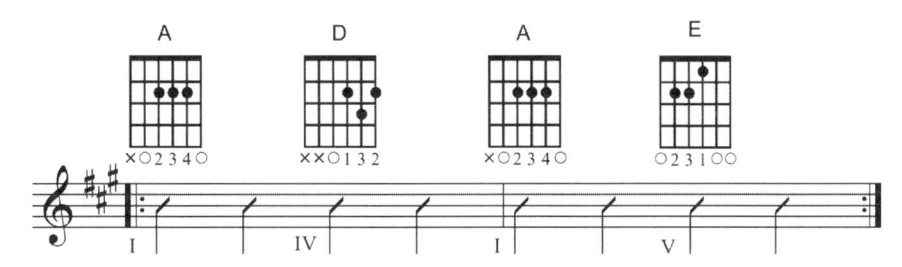

[A chord — ×0 2 3 4 0] [D chord — ×× 0 1 3 2] [A chord — ×0 2 3 4 0] [E chord — 0 2 3 1 0 0]

I   IV   I   V

I-V-IV-V

I   V   IV   V

You can hear the variation on I, IV, and V in the same keys in the song "Crimson and Clover."

1. The key of C major:

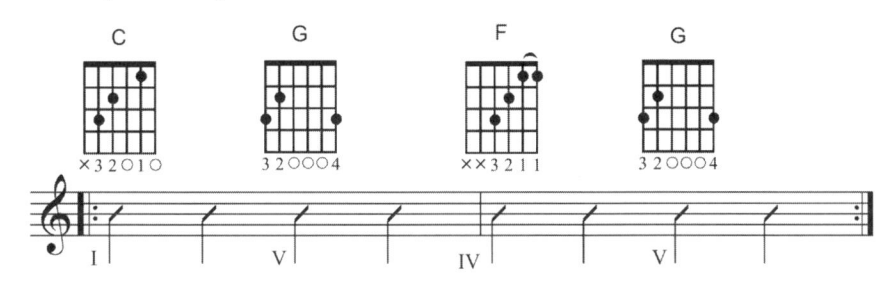

[C chord — ×3 2 0 1 0] [G chord — 3 2 0 0 0 4] [F chord — ×× 3 2 1 1] [G chord — 3 2 0 0 0 4]

I   V   IV   V

2. The key of D major:

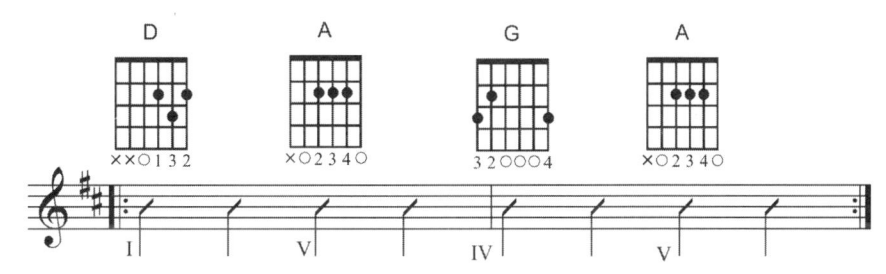

[D chord — ×× 0 1 3 2] [A chord — ×0 2 3 4 0] [G chord — 3 2 0 0 0 4] [A chord — ×0 2 3 4 0]

I   V   IV   V

15

Guitar for Songwriters

3. The key of E major, using the V7 chord:

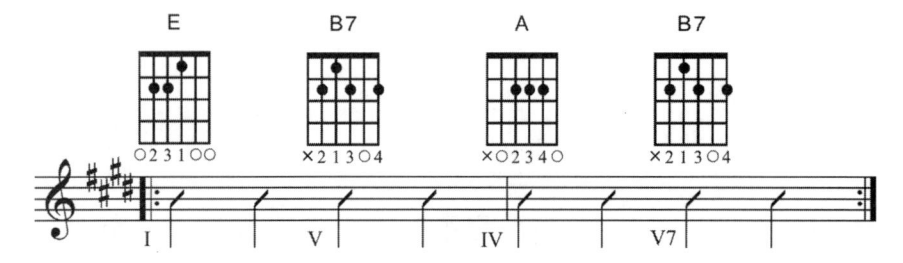

   E — B7 — A — B7
   I — V — IV — V7

4. The key of G major:

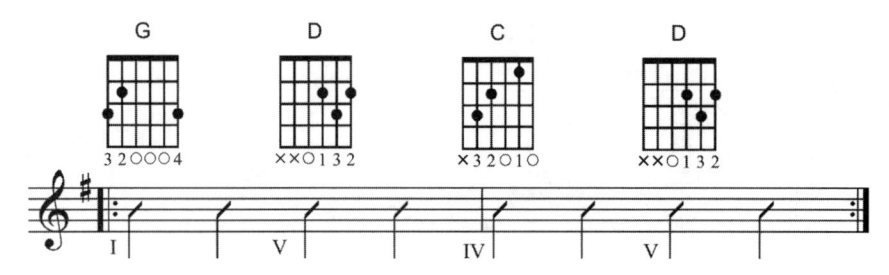

   G — D — C — D
   I — V — IV — V

5. The key of A major:

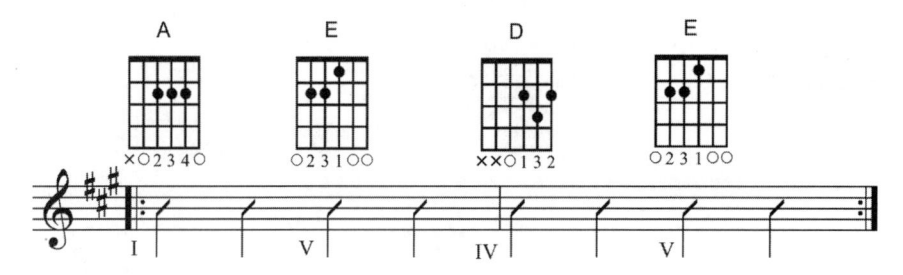

   A — E — D — E
   I — V — IV — V

I, IV, and V in Minor

Following are the same progressions using all minor chords. The distance between chords is the same, but the minor chords give them quite a different sound.

Im-IVm-Vm-IVm

1. The key of C minor:

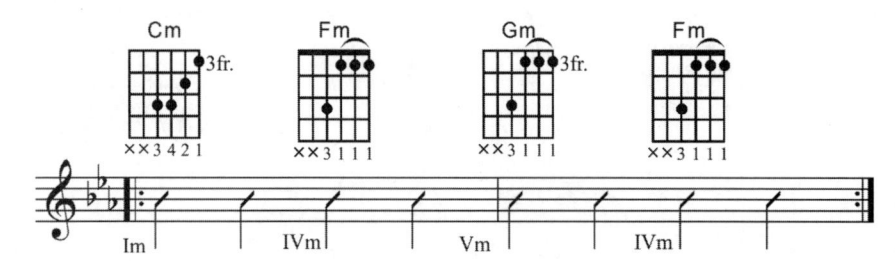

   Cm — Fm — Gm — Fm
   Im — IVm — Vm — IVm

Chapter 2 I, IV, and V

2. The key of D minor:

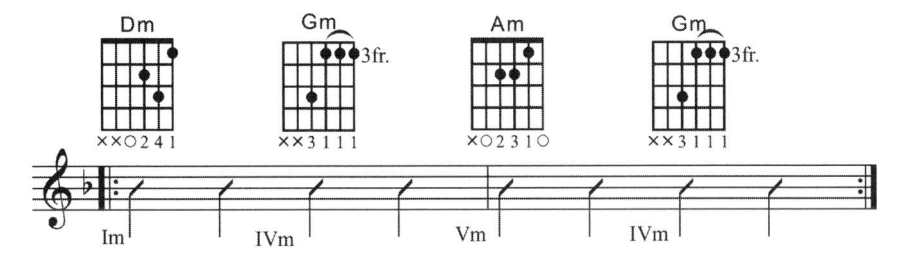

   Im — IVm — Vm — IVm

3. The key of E minor:

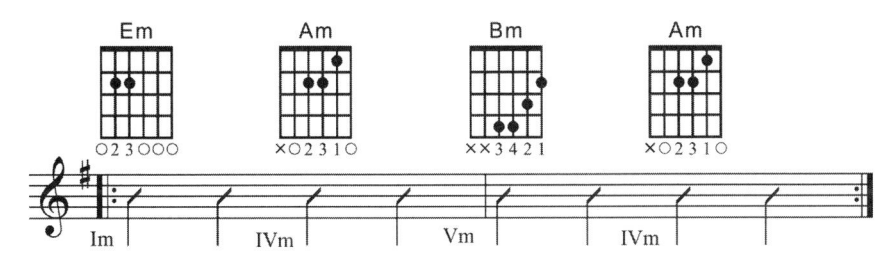

   Im — IVm — Vm — IVm

4. The key of G minor:

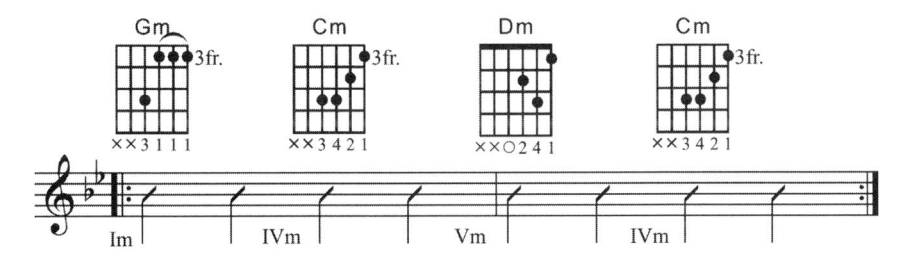

   Im — IVm — Vm — IVm

5. The key of A minor:

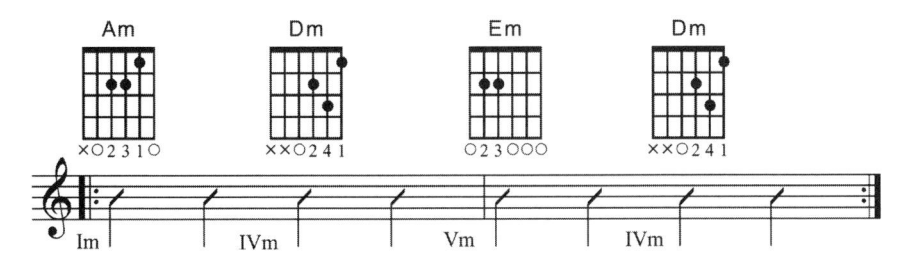

   Im — IVm — Vm — IVm

Im-IVm-Im-Vm

1. The key of C minor:

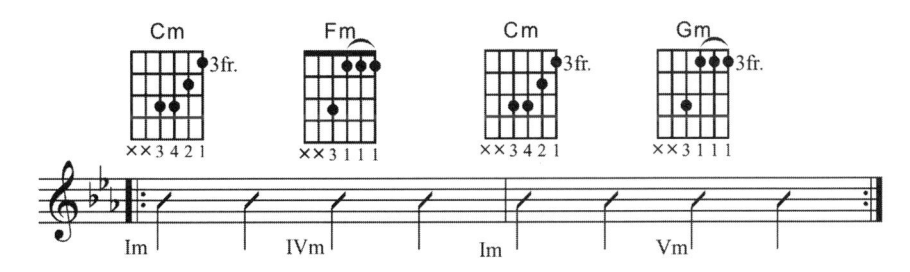

   Im — IVm — Im — Vm

Guitar for Songwriters

2. The key of D minor:

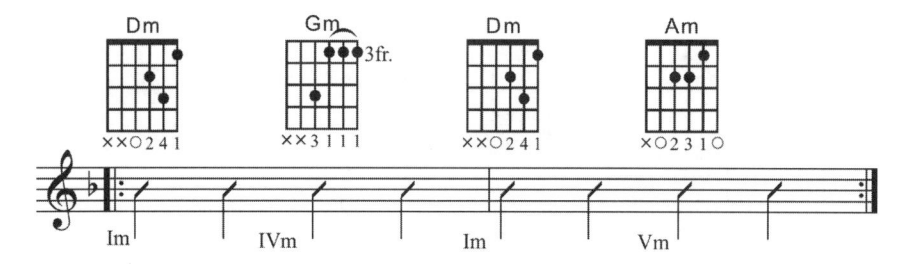

3. The key of E minor:

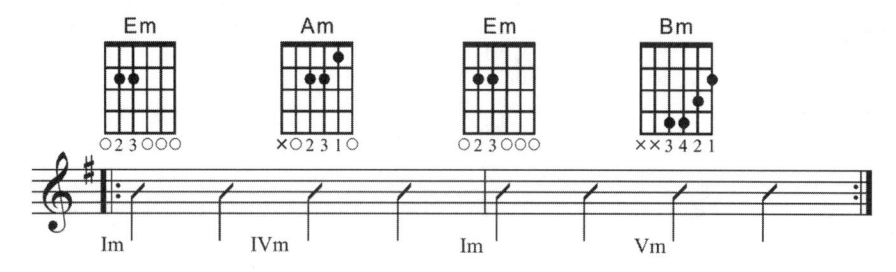

4. The key of G minor:

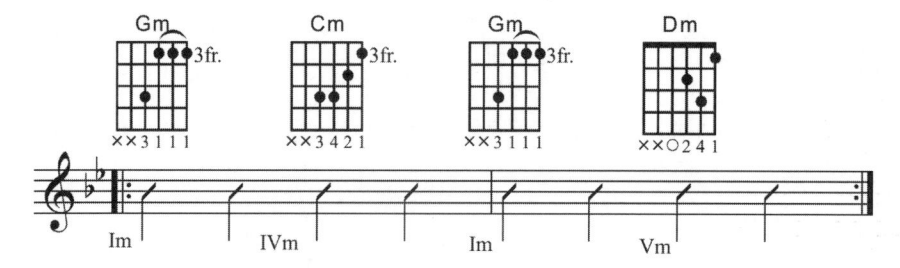

5. The key of A minor:

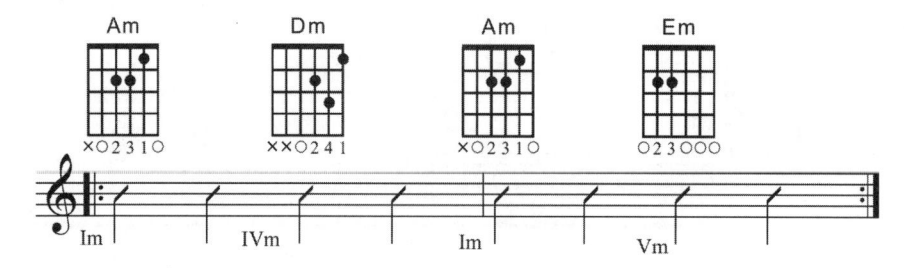

Im-Vm-IVm-Vm

1. The key of C minor:

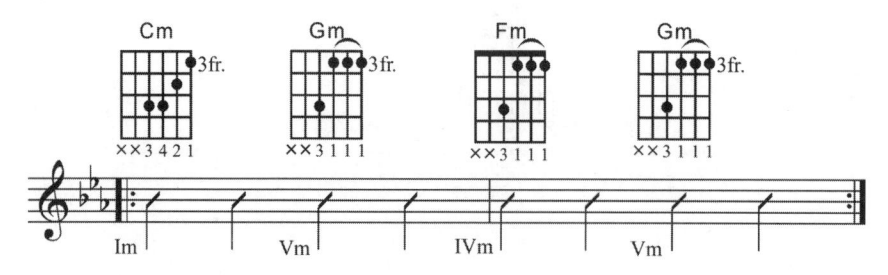

Chapter 2 I, IV, and V

2. The key of D minor:

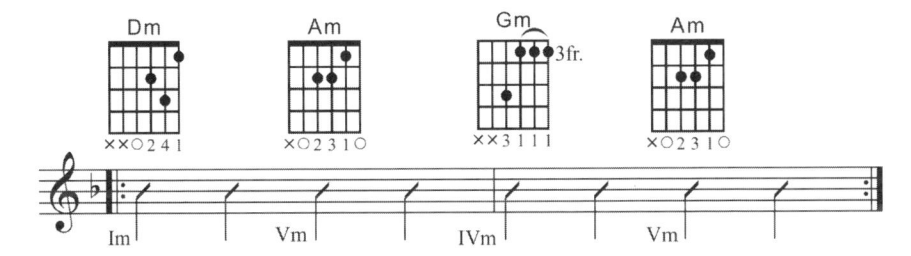

3. The key of E minor:

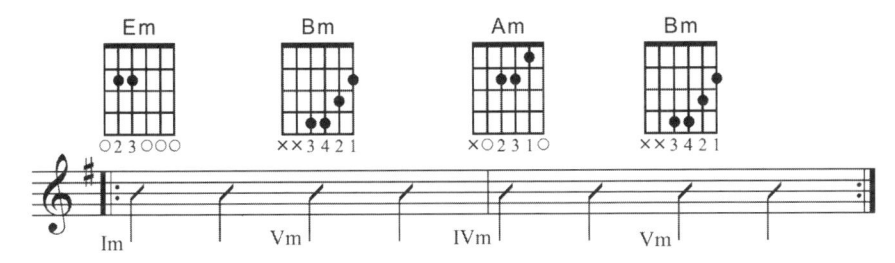

4. The key of G minor:

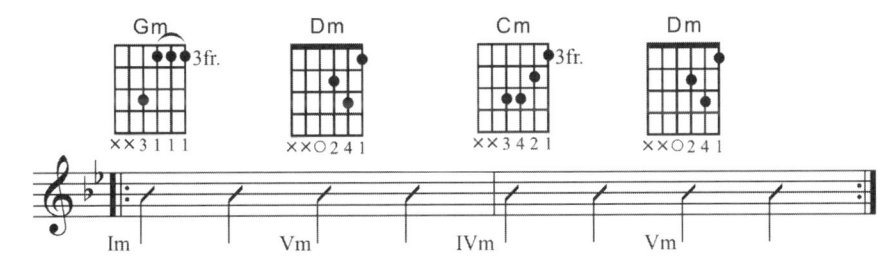

5. The key of A minor:

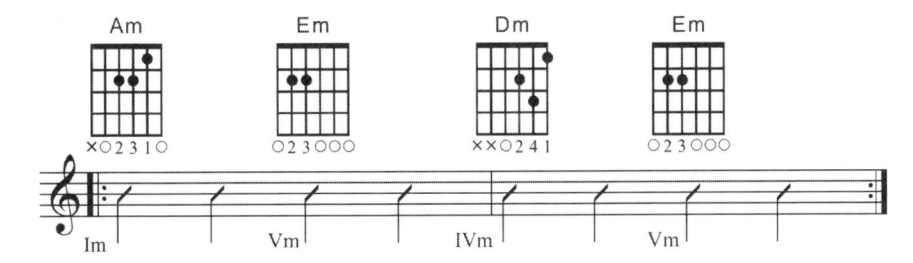

I, IV, and V with Seventh Chords

I've omitted the key of C for the time being, because the IV7 chord in that key, F7, is a little more difficult to hold. Otherwise, these are the same progressions as before, adding the distinctive sound of dominant seventh chords.

19

Guitar for Songwriters

I7-IV7-V7-IV7

1. The key of D:

D7	G7	A7	G7
I7	IV7	V7	IV7

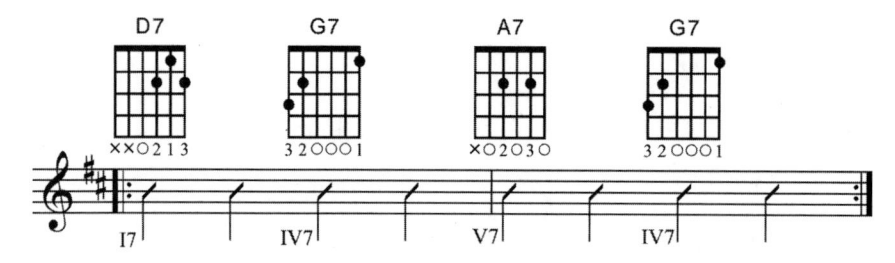

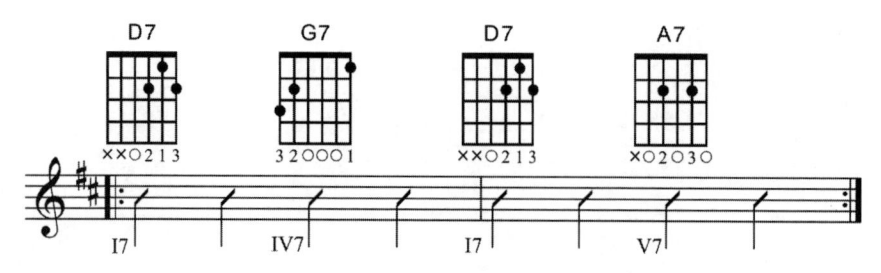

2. The key of E:

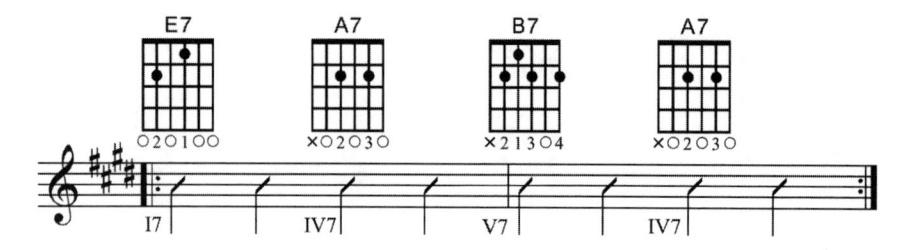

E7	A7	B7	A7
I7	IV7	V7	IV7

3. The key of G:

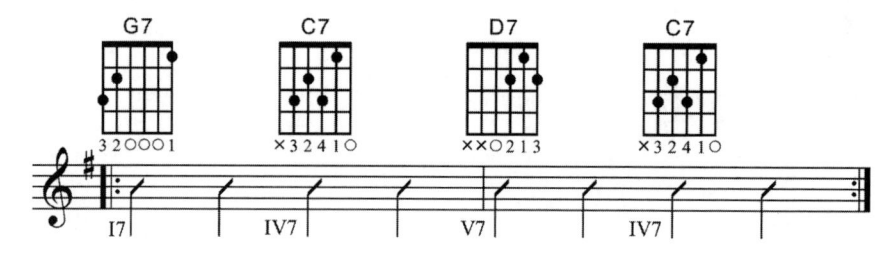

G7	C7	D7	C7
I7	IV7	V7	IV7

4. The key of A:

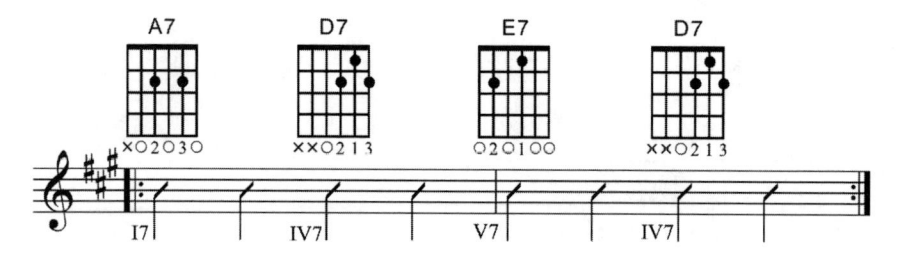

A7	D7	E7	D7
I7	IV7	V7	IV7

I7-IV7-I7-V7

1. The key of D:

D7	G7	D7	A7
I7	IV7	I7	V7

Chapter 2 I, IV, and V

2. The key of E:

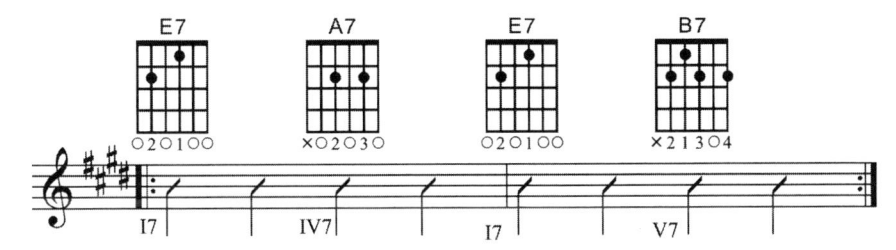

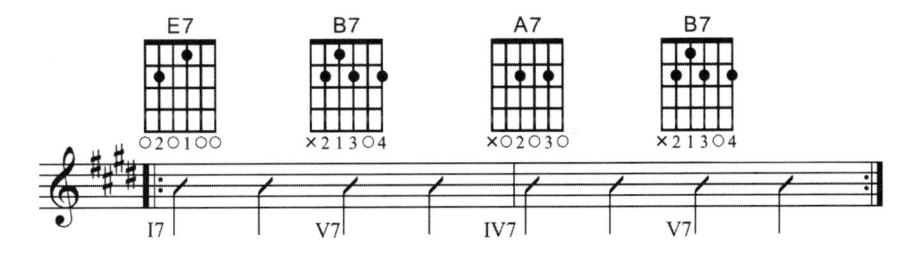

[E7 — I7]   [A7 — IV7]   [E7 — I7]   [B7 — V7]

3. The key of G:

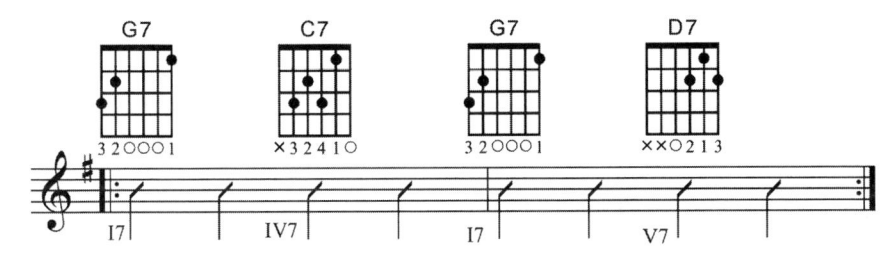

[G7 — I7]   [C7 — IV7]   [G7 — I7]   [D7 — V7]

4. The key of A:

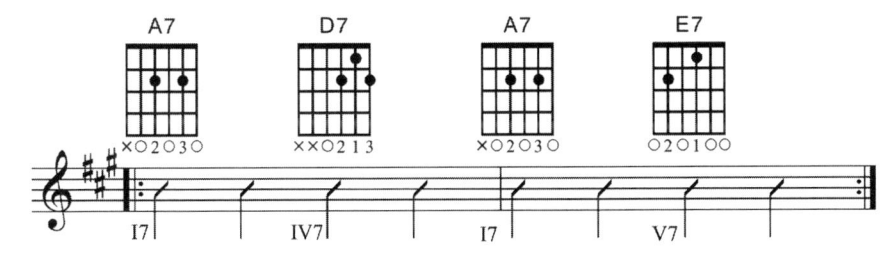

[A7 — I7]   [D7 — IV7]   [A7 — I7]   [E7 — V7]

I7-V7-IV7-V7

1. The key of D:

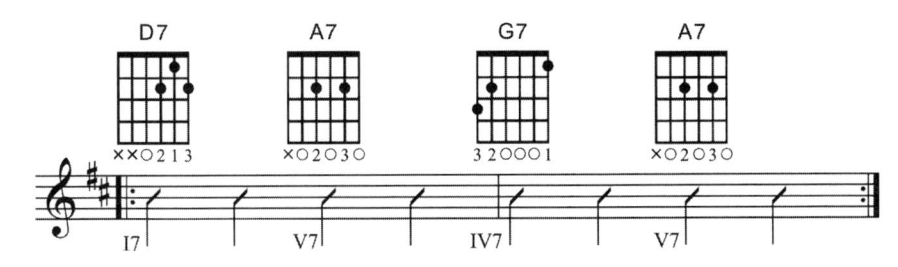

[D7 — I7]   [A7 — V7]   [G7 — IV7]   [A7 — V7]

2. The key of E:

[E7 — I7]   [B7 — V7]   [A7 — IV7]   [B7 — V7]

Guitar for Songwriters

3. The key of G:

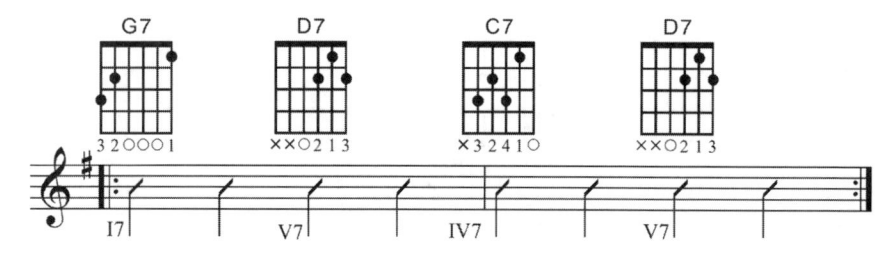

   G7 — D7 — C7 — D7
   I7 — V7 — IV7 — V7

4. The key of A:

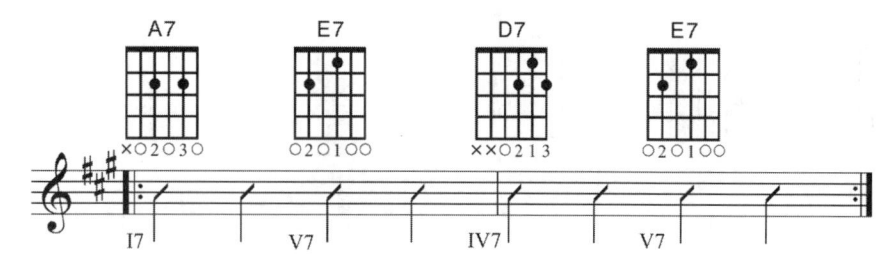

   A7 — E7 — D7 — E7
   I7 — V7 — IV7 — V7

I, IV, and V with Mixed Chord Types

Here are a few progressions using a mixture of major, minor, and seventh chords for I, IV, and V in easy keys.

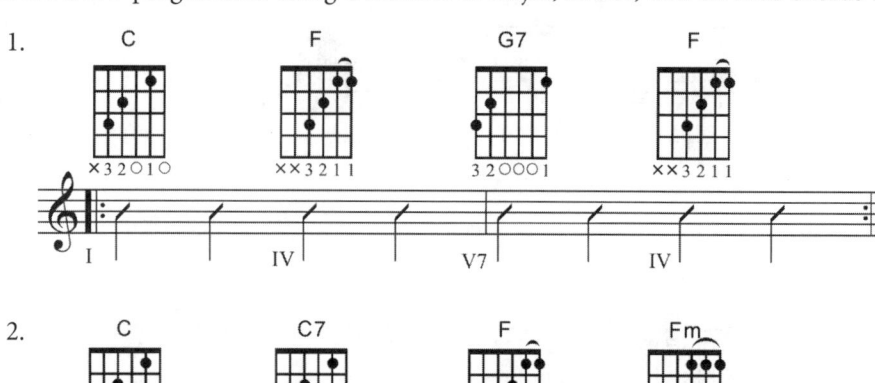

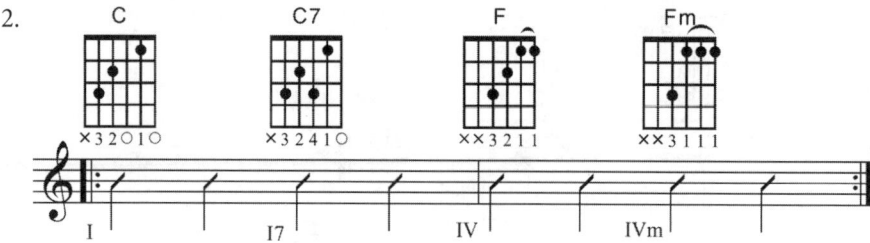

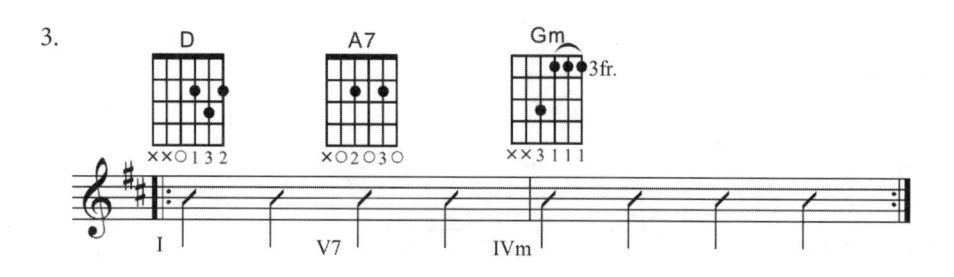

1. C — F — G7 — F
   I — IV — V7 — IV

2. C — C7 — F — Fm
   I — I7 — IV — IVm

3. D — A7 — Gm
   I — V7 — IVm

22

Chapter 2 I, IV, and V

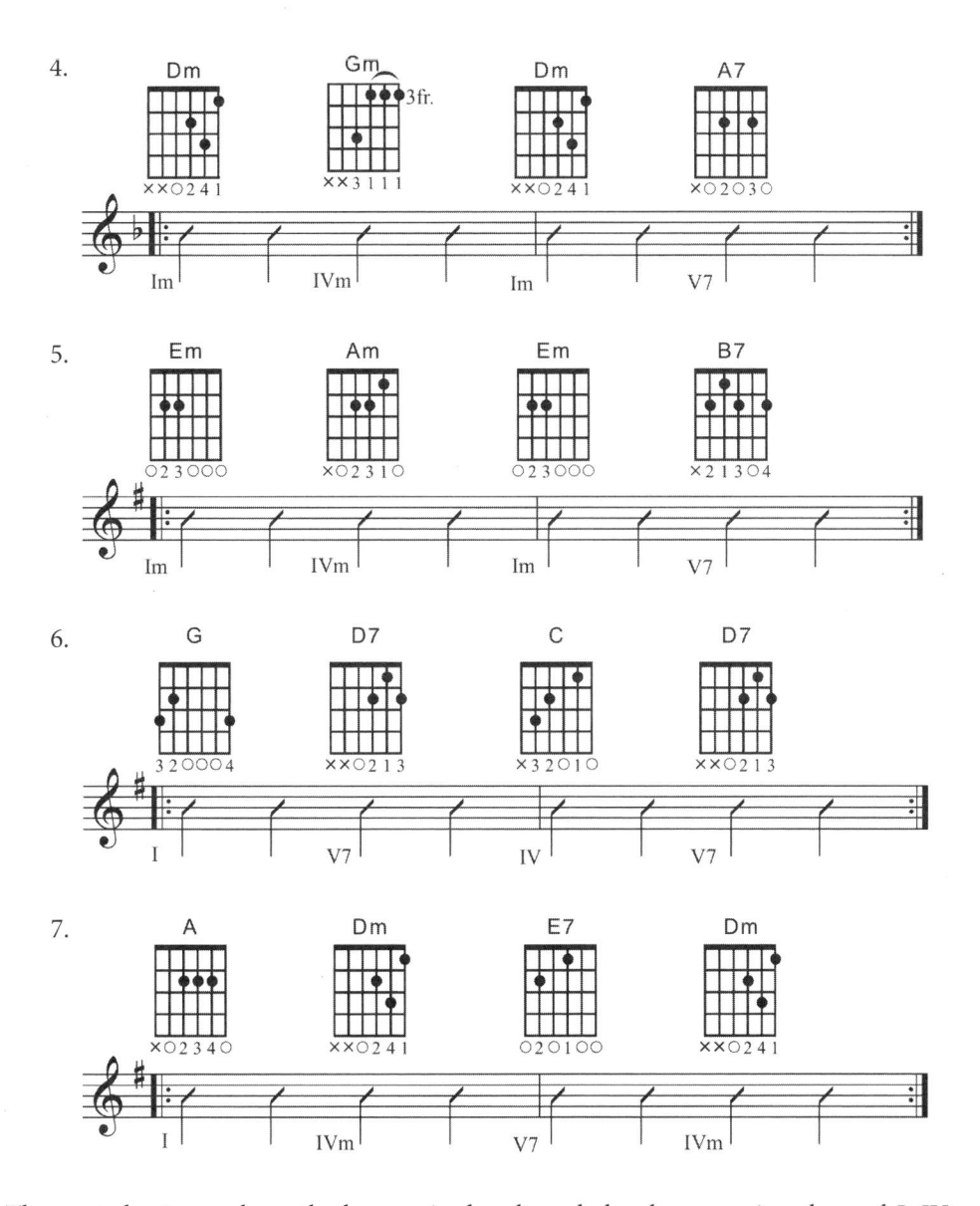

4. Dm | Gm | Dm | A7
   Im | IVm | Im | V7

5. Em | Am | Em | B7
   Im | IVm | Im | V7

6. G | D7 | C | D7
   I | V7 | IV | V7

7. A | Dm | E7 | Dm
   I | IVm | V7 | IVm

The next chapter explores the harmonized scale and chord progressions beyond I, IV, and V.

3
The Harmonized Scale

Although thousands of songs use only three chords (I, IV, and V), there are of course many other chords common to any key. The next most common chords can be found in the harmonized scale—the chords based on the notes of a scale.

Look at the notes of a C major scale: **C D E F G A B C**

Assign a Roman numeral to each note in the scale: C is I, D is II, E is III, F is IV, G is V, A is VI, B is VII, and then you are back to C.

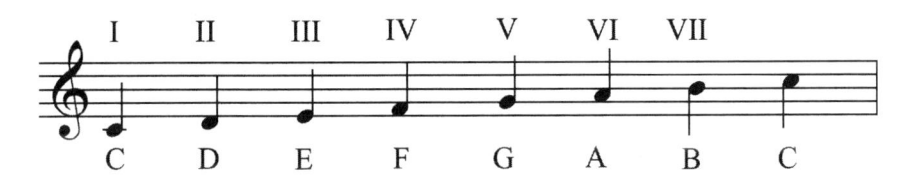

Build a chord on each of these notes by adding notes a third and a fifth above each of these scale tones. Use only the notes from the C major scale. (Chapter 8, "Chord Construction: How to Build Chords and Find Good Voicings," will explain how chords are built and how to identify major, minor, and dominant seventh chords.) Looking at the resulting chords, you will find that the chord built on the C note is a major chord, D is minor, E is minor, F is major, G is major, A is minor, and B is diminished. (The ° symbol is sometimes used for diminished.)

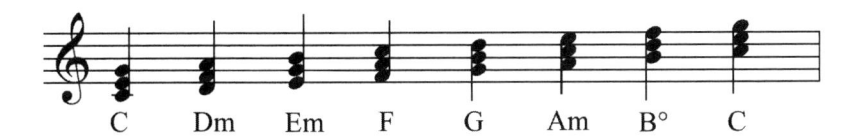

This is called the *harmonized* scale. It shows the chords that naturally occur in a key—because they are built on the notes of the scale and use only notes from that key.

If you refer to chords by numbers rather than by the letter names, you are then using terms that can easily be translated to other keys. I, IV, and V describe a relationship between chords, rather than naming specific chords. When you specify a key, then you can name the chords. The IV chord means the chord built on the fourth note of a scale. The IV chord in the key of G means the C major chord—based on the fourth note in a G major scale. The IV chord in the key of D is G major, because G is the fourth note of the D major scale.

Some people notate a minor chord by using a lowercase Roman numeral, such as ii. Others use uppercase Roman numerals to indicate the scale tone followed by "m" for minor, such as IIm. That would mean the minor chord built on the second note of the scale in whatever key you are in. In this book, I'll always use "m" to refer to minor chords. An upper case "M" is sometimes used to indicate major, so it's safer to use a lowercase "m" for minor.

Guitar for Songwriters

```
I    IIm   IIIm   IV    V    VIm   VII°   I
C    Dm    Em     F     G    Am    B°     C
```

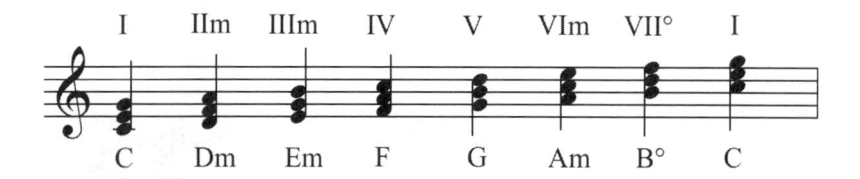

Why go to all this trouble? Why not just say C, F, or G7? Because similar progressions occur in thousands of songs, only with slight variations or in different keys. If you get comfortable with this way of thinking, it becomes easier to remember songs and to learn new ones. Most musicians with "good ears" hear the relationships between notes or chords. They can't necessarily tell the actual notes being played, but they know the distances between them. After a while, you'll find yourself "hearing" some chord changes—anticipating a change to the IV chord or a return to the I chord. A blues, for example, normally goes between I, IV, and V7 in a certain sequence. Thinking in "numbers" makes it easier to transpose the blues to other keys, to hear similarities or differences in various songs, or to remember a piece.

> *Most musicians with "good ears" hear the relationships between notes or chords. They can't necessarily tell the actual notes being played, but they know the distances between them.*

Another advantage of this system is on the bandstand. It is often easier and clearer to call "five" across to the bass player, rather than "G," which might be misheard as "C," "D," or some other letter that rhymes. Trumpet and saxophone players play what are called *transposing instruments*, and they think in different keys than the guitar does for the same song. Using a number instead of a specific chord means your fellow musicians don't have to transpose when you call out a chord.

Getting back to the C scale, again the chords that occur naturally in the key of C are C major, D minor, E minor, F major, G major, A minor, and B diminished. In other words, using only the notes in the C scale, without using any sharps or flats, you find those chords. The G is often a G7 in the key of C, and the B diminished is rarely seen. I'll explain this later, although you don't need to understand the reason to be able to take advantage of the information.

What's important is this: The chords found most often in the key of C are C, Dm, Em, F, G7, and Am.

> *The chords found most often in the key of C are C, Dm, Em, F, G7, and Am.*

Using the Roman numerals, you can apply this knowledge to all keys: The chords found most often in any key are I, IIm, IIIm, IV, V7, and VIm.

To apply this to key of D, for instance, just choose the first six notes of the D scale and add the proper chord suffix—major, minor, or seventh. The most common chords in the key of D are D, Em, F♯m, G, A7, and Bm.

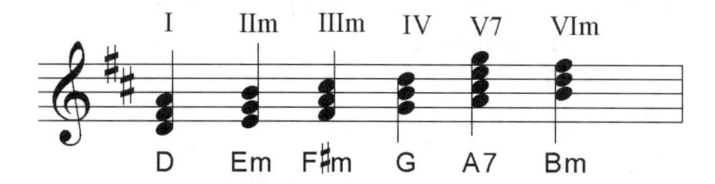

```
I    IIm   IIIm   IV    V7   VIm
D    Em    F♯m    G     A7   Bm
```

> *The chords found most often in any key are I, IIm, IIIm, IV, V7, and VIm.*

Chapter 3 The Harmonized Scale

Why is the V chord a 7th and not just a major? In the key of C, why is it a G7 and not a G? Add one more note a third higher to the G chord, and you have a G7 (GBDF). If you look at the top three notes of the G7 chord, you will find that they are the same as the notes of the B° (BDF). The B° chord is fairly rare in most songs and is usually considered part of a G7.

Table 3.1 shows the most common chords in all keys. Practicing the chords that go together in a key is more helpful than practicing chords at random. The section of this book on bar chords will give you good forms for playing in the more difficult keys.

Table 3.1 The Harmonized Scale in All Keys

Key	I	IIm	IIIm	IV	V7	VIm	(VII°)(rare)
C	C	Dm	Em	F	G7	Am	(B°)
C♯	C♯	D♯m	E♯m	F♯	G♯7	A♯m	(B♯°)
D♭	D♭	E♭m	Fm	G♭	A♭7	B♭m	(C°)
D	D	Em	F♯m	G	A7	Bm	(C♯°)
E♭	E♭	Fm	Gm	A♭	B♭7	Cm	(D°)
E	E	F♯m	G♯m	A	B7	C♯m	(D♯°)
F	F	Gm	Am	B♭	C7	Dm	(E°)
F♯	F♯	G♯m	A♯m	B	C♯7	D♯m	(E♯°)
G♭	G♭	A♭m	B♭m	C♭	D♭7	E♭m	(F°)
G	G	Am	Bm	C	D7	Em	(F♯°)
A♭	A♭	B♭m	Cm	D♭	E♭7	Fm	(G°)
A	A	Bm	C♯m	D	E7	F♯m	(G♯°)
B♭	B♭	Cm	Dm	E♭	F7	Gm	(A°)
B	B	C♯m	D♯m	E	F♯7	G♯m	(A♯°)
C♭	C♭	D♭m	E♭m	F♭	G♭7	A♭m	(B♭°)

The keys of F♯ and G♭ are the same keys with a different spelling. The keys of C♯ and C♭ are rarely seen, because the corresponding keys of D♭ and B have fewer flats or sharps.

Use the harmonized scale to become familiar with the most common chords in any key.

Guitar for Songwriters

Some Common Progressions Using the Harmonized Scale

The exercises in the following sections use the easiest guitar keys. After learning bar chords, transpose them into the remaining keys.

I-IIm-IIIm-IV

Bob Dylan's "Like a Rolling Stone" uses this progression for the first four chords.

1. The key of C:

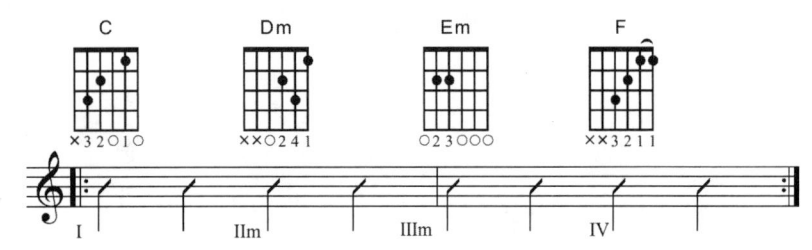

2. The key of D:

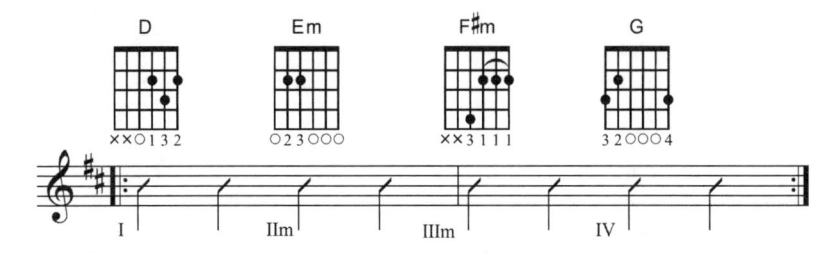

3. The key of E:

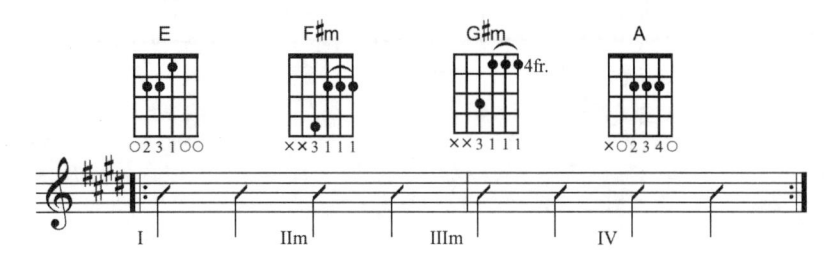

28

Chapter 3 The Harmonized Scale

4. The key of G:

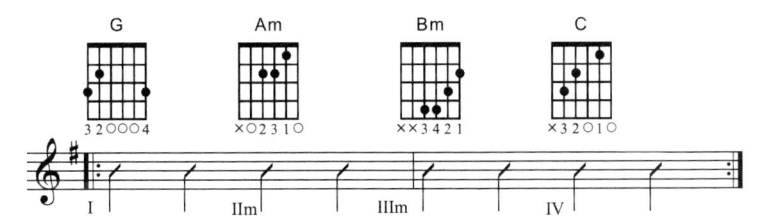

G	Am	Bm	C
I	IIm	IIIm	IV

5. The key of A:

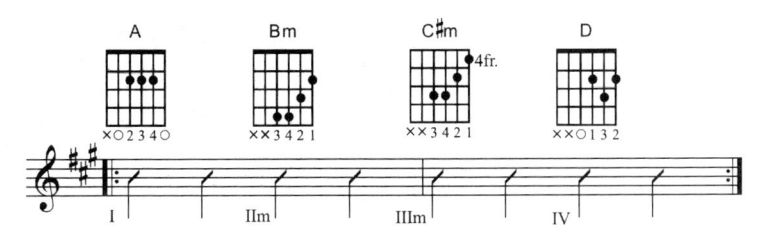

A	Bm	C#m	D
I	IIm	IIIm	IV

I–VIm–IIm–V7

| I | VIm | IIm | V7 |

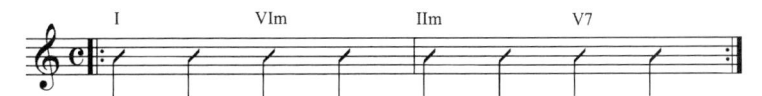

This pattern is very common in introductions and turnarounds, and in old rock and roll ballads, such as "All I Have to Do Is Dream."

1. The key of C:

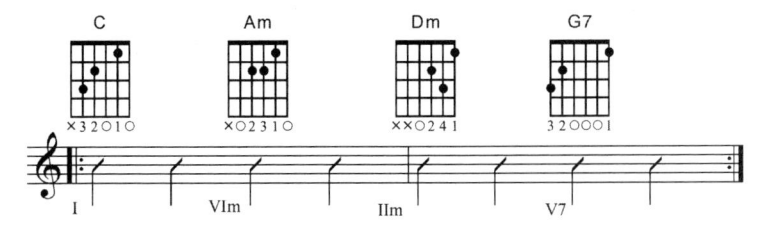

C	Am	Dm	G7
I	VIm	IIm	V7

2. The key of D:

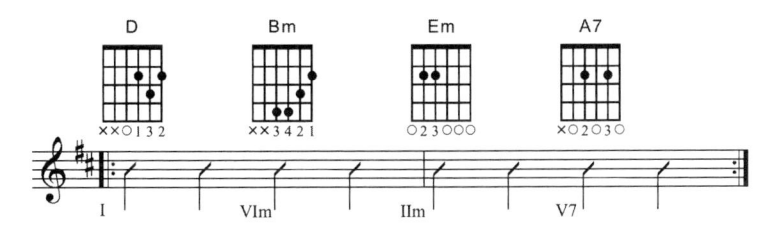

D	Bm	Em	A7
I	VIm	IIm	V7

29

Guitar for Songwriters

3. The key of E:

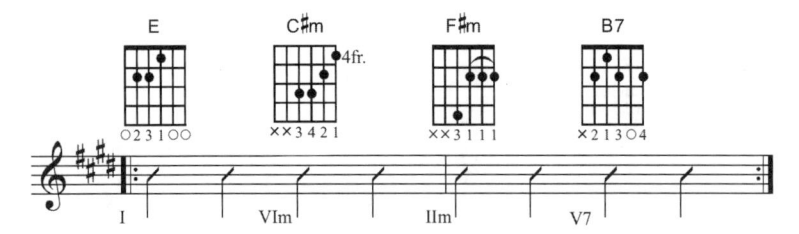

   E — C#m — F#m — B7
   I — VIm — IIm — V7

4. The key of G:

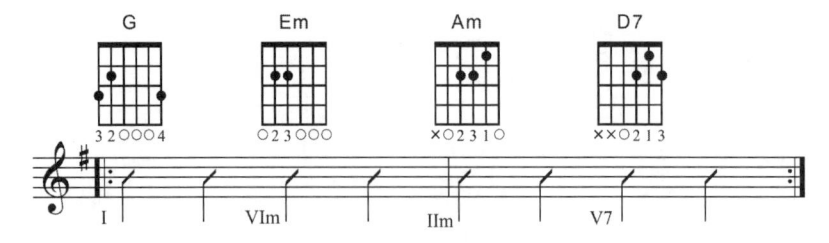

   G — Em — Am — D7
   I — VIm — IIm — V7

5. The key of A:

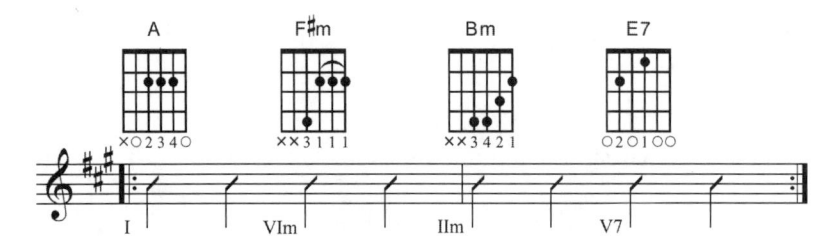

   A — F#m — Bm — E7
   I — VIm — IIm — V7

I-IIIm-IV-V7

Here is another progression to help you get comfortable with the main chords in a key.

I — IIIm — IV — V7

1. The key of C:

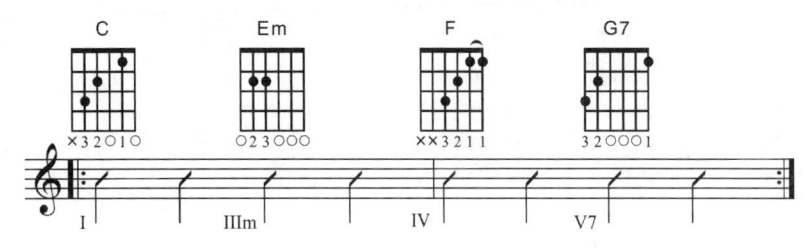

   C — Em — F — G7
   I — IIIm — IV — V7

30

Chapter 3 The Harmonized Scale

2. The key of D:

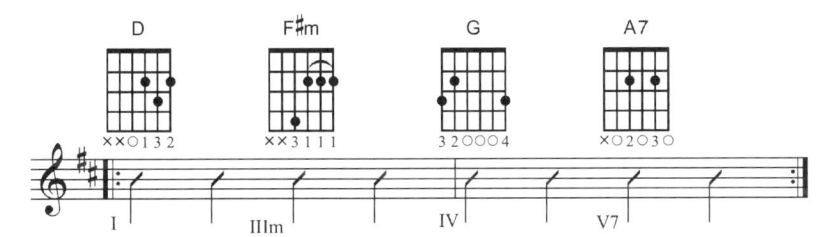

[Chord diagrams: D (xx0132), F#m (xx3111), G (320004), A7 (x02030) — I, IIIm, IV, V7]

3. The key of E:

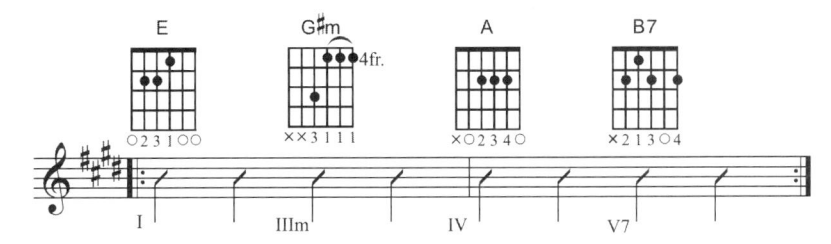

[Chord diagrams: E (023100), G#m (xx3111, 4fr.), A (x02340), B7 (x21304) — I, IIIm, IV, V7]

4. The key of G:

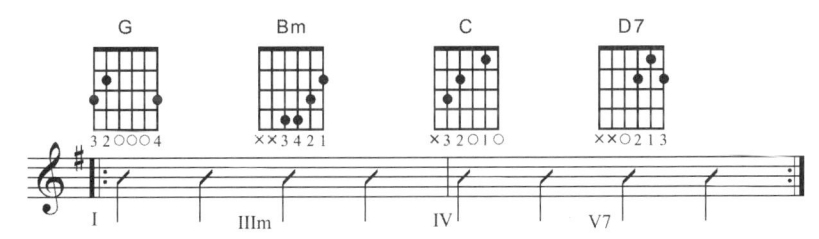

[Chord diagrams: G (320004), Bm (xx3421), C (x32010), D7 (xx0213) — I, IIIm, IV, V7]

5. The key of A:

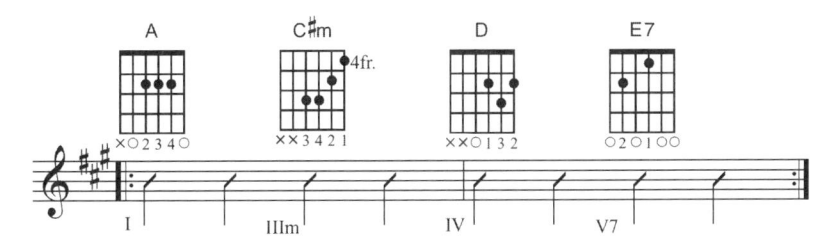

[Chord diagrams: A (x02340), C#m (xx3421, 4fr.), D (xx0132), E7 (020100) — I, IIIm, IV, V7]

I-I7-IV-IVm

Roman numerals can also be used to describe chords that aren't part of the regular harmonized scale. I7 and IVm don't normally appear in a major key, but this is still a common progression. The Beatles used it in many songs, and it shows up in part of the Mickey Mouse Club theme song.

[Notation: I, I7, IV, IVm]

31

Guitar for Songwriters

1. The key of C:

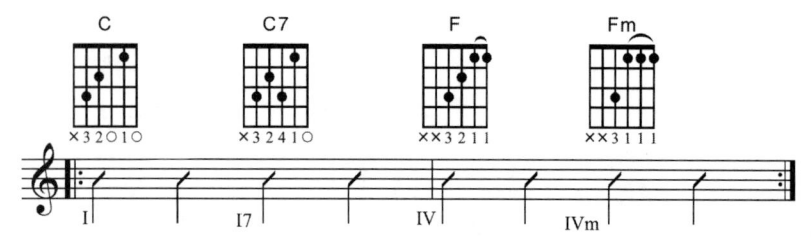

C	C7	F	Fm
x32010	x32410	xx3211	xx3111
I	I7	IV	IVm

2. The key of D:

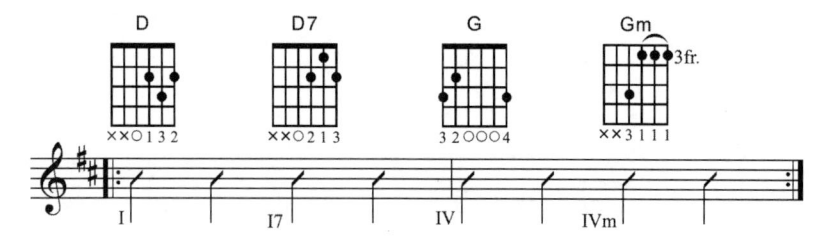

D	D7	G	Gm (3fr.)
xx0132	xx0213	320004	xx3111
I	I7	IV	IVm

3. The key of E:

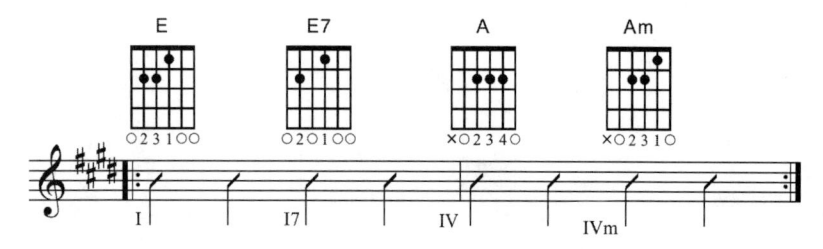

E	E7	A	Am
023100	020100	x02340	x02310
I	I7	IV	IVm

4. The key of G:

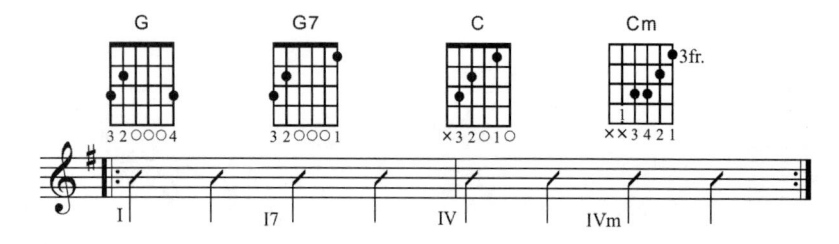

G	G7	C	Cm (3fr.)
320004	320001	x32010	xx3421
I	I7	IV	IVm

5. The key of A:

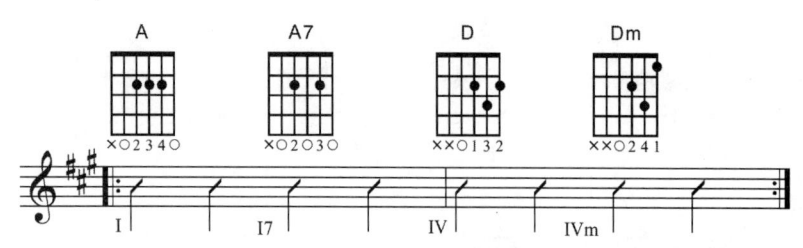

A	A7	D	Dm
x02340	x02030	xx0132	xx0241
I	I7	IV	IVm

Chapter 3 The Harmonized Scale

The Harmonized Scale in Minor Keys

Experimenting with scales will reveal that, although there is only one formula for a major scale, there are several types of minor scales. This means that you may come across different chords when playing in a minor key, depending on what type of scale is being used.

There are different possible ways to write the harmonized scale in minor, but here is the most common: Im, IIm7(♭5), ♭III, IVm, V7, ♭VI, and ♭VII. In C minor, the most common chords would therefore be Cm, Dm7♭5, E♭, Fm, G7, A♭, and B♭, although it wouldn't be unusual to see other chords also. (The IIm7(♭5) is closely related to the IVm and is seldom seen in simpler songs.)

> *The most common version of the harmonized scale in minor is Im, IIm7(♭5), ♭III, IVm, V7, ♭VI, and ♭VII.*

The minor seventh flat five chord—m7(♭5)—is a complicated name for a chord that is sometimes quite easy to hold. It is closely related to the IVm chord, which is often used in its place in simpler songs. Don't be scared off by the big name. We'll analyze these chords later, in the chapters on chord construction.

> **NOTE:** These scale tones are derived from the major scale. "♭III" means the chord built a half step lower than the third note of the major scale. The third note of a C scale is E, so ♭III in the key of Cm would be E♭. The third note in the key of D major is F♯, so ♭III would be F♮.

Table 3.2 Harmonized Minor Scale

Key	Im	IIm7(♭5)	♭III	IVm	V7	♭VI	♭VII
Cm	Cm	Dm7(♭5)	E♭	Fm	G7	A♭	B♭
C♯m	C♯m	D♯m7(♭5)	E	F♯m	G♯7	A	B
Dm	Dm	Em7(♭5)	F	Gm	A7	B♭	C
E♭m	E♭m	Fm7(♭5)	G♭	A♭m	B♭7	C♭	D♭
Em	Em	F♯m7(♭5)	G	Am	B7	C	D
Fm	Fm	Gm7(♭5)	A♭	B♭m	C7	D♭	E♭
F♯m	F♯m	G♯m7(♭5)	A	Bm	C♯7	D	E
Gm	Gm	Am7(♭5)	B♭	Cm	D7	E♭	F
G♯m	G♯m	A♯m7(♭5)	B	C♯m	D♯7	E	F♯
A♭m	A♭m	B♭m7(♭5)	C♭	D♭m	E♭7	F♭	G♭
Am	Am	Bm7(♭5)	C	Dm	E7	F	G
B♭m	B♭m	Cm7(♭5)	D♭	E♭m	F7	G♭	A♭
Bm	Bm	C♯m7(♭5)	D	Em	F♯7	G	A

Guitar for Songwriters

Some Common Progressions in Minor Keys

The exercises in the following sections are in the simplest minor keys for the guitar. After learning bar chords, transpose them to other keys.

Im-IVm-bVI-V7

1. The key of Em:

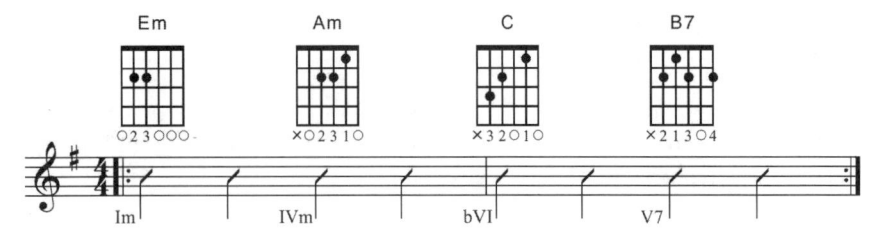

2. The key of Am:

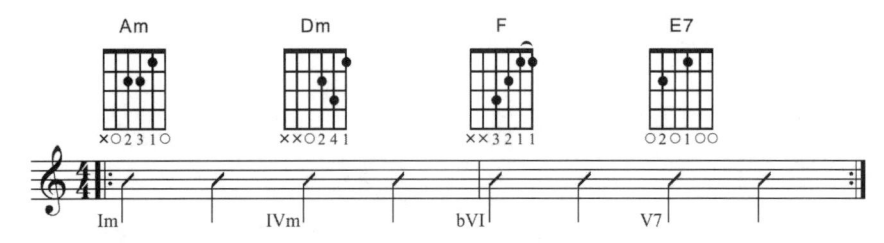

3. The key of Dm:

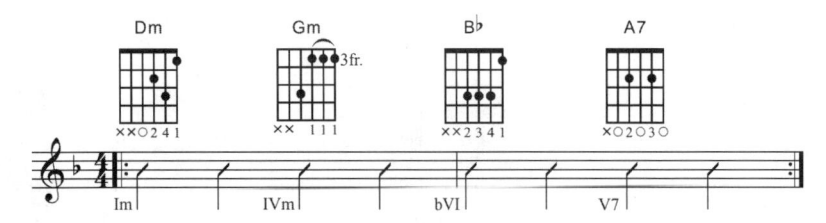

The B♭ major chord shown here is one of many possible voicings. Later in this book, I'll present other options that sound fuller but are a little more difficult to hold.

Im-bIII-IVm-V7

Chapter 3 The Harmonized Scale

1. The key of Em:

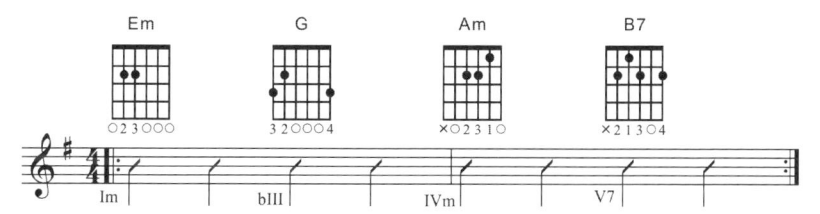

Em	G	Am	B7
Im	bIII	IVm	V7

2. The key of Am:

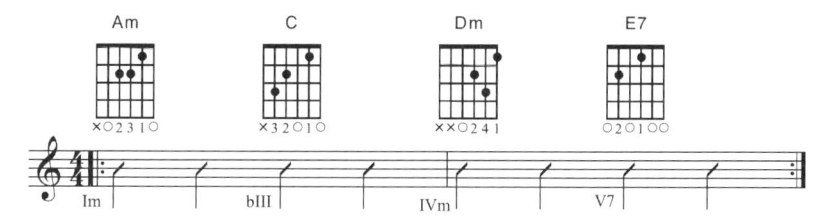

Am	C	Dm	E7
Im	bIII	IVm	V7

3. The key of Dm:

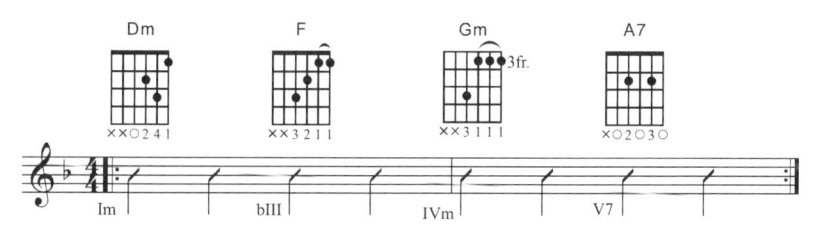

Dm	F	Gm	A7
Im	bIII	IVm	V7

Im-bVII-bVI-V7

This is a common pattern that was used in the old surfer tune, "Walk Don't Run."

| Im | bVII | bVI | V7 |

1. The key of Em:

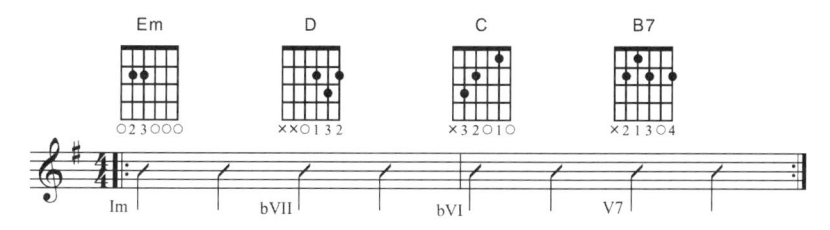

Em	D	C	B7
Im	bVII	bVI	V7

2. The key of Am:

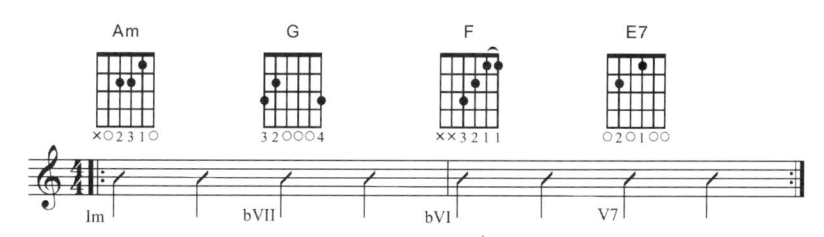

Am	G	F	E7
Im	bVII	bVI	V7

35

Guitar for Songwriters

3. The key of Dm:

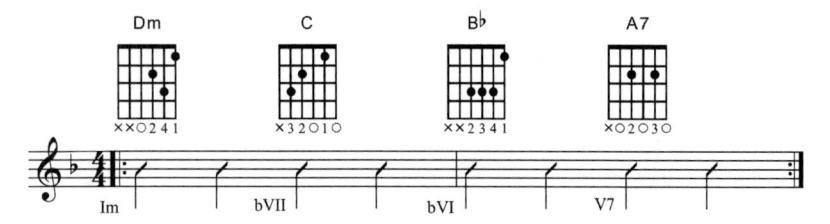

   | Dm | C | B♭ | A7 |

   Im — bVII — bVI — V7

Im-IVm-IIm7(♭5)-V7

The IIm7(♭5) chord may have a long name, but that doesn't mean it's difficult to hold. It has several notes in common with IVm.

Im — IVm — IIm7(b5) — V7

1. The key of Em:

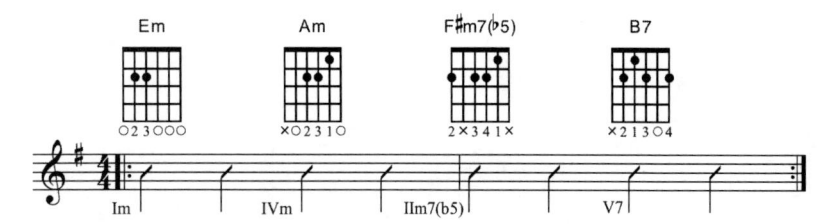

   | Em | Am | F♯m7(♭5) | B7 |

   Im — IVm — IIm7(b5) — V7

   For F♯m7(♭5), also called F♯ø or F♯ half-diminished, mute the first and fifth strings by leaning the first and second fingers of your left hand slightly.

2. The key of Am:

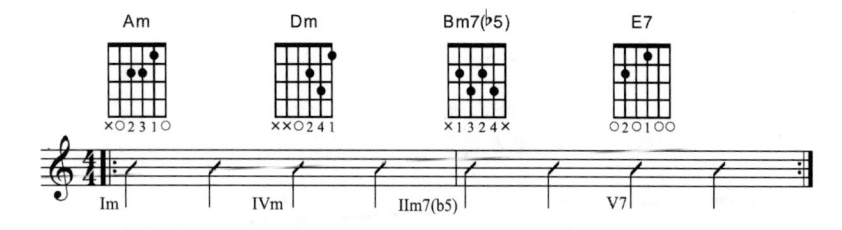

   | Am | Dm | Bm7(♭5) | E7 |

   Im — IVm — IIm7(b5) — V7

3. The key of Dm:

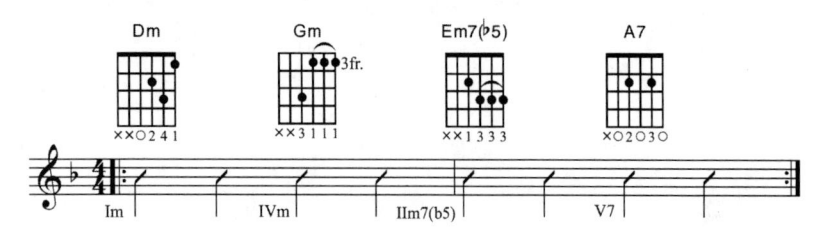

   | Dm | Gm | Em7(♭5) | A7 |

   Im — IVm — IIm7(b5) — V7

Power Chords

POWER CHORDS ARE TWO- AND THREE-STRING CHORDS SOMETIMES USED IN CERTAIN STYLES OF ROCK GUITAR PLAYING, like punk and heavy metal, mostly with an electric guitar and some distortion. In music books, they are usually notated with a letter and the number 5, to indicate the root of the chord and the fifth note of that scale. C5 contains the notes C and a G (the fifth note of the C scale). D5 has the notes D and A in it, while G5 has G and D. If the chord has three strings, the third note being held is a repeat of the root, an octave higher.

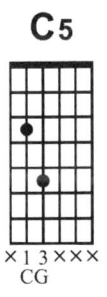

C5

C and G—the first and fifth notes in a C major scale—are the notes in a C5 chord.

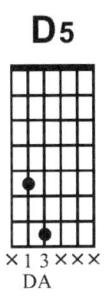

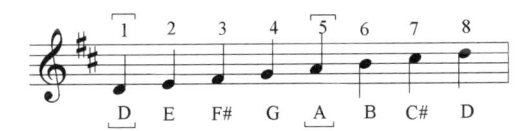

D5

D and A—the first and fifth notes in a D major scale—are the notes in a D5 chord.

37

Guitar for Songwriters

G5

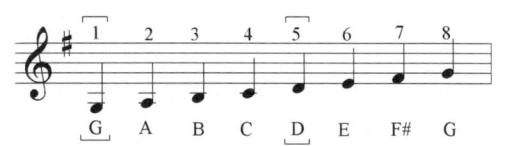

The notes in G5 are G and D.

A three-string power chord has a root, the fifth note of the scale, and another root an octave higher.

C5

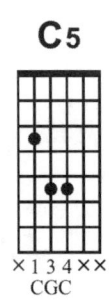

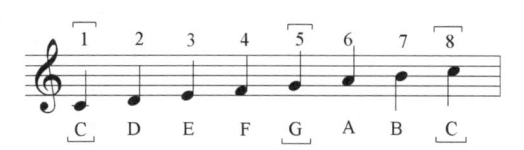

Although limited, these chords demonstrate one of the real strengths of the guitar. Simply by moving these chords to different positions on the neck, you form new chords. This principle also applies to bar chords and many other types of chords on the guitar.

> *By moving these chords to different positions on the neck, you form new chords.*

F5 1fr.   **F#5** 2fr.   **G5** 3fr.   **A♭5** 4fr.   **A5** 5fr.   **B♭5** 6fr.

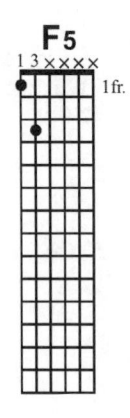

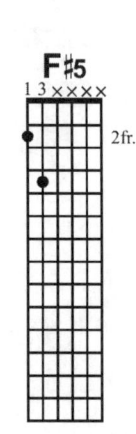

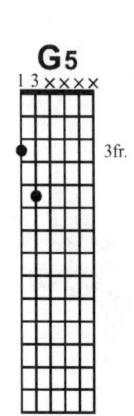

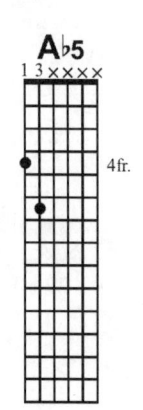

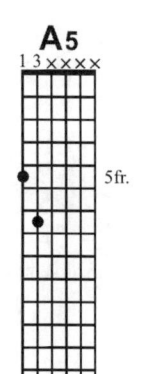

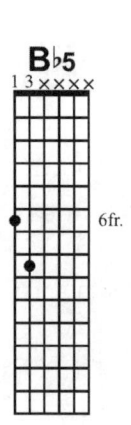

Chapter 4 Power Chords

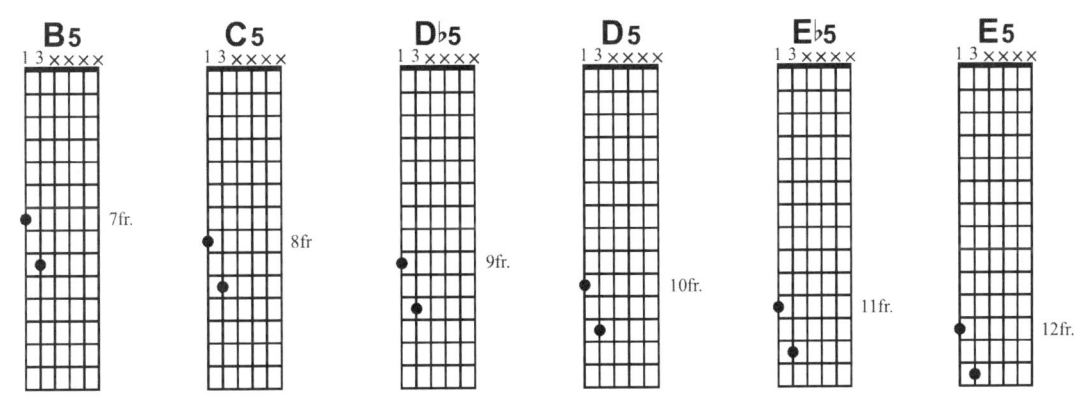

B5 1 3 × × × × 7fr.
C5 1 3 × × × × 8fr.
D♭5 1 3 × × × × 9fr.
D5 1 3 × × × × 10fr.
E♭5 1 3 × × × × 11fr.
E5 1 3 × × × × 12fr.

You can play this chord in any key by moving it up the neck.

These chords sound good for the right kind of music. On an electric guitar with the amp cranked up, they often sound better than a chord with more notes. They are easy to learn, using only two or three fingers and moving the same shape all over the neck. But they don't work at all for most styles of music—from B.B. King to the Beatles to bebop.

Following are power chords on the fourth and fifth strings.

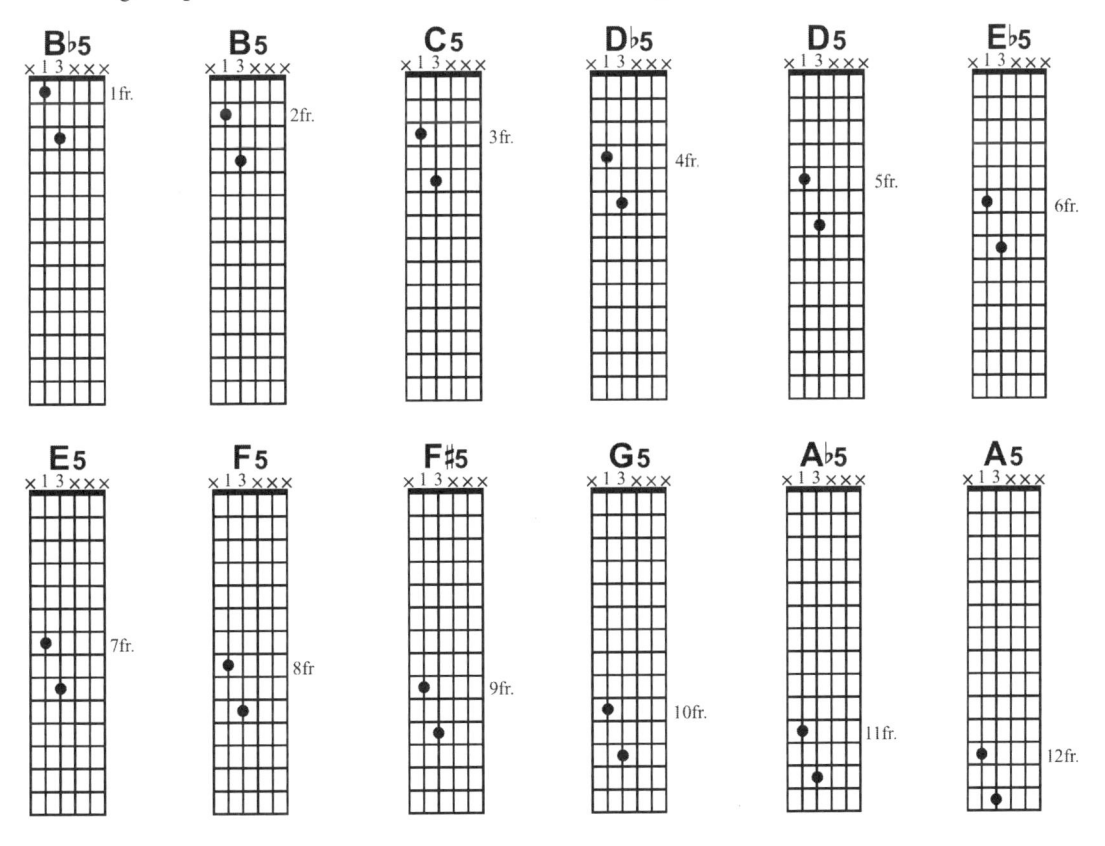

B♭5 × 1 3 × × × 1fr.
B5 × 1 3 × × × 2fr.
C5 × 1 3 × × × 3fr.
D♭5 × 1 3 × × × 4fr.
D5 × 1 3 × × × 5fr.
E♭5 × 1 3 × × × 6fr.

E5 × 1 3 × × × 7fr.
F5 × 1 3 × × × 8fr.
F#5 × 1 3 × × × 9fr.
G5 × 1 3 × × × 10fr.
A♭5 × 1 3 × × × 11fr.
A5 × 1 3 × × × 12fr.

At this time, it's appropriate to learn the names of the notes on the fifth and sixth strings. The root of these power chords is the note held by your first finger. If you know the name of that note, you can name the power chord. For example, the note G is on the sixth string at the third fret. Hold the power chord with your first finger on that G, and you are holding G5. D5 is the chord starting with your first finger on the D note, on the fifth string at the fifth fret.

Guitar for Songwriters

The root of these chords is the note held by your first finger.

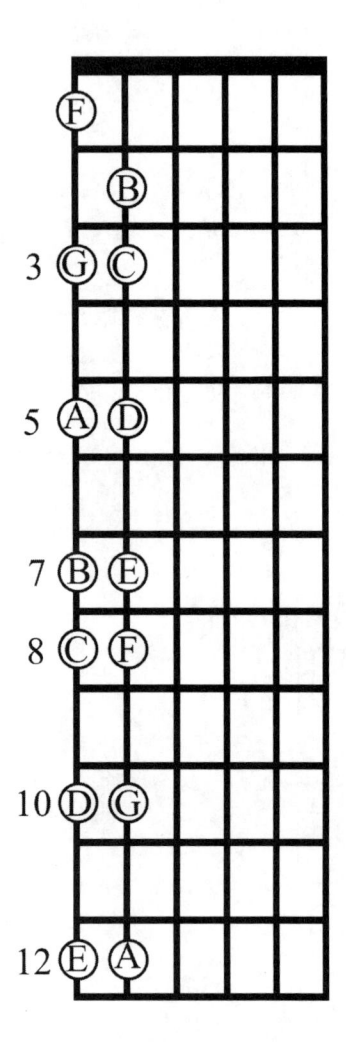

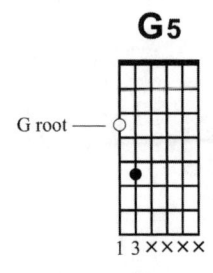

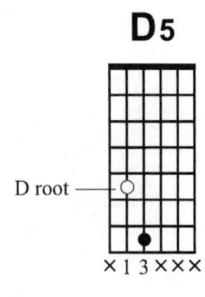

G5

G root — (open)

1 3 × × × ×

D5

D root — (open)

× 1 3 × × ×

Chapter 4 Power Chords

Power chords lack the note that makes a chord major or minor. This ambiguity can be seen as a weakness or a strength—a power chord is not as complex as other chords, but it is easy to learn and can be used in place of either chord type. It generally doesn't sound very good to mix power and other types of chords within a song.

1. This exercise uses the form with fingers on the fifth and sixth strings. When you slide between the chords, relax your hand. In other words, keep touching the strings as you move up or down the neck, but don't apply any pressure.

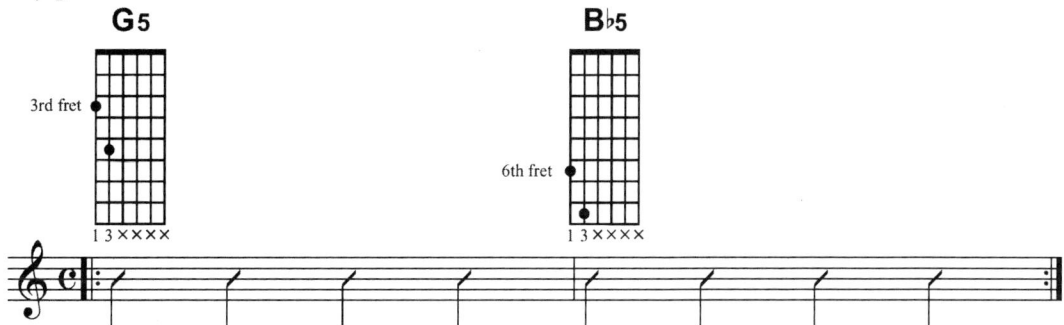

You can hear how exercise #1 sounds by downloading the audio file Example02 from http://cengageptr.com/guitarforsongwriters.

2. This exercise uses the form on the fourth and fifth strings.

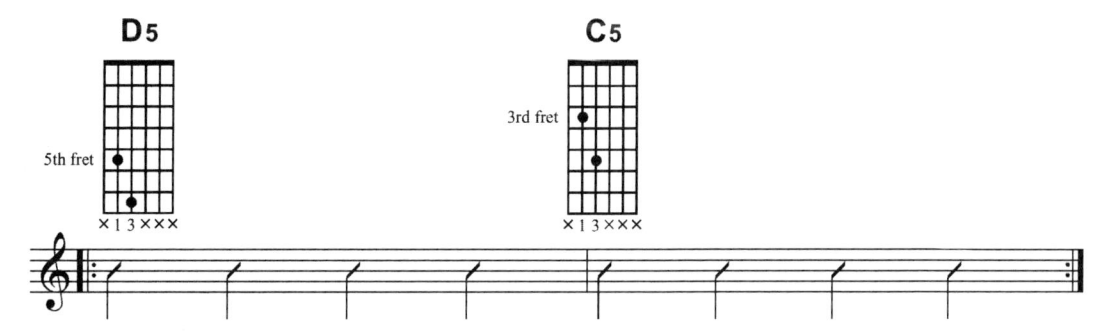

3. It is often easier to switch strings rather than slide a large distance along the neck.

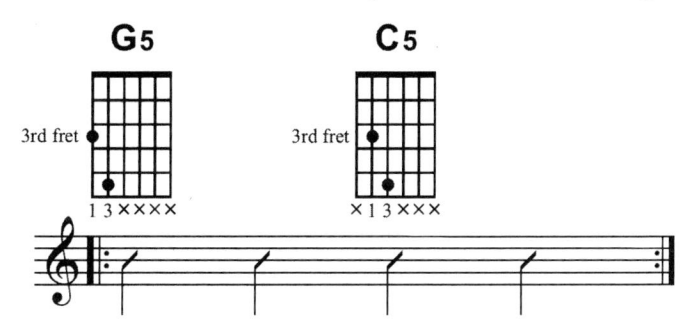

Guitar for Songwriters

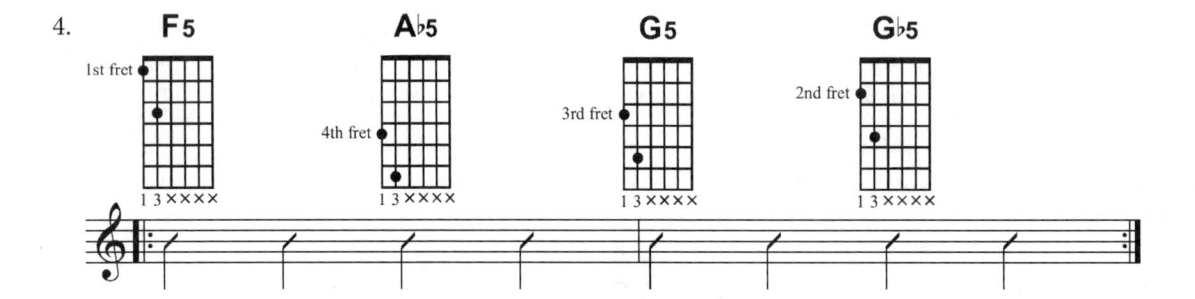

4. F5   A♭5   G5   G♭5

The following exercises show the positions for the chords, but not which strings. Refer to the fingerboard diagram earlier in this chapter if necessary.

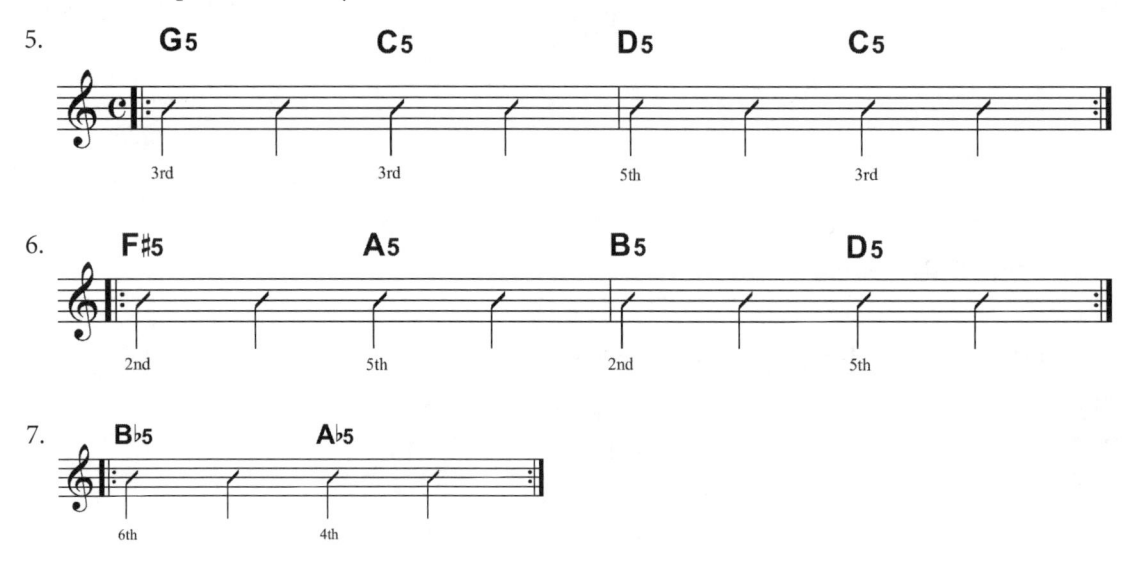

5. G5 (3rd)   C5 (3rd)   D5 (5th)   C5 (3rd)

6. F♯5 (2nd)   A5 (5th)   B5 (2nd)   D5 (5th)

7. B♭5 (6th)   A♭5 (4th)

In the next chapter, we'll explore the right hand and ways to add personality to your playing.

Accompaniment Styles

S O FAR, WE HAVE ONLY LOOKED AT THE LEFT HAND, at the fingers holding the chords. But the right hand is the one that adds personality—it can make a song sound driving or peaceful, it can swing or syncopate, it can be loud or soft, or it can sound confident or shaky. In this chapter, we'll touch upon a number of techniques for the right hand.

Strumming

Strumming chords involves a number of subtle movements that can best be learned by listening and trying to duplicate the sounds you hear. The techniques presented here are only a beginning. The details—accents, muting, knowing which strings to hit and how hard—must be refined with practice.

Upon listening closely to a guitarist playing chords, you will quickly realize that not all beats are created equal. Within most measures, there are loud strums, soft ones, strums that are almost nonexistent, and strums that are more percussive than harmonic. Strumming in the right direction is necessary to make these elements fall into place.

The basic down strum is the strongest—moving your pick or fingers from the bass strings to the higher-pitched strings. You usually strum down on the beat, moving your hand along with your foot. The symbol ⊓ indicates a down strum. V indicates an up strum.

When playing eighth notes (two notes per beat), you normally strum down on the beat (when your foot is going down) and up off the beat (when your foot is coming up).

Notice that pattern 5 below requires playing two up strokes in a row, and pattern 6 is almost all up strokes. Your hand will still move with your foot, going down on the beat but not hitting any strings. This puts you in position for the next up stroke. If you are doing it correctly, everything should be nice and relaxed.

> The following strums are demonstrated in Example03 through Example08 at
> http://cengageptr.com/guitarforsongwriters.

1. All down strokes.

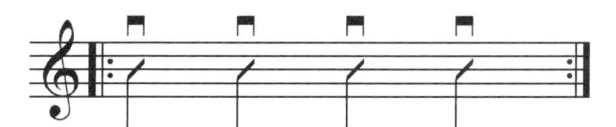

Guitar for Songwriters

2. Alternating down and up strokes.

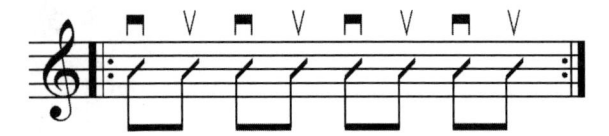

3. A down stroke on beat one and alternating down and up strokes on the other beats.

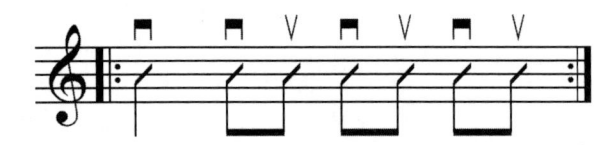

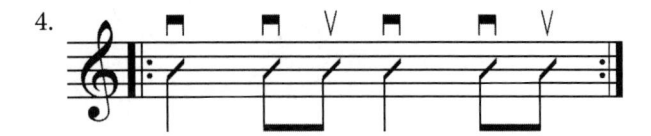

4.

5. The all-purpose generic strum—it seems to fit almost anything!

6. This one is very syncopated—except for beat one, all strums are upstrokes, occurring off the beat.

Muting and Accents

Chords can sound much more effective and dramatic when they aren't constantly ringing out. Muting them provides tiny silences that really enhance the sound. You can stop a chord from sounding using a combination of left and right hands—relax your left hand to take the pressure off the strings, lean your fingers slightly to mute adjacent strings, and at the same time lay the heel of your right hand across any open strings that may still be ringing.

- ▶ • **Staccato:** Make the notes "short" by cutting them off as soon as you play them.
- ▶ x **Muted:** Hit "dead" strings to get a percussive sound.
- ▶ > **Accent:** Play this louder than the surrounding notes.

Chapter 5 Accompaniment Styles

> You can hear the next six examples of muting and accents by downloading Example09 through Example14 from http://cengageptr.com/guitarforsongwriters.

1. Play some chords and then stop the strings immediately after. Start with the G5 chord at the third position. Only pick on the bass strings, and it should be fairly easy to mute.

2. Now mute the strings before striking them on the second and fourth beats.

3. Accent a beat by making it louder than the others around it.

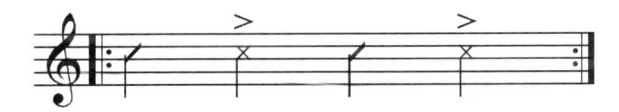

4. Here is a combination of accents and muted strings.

5. This is similar, but twice as fast and with the accent in a different place.

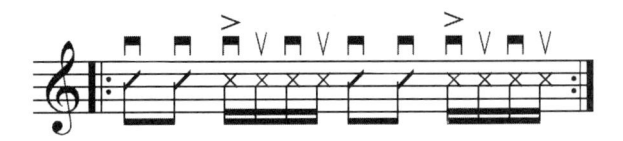

6. This is the classic "Bo Diddley" strum. If you're not familiar with him, look him up!

Guitar for Songwriters

Bass Notes

If you're not playing with a bass player, playing a bass note on the first beat of a chord can be very effective. Instead of strumming on the first beat, play the lowest note of the chord, usually the fifth or sixth string. Then strum the higher-pitched strings as usual for the rest of the measure, muting strings or doing whatever sounds good to you. (Power chords don't have enough strings in them for this to make sense.) Try to get some separation between the bass notes and the chords—in other words, don't play the bass strings as part of the strumming.

Normally you would try to hit the lowest root of the chord for the bass note. That is often the lowest note you're holding. Experiment using different notes as the bass, and learn to trust your ear. If it sounds good, that's a good bass note to use!

> The next five exercises can be heard as Example15 through Example19 at http://cengageptr.com/guitarforsongwriters.

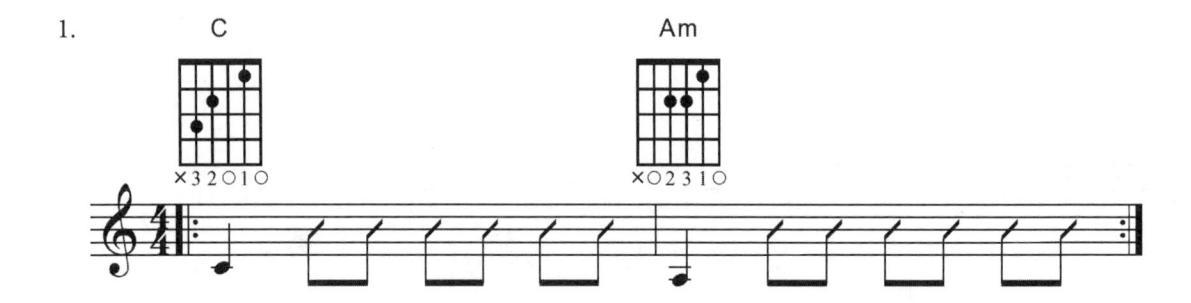

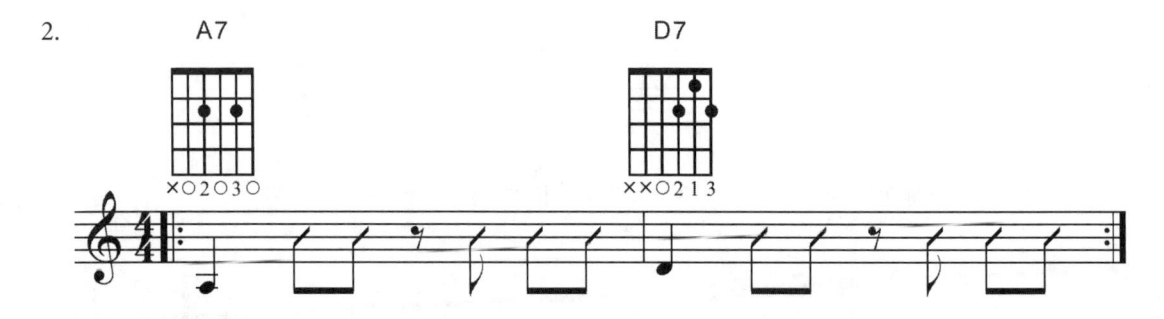

1. C   Am

2. A7   D7

You can also play two bass notes per measure, alternating between the root and the fifth of the chord (the fifth and sixth strings in this example). For some chords, you don't need to move any fingers. For C major, play the second bass note by moving your third finger to the sixth string.

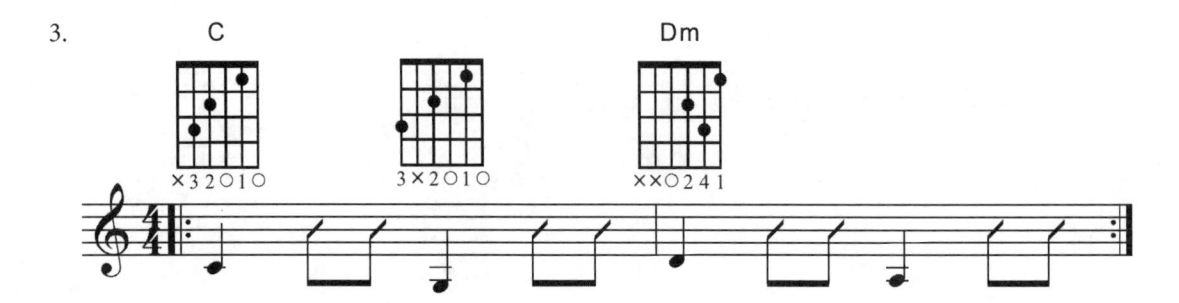

3. C   Dm

Chapter 5 Accompaniment Styles

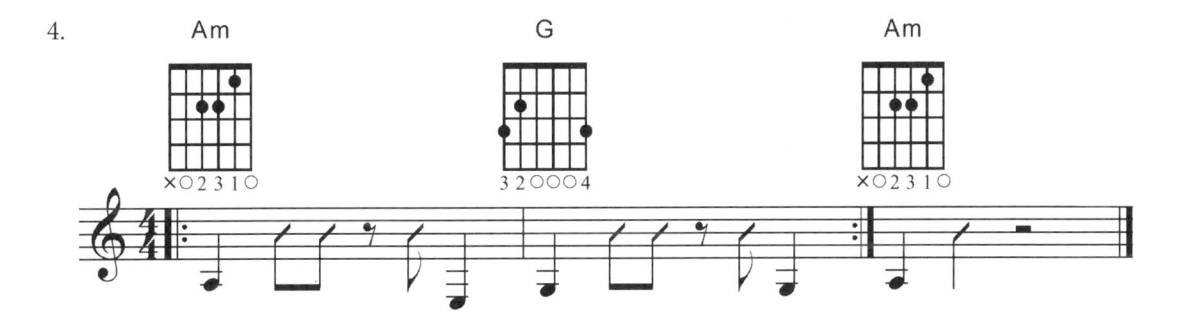

4. Am G Am

This exercise is more syncopated, with three bass notes per four-beat measure.

5. C

Am C

Descending Bass Lines

The following two examples show a chord with a descending bass line. Sometimes called *slash chords*, two letters separated by a slash indicate a chord and the bass note. C/B means the C major chord with B as the bass note. When you see slash chords, be on the alert for a nice bass progression. Emphasize the bass notes a little more to bring out that line.

These descending bass lines can be heard in Example20 and Example21, available at http://cengageptr.com/guitarforsongwriters.

Guitar for Songwriters

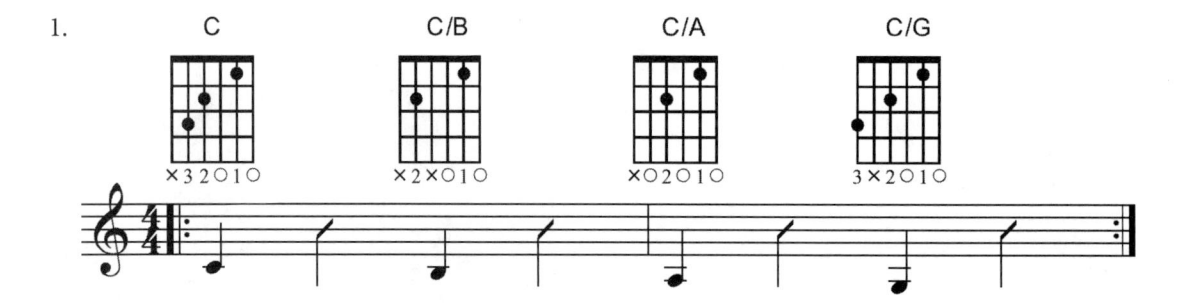

1.

[Chord diagrams: C (x32010), C/B (x2x010), C/A (x02010), C/G (3x2010) with notation staff in 4/4]

2. Be sure to hit only the first four strings on the first three chords. Bring out the descending bass line.

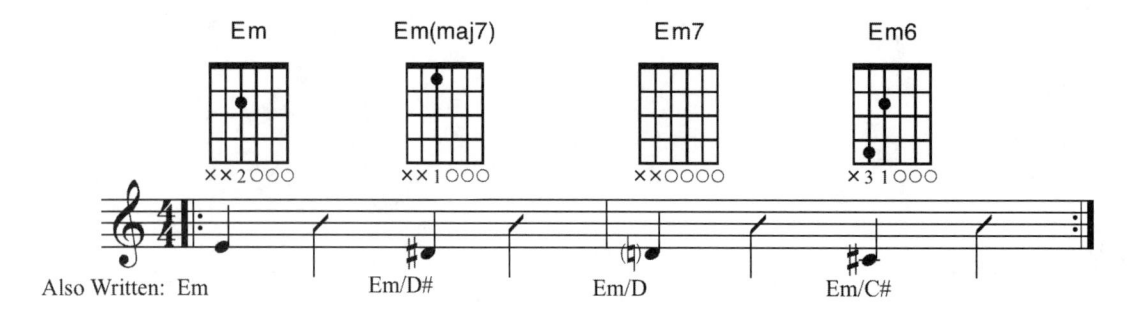

[Chord diagrams: Em (xx2000), Em(maj7) (xx1000), Em7 (xx0000), Em6 (x31000) with notation staff in 4/4]

Also Written: Em   Em/D#   Em/D   Em/C#

Fingerpicking

Fingerpicking uses the thumb and two or three fingers of the right hand to play individual strings of a chord. It is generally quieter than strumming with a pick, with a more personal sound that works especially well on slower, quieter pieces.

The thumb takes care of the bass notes, usually on the fourth, fifth, or sixth string. The index and middle fingers play the other strings. Many people also use their ring finger, but few use the pinkie, since it is so much shorter.

Right-Hand Fingers:

▶ T: Thumb
▶ I: Index
▶ M: Middle
▶ R: Ring

Fingerpicking Exercises: Pattern 1

Here is a basic pattern with the thumb, index, middle, and ring fingers playing in sequence. The thumb alternates between the root and the fifth of the chord. On the C chord, you need to shift your third finger to hit the fifth, but on many chords you don't move any fingers.

> **NOTE:** Classical guitarists use P, I, M, and A to indicate thumb, index, middle, and ring fingers of the right hand. The initials come from the Spanish words for those fingers.

Chapter 5 Accompaniment Styles

Listen to Example22 at http://cengageptr.com/guitarforsongwriters.

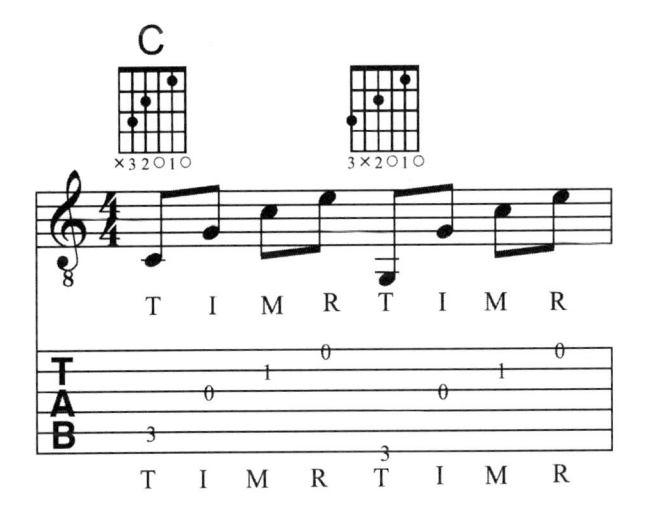

About Tablature: "TAB" on the second staff stands for "tablature," a system of notation for stringed instruments. The lines represent the six strings of the guitar, with high E (the first string) on top. The numbers are the frets. A three on the second line is telling you to hold the second string at the third fret.

Here is that pattern applied to a few progressions.

The next two exercises can be heard as Example23 and Example24 at http://cengageptr.com/guitarforsongwriters.

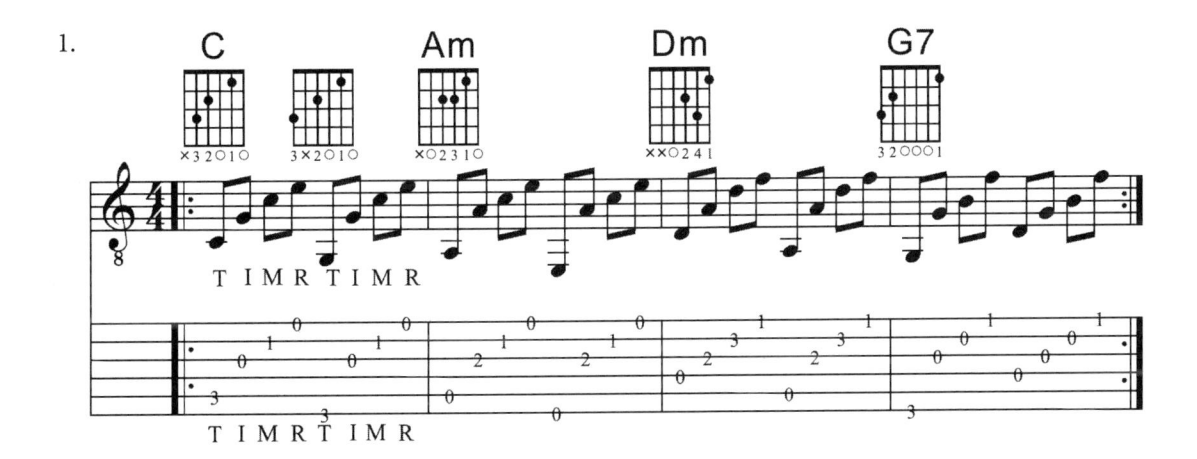

1.

Guitar for Songwriters

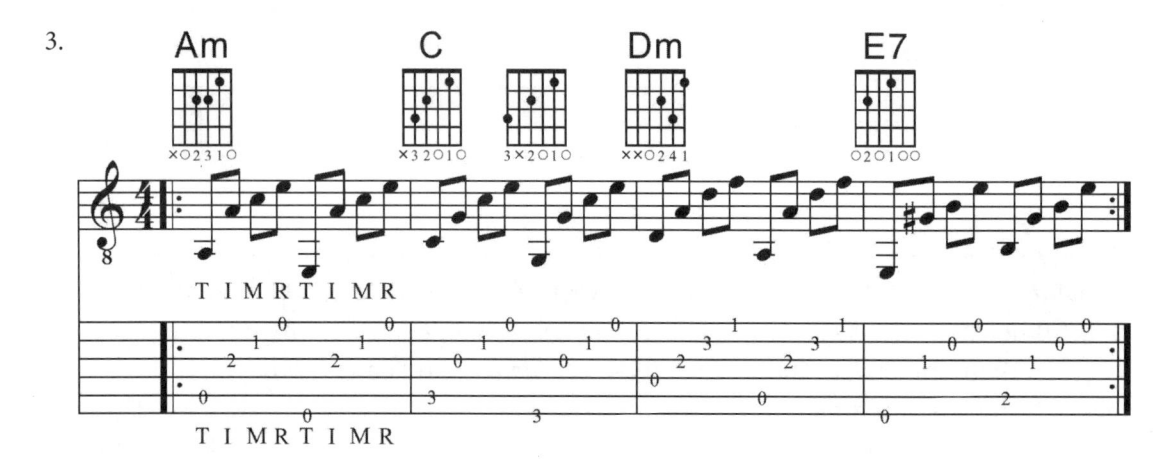

Fingerpicking Exercises: Pattern 2

The next pattern uses the ring and middle fingers playing at the same time, with the ring on the first string and the middle on the second.

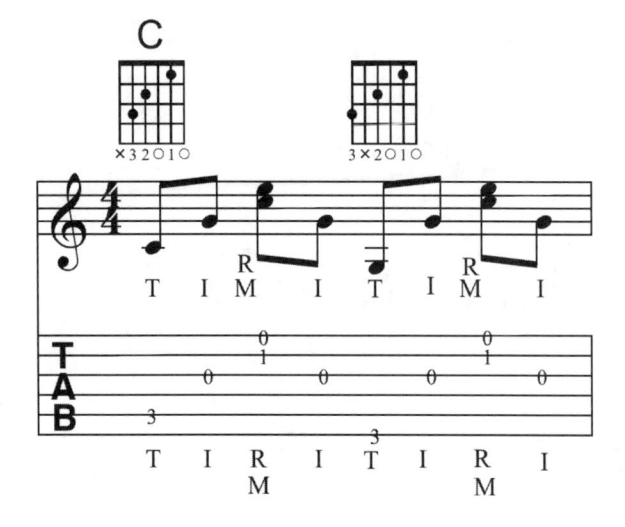

50

Chapter 5 Accompaniment Styles

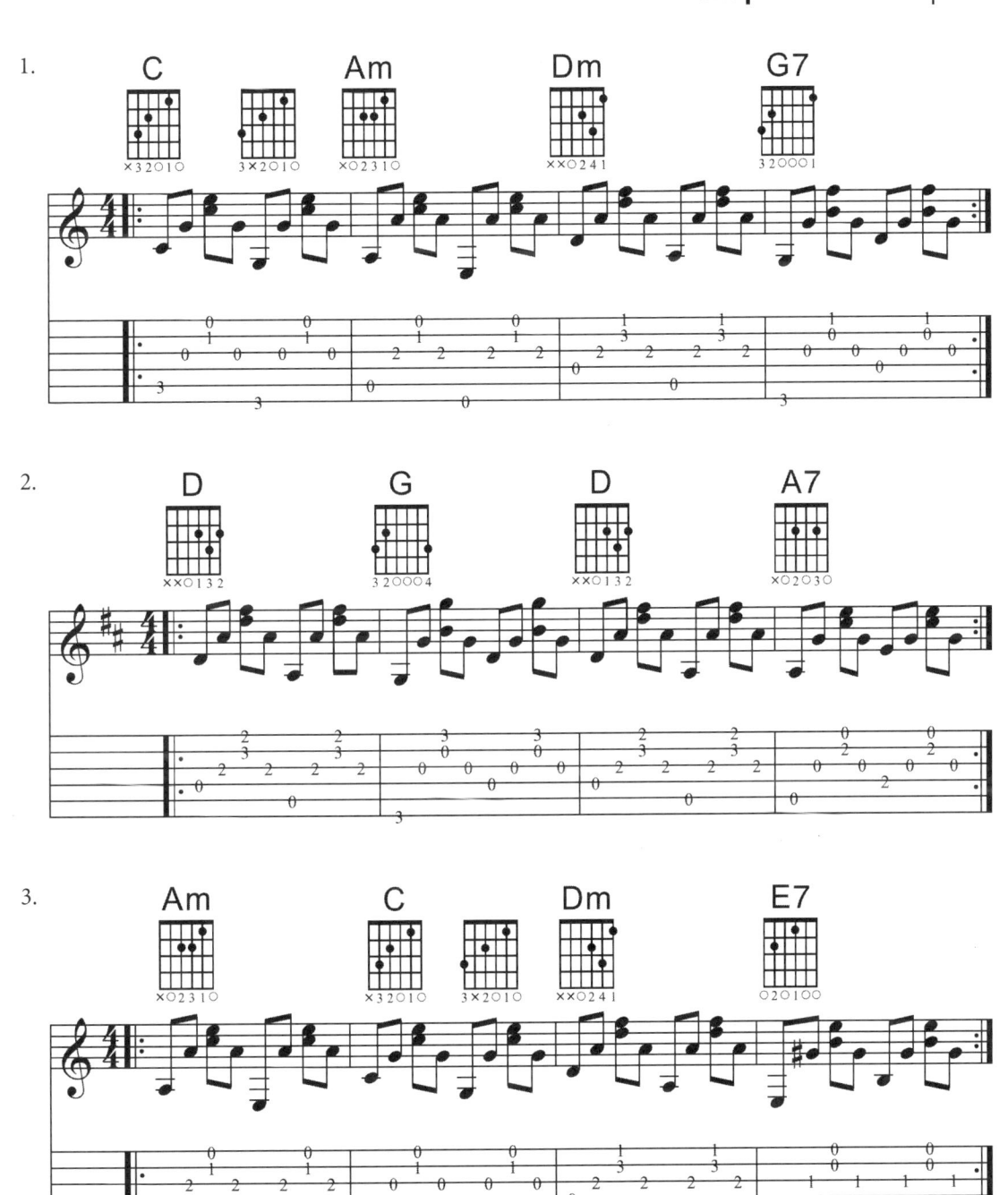

Guitar for Songwriters

Fingerpicking Exercises: Pattern 3

This pattern has the thumb playing only on the first beat of each measure.

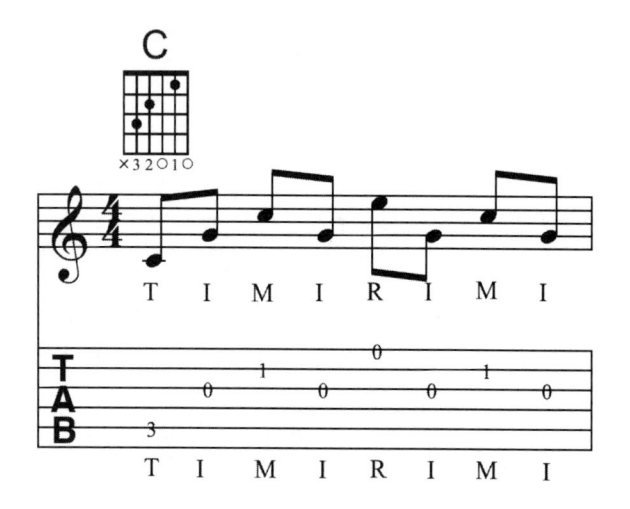

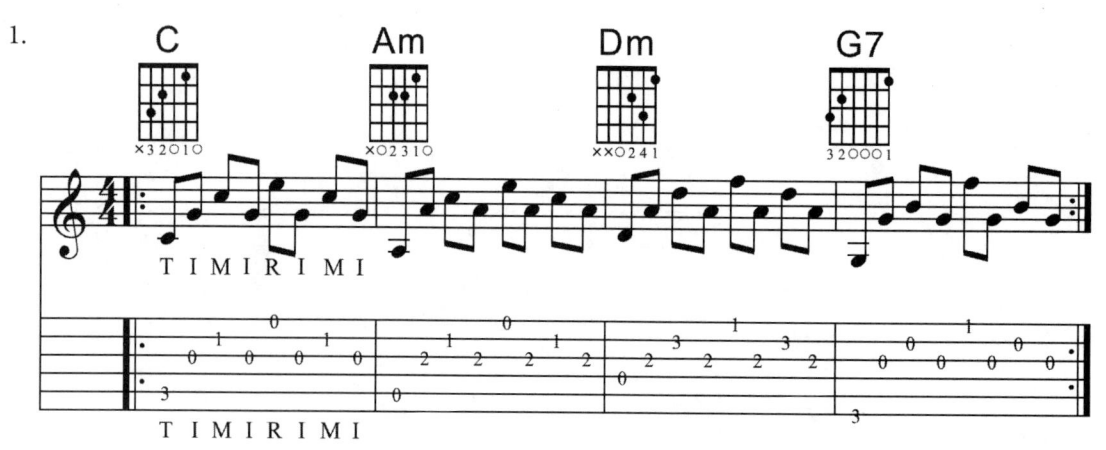

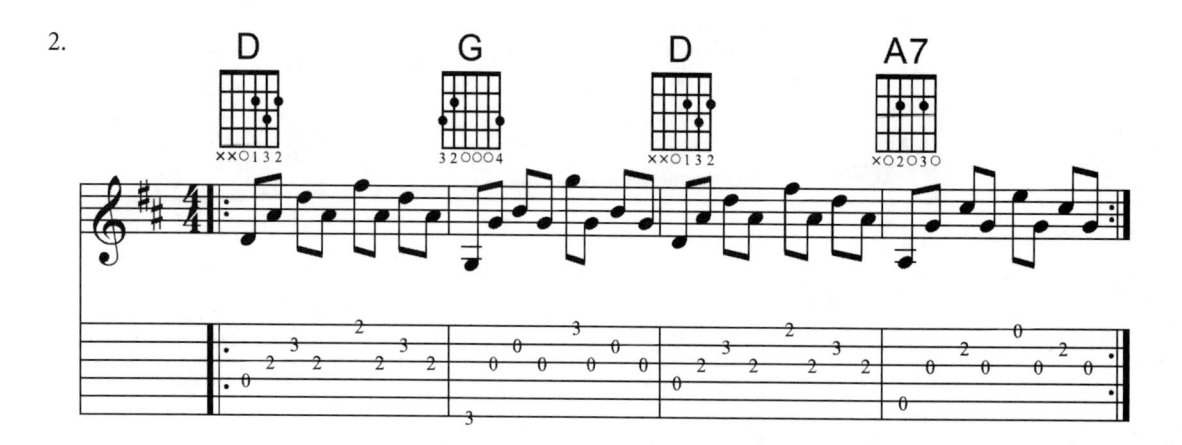

Chapter 5 Accompaniment Styles

3.

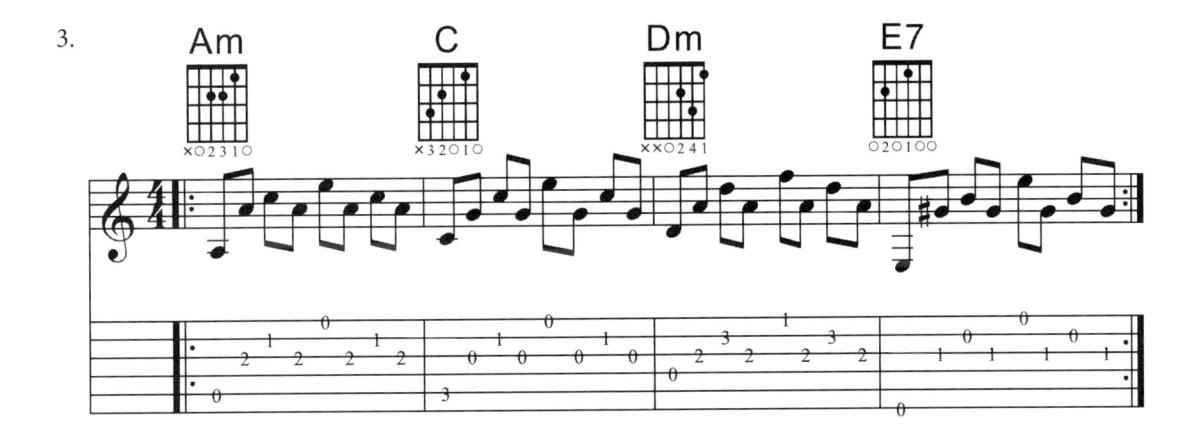

Common Fingerpicking Patterns

By now, you should have the basic idea of fingerpicking. It's easy to come up with your own patterns, but this section covers some of the more common ones.

> These 10 common fingerpicking patterns are Example25 through Example34 at http://cengageptr.com/guitarforsongwriters.

The first three patterns are steady eighth notes with a bass note on beats one and three.

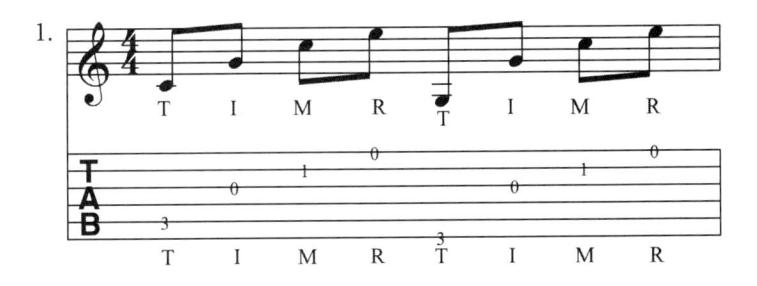

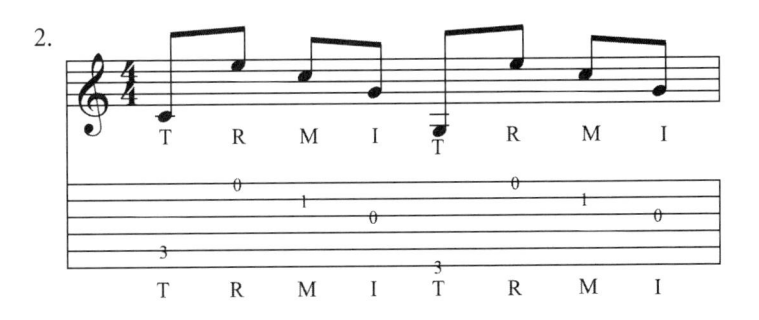

1.

2.

53

Guitar for Songwriters

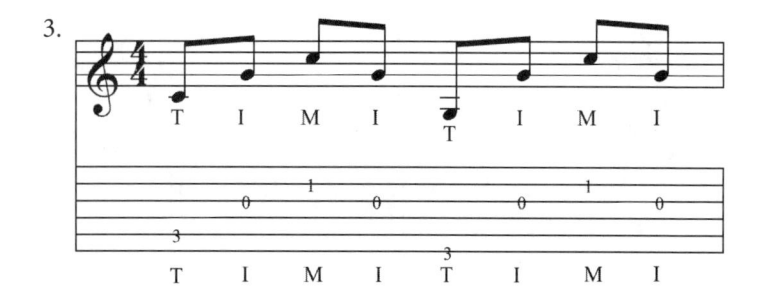

3.

The next two patterns have two notes being played at once.

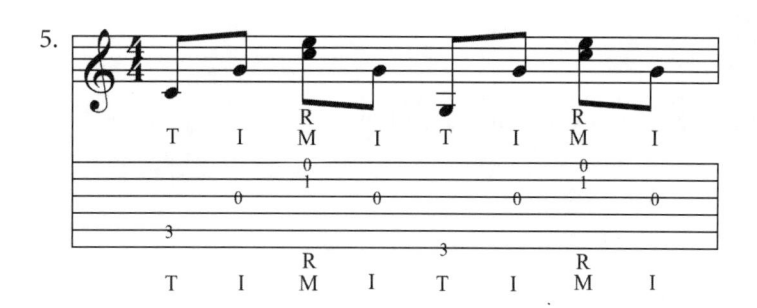

4.

5.

6. In this pattern, the thumb plays only on the first beat of each measure.

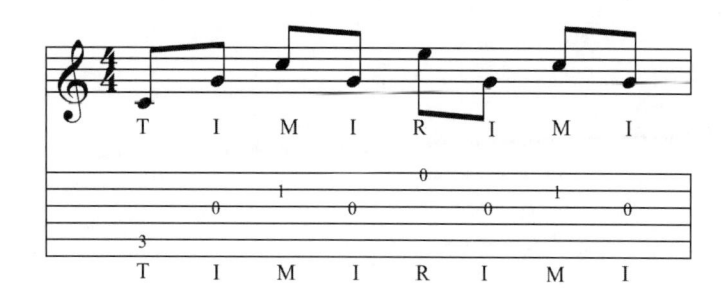

Chapter 5 Accompaniment Styles

7. All fingers play on the first beat of this syncopated pattern.

The next three patterns are in three-four time.

8.

9.

10.

Styles

Different styles of music are identified by the type of beat and the accents, as well as the chords used. Your ear is the best guide to finding the sound you want, but the following sections provide basic descriptions of a few types of music.

Guitar for Songwriters

Rock

The chords in many rock songs are played with a straight-eighths feel—that is, with all of the notes evenly spaced. This is very different from a swing feel. Beats two and four are very heavy—this is called a strong backbeat. It is generally played loud, with lots of energy. The most common chords are power chords or simple major and minor chords, although there are very many exceptions to this. A lot of so-called rock music borrows from other styles.

> These examples of styles make more sense when you hear them. The following exercises can be heard in Example35 through Example39 at http://cengageptr.com/guitarforsongwriters.

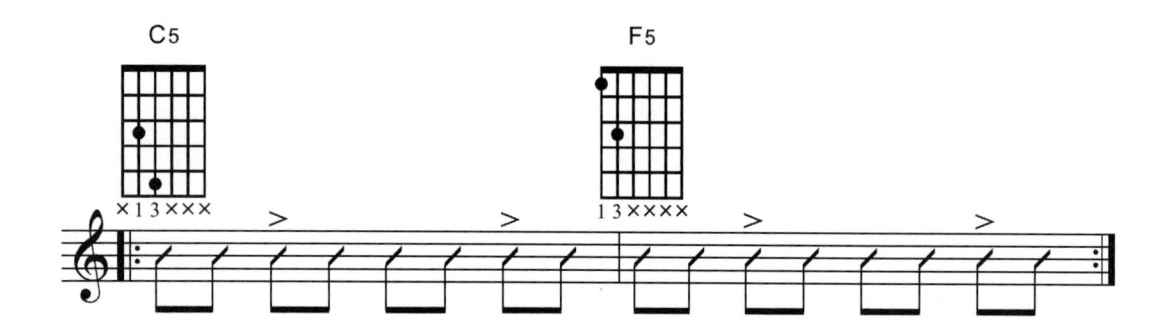

Swing

A swing beat is not divided evenly. When playing eighth notes, it is long-short. The chord played *on* the beat is held longer than the one played *off* the beat. Beats two and four are accented. The sound is light and relaxed. The chords are more sophisticated, often using major and minor sevenths, ninths, flat ninths, and beyond. The progressions in the chapter on jazz chords usually sound good with a swing feel.

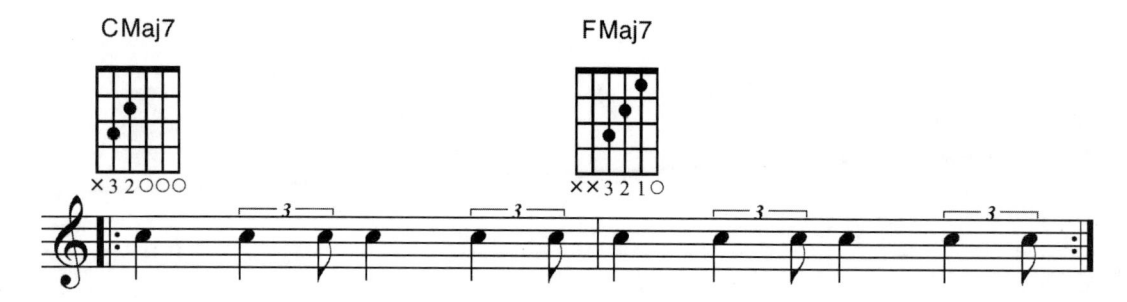

Reggae/Ska

Chords are played mostly on beats two and four, emphasizing the higher-pitched notes and played very staccato (cut short). The bass fills a lot of the spaces.

Chapter 5 Accompaniment Styles

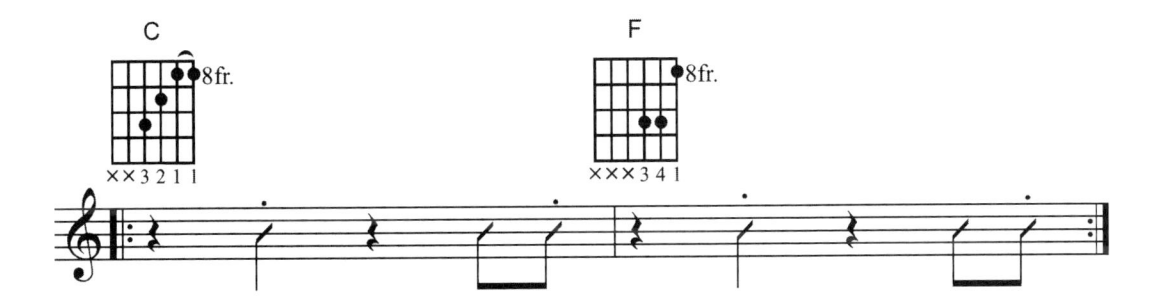

Country

Country music has expanded greatly in recent years, and a lot of it sounds like rock with a few different instruments. The older country style involves straight eighths with a strong bass note on beats one and three. The chords are usually pretty simple—major, minor, and seventh.

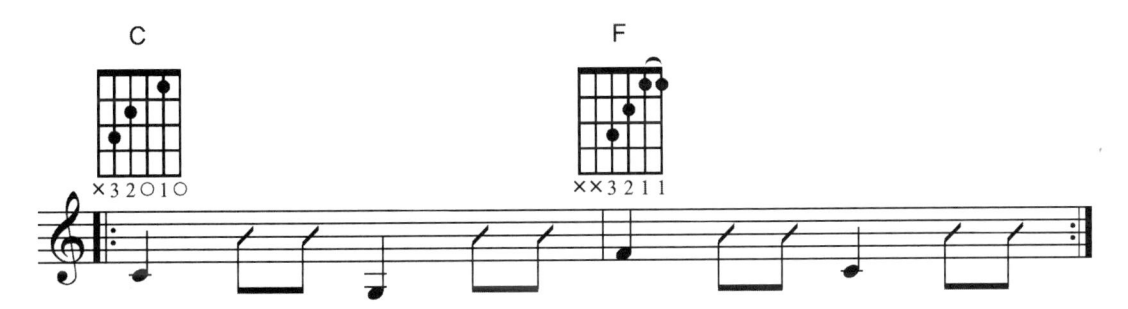

Latin

Latin music has many subcategories, such as samba, bossa nova, rhumba, mambo, and salsa, but it almost always includes syncopation. Many accents fall *off* the beat, and there are often more chords played on the up-beat (when your foot is coming up) than on the down-beat, when your foot is tapping. Many chords are "anticipated"—that is, they come half a beat early, on the "and" of beat 4. The chords are often the richer-sounding jazz chords.

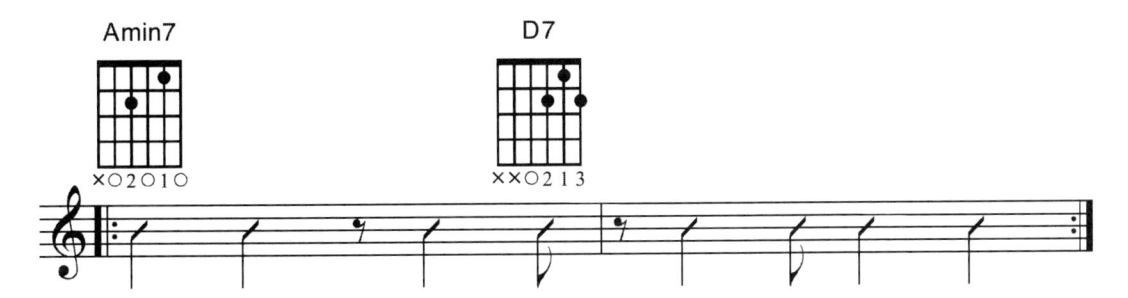

Blues

There are so many ways to play the blues that you can find examples in just about any style of music. There are blues using straight eighths, with a swing feel, with power chords, with jazz chords, and just about any other style you can imagine. We'll explore a few of these in the final chapter.

The next chapter looks at bar chords, the path to playing in all keys all over the neck.

Bar Chords Part I: The Basics—Major, Minor, and Seventh Chords in All Keys

Most guitarists come across chords such as E♭ or A♭m at some point, and they aren't quite sure of the best way to deal with them. They see guitarists playing chords all over the neck with little difficulty and wonder how they managed to learn so many chords.

The secret, quite often, is *bar chords*.

To *bar* on the guitar means to lay your finger across several strings at the same time. It can also be spelled *barre*.

If you hold a regular C major chord and try to slide it up the neck, it doesn't work because some notes change while the open strings don't. But if you have a chord with no open strings, everything changes equally when you move up the neck. This is the principle behind bar chords.

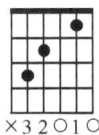

×3 2 0 1 0
A standard C chord.

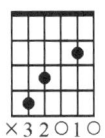

×3 2 0 1 0
You can't slide this up the neck. The fingered notes change, but the open strings don't.

The chord shown below is one of the basic bar chord forms. It is a major chord and can be held anywhere on the neck, as long as your fingers can squeeze between the frets. The notes marked with an "O" are the roots. In this case, each one of these roots is an F, and the chord is an F major chord.

Guitar for Songwriters

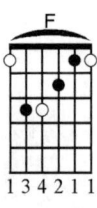

F

`1 3 4 2 1 1`

An F major bar chord with no open strings. (Remember, 0 = root.)

Slide this chord one fret higher, and it becomes an F♯ major chord, because all notes change equally. The roots are F♯s. (This is the same as a G♭ major chord.)

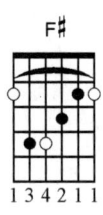

F♯

`1 3 4 2 1 1`

In the second position, this becomes an F♯ major bar chord.

In the third position, the roots are Gs. The chord is a G major chord. Compare it with a standard, open-position G chord. They sound similar, although not exactly the same. One guitarist could play the bar G while another played the open-string version, and they would blend.

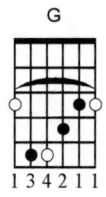

G

`1 3 4 2 1 1`

Move it up another fret, and it becomes G major.

If you learn the names of the notes on the sixth string, you will know the name of this chord at any position. This is because it has a root on the sixth string. The other roots in the diagrams, on the first and fourth strings, are the same notes in different octaves.

Form 1 Bar Chords with the Root on the Sixth String

These major, minor, and seventh chord forms have roots on the first string and the sixth string. The major and minor forms also have an additional root on the fourth string. To find any chord, locate the root note you want on the sixth string and hold the chord in that position. For example, to find a C major chord, hold the major form shown below at the eighth position (with the first finger at the eighth fret). A Cm would be the minor form held at the same position, or a C7 would be the seventh form, also at the eighth position. These chords will be called Form 1.

Chapter 6 Bar Chords Part I: The Basics

Major

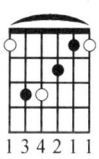

1 3 4 2 1 1

Minor

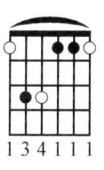

1 3 4 1 1 1

Dominant Seventh

1 3 1 2 1 1

Roots for Form 1 Bar Chords:

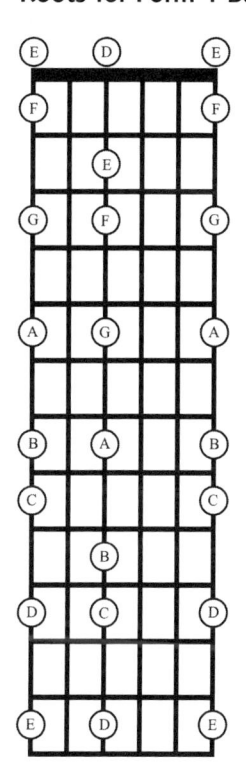

Notice there is only a half step (one fret) between B and C, and between E and F. There is a whole step (two frets) between all other notes.

Guitar for Songwriters

Be careful not to confuse flats and minor chords. An A♭ chord is still a major chord. The types of chords listed here are major, minor, and seventh. The flats and sharps affect the location of a note, not the type of chord.

Form 1 Bar Chord Diagrams

As you can see, all of the major chords are the same, just moved to different positions on the neck. The same goes for the minor and seventh chords. The note on the sixth string is a root of the chord.

Major

Besides the sixth string, the root for this type of major chord can be found on the fourth and first strings (an octave apart). If you know the name of the note you are holding on any of these strings, that is the name of the major chord you are holding.

Root on the sixth, fourth, and first strings:

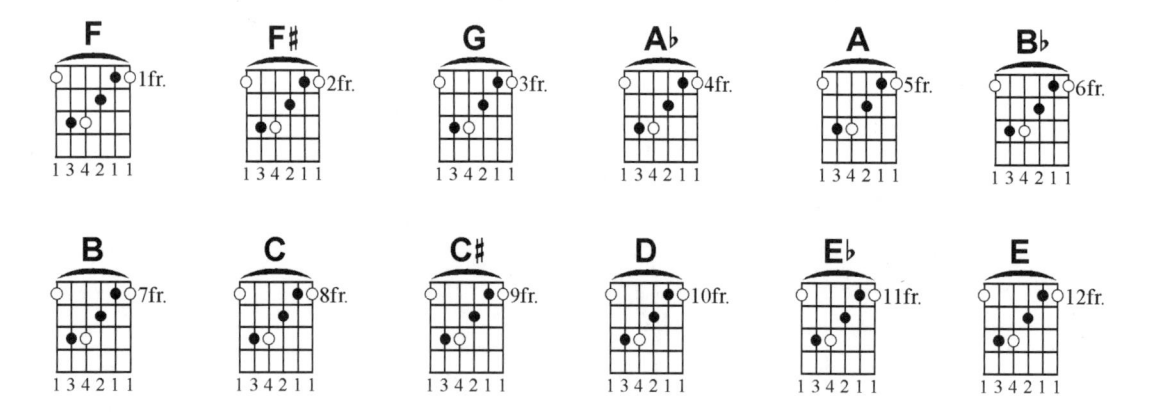

These chords are difficult to hold in the higher positions, where the frets are much closer together. Form 2 and Form 3 bar chords, in the next sections, sometimes work better for certain chords.

Minor

Root on the sixth, fourth, and first strings:

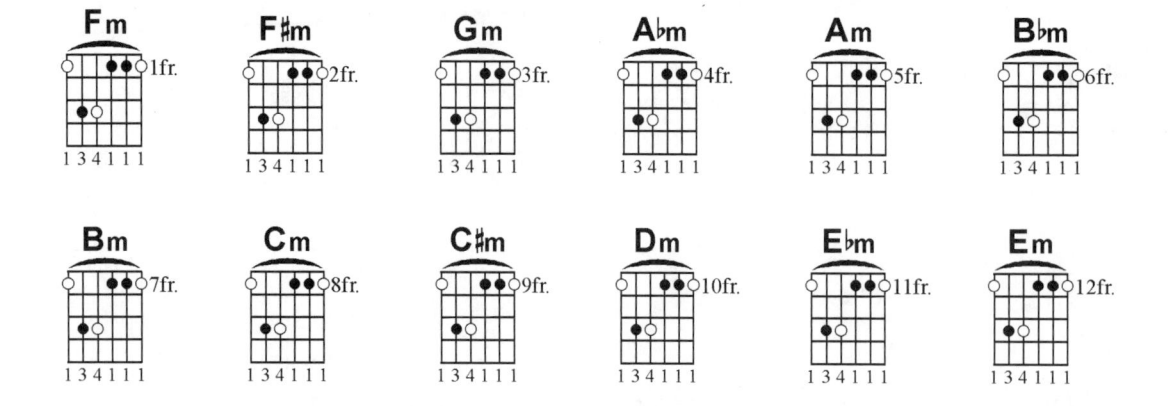

Chapter 6 Bar Chords Part I: The Basics

Dominant Seventh

Root on the sixth and first strings:

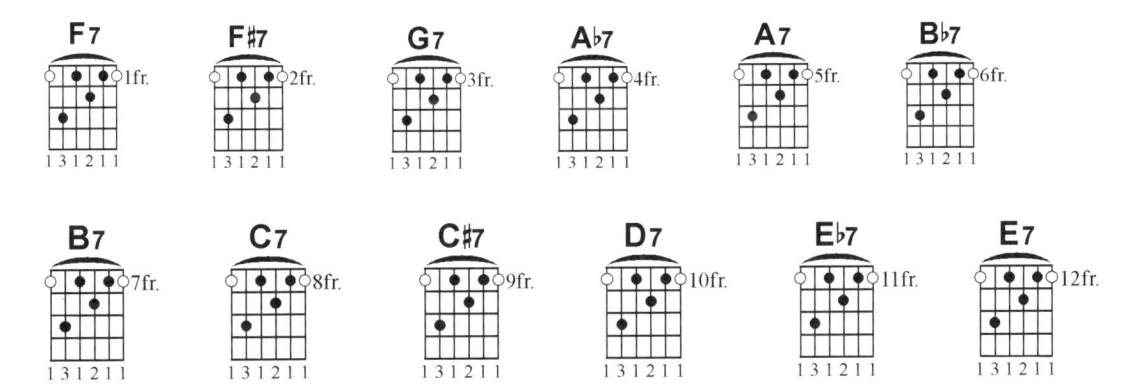

F7 — 1fr. — 1 3 1 2 1 1
F#7 — 2fr. — 1 3 1 2 1 1
G7 — 3fr. — 1 3 1 2 1 1
A♭7 — 4fr. — 1 3 1 2 1 1
A7 — 5fr. — 1 3 1 2 1 1
B♭7 — 6fr. — 1 3 1 2 1 1
B7 — 7fr. — 1 3 1 2 1 1
C7 — 8fr. — 1 3 1 2 1 1
C#7 — 9fr. — 1 3 1 2 1 1
D7 — 10fr. — 1 3 1 2 1 1
E♭7 — 11fr. — 1 3 1 2 1 1
E7 — 12fr. — 1 3 1 2 1 1

Getting Comfortable with Bar Chords

At first, bar chords are very difficult to hold. They require more pressure than chords with open strings to make them sound clear. Your hand will probably become quite fatigued at the beginning. Here are some tips to make playing bar chords easier.

Keep in mind that bar chords are more difficult at the end of the neck (near the first fret). It is harder to push the strings down near the nut than farther up the neck, where there is less resistance.

Bar chords are also harder to hold as you approach the tenth fret or so. The frets get closer together the farther up the neck you go, and it gets difficult to fit your fingers between the frets.

This means that bar chords will be easiest in the middle of the neck, perhaps between the third and seventh positions.

Many people have trouble shifting bar chords at first. You must release the pressure on the strings before sliding. You should not hear any notes sliding as you shift chords (although you may hear some string noise). Your thumb can lightly touch the back of the neck, or you can lift it slightly, but you must be sure it's not dragging as you shift.

It's helpful to separate the movements when you first practice shifting bar chords. After strumming a chord and before moving to the next one, relax your hand so the strings are no longer being pressed. Keep your fingers on the strings, but slide them without any pressure on the strings. You will have to relax your thumb also, and be sure it slides the same distance as your fingers instead of dragging behind. Try this: strum, relax, shift.

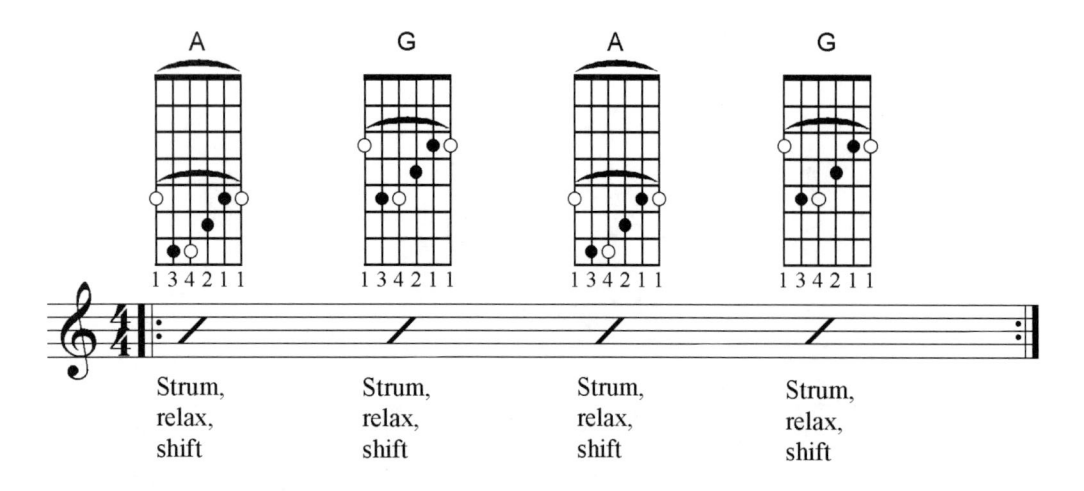

Guitar for Songwriters

A	G	A	G
1 3 4 2 1 1	1 3 4 2 1 1	1 3 4 2 1 1	1 3 4 2 1 1

Strum, relax, shift. | Strum, relax, shift. | Strum, relax, shift. | Strum, relax, shift.

Hear this pattern demonstrated in Example40 at http://cengageptr.com/guitarforsongwriters.

Strum, relax, shift.

Relax your hand before shifting the chord. Practice each exercise several times without stopping. A steady beat is more important than having every note sound clearly. These exercises are difficult at first, so don't overdo it. Practice them for a few minutes several times a day.

Form 1 Bar Chord Exercises

The following exercises are designed to help you become more comfortable shifting these chords between different positions. Familiarity with these forms is essential before moving on.

1. A 5fr. / G 3fr.
   1 3 4 2 1 1 / 1 3 4 2 1 1

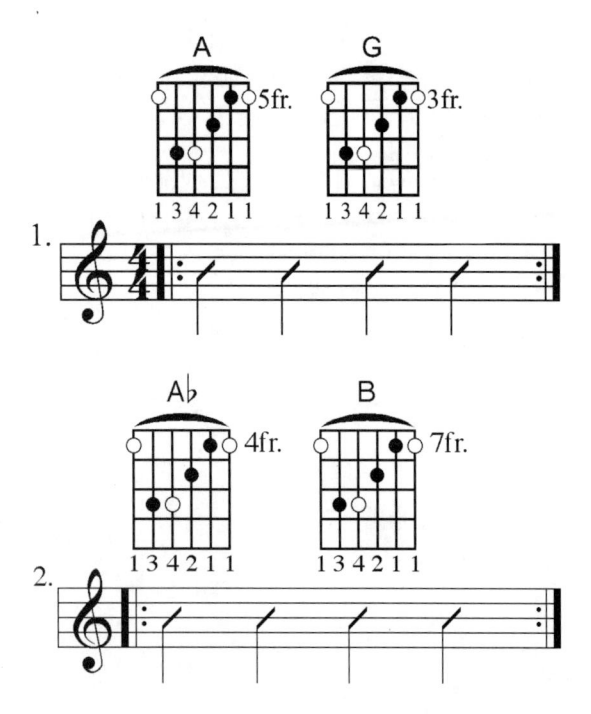

2. A♭ 4fr. / B 7fr.
   1 3 4 2 1 1 / 1 3 4 2 1 1

Chapter 6 Bar Chords Part I: The Basics

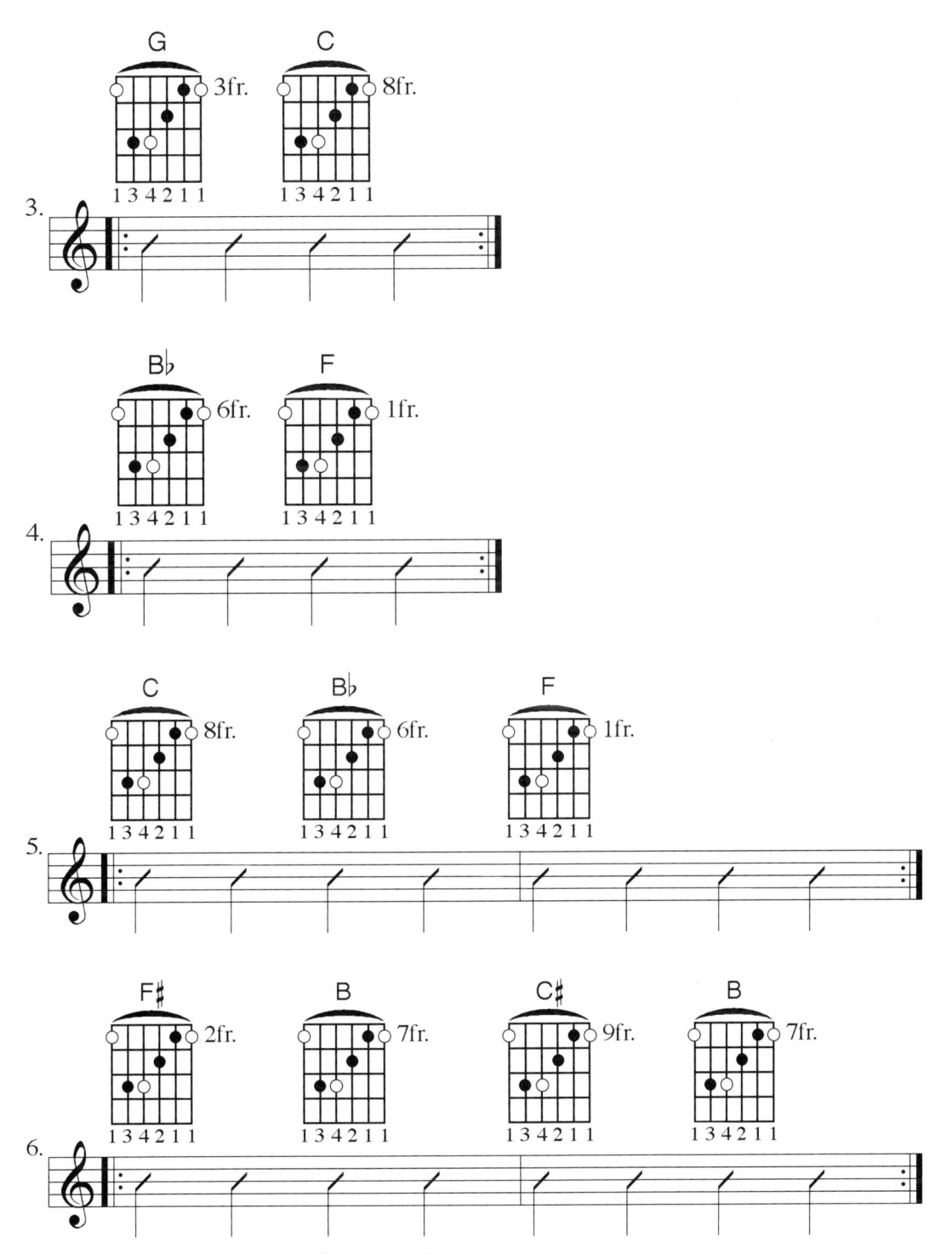

3.

4.

5.

6.

This is a way to play the I-IV-V-IV progression seen earlier in this book.

Guitar for Songwriters

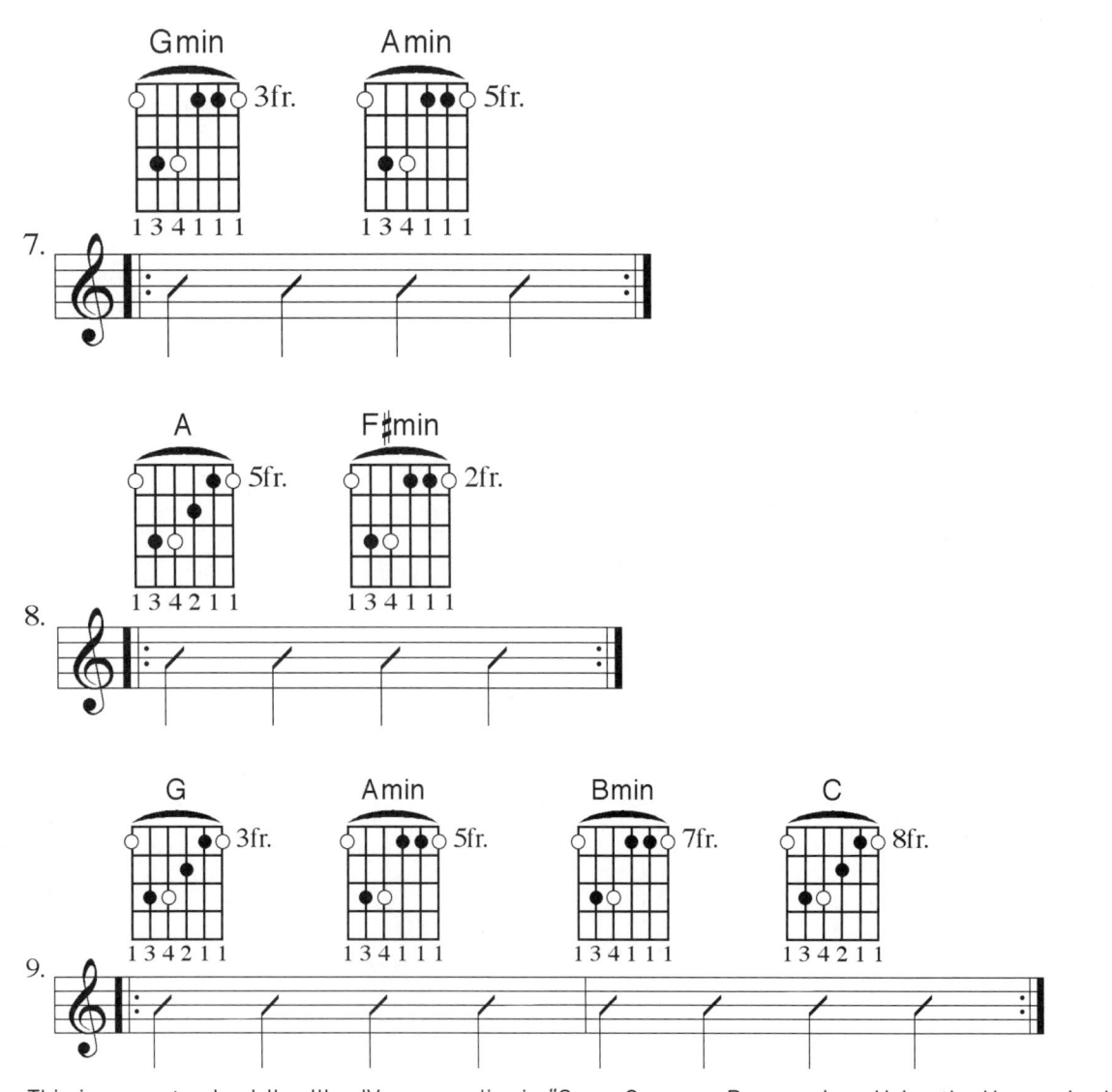

7. Gmin (3fr.) — Amin (5fr.)

8. A (5fr.) — F#min (2fr.)

9. G (3fr.) — Amin (5fr.) — Bmin (7fr.) — C (8fr.)

This is a way to play I-IIm-IIIm-IV seen earlier in "Some Common Progressions Using the Harmonized Scale."

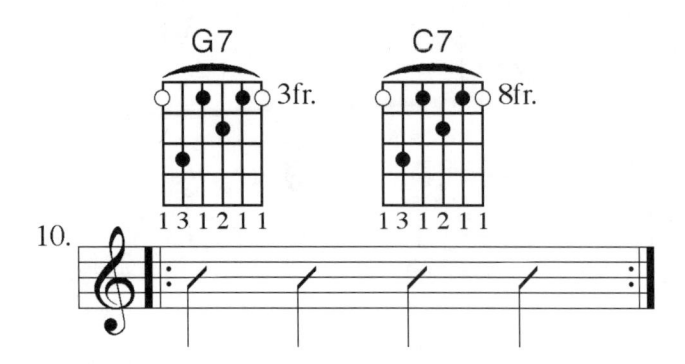

10. G7 (3fr.) — C7 (8fr.)

Chapter 6 Bar Chords Part I: The Basics

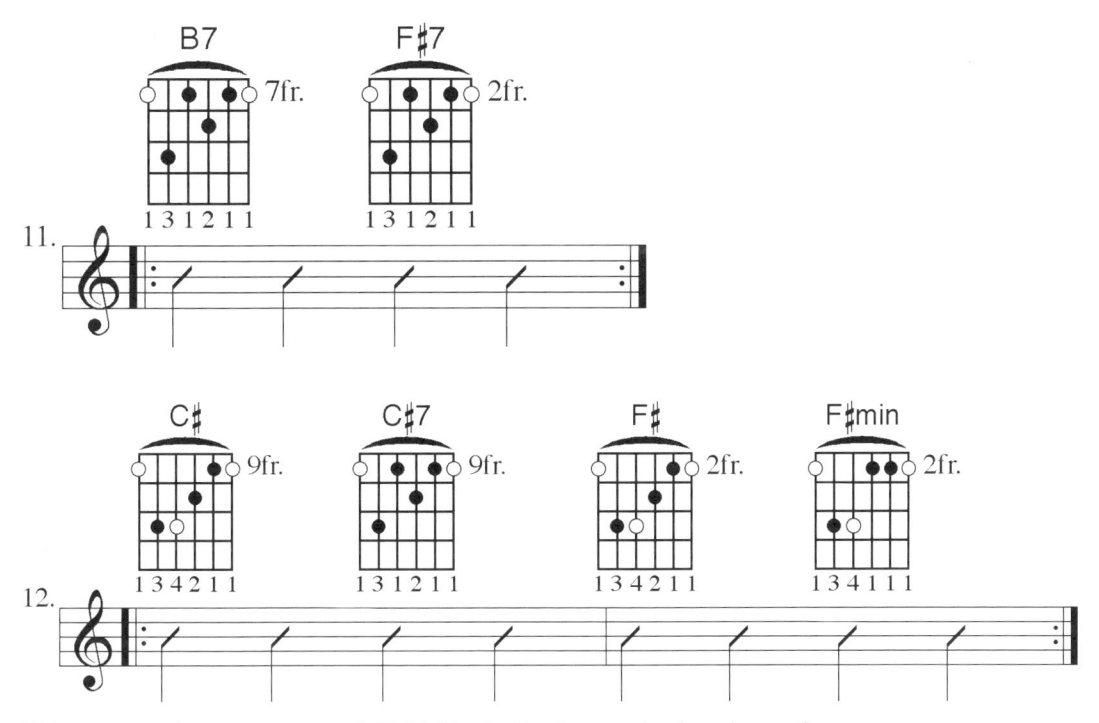

11. [B7 7fr. 1 3 1 2 1 1] [F#7 2fr. 1 3 1 2 1 1]

12. [C# 9fr. 1 3 4 2 1 1] [C#7 9fr. 1 3 1 2 1 1] [F# 2fr. 1 3 4 2 1 1] [F#min 2fr. 1 3 4 1 1 1]

This progression was seen as I-I7-IV-IVm in the harmonized scale section.

Muting

Bar chords can tire you out quite rapidly if you don't know a few tricks about playing them. If you don't know about muting, you're probably working too hard.

It is rare that you would play a bar chord for any period of time without relaxing your left hand and cutting a chord short. A very simple exercise is to stay on one chord and relax your left hand after every other beat.

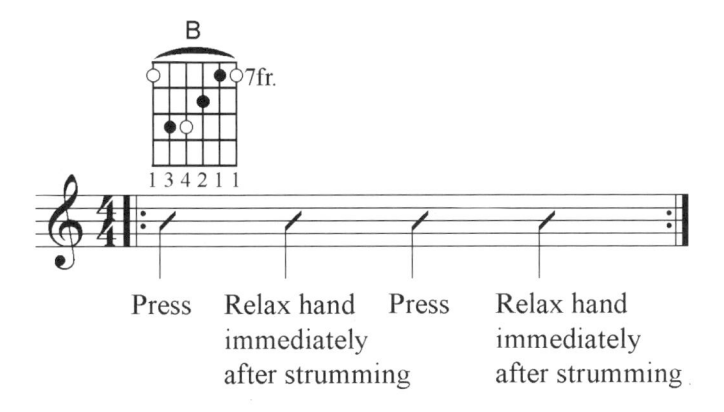

[B 7fr. 1 3 4 2 1 1]

Press — Relax hand immediately after strumming — Press — Relax hand immediately after strumming

Another technique is to mute the strings—to relax your left hand while strumming on strings that are dead (not pressed down).

Guitar for Songwriters

> This example of muting is Example41 at http://cengageptr.com/guitarforsongwriters. Chapter 5 has more examples of muting and accents that can also be heard on the website.

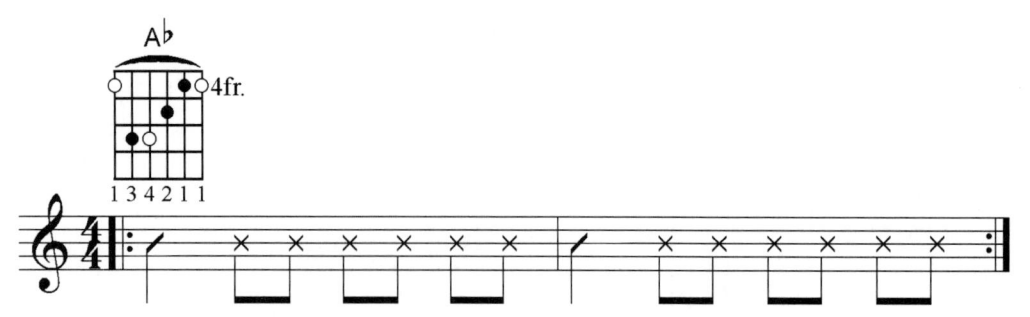

Sound the strings only on beat one. Mute the strings where marked with an "x" to give a percussive sound.

Damping or muting chords will give your hand a rest that will enable you to play much longer without tiring. Get in the habit of chopping some chords off, and you will gain a lot of endurance—and the music won't sound so cluttered.

Form 2 Bar Chords with the Root on the Fifth String

The following sections provide another set of bar chords, called Form 2. These have the root on the fifth and third strings and give you an alternative to the Form 1 chords, which are too far up the neck to hold comfortably. For instance, a Form 1 E♭ chord is at the eleventh fret, while the Form 2 E♭ is at the sixth fret.

Major

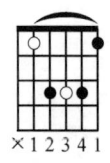

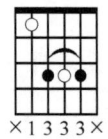

Alternate way to hold the Form 2 major chord.

This alternate form is easier to hold for those with big fingers or when you need to hold the chord for only a beat or two. Bar your third finger over the first four strings, but don't hit the first string when strumming.

Chapter 6 Bar Chords Part I: The Basics

Minor

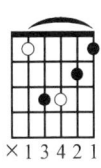

× 1 3 4 2 1

Dominant Seventh

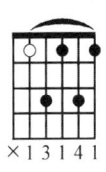

× 1 3 1 4 1

Roots for Form 2 Bar Chords:

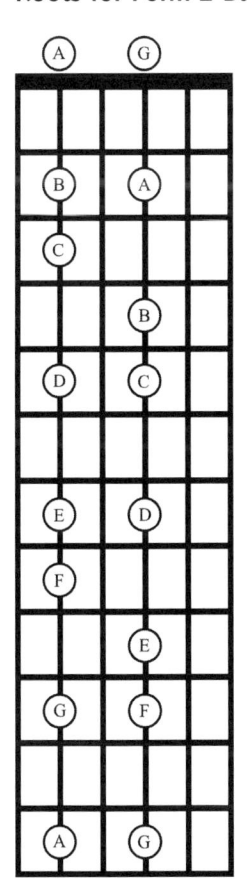

You can find the roots of the Form 2 bar chords on the third and fifth strings.

Guitar for Songwriters

Form 2 Bar Chord Diagrams

Find the root on the fifth string to identify the Form 2 chords.

Major

Root on the fifth and third strings:

B♭ 1fr.	B 2fr.	C 3fr.	C♯ 4fr.	D 5fr.	E♭ 6fr.
×1 2 3 4 1	×1 2 3 4 1	×1 2 3 4 1	×1 2 3 4 1	×1 2 3 4 1	×1 2 3 4 1

E 7fr.	F 8fr.	F♯ 9fr.	G 10fr.	A♭ 11fr.	A 12fr.
×1 2 3 4 1	×1 2 3 4 1	×1 2 3 4 1	×1 2 3 4 1	×1 2 3 4 1	×1 2 3 4 1

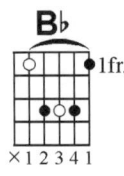

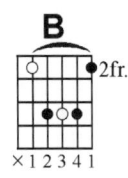

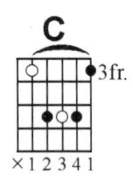

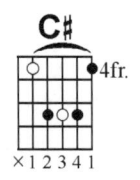

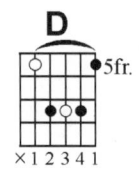

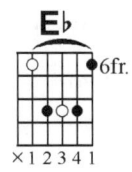

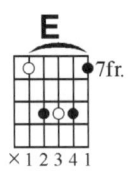

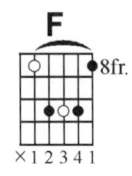

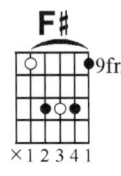

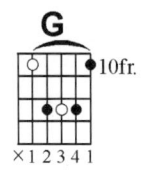

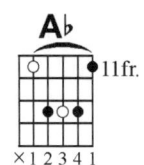

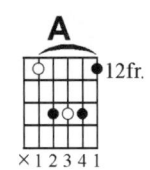

Minor

Root on the fifth and third strings:

B♭m 1fr.	Bm 2fr.	Cm 3fr.	C♯m 4fr.	Dm 5fr.	E♭m 6fr.
×1 3 4 2 1	×1 3 4 2 1	×1 3 4 2 1	×1 3 4 2 1	×1 3 4 2 1	×1 3 4 2 1

Em 7fr.	Fm 8fr.	F♯m 9fr.	Gm 10fr.	A♭m 11fr.	Am 12fr.
×1 3 4 2 1	×1 3 4 2 1	×1 3 4 2 1	×1 3 4 2 1	×1 3 4 2 1	×1 3 4 2 1

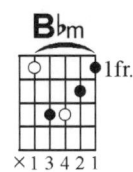

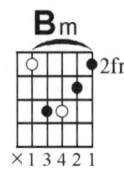

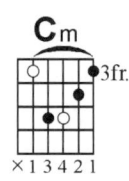

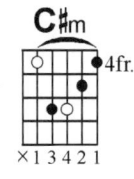

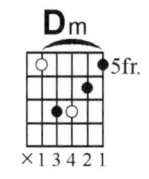

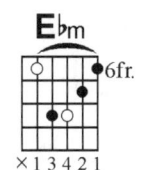

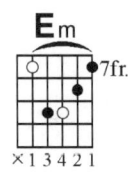

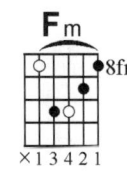

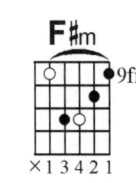

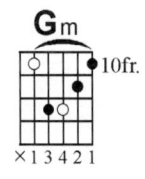

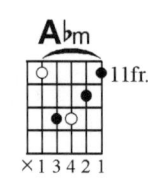

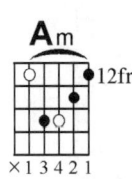

Chapter 6 Bar Chords Part I: The Basics

Dominant Seventh

Root on the fifth string:

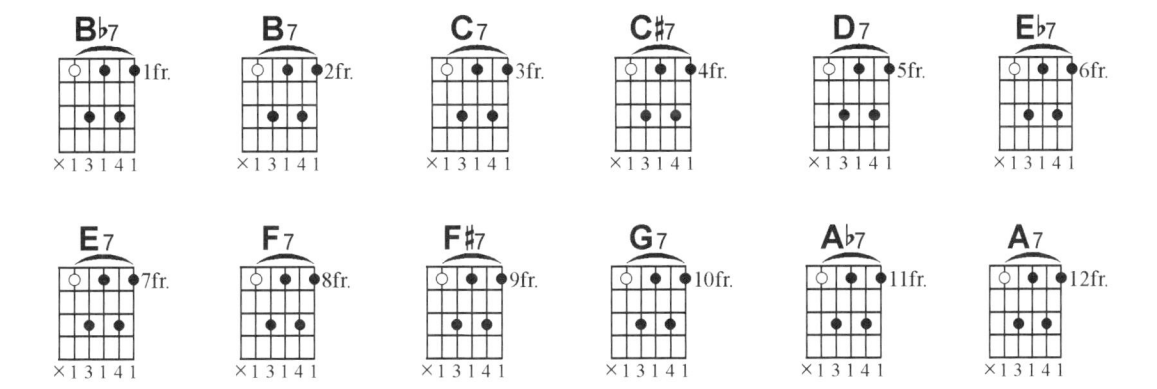

B♭7 — 1fr. × 1 3 1 4 1
B7 — 2fr. × 1 3 1 4 1
C7 — 3fr. × 1 3 1 4 1
C♯7 — 4fr. × 1 3 1 4 1
D7 — 5fr. × 1 3 1 4 1
E♭7 — 6fr. × 1 3 1 4 1

E7 — 7fr. × 1 3 1 4 1
F7 — 8fr. × 1 3 1 4 1
F♯7 — 9fr. × 1 3 1 4 1
G7 — 10fr. × 1 3 1 4 1
A♭7 — 11fr. × 1 3 1 4 1
A7 — 12fr. × 1 3 1 4 1

Form 2 Bar Chord Exercises

Don't forget to relax your hand before shifting chords. Also try the alternate version of the Form 2 major chord, with a third finger bar. Many people find this form easier to hold.

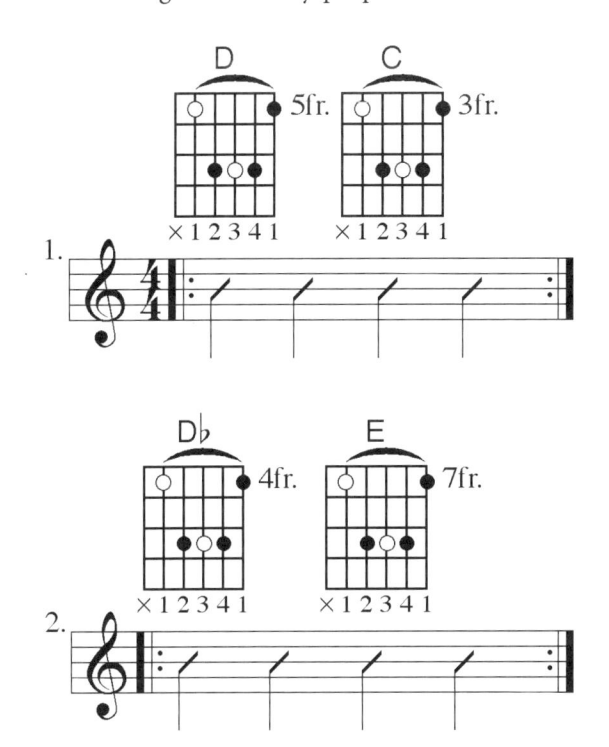

1. D — 5fr. × 1 2 3 4 1
   C — 3fr. × 1 2 3 4 1

2. D♭ — 4fr. × 1 2 3 4 1
   E — 7fr. × 1 2 3 4 1

71

Guitar for Songwriters

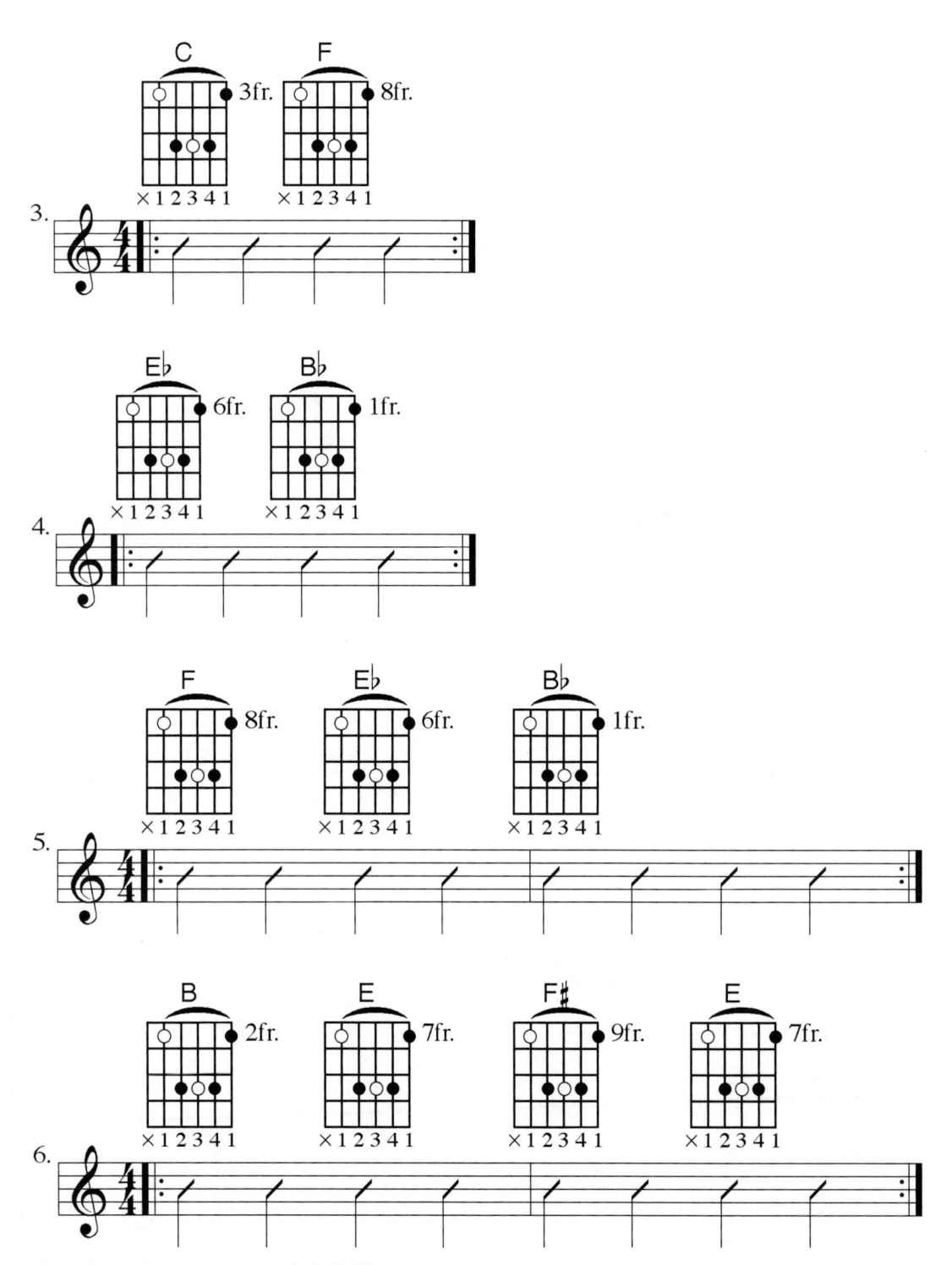

Here is another way to play I-IV-V-IV.

Chapter 6 Bar Chords Part I: The Basics

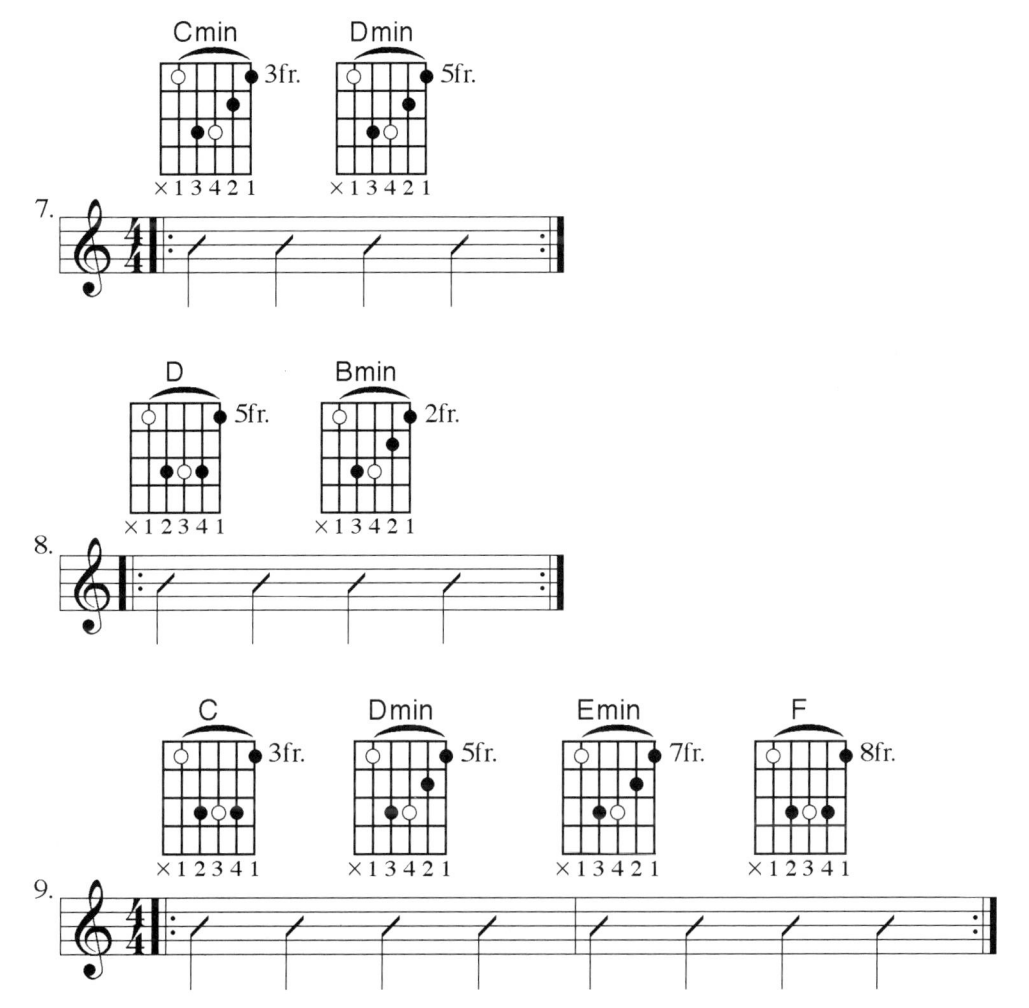

7. Cmin — Dmin

8. D — Bmin

9. C — Dmin — Emin — F

This is I-IIm-IIIm-IV using Form 2 bar chords.

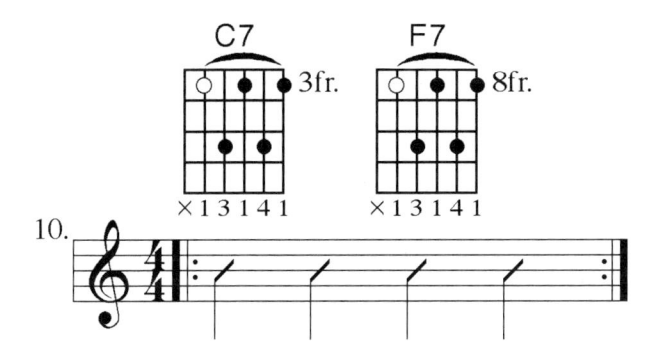

10. C7 — F7

Guitar for Songwriters

11.

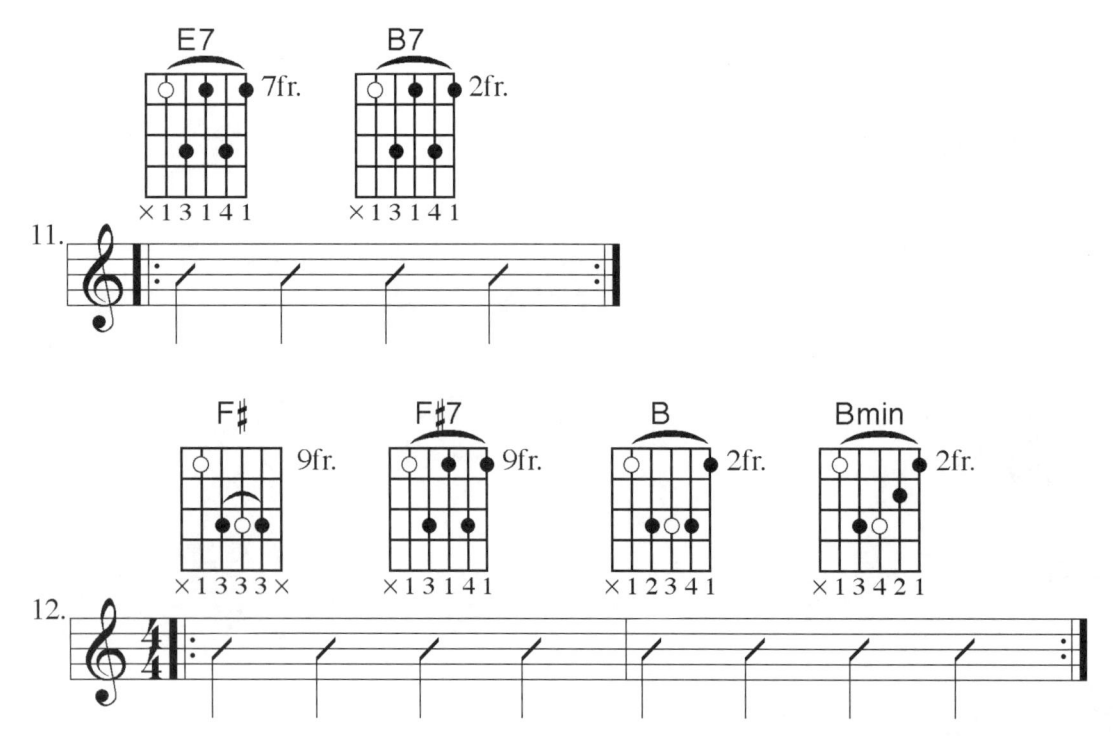

[Chord diagrams: E7 7fr. ×1 3 1 4 1, B7 2fr. ×1 3 1 4 1]

12.

[Chord diagrams: F# 9fr. ×1 3 3 3 ×, F#7 9fr. ×1 3 1 4 1, B 2fr. ×1 2 3 4 1, Bmin 2fr. ×1 3 4 2 1]

This exercise uses the alternate version of the Form 2 major chord for F♯, with the third finger bar. The other form is too difficult to hold in this position on many guitars. The progression is I-I7-IV-IVm, seen earlier in the harmonized scale section.

Form 3 Bar Chords

The following sections provide a third set of chords that can be moved up the neck. The root is on the fifth and second strings, except for the minor form, which has the root on the second string only.

Major

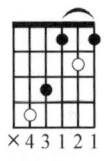

[Chord diagram: ×4 3 1 2 1]

Major

[Chord diagram: ×4 3 1 2 ×]

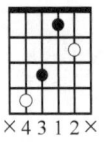

Alternate fingering for the Form 3 bar chord. Omit the bar and mute the first string by leaning the first finger. Play only the second through fifth strings in this version.

Chapter 6 Bar Chords Part I: The Basics

Minor

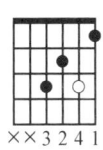

×× 3 2 4 1

There is no good version of this chord to hold with the root in the bass. This chord may sound a little less satisfying without that bass root.

Dominant Seventh

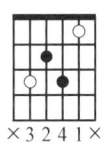

× 3 2 4 1 ×

Technically speaking, this chord and the minor chord above are not really bar chords, since the first finger is not barring across several strings. But they serve the same purpose in that they can be moved up and down the neck.

Roots for Form 3 Bar Chords:

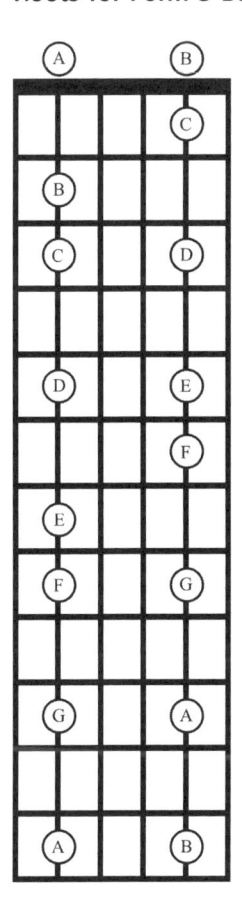

You can find the roots of the Form 3 bar chords on the second or fifth string.

Guitar for Songwriters

Form 3 Bar Chord Diagrams

This third set of movable chords has the root on the fifth string or, for the minor form, on the second string.

Major

Root on the fifth and second strings:

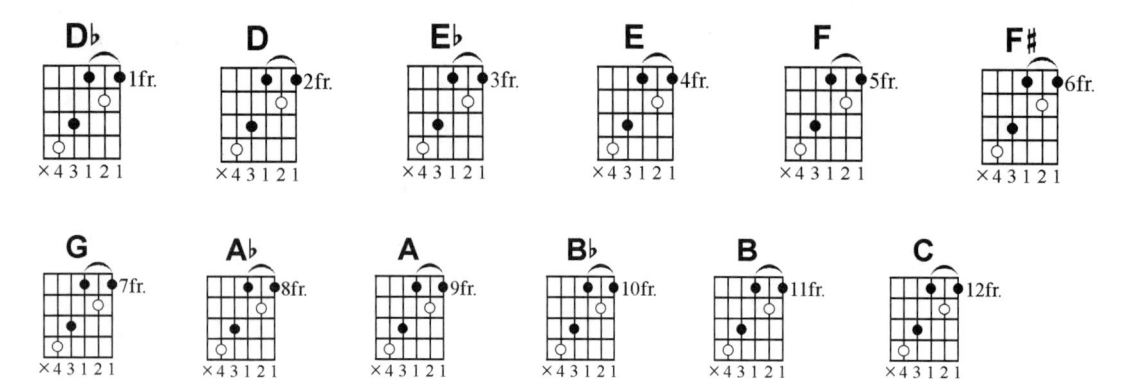

Db 1fr. D 2fr. Eb 3fr. E 4fr. F 5fr. F# 6fr.

G 7fr. Ab 8fr. A 9fr. Bb 10fr. B 11fr. C 12fr.

Minor

Root on the second string:

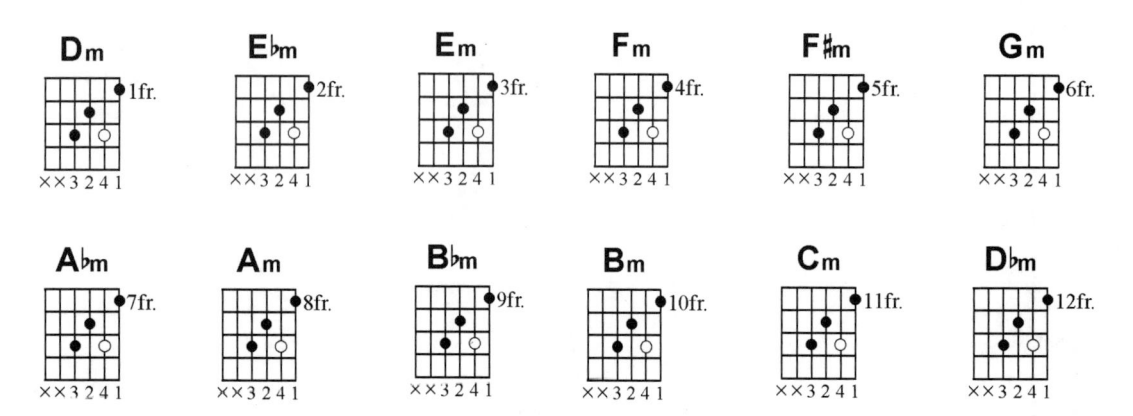

Dm 1fr. Ebm 2fr. Em 3fr. Fm 4fr. F#m 5fr. Gm 6fr.

Abm 7fr. Am 8fr. Bbm 9fr. Bm 10fr. Cm 11fr. Dbm 12fr.

Chapter 6 Bar Chords Part I: The Basics

Dominant Seventh

Root on the fifth and second strings:

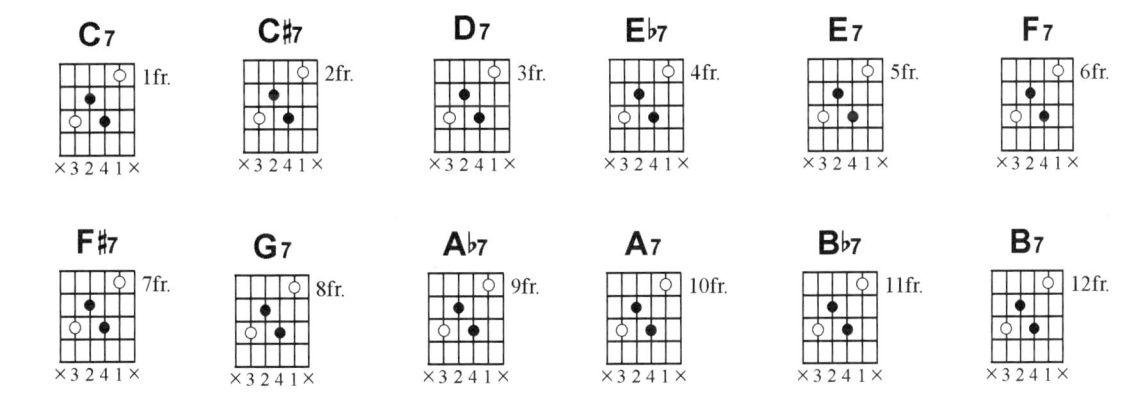

C7 1fr.	C#7 2fr.	D7 3fr.	Eb7 4fr.	E7 5fr.	F7 6fr.
×3241×	×3241×	×3241×	×3241×	×3241×	×3241×

F#7 7fr.	G7 8fr.	Ab7 9fr.	A7 10fr.	Bb7 11fr.	B7 12fr.
×3241×	×3241×	×3241×	×3241×	×3241×	×3241×

Form 3 Bar Chord Exercises

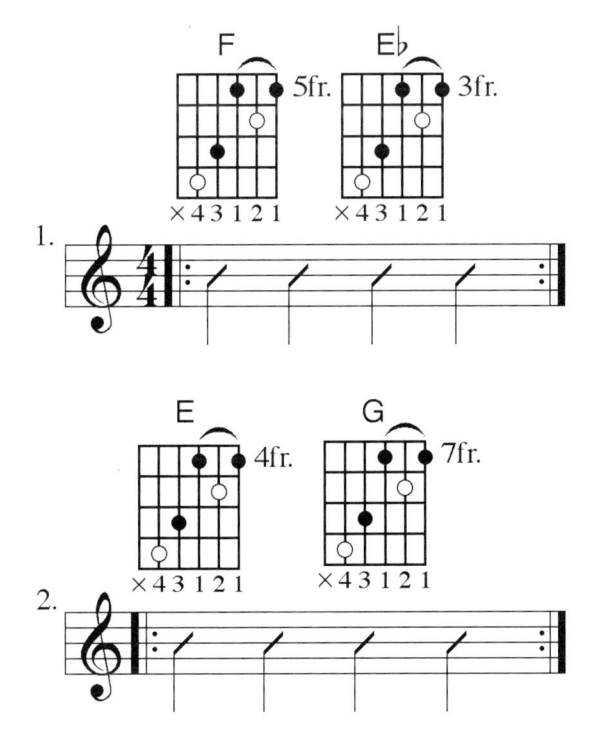

1. F (5fr.) ×43121   Eb (3fr.) ×43121

2. E (4fr.) ×43121   G (7fr.) ×43121

Guitar for Songwriters

3. [Eb 3fr. / Ab 8fr.] ×43121

4. [Gb 6fr. / Db 1fr.] ×43121

5. [Ab 8fr. / Gb 6fr. / Db 1fr.] ×43121

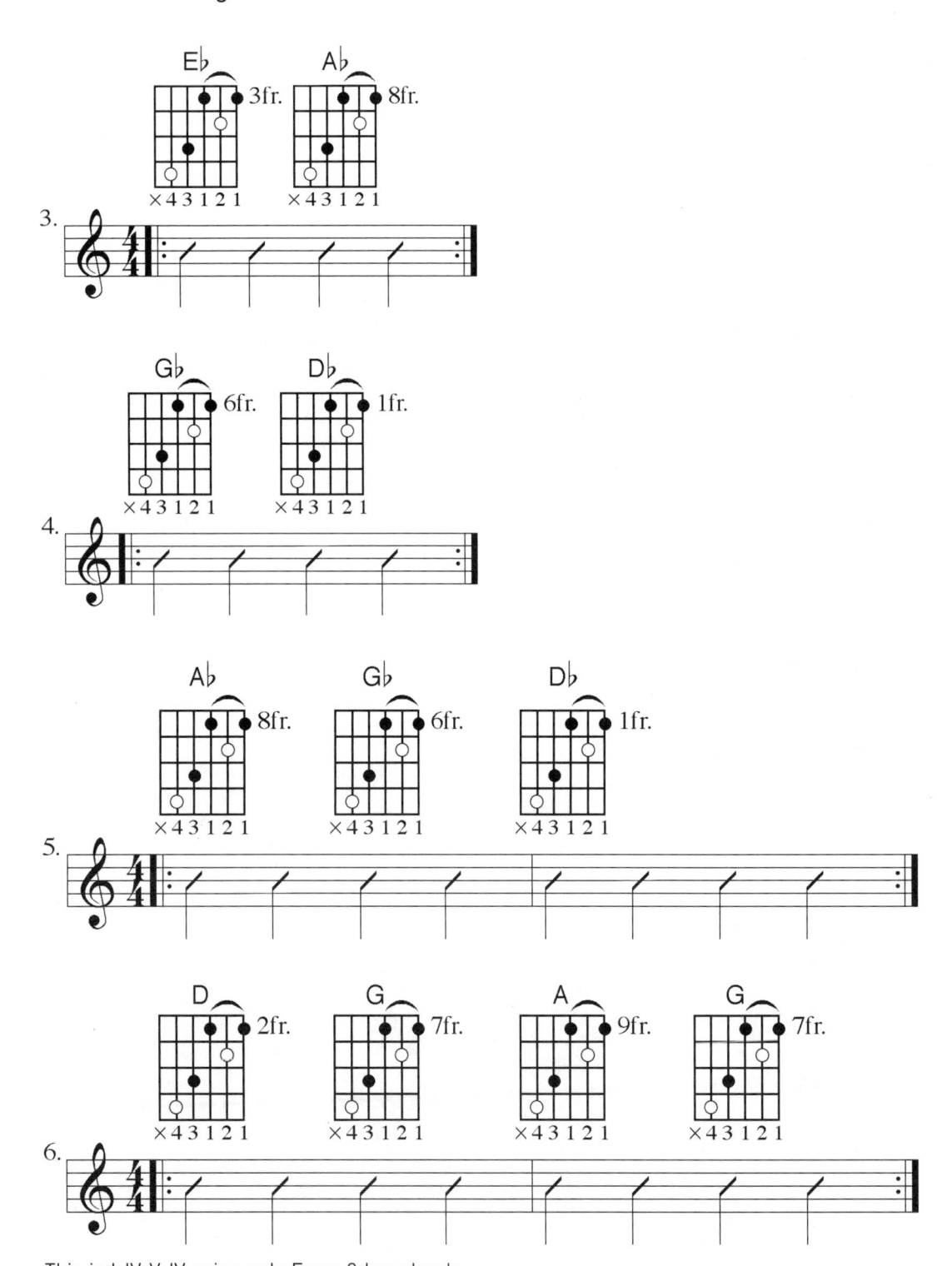

6. [D 2fr. / G 7fr. / A 9fr. / G 7fr.] ×43121

This is I-IV-V-IV using only Form 3 bar chords.

78

Chapter 6 Bar Chords Part I: The Basics

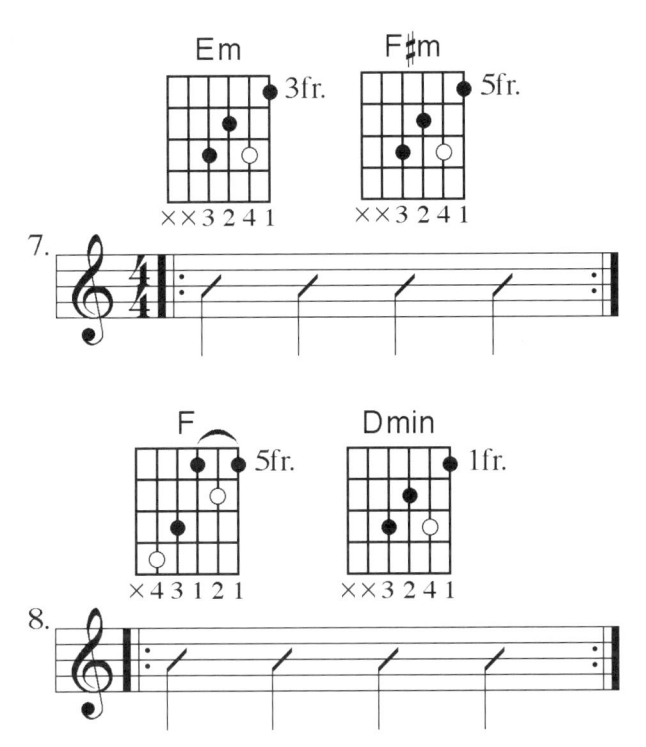

7.

8.

A Form 2 Dm would actually be much more practical here. You could keep your second and third fingers down.

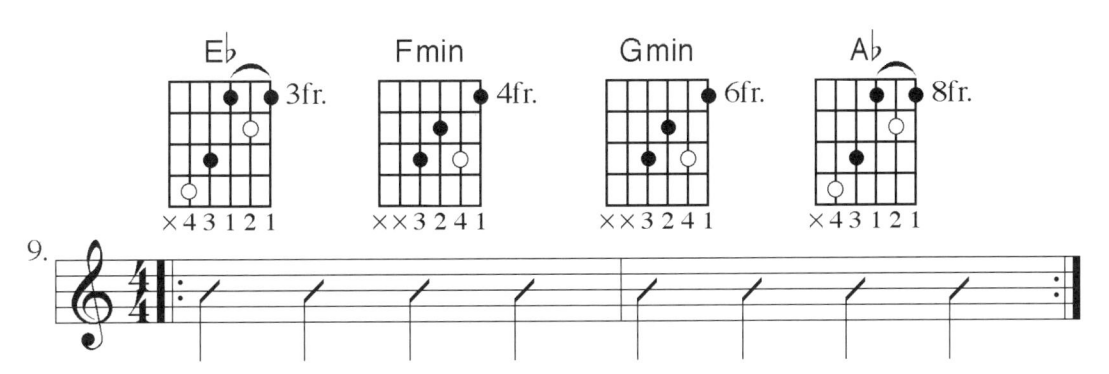

9.

This is the I-IIm-IIIm-IV progression seen earlier.

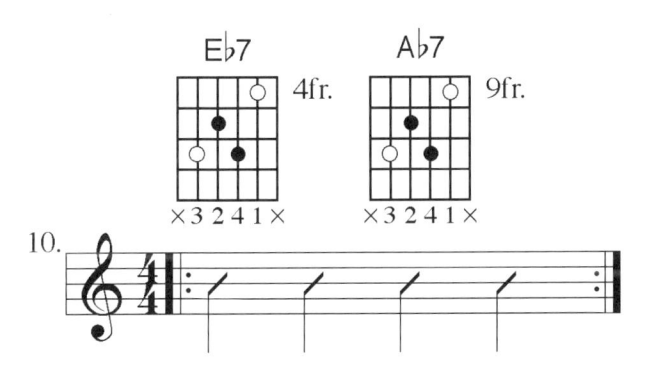

10.

79

Guitar for Songwriters

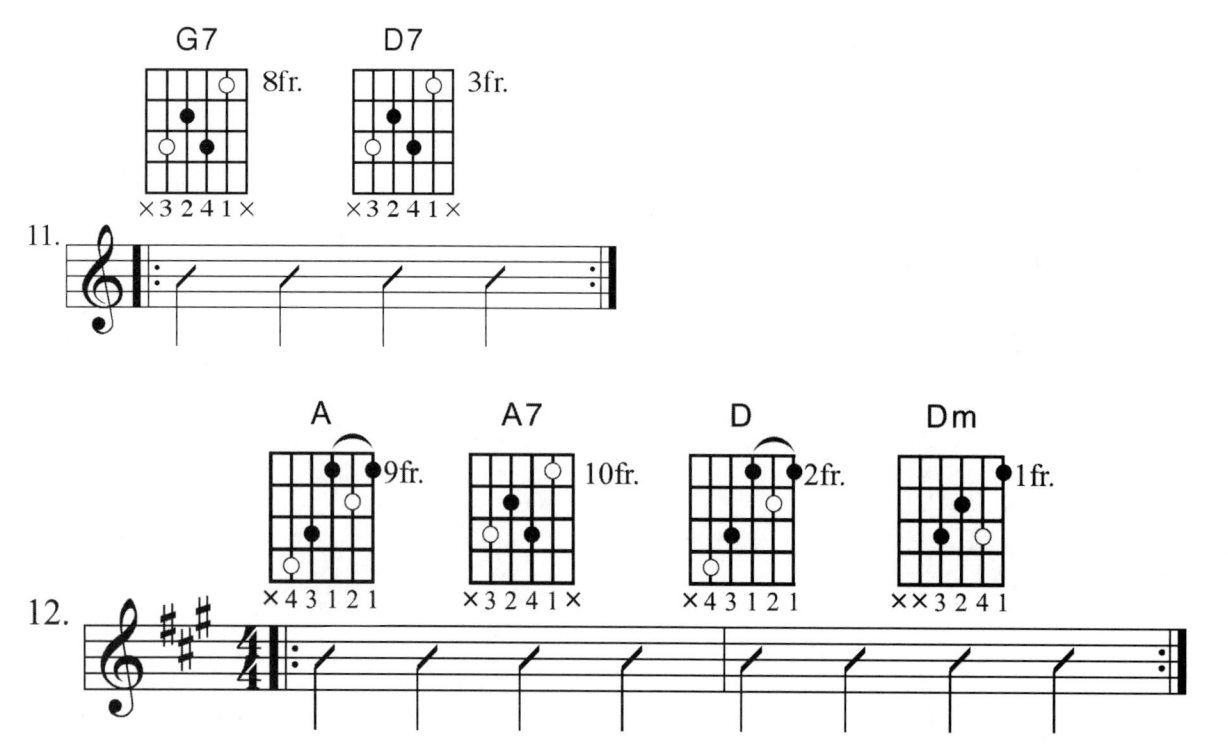

11. [G7 (8fr.) | D7 (3fr.)]

12. [A (9fr.) | A7 (10fr.) | D (2fr.) | Dm (1fr.)]

Although this particular exercise would be much easier with open-string chords, it is important to be familiar with chords in all parts of the neck. This is another way to play I-I7-IV-IVm.

The next chapter looks at bar chords in more detail, exploring ways to put them together in many common progressions. How do you change keys using bar chords? Are there patterns that keep recurring?

Bar Chords Part II: Putting Them Together

B AR CHORDS GIVE YOU THREE FORMS TO CHOOSE FROM FOR ANY MAJOR, MINOR, OR SEVENTH CHORD. Now it's time to put them together. You can use them to play in more difficult keys or to transpose to a different key. You can find fingerings that make previously awkward chord changes much easier. This chapter is intended to help you put bar chords to work for you.

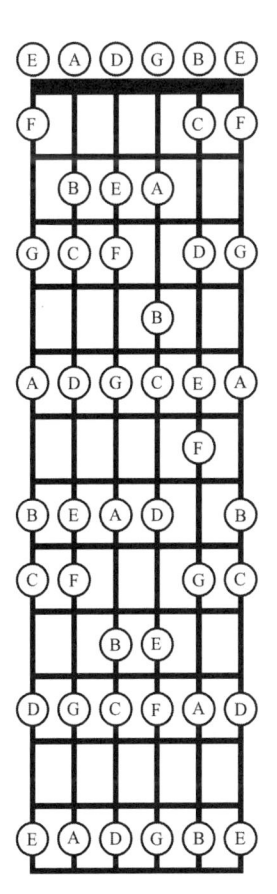

Guitar for Songwriters

Bar Chord Diagrams, All Forms

Below are the major, minor, and seventh chords in all three forms.

Form 1

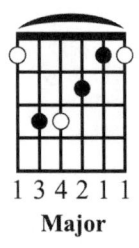

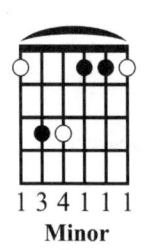

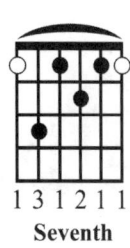

1 3 4 2 1 1
Major

1 3 4 1 1 1
Minor

1 3 1 2 1 1
Seventh

Form 2

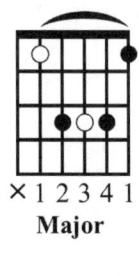

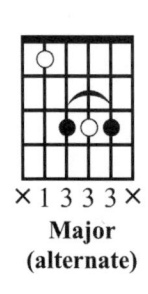

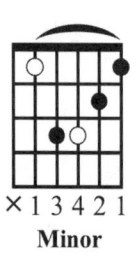

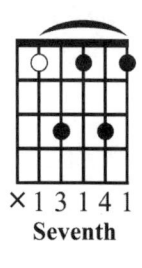

× 1 2 3 4 1
Major

× 1 3 3 3 ×
Major (alternate)

× 1 3 4 2 1
Minor

× 1 3 1 4 1
Seventh

Form 3

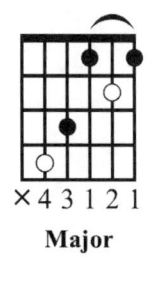

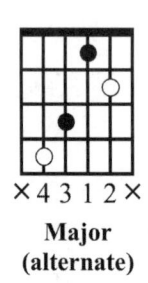

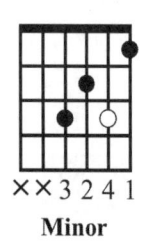

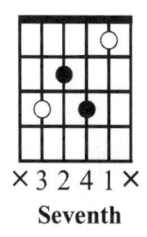

× 4 3 1 2 1
Major

× 4 3 1 2 ×
Major (alternate)

× × 3 2 4 1
Minor

× 3 2 4 1 ×
Seventh

Using Bar Chords to Transpose

It's easy to change keys when using only bar chords. Move all the chords in an exercise equally, up or down the neck, and you are playing the same progression in a new key. The following examples show the same progression in three different keys, G, F♯, and A♭. The same fingering is used in each example, simply shifted to a different position.

Chapter 7 Bar Chords Part II: Putting Them Together

1. The key of G. This exercise could easily be played with chords using open strings. However, with bar chords it can be transposed with very little effort.

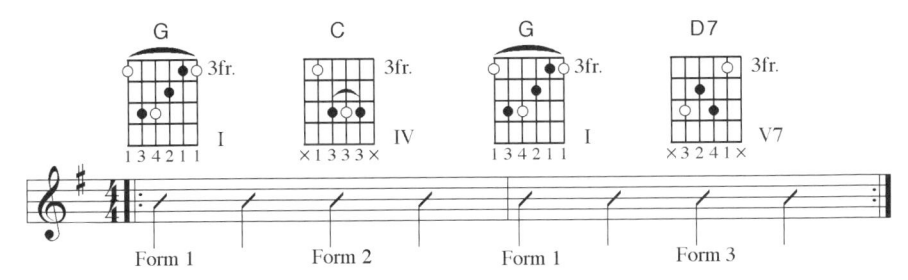

2. The key of F♯. Here is the same progression, a half-step lower. Just shift your hand one position to the left.

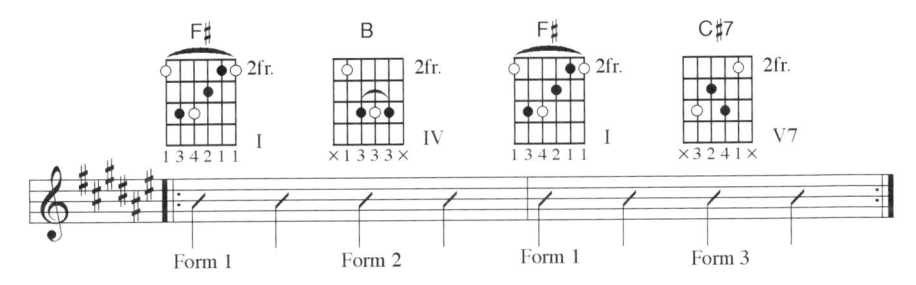

3. The key of A♭. Shift your hand one position in the opposite direction to transpose the exercise up a half-step.

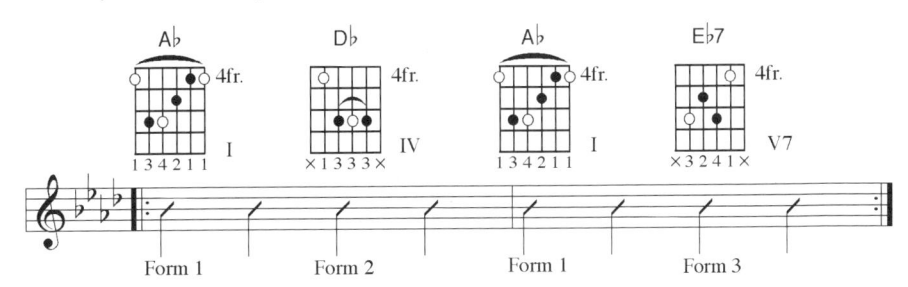

Bar Chord Exercises Using All Forms

The following exercises combine the different forms to demonstrate the versatility of bar chords. All keys are open to you now. Try transposing these exercises to other keys. Then play different songs with bar chords, looking for forms that minimize jumping around the neck.

1. The key of A

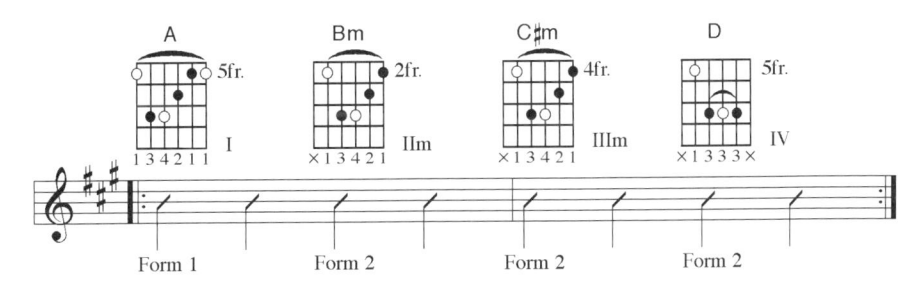

Guitar for Songwriters

2. The key of C

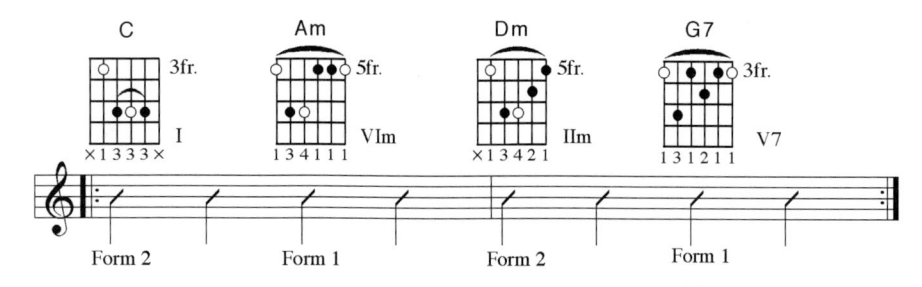

3. The key of E♭

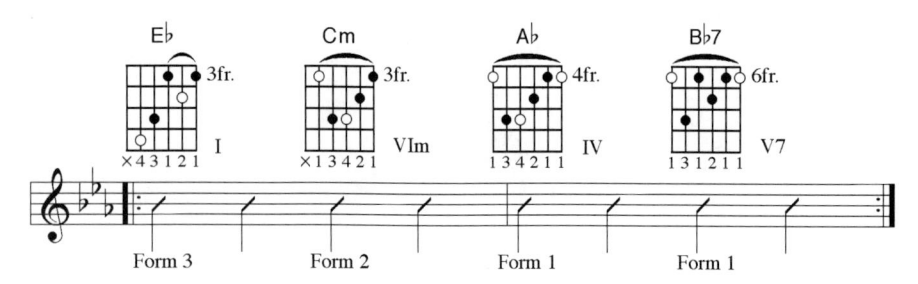

4. The key of F

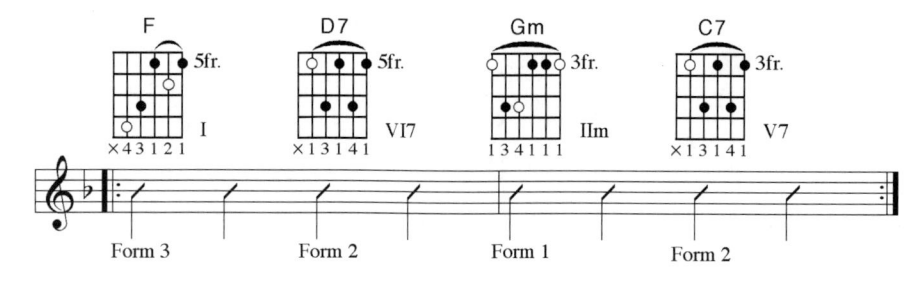

5. The key of A♭m

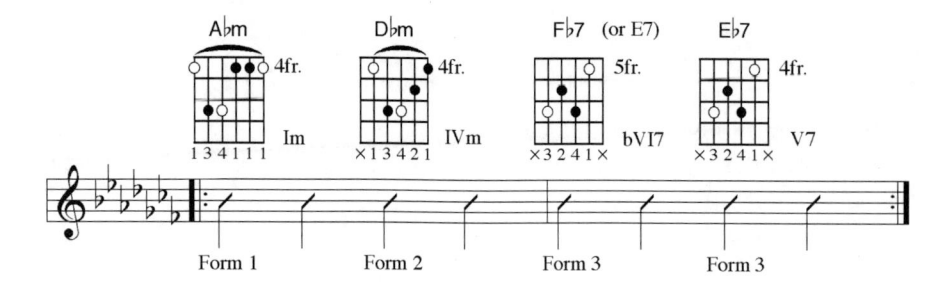

6. The key of Gm

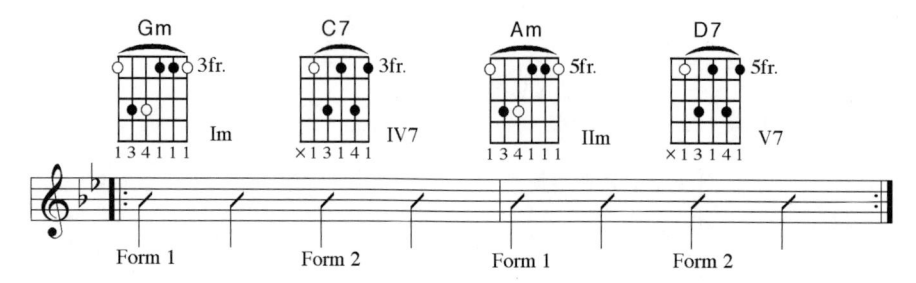

Chapter 7 Bar Chords Part II: Putting Them Together

7. The key of A

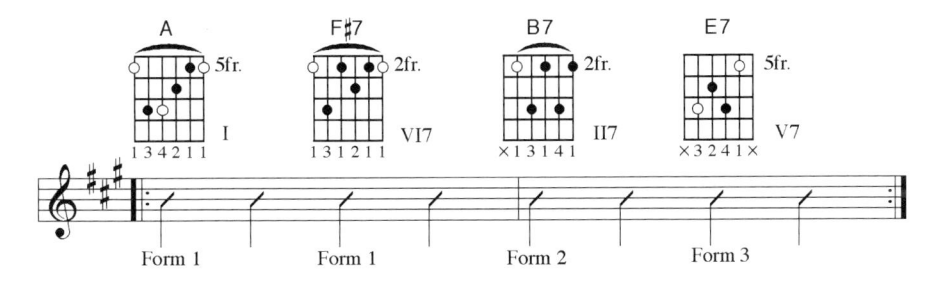

[Chord diagrams: A (5fr, Form 1, I), F#7 (2fr, Form 1, VI7), B7 (2fr, Form 2, II7), E7 (5fr, Form 3, V7)]

8. The key of Cm

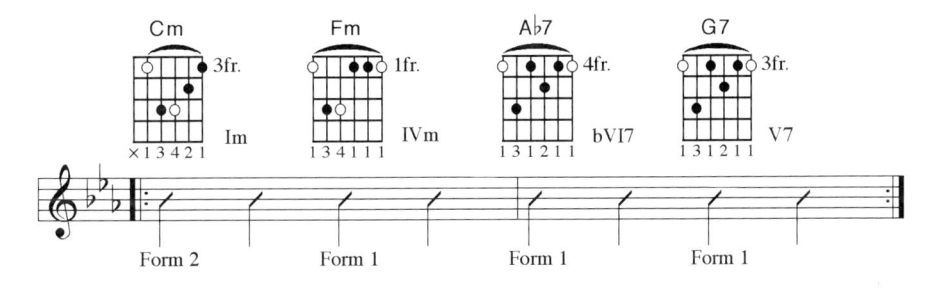

[Chord diagrams: Cm (3fr, Form 2, Im), Fm (1fr, Form 1, IVm), Ab7 (4fr, Form 1, bVI7), G7 (3fr, Form 1, V7)]

9. The key of Bb

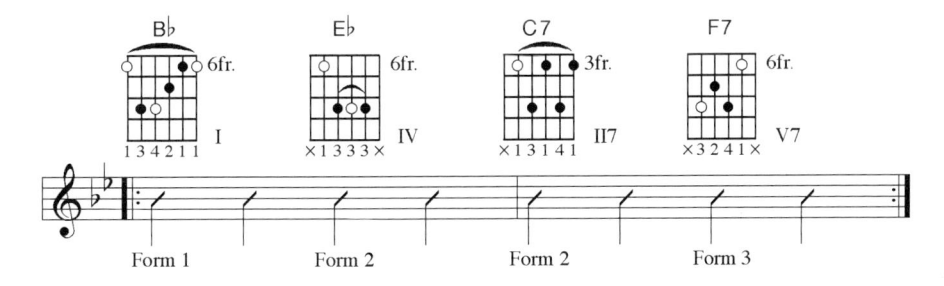

[Chord diagrams: Bb (6fr, Form 1, I), Eb (6fr, Form 2, IV), C7 (3fr, Form 2, II7), F7 (6fr, Form 3, V7)]

Harmonized Scale Progressions Using Form 1 and 2 Bar Chords

The following sections feature two of the harmonized scale progressions studied earlier, but this time in keys that work better with bar chords. Transpose each exercise into as many other keys as are practical.

I-IIm-IIIm-IV

Guitar for Songwriters

1. The key of F

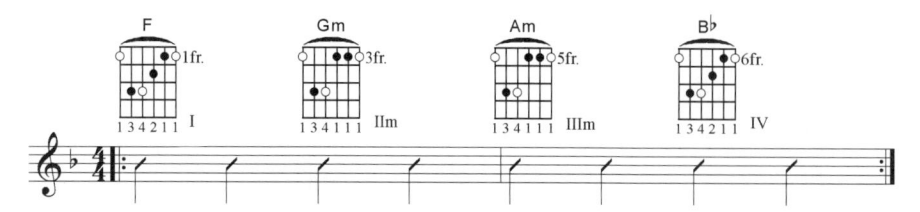

2. The key of B♭

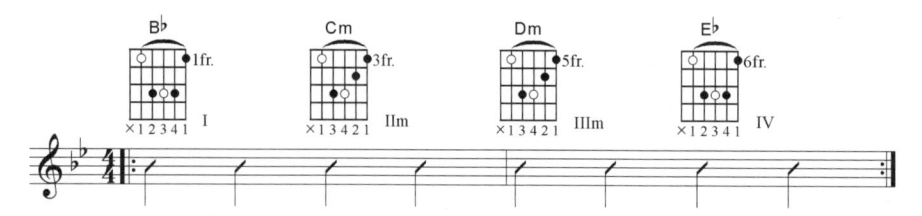

3. The key of A♭

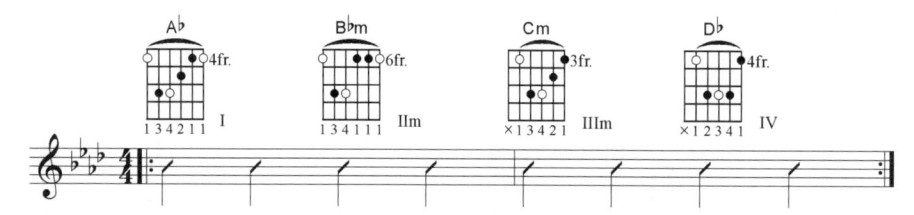

I-VIm-IIm-V7

Musicians often say "One, six, two, five" to indicate this pattern, commonly used in introductions and turnarounds and in old rock-and-roll ballads.

4. The key of F♯

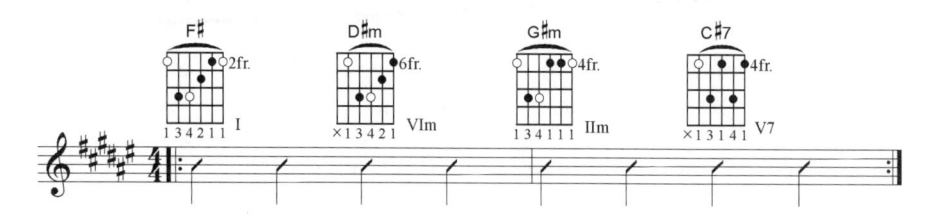

5. The key of D

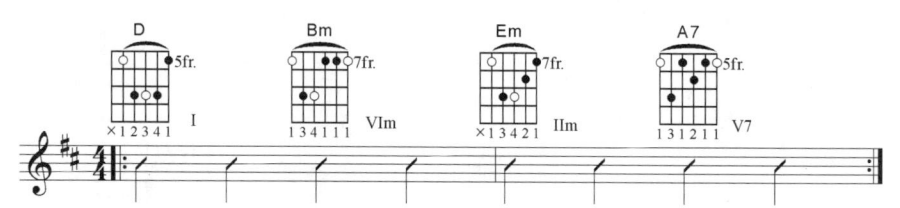

Chapter 7 Bar Chords Part II: Putting Them Together

6. The key of B

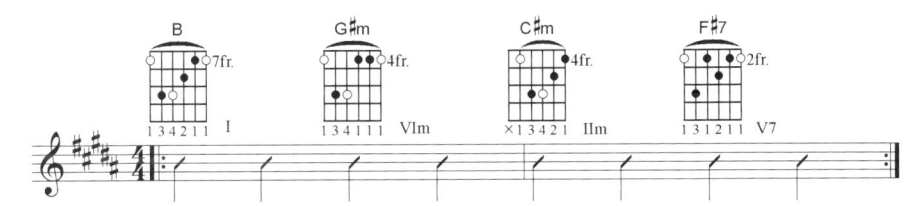

Finding I, IV, and V Quickly with Bar Chords

Since the I, IV, and V7 chords are so common, it's worth memorizing the relationships between the roots. If the I chord has a root on the sixth string, the IV chord root will be on the same fret on the fifth string. The root of the V chord will be two frets above that on the fifth string.

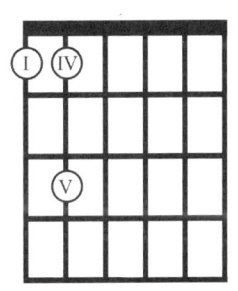

Using that knowledge, the three chords below can be used together in any position to play I, IV, and V7. Notice that they are all at the same position in relation to each other on the neck.

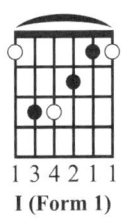

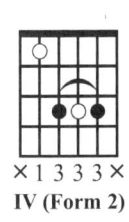

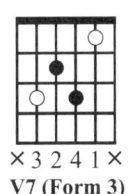

1 3 4 2 1 1   × 1 3 3 3 ×   × 3 2 4 1 ×
I (Form 1)   **IV (Form 2)**   **V7 (Form 3)**

If the I chord has a root on the fifth string, the IV chord root is on the sixth string two frets lower, while the V chord is on the sixth string at the same fret as the I chord.

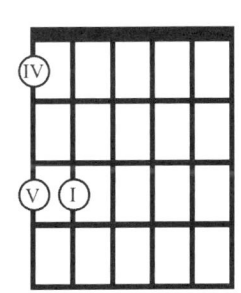

Guitar for Songwriters

Starting with the Form 2 major chord, the three chords below can represent I, IV, and V7. The IV chord is two frets lower than the I, while the V7 chord is at the same position as the I chord.

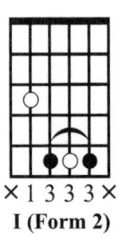

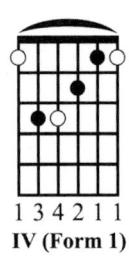

× 1 3 3 3 ×   1 3 4 2 1 1   1 3 1 2 1 1
I (Form 2)   IV (Form 1)   V7 (Form 1)

The chords below show the same relationship, starting with the Form 3 major chord. The IV chord is one fret higher than the I, and the V7 chord is three frets higher than the I.

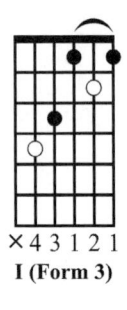

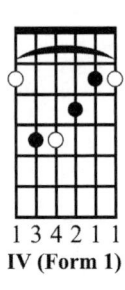

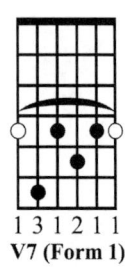

× 4 3 1 2 1   1 3 4 2 1 1   1 3 1 2 1 1
I (Form 3)   IV (Form 1)   V7 (Form 1)

Learn these patterns with minor and dominant seventh chords as well. Eventually, you should learn to find the nearest IV or V chord from any form of a chord, including three- and four-string chords.

Exercises with I, IV, and V7 Bar Chords in All Keys

When I introduced the concept of I, IV, and V chords in this book, I gave exercises in the keys that are easy on the guitar. Using bar chords, you can now play these in any key. Mastering these exercises will greatly improve your playing.

Table 7.1   I, IV, and V7 in All Keys

Key	I	IV	V7
C	C	F	G7
Db	Db	Gb	Ab7
D	D	G	A7
Eb	Eb	Ab	Bb7
E	E	A	B7

Chapter 7 Bar Chords Part II: Putting Them Together

Table 7.1 I, IV, and V7 in All Keys (Continued)

Key	I	IV	V7
F	F	B♭	C7
F♯	F♯	B	C♯7
G♭	G♭	C♭	D♭7
G	G	C	D7
A♭	A♭	D♭	E♭7
A	A	D	E7
B♭	B♭	E♭	F7
B	B	E	F♯7

The keys of F♯ and G♭ are really enharmonic spellings of the same key, which means they are two different ways to spell tones that sound the same. An F♯ is held at the same place on the guitar as a G♭. The keys of F♯ and G♭ have six sharps or six flats in their scales, so you are equally likely to see either key. Although other scales could also be spelled two different ways, you usually will see the key that has fewer sharps or flats. Even though C♯ and D♭ are the same, you see the key of D♭ more often because it has five flats in the scale, versus seven sharps in the key of C♯.

The following exercises apply these I-IV-V bar chord relationships to chord progressions explored earlier in this book.

This first set starts with the Form 1 bar chord.

I-IV-V7-IV

We first examined this pattern in Chapter 2. In the following exercises, it is played in the key of F at the first position, then in F♯ with the same chords at the second position. It continues through the keys by moving the chords up one position in each exercise.

1. The key of F

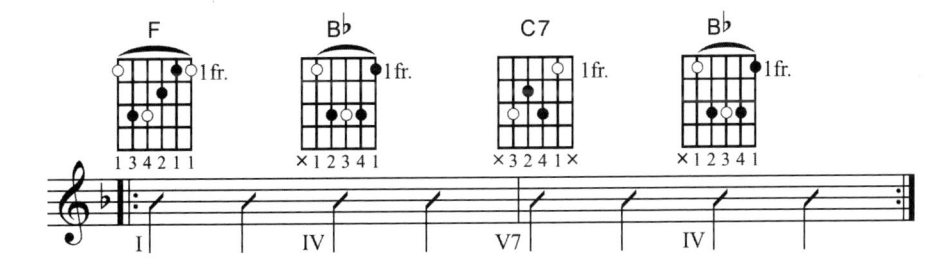

Guitar for Songwriters

2. The key of F#

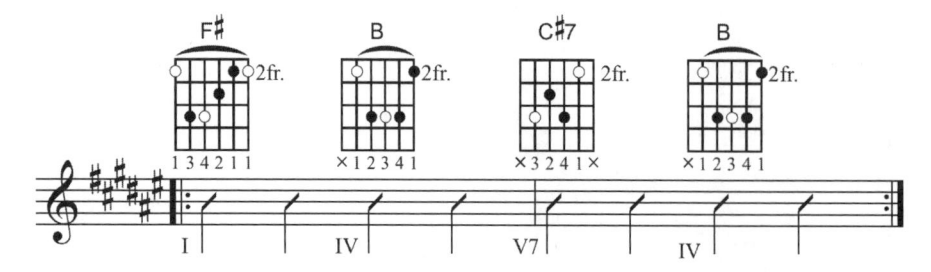

3. The key of G

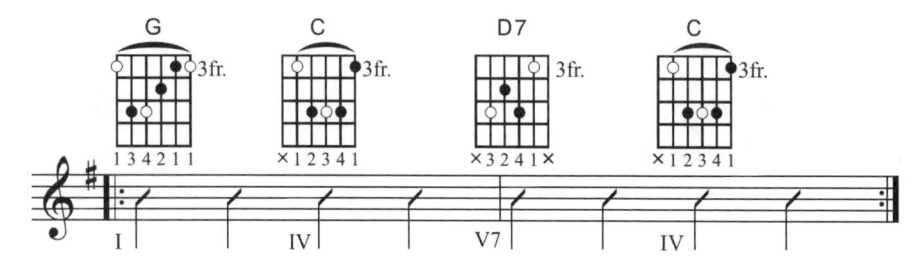

4. The key of A♭

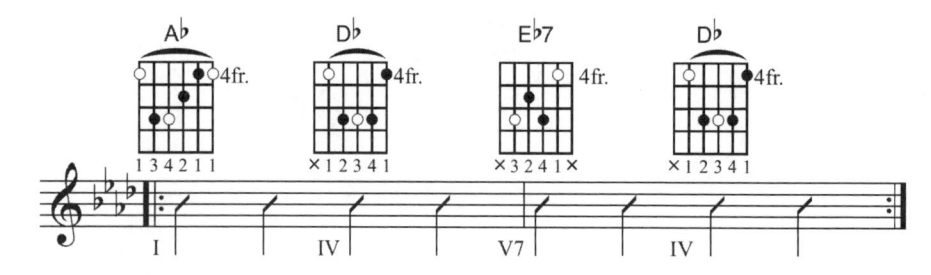

The pattern continues with the key of A at the fifth fret, B♭ at the sixth fret, B at the seventh, and so on.

I-IV-I-V7

This section provides another combination of I, IV, and V7 chords. The exercises start with the Form 2 bar chord.

1. The key of C

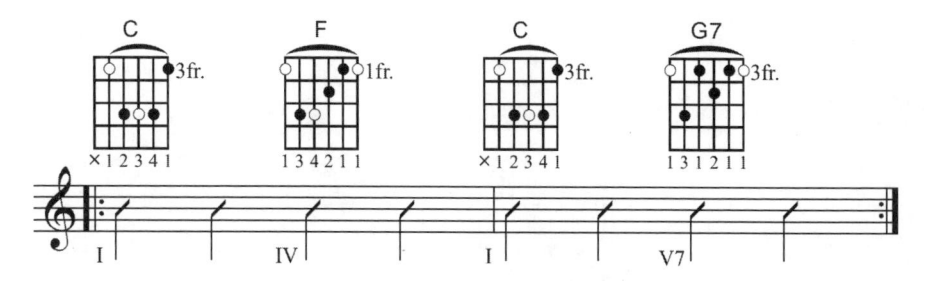

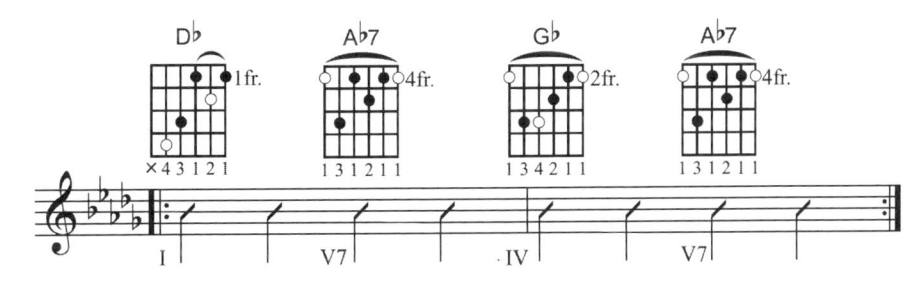

Chapter 7 Bar Chords Part II: Putting Them Together

2. The key of D♭

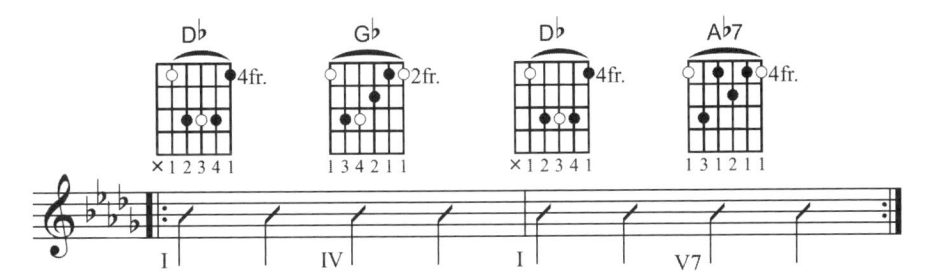

3. The key of D

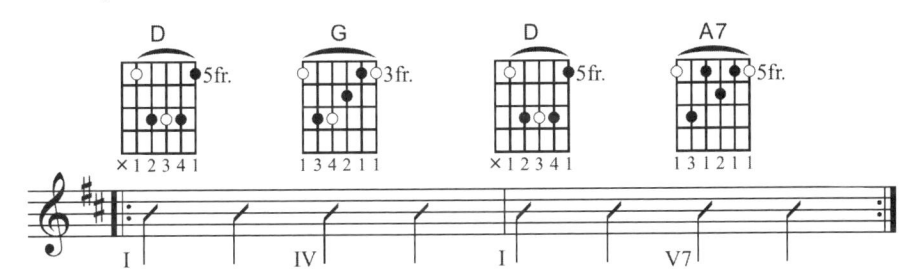

4. The key of E♭

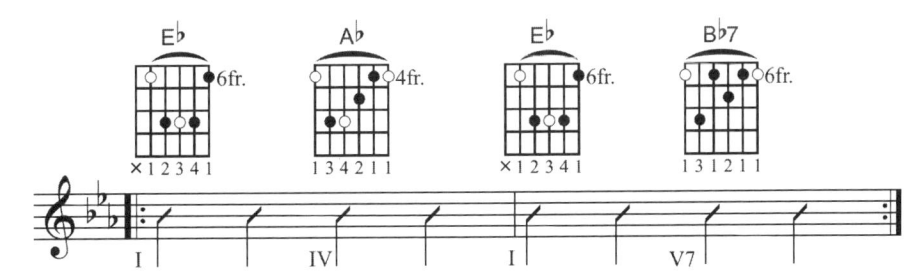

Continue to move this pattern up the neck to play in the keys of E, F, F♯, and G.

I-V7-IV-V7

This variation on I, IV, and V7 starts with the Form 3 bar chord.

1. The key of D♭

Guitar for Songwriters

2. The key of D

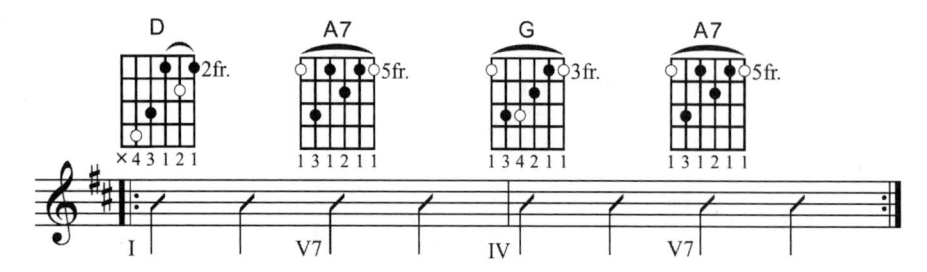

3. The key of E♭

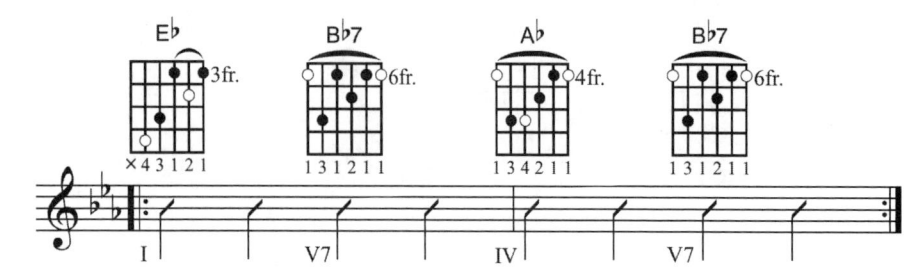

4. The key of E

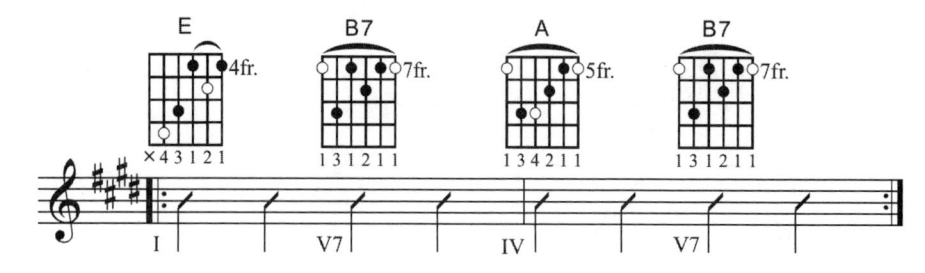

Continue to move this pattern up the neck to play in the keys of F, F♯, and G.

The next chapter examines chord construction. How are chords built? What are the notes in a chord? What is the difference between a major chord and a minor chord? Is there a way to find a chord somewhere else on the neck?

8

Chord Construction: How to Build Chords and Find Good Voicings

WITH A LITTLE KNOWLEDGE OF MUSIC THEORY, you can find chords anywhere on the neck. This chapter tells you how to find the notes in a chord and how to apply that to the guitar.

How Chords Are Built

To find any chord on the guitar, you need to know three things:

▷ The major scale for every key
▷ The notes on the neck of the guitar
▷ The formula for the type of chord you want (major, minor, seventh, and so on)

Page 81 provides a chart of the notes on the neck. We'll explore the formulas in the pages ahead.

Chords are built from the notes of scales. A major chord uses the root (the tonic, or first note of the scale), the third note, and the fifth note of a major scale. A C major chord contains the notes C, E, and G—the root, the third note, and the fifth note of a C major scale. A D major chord uses the root, third, and fifth of the D major scale—D, F♯, and A. A B♭ major chord contains B♭, D, and F—the root, third, and fifth of the B♭ major scale.

Other types of chords, such as minor or seventh chords, use different formulas, but you still start from the major scale in finding the notes to any chord.

There are a few basic but very important rules about constructing chords:

▷ The notes in a chord can be repeated as many times as you like.
▷ The notes can be in any order.

If you had the notes E, G, and C, it would still be a C major chord. The same goes for C, G, C, G, C, G, and E. Or G, C, G, E, C, and G. Any combination of those three notes forms a C major chord.

> *The notes in a chord can be repeated as many times as you like. The notes can be in any order.*

93

Guitar for Songwriters

Consider the significance of this for the guitar: Since there are Cs, Es, and Gs all over the neck, you are never far from a C chord.

Here are just a few of the possible fingerings for a C major chord on the guitar. Moving up the neck will give you dozens more possibilities. They are called different *voicings*—different combinations of the notes that all make valid C major chords.

> **NOTE:** A voicing is the particular arrangement of notes to produce a chord.

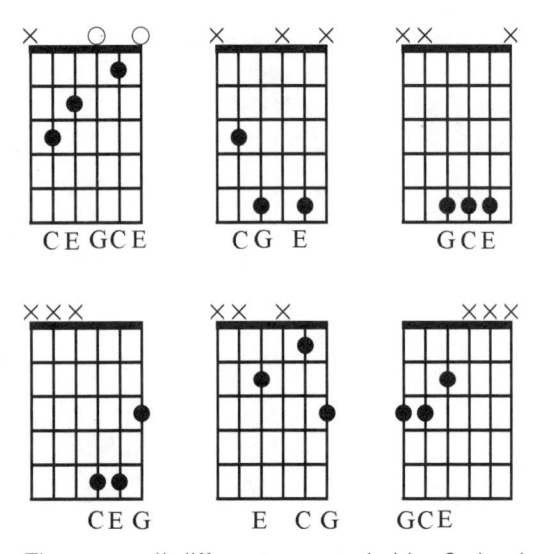

These are all different ways to hold a C chord.

To find a D major chord, or E major, or any other major chord, you follow the same process: Find the root, third, and fifth notes of that major scale. Then find those notes in any order on the neck of the guitar.

Major Chords

Major chords are formed by choosing the root, third note, and fifth note of the major scale that corresponds to the chord you want. For a C major chord, choose the root (tonic, or first note), third, and fifth of the C major scale (C E G). For a D major chord, the root, third, and fifth of a D major scale are D, F♯, and A.

When playing these chords, you can put the notes in any order and repeat them as many times as you want. We'll examine this more closely in the section on voicings.

Chapter 8 Chord Construction: How to Build Chords and Find Good Voicings

> *Major chords are formed by choosing the root, third note, and fifth note of the major scale that corresponds to the chord you want.*

Table 8.1 Notes in Major Chords

Chord	Root	3rd	5th
C	C	E	G
C♯	C♯	E♯	G♯
D♭	D♭	F	A♭
D	D	F♯	A
E♭	E♭	G	B♭
E	E	G♯	B
F	F	A	C
F♯	F♯	A♯	C♯
G♭	G♭	B♭	D♭
G	G	B	D
A♭	A♭	C	E♭
A	A	C♯	E
B♭	B♭	D	F
B	B	D♯	F♯
C♭	C♭	E♭	G♭

At some point, you must memorize this information if you want to become adept at using chords. Minor chords, seventh chords, and all other types are calculated starting from the major chord. If you can name the major chords, it's fairly easy to figure out other types of chords.

Some Voicings of Major Chords

Keeping in mind that the three notes of a major chord can be assembled in any order and repeated as often as desired, there are dozens, if not hundreds, of possible ways to play any major chord on the guitar. Most of these fingerings are easier to remember if related to the basic bar chord forms. They are often just shortened versions of the bar chords—fewer strings to play, with a slightly smaller sound but easier to hold, especially if you're going to hold the chord for just a beat or two.

Guitar for Songwriters

Form 1 Variations

These chord forms are all related to the Form 1 bar chord. Don't hold a bar on these unless it is required—you'll find the chord much easier to move around.

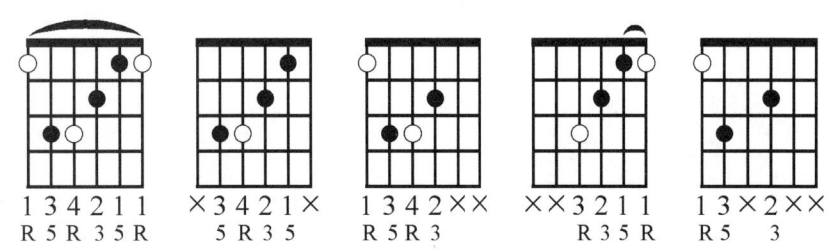

```
1 3 4 2 1 1      × 3 4 2 1 ×      1 3 4 2 × ×      × × 3 2 1 1      1 3 × 2 × ×
R 5 R 3 5 R       5 R 3 5           R 5 R 3           R 3 5 R          R 5    3
```

The chord on the right is a good example of an open voicing—there is distance between the chord tones, and it can cut through without sounding muddy. It is also called a *tenth* chord, because of the interval of a tenth between the top and bottom notes. These types of chords were often used by guitarists in the old big bands to give the solid "chunk-chunk" sound that propelled those bands.

Form 2 Variations

Based on the Form 2 bar chord, these chords have the root on either the fifth or third string. For the second chord above, bar your third finger across four strings but do not strum the first string. The chord on the right, again, is a tenth chord.

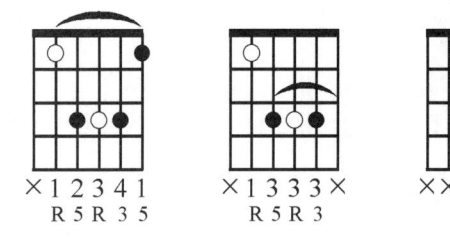

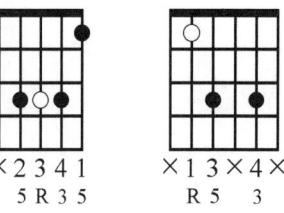

```
× 1 2 3 4 1      × 1 3 3 3 ×      × × 2 3 4 1      × 1 3 × 4 ×
  R 5 R 3 5        R 5 R 3            5 R 3 5        R 5    3
```

Form 3 Variations

These variations on the Form 3 bar chord have the root on the second string and sometimes on the fourth or fifth string. Most of them do not use an actual bar, but they can still be moved along the neck. When an inner string is marked with an *x*, mute it by leaning your other left-hand fingers slightly.

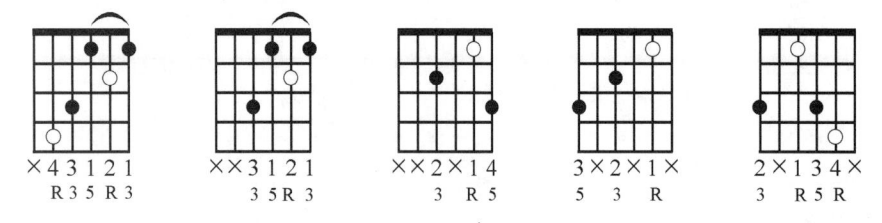

```
× 4 3 1 2 1      × × 3 1 2 1      × × 2 × 1 4      3 × 2 × 1 ×      2 × 1 3 4 ×
  R 3 5 R 3          3 5 R 3          3   R 5         5   3   R        3   R 5 R
```

G Form Variations

These chords are related to the open position G chord—if you imagine moving that chord up the neck and using a first-finger bar in place of the open strings.

96

Chapter 8 Chord Construction: How to Build Chords and Find Good Voicings

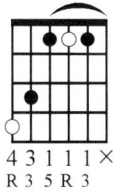

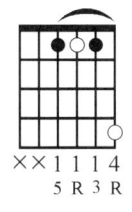

```
4 3 1 1 1 ×        × 3 1 1 4 ×        × × 1 1 1 4
R 5 5 R 3            3 5 R 5              5 R 3 R
```

These examples are by no means all of the possible ways to hold a major chord on the guitar. But none of these forms will do you any good if you can't progress smoothly to other chords. Knowledge of progressions and voice leading will help you find the right time for the right chord.

Minor Chords

Once you have the major chords down, it's not difficult to analyze other types of chords. The minor chord uses the root, the flatted third, and the fifth note of the major scale of the chord you are constructing. A Cm chord has the notes C, E♭, and G, as opposed to C, E, and G for the C major. If you know the major chord, you can just flat the third.

> **NOTE:** Minor chords are formed by choosing the root, the flatted third, and the fifth note of the major scale that corresponds to the chord you want.

For a Dm, flatting the F♯ would give F (not F♭).

Table 8.2 Notes in Minor Chords

Chord	Root	Flat 3rd	5th
Cm	C	E♭	G
C♯m	C♯	E	G♯
D♭m	D♭	F♭	A♭
Dm	D	F	A
E♭m	E♭	G♭	B♭
Em	E	G	B
Fm	F	A♭	C
F♯m	F♯	A	C♯
G♭m	G♭	B♭♭	D♭
Gm	G	B♭	D
G♯m	G♯	B	D♯

(Continued)

Guitar for Songwriters

Table 8.2 Notes in Minor Chords (*Continued*)

Chord	Root	Flat 3rd	5th
A♭m	A♭	C♭	E♭
Am	A	C	E
B♭m	B♭	D♭	F
Bm	B	D	F♯

B♭♭ is called "B double flat" and is the same note on the guitar as an A. It would not be called A when spelling a G♭m chord, because an A is the second of the chord, not the third.

Some Voicings of Minor Chords

Minor chords are easier to remember if related to the corresponding major chord. A minor chord is like a major chord with the third note of the scale flatted—root, flatted third, and fifth. Compare these voicings to the corresponding major chords.

Form 1 Variations

These are related to the Form 1 bar chord.

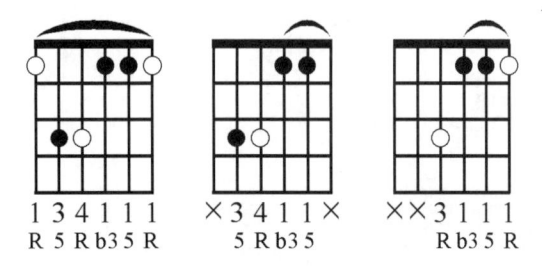

```
1 3 4 1 1 1        × 3 4 1 1 ×        × × 3 1 1 1
R 5 R b3 5 R         5 R b3 5           R b3 5 R
```

Form 2 Variations

The Form 2 minor bar chord is the basis for these voicings.

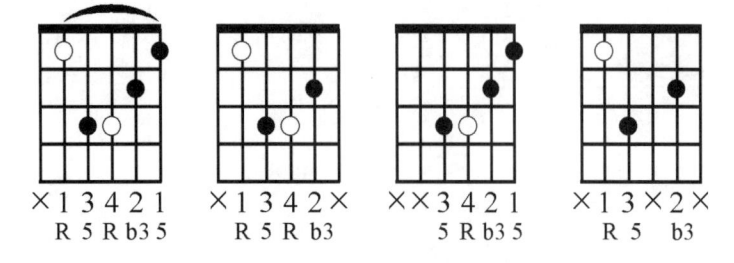

```
× 1 3 4 2 1      × 1 3 4 2 ×      × × 3 4 2 1      × 1 3 × 2 ×
R 5 R b3 5        R 5 R b3           5 R b3 5         R 5   b3
```

98

Chapter 8 Chord Construction: How to Build Chords and Find Good Voicings

Form 3 Variations

It is difficult to find a fingering for this form, which includes the root in the bass. For that reason, these forms work better when playing with a bass player or when the tonality has already been strongly established by playing other forms of the chord with the root in the bass.

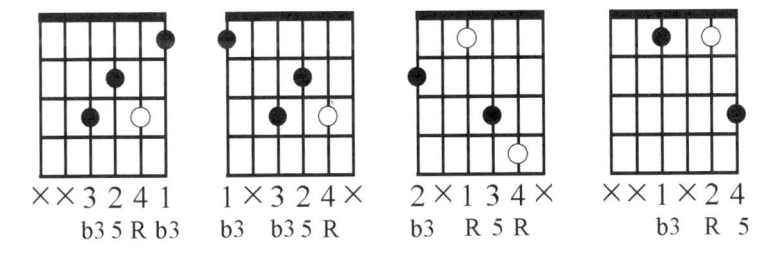

```
× × 3 2 4 1      1 × 3 2 4 ×      2 × 1 3 4 ×      × × 1 × 2 4
 b3 5 R b3        b3  b3 5 R       b3  R 5 R         b3  R 5
```

G Form Variations

These minor chords are related to the open string G chord.

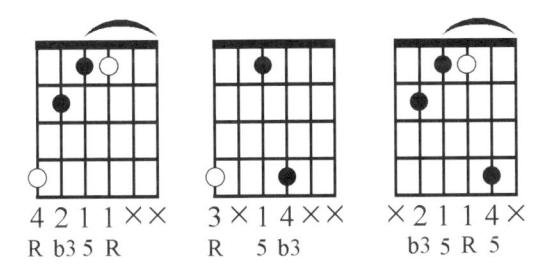

```
4 2 1 1 × ×      3 × 1 4 × ×      × 2 1 1 4 ×
 R b3 5 R         R   5 b3         b3 5 R 5
```

Dominant Seventh Chords

When a song calls for a G7 chord, it actually means "G dominant 7th," although usually only theory students say the longer name. Dominant 7th chords are different from major 7ths, which we'll discuss later.

Dominant 7ths are formed with the root, third, fifth, and flatted seventh note of the major scale that corresponds to the chord you want. So they are like a major chord, with one more note. For a C7, the notes are C, E, G, and B♭—a C major chord and the flatted seventh. For a D7 chord, the notes are D, F♯, A, and C. (The seventh note of the D scale is C♯; flatted, it becomes C natural.)

A quick way to find the flatted seventh is to count down a whole step from the root. You can find the flatted seventh of a C scale, for example, by counting up seven notes to B and then flatting it to B♭. Or you can count down a whole step (two frets) from C to B♭.

> **NOTE:** Dominant 7th chords are formed by choosing the root, third, fifth, and flatted seventh notes of the major scale that corresponds to the chord you want.

Guitar for Songwriters

Table 8.3 Notes in Dominant Seventh Chords

Chord	Root	3rd	5th	Flat 7th
C7	C	E	G	Bb
C#7	C#	E#	G#	B
Db7	Db	F	Ab	Cb
D7	D	F#	A	C
Eb7	Eb	G	Bb	Db
E7	E	G#	B	D
F7	F	A	C	Eb
F#7	F#	A#	C#	E
Gb7	Gb	Bb	Db	Fb
G7	G	B	D	F
G#7	G#	B#	D#	F#
Ab7	Ab	C	Eb	Gb
A7	A	C#	E	G
Bb7	Bb	D	F	Ab
B7	B	D#	F#	A

Some Voicings of Dominant Seventh Chords

There are a few points to keep in mind regarding dominant 7th chords. First of all, a C7 or G7 is a dominant 7th chord, which is different from a major 7th. You could say either C seven, C seventh, or C dominant seventh—they all refer to the same chord. CMaj7 is a different type of chord.

The formula for a dominant 7th chord is the root, third, fifth, and flatted seventh. The fifth or the root is sometimes omitted, because it is often difficult to include all four chord tones. You would rarely omit the third, since that note determines the difference between major and minor, and you wouldn't omit the seventh, or you would just have a major chord.

It may seem strange to list the notes included in a chord and then say you can leave some out. In the context of playing a song, it can work for a number of reasons. First of all, if you're playing with other people, chances are someone else will sound those missing notes. Secondly, if you are playing different voicings of the chords at different times, you will have played those notes before and will have established the tonality. We remember the sounds we heard before and relate the new chord to those sounds.

Chapter 8 Chord Construction: How to Build Chords and Find Good Voicings

Form 1 Variations

Below are a few of the many possible voicings of a dominant 7th chord based on Form 1.

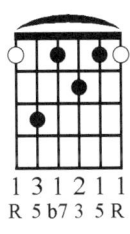

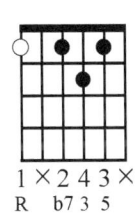

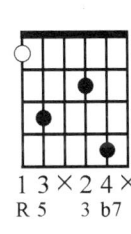

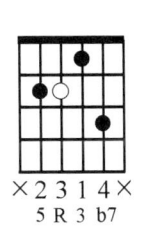

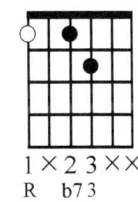

1 3 1 2 1 1   1 × 2 4 3 ×   1 3 × 2 4 ×   × 2 3 1 4 ×   × × 1 2 1 1   1 × 2 3 × ×
R 5 b7 3 5 R   R   b7 3 5   R 5   3 b7   5 R 3 b7   b7 3 5 R   R   b7 3

Form 2 Variations

There is no root in the variations with an × marking where the root would be. Played in context, where the root has been sounded earlier by you or a bass player, this can still work.

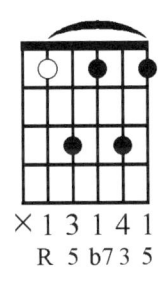

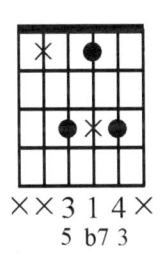

× 1 3 1 4 1   × × 3 1 4 ×
R 5 b7 3 5   5 b7 3

Form 3 Variations

These voicings are easy to hold and can be very handy when progressing to the Form 1 major chord.

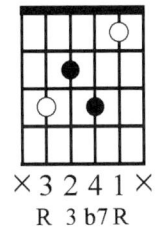

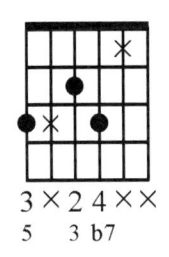

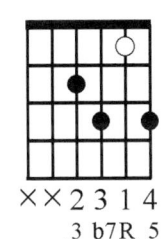

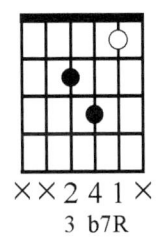

× 3 2 4 1 ×   3 × 2 4 × ×   × × 2 3 1 4   × × 2 4 1 ×
R 3 b7 R   5   3 b7   3 b7 R 5   3 b7 R

G Form Variations

The form on the right would usually resolve by having the seventh in the bass move down to the third of the next chord.

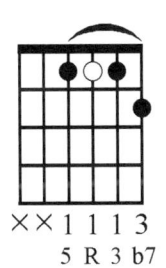

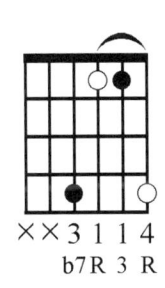

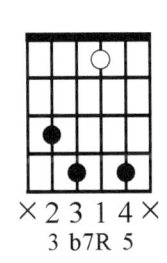

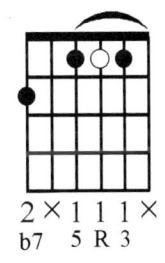

× × 1 1 1 3   × × 3 1 1 4   × 2 3 1 4 ×   2 × 1 1 1 ×
5 R 3 b7   b7 R 3 R   3 b7 R 5   b7 5 R 3

101

Other Dominant Seventh Forms

When you know the notes you need, you can find chords beyond the vicinity of the basic bar forms. The chords below are very handy, but they are harder to relate to chord forms we have covered.

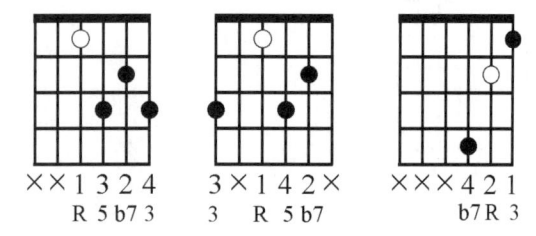

```
× × 1 3 2 4         3 × 1 4 2 ×         × × × 4 2 1
  R 5 b7 3          3   R 5 b7              b7 R 3
```

Chord Voicings

As discussed in more detail in the section on chord construction, a chord has to have certain notes in it, but the notes can be repeated and can be in any order. A C chord must have the notes C, E, and G, but they could be played EGC, or GEGEC, or any other combination of those notes. The particular way you play a chord is the voicing.

You could play a straight triad—the notes of a major or minor triad in their closest proximity to each other, such as CEG. This is called *close harmony* or a *close voicing*. *Open harmony* or *voicing* involves taking the middle note and raising it an octave—CGE—so the notes are spread out over a wider range. The tenth chords played by Freddie Green in the Count Basie orchestra are good examples of open voicings that cut through without sounding muddy.

Chords with notes other than the root in the bass are called *inversions*. A chord with the third in the bass is called *first inversion*, and one with the fifth in the bass is called *second inversion*. Chords with the root in the bass are said to be in root position.

You don't really need to be aware of the terms for different types of chords, but you should be aware of the sounds. Certain voicings sound fuller; others leave more space and are lighter but can cut through the sounds of other instruments. The fewer instruments playing with you, the fuller the sound you will generally want.

If you are the only instrument accompanying a group of singers, you will probably play five- and six-string root position chords that will really lay a foundation for them. If you are playing with piano, bass, and drums, you will more likely play smaller chords, in a higher register, providing little punctuations but leaving space for the bass and drums to lay the foundation and for the piano to play some chords also.

Another thing to keep in mind when playing chords is voice leading. Each note in a chord could be considered a separate voice. The chord will sound best when each voice has somewhere to go, without making large leaps. In other words, a chord progression will sound better when you generally use the same number of strings in each chord and stay in the same general area of the neck. A full six-string E chord with open strings followed by an E♭ chord on the first three strings at the eleventh position isn't going to make a lot of musical sense.

> *A chord progression will sound better when you generally use the same number of strings in each chord and stay in the same general area of the neck.*

This is why there is such an emphasis on progressions and exercises in this book. Chords don't exist as separate units out in space. They are part of a progression of chords making up a song, and they need to flow together well. The most common chord patterns are given in this book with specific chord voicings that will go together well.

Chapter 8 Chord Construction: How to Build Chords and Find Good Voicings

After you have tried the exercises in this book, try constructing chords of your own and combining them using good voice leading.

Notes to Omit

With only six strings and four fingers, there is a limited number of note combinations you can hold on the guitar. If you're trying to construct a chord, there will come a time when it's better to leave one or two notes out of the chord.

Probably the most important note of any chord is the third. This is the note that makes the difference between major and minor. It's very rare that you would leave out the third on anything other than a power chord.

The root is obviously very important, but there are times when it can be omitted. If you're playing with a bass player or another chordal instrument, such as piano, chances are they will be playing a root. Also, if there are a lot of chord changes, the root may already be established in your ear and can be left out now and then.

The seventh is an important tone—it can add real color to a chord. It would rank near the root in terms of notes not to omit.

This leaves the fifth. It is the note most often left out of chords.

Higher harmonies, such as ninths and thirteenths, could be left out if necessary. They are wonderful color tones, but only if the third and seventh are being played also.

I-IV Examples with Different Voicings

There are dozens of ways to play any chord progression. These exercises give combinations that work well on the guitar. Some have a fuller sound; others might work better for a light sound or when playing with a number of other instruments, when you don't want to muddy the sound. Think of these as related pairs of chords. Analyze each voicing to see whether any notes are omitted.

You usually want your chords to have roughly the same number of strings and be in the same general area of the neck. It may stand out to have thin- and thick-sounding chords following each other.

The first eight exercises are in the key of C. The rest are in G. Try transposing the exercises into the suggested keys.

1. Works from the key of C to the key of G.

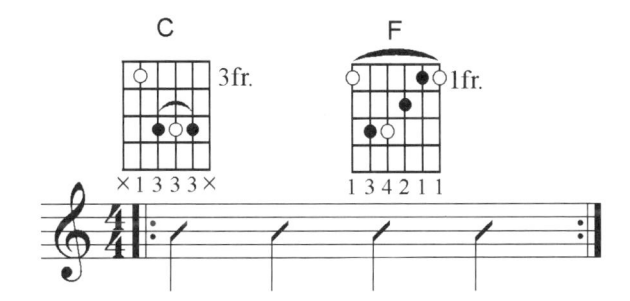

Guitar for Songwriters

2. Works from F to about D♭.

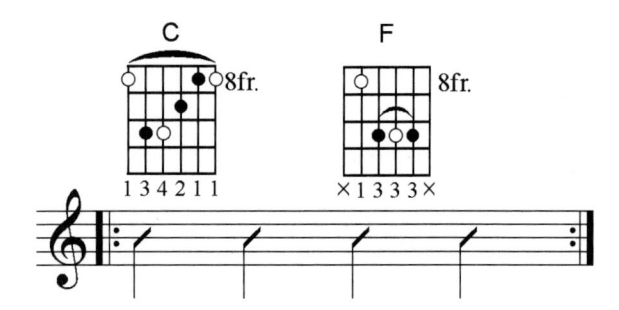

3. Try from A♭ to E♭.

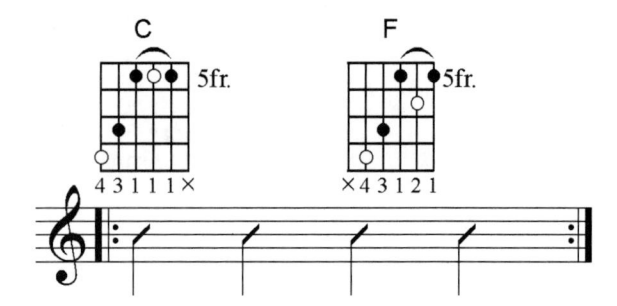

4. A♭ to E♭.

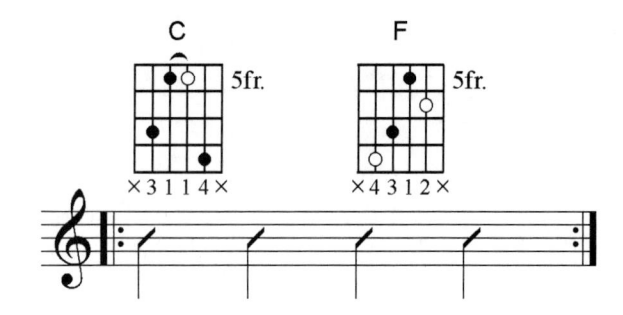

5. Try from A♭ to E. These forms with fewer strings are more maneuverable and work well when playing faster tempos.

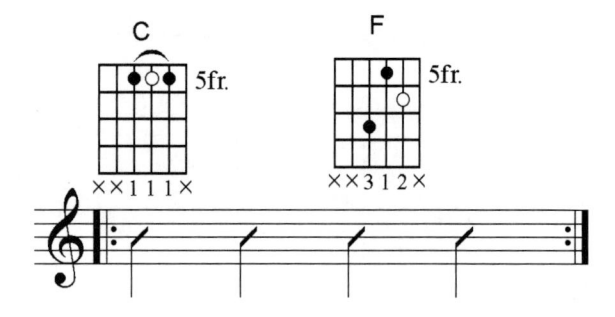

Chapter 8 Chord Construction: How to Build Chords and Find Good Voicings

6. Try from the key of A♭ to the key of E.

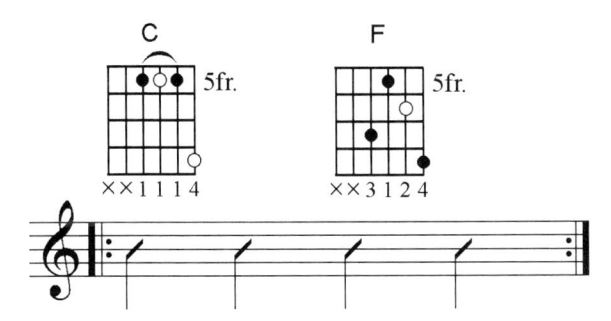

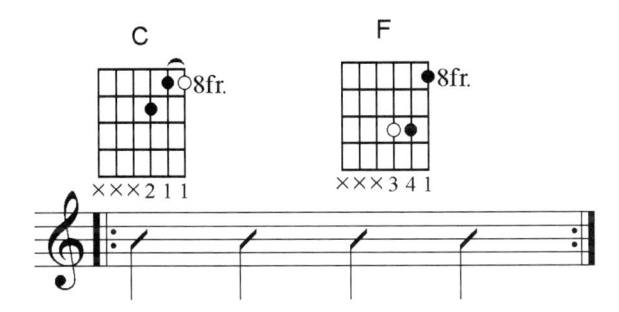

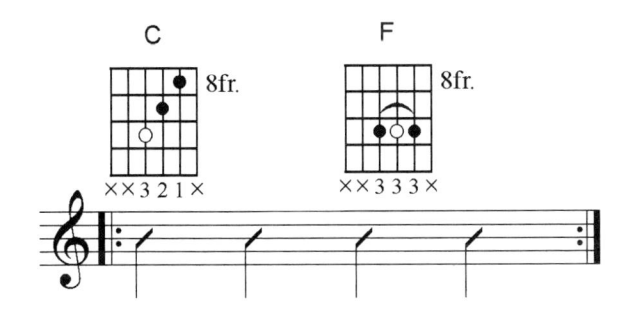

7. F to D♭.

8. F to D♭.

9. E♭ to B. These examples would be too high to hold comfortably in the key of C, but they work well in many other keys.

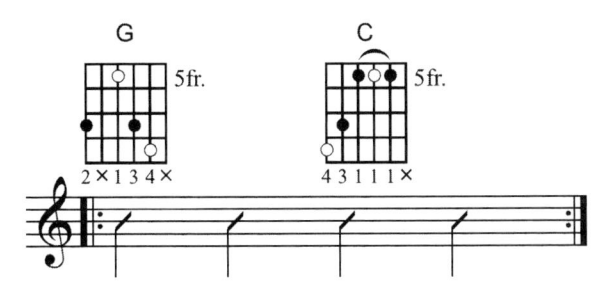

105

Guitar for Songwriters

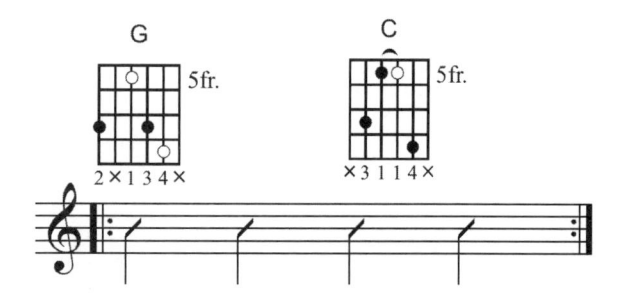

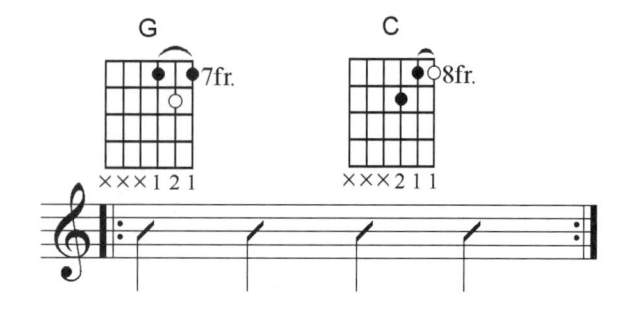

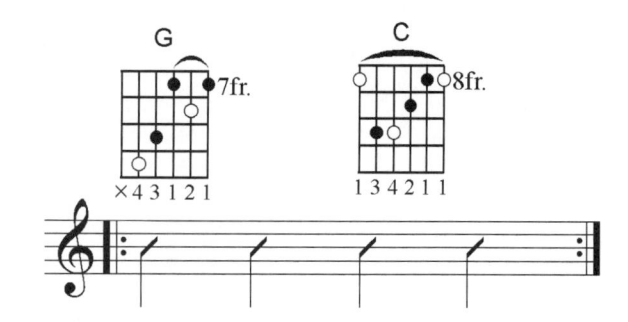

10. E♭ to B.

11. D♭ to A.

12. D♭ to A♭.

Ways to Play I-IV-V7-IV Up the Neck

We have already observed that C, F, and G7 will often be used in songs in the key of C. Applying this to the guitar, it is important to use voicings of the chords that work together well. Again, this generally means chords that have about the same number of strings and are in the same area of the neck. The next 10 exercises can be transposed to most keys, although there will be a few keys for each example where the chords are too high up the neck to be held comfortably.

Chapter 8 Chord Construction: How to Build Chords and Find Good Voicings

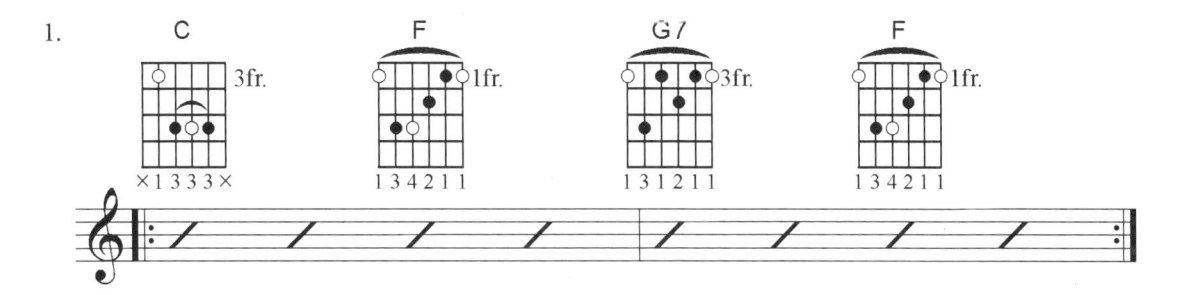

1.

2. This G7 has the fifth in the bass.

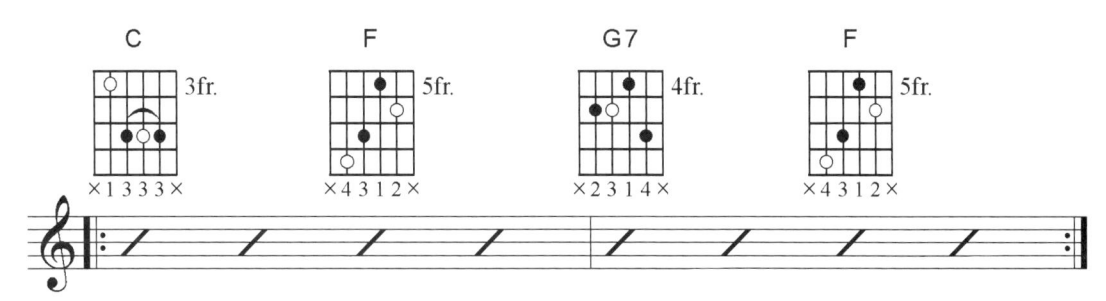

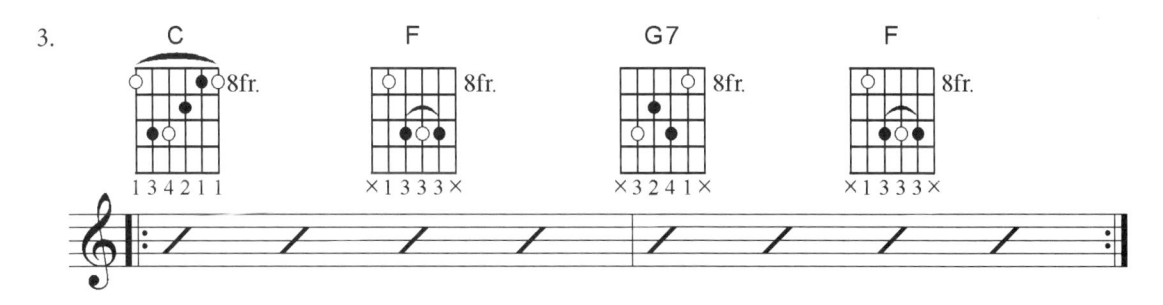

3.

4. This C chord has the third in the bass.

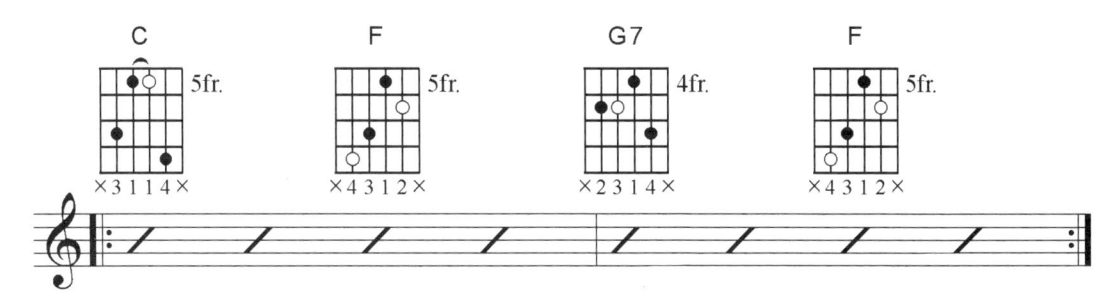

5. It sometimes works to use a G instead of a G7.

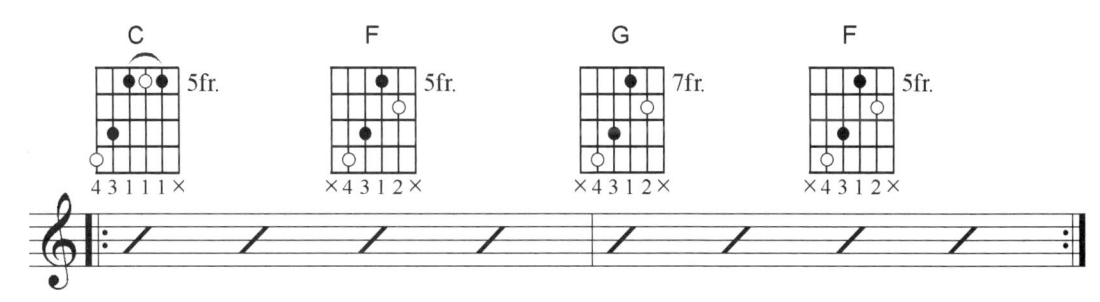

Guitar for Songwriters

6. These chords work very well when playing with a bass player, since they are in a higher range that won't compete with the bass.

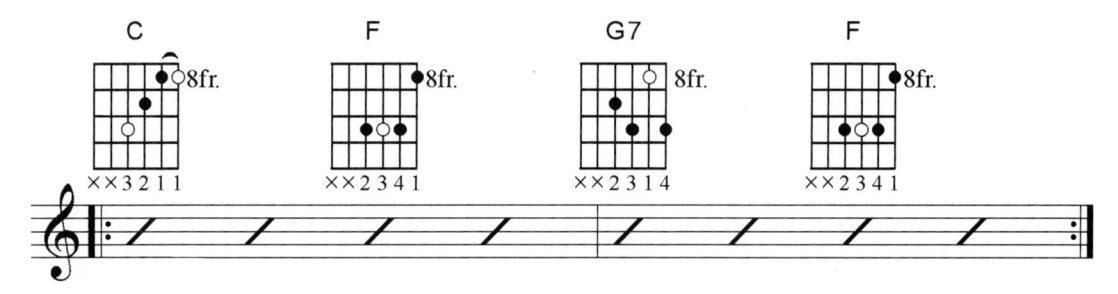

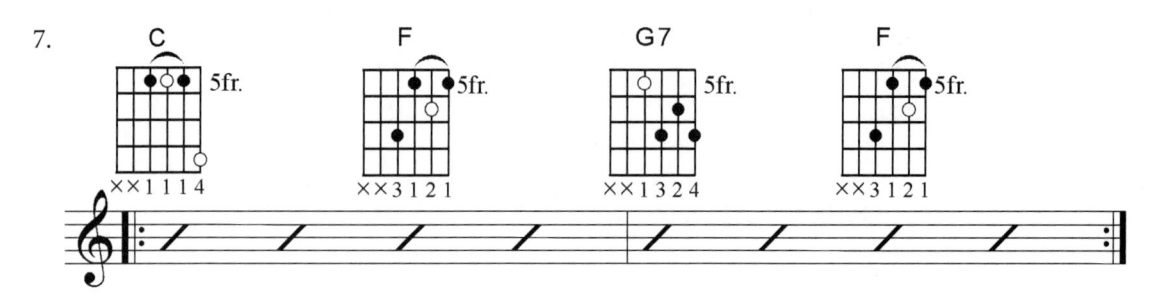

7.

8. These forms are shown in the key of F because they are too far up the neck for the key of C.

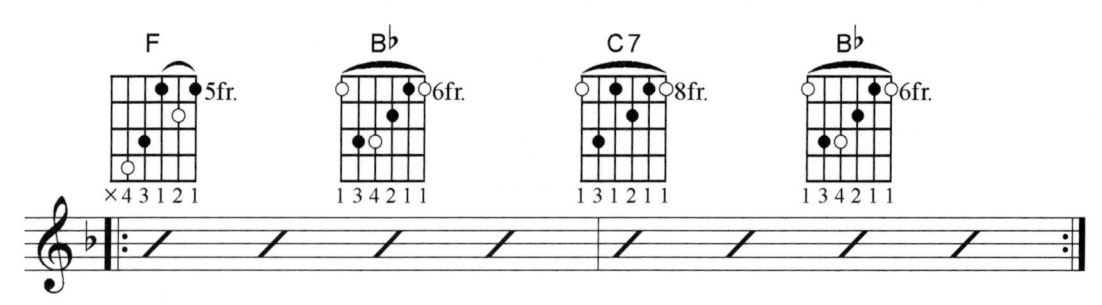

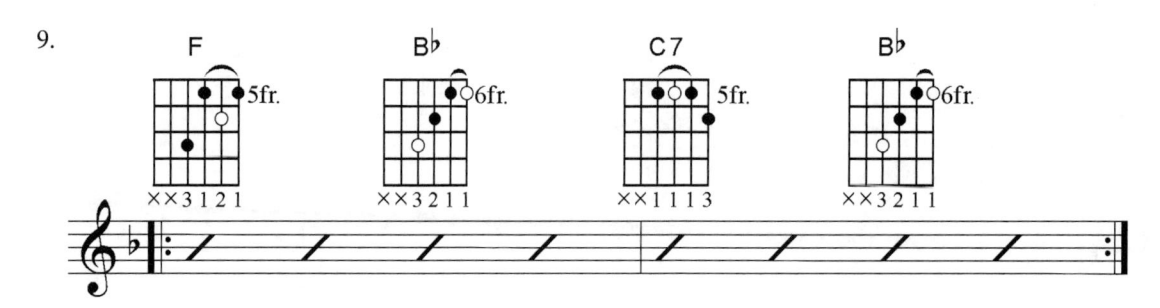

9.

10. C is used here in place of C7.

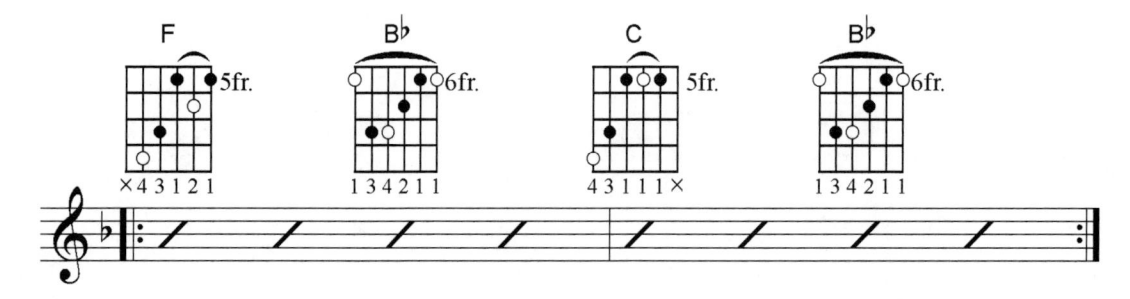

108

Chapter 8 Chord Construction: How to Build Chords and Find Good Voicings

Playing I, IV, and V in Minor Keys

In general, the minor key equivalent of I-IV-V7 is Im-IVm-V7. In the key of C minor, that would be Cm-Fm-G7. Notice that the V chord is a dominant seventh, the same as in the major key, while the I and IV chords have both become minor.

Here are the Im, IVm, and V7 chords for all keys:

Table 8.4 Im, IVm and V7 in All Keys

Key	Im	IVm	V7
Cm	Cm	Fm	G7
C♯m	C♯m	F♯m	G♯7
D♭m	D♭m	G♭m	A♭7
Dm	Dm	Gm	A7
E♭m	E♭m	A♭m	B♭7
Em	Em	Am	B7
Fm	Fm	B♭m	C7
F♯m	F♯m	Bm	C♯7
Gm	Gm	Cm	D7
G♯m	G♯m	C♯m	D♯7
A♭m	A♭m	D♭m	E♭7
Am	Am	Dm	E7
B♭m	B♭m	E♭m	F7
Bm	Bm	Em	F♯7

Guitar for Songwriters

Im-IVm Examples

In minor keys, the I and IV chords are both minor. Most of the following examples will be very close to patterns used for I to IV in major keys given earlier. Transpose them to see which keys will work on the guitar.

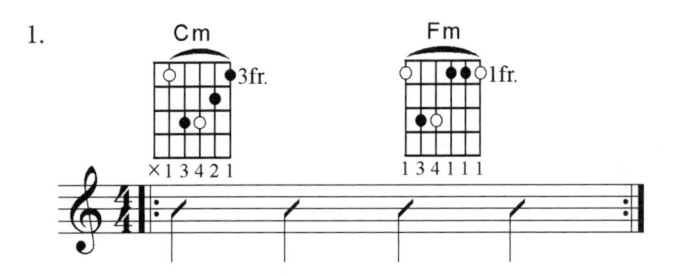

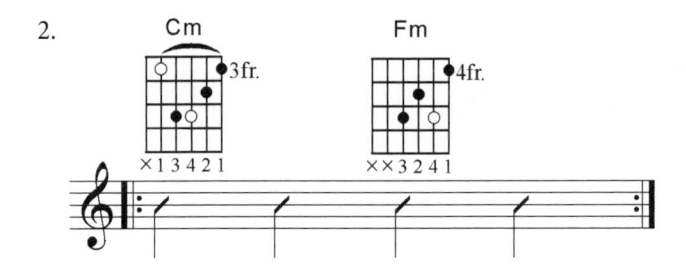

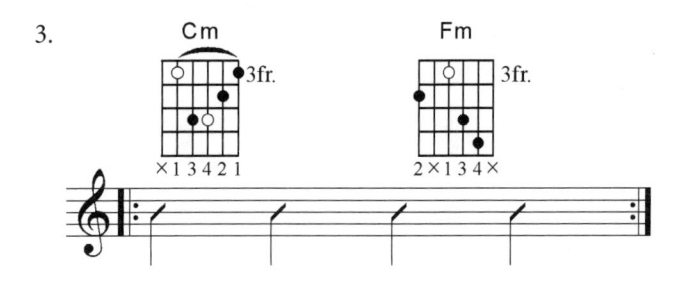

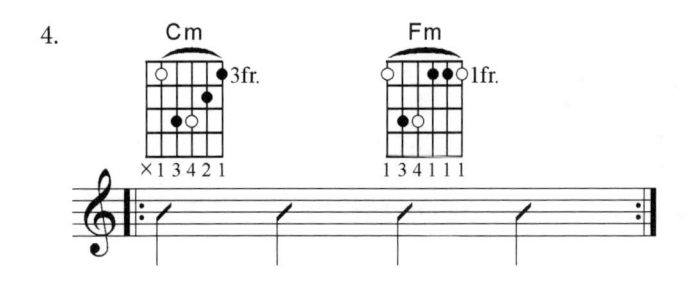

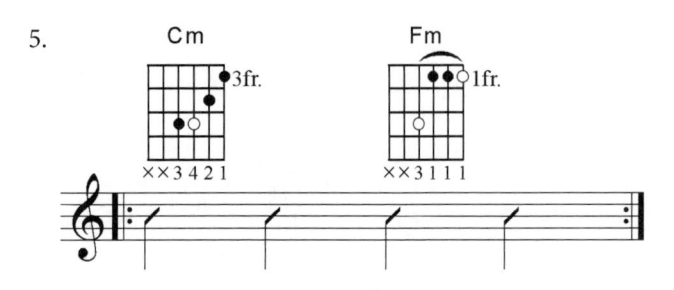

110

Chapter 8 Chord Construction: How to Build Chords and Find Good Voicings

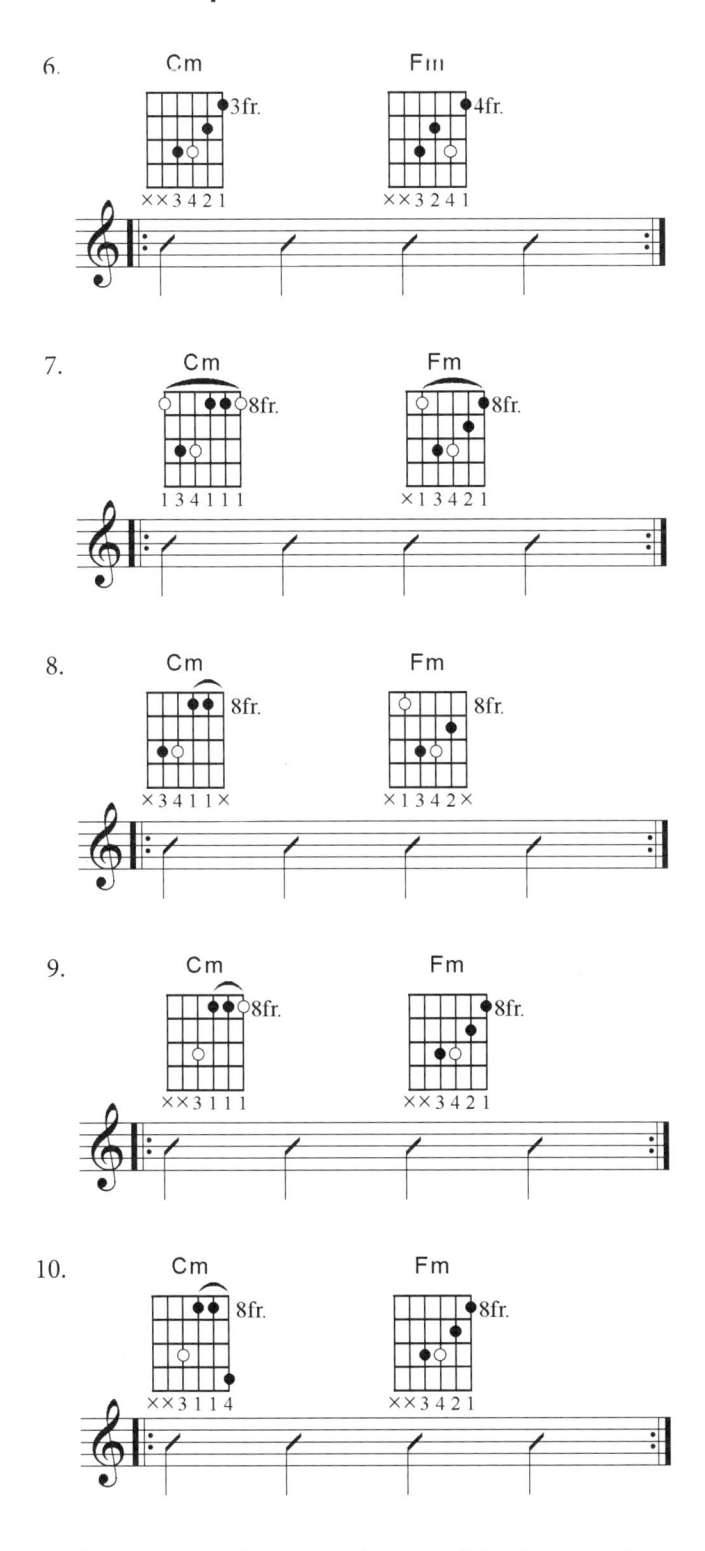

These last two examples are in the key of Gm because they are too high up the neck to play comfortably in Cm.

Guitar for Songwriters

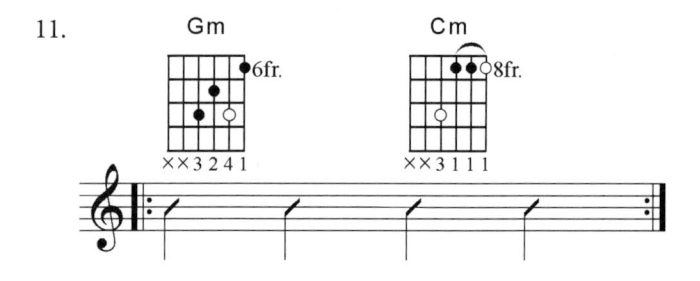

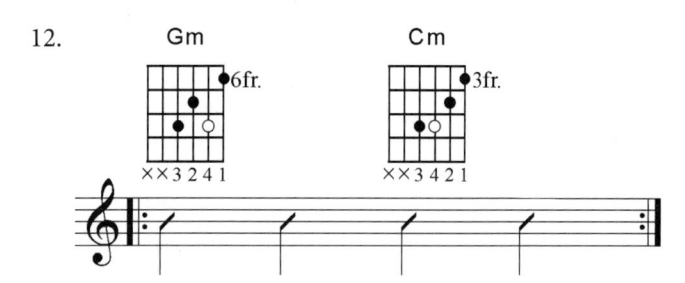

11.

12.

Ways to Play Im-IVm-V7-IVm Up the Neck

The following chord progressions use Im, IVm, and V7, the most common chords found in minor keys. Transpose each exercise into all keys.

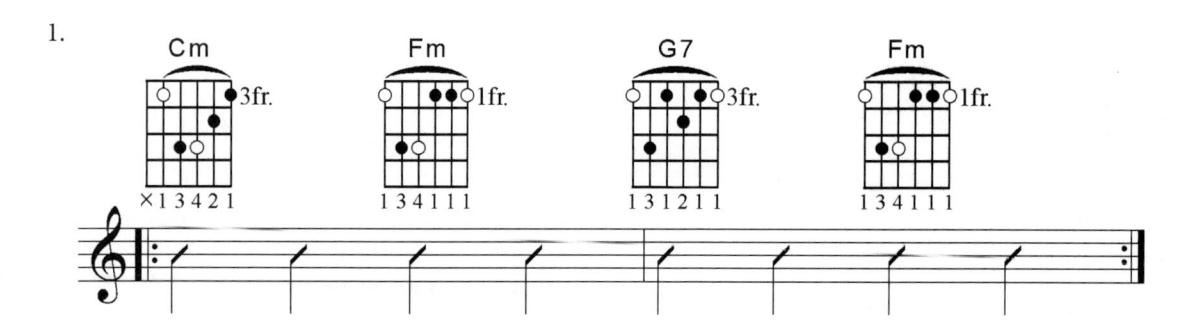

1.

2. Keep the little finger down and slide the others to move between Fm and G7.

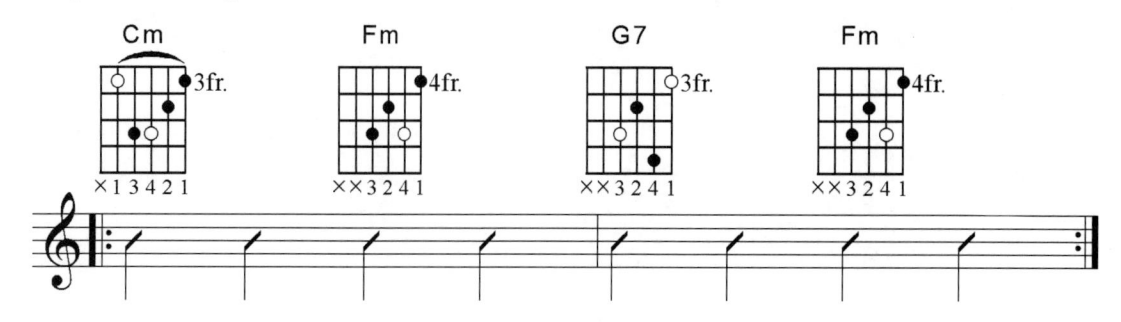

Chapter 8 Chord Construction: How to Build Chords and Find Good Voicings

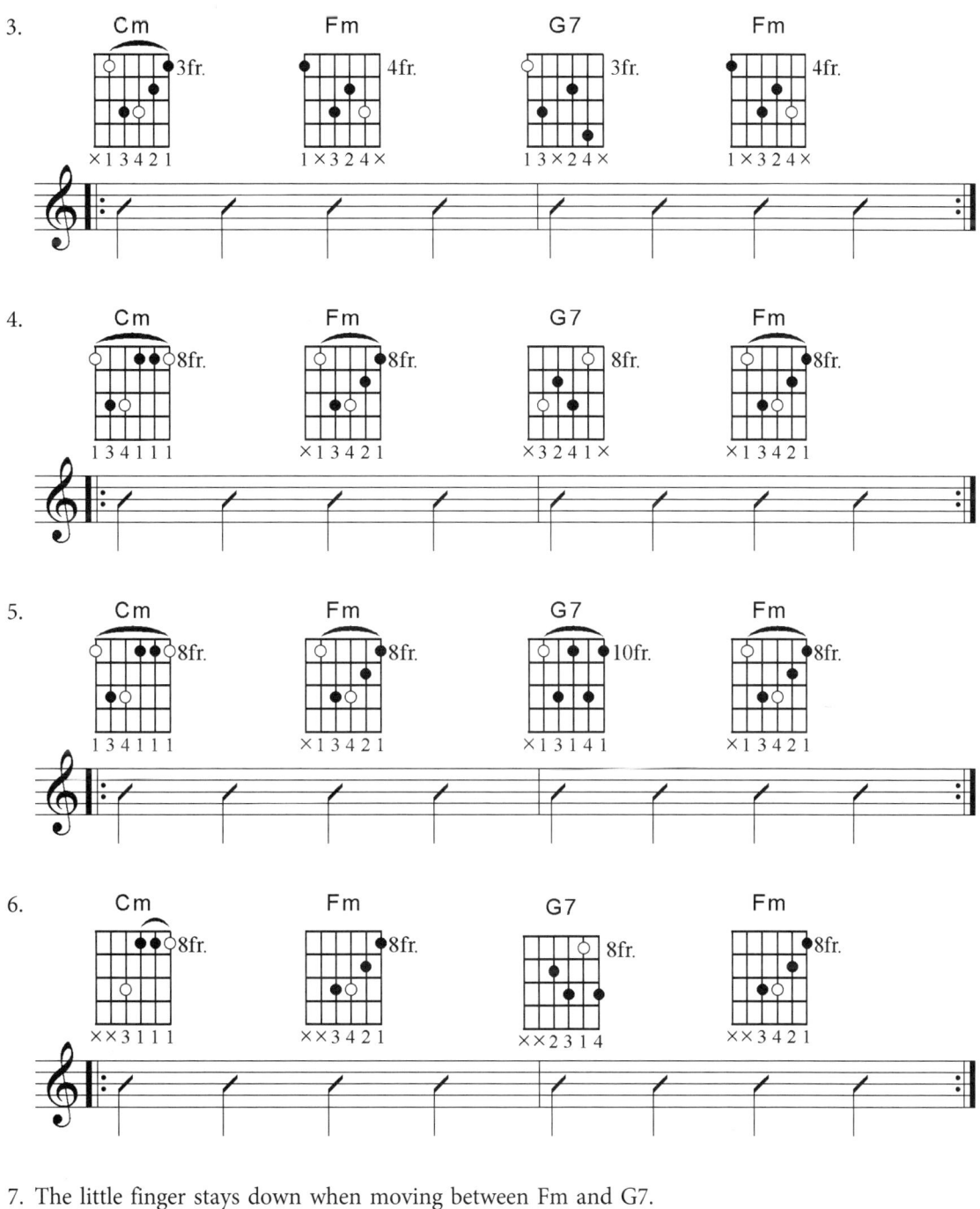

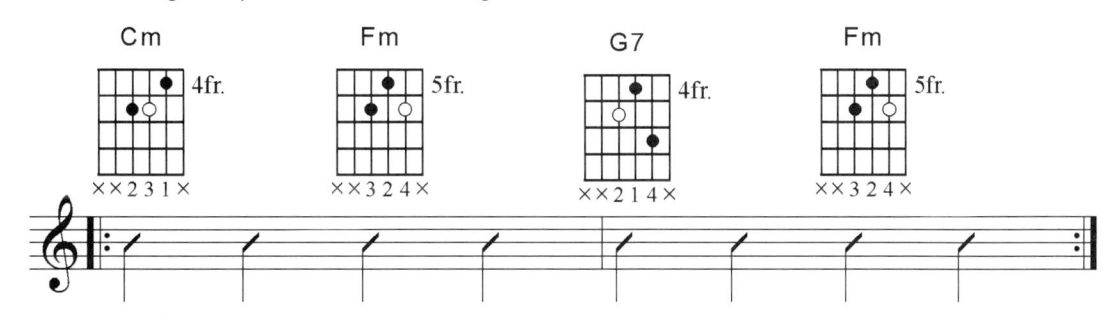

7. The little finger stays down when moving between Fm and G7.

Guitar for Songwriters

8. Slide the first and second fingers while holding down the fourth finger to move between Fm and G7.

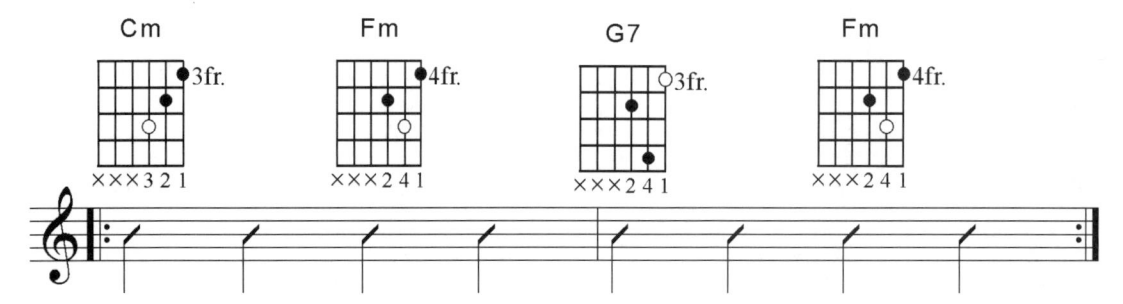

These forms are shown in the key of Gm because they are too high up the neck for the key of Cm.

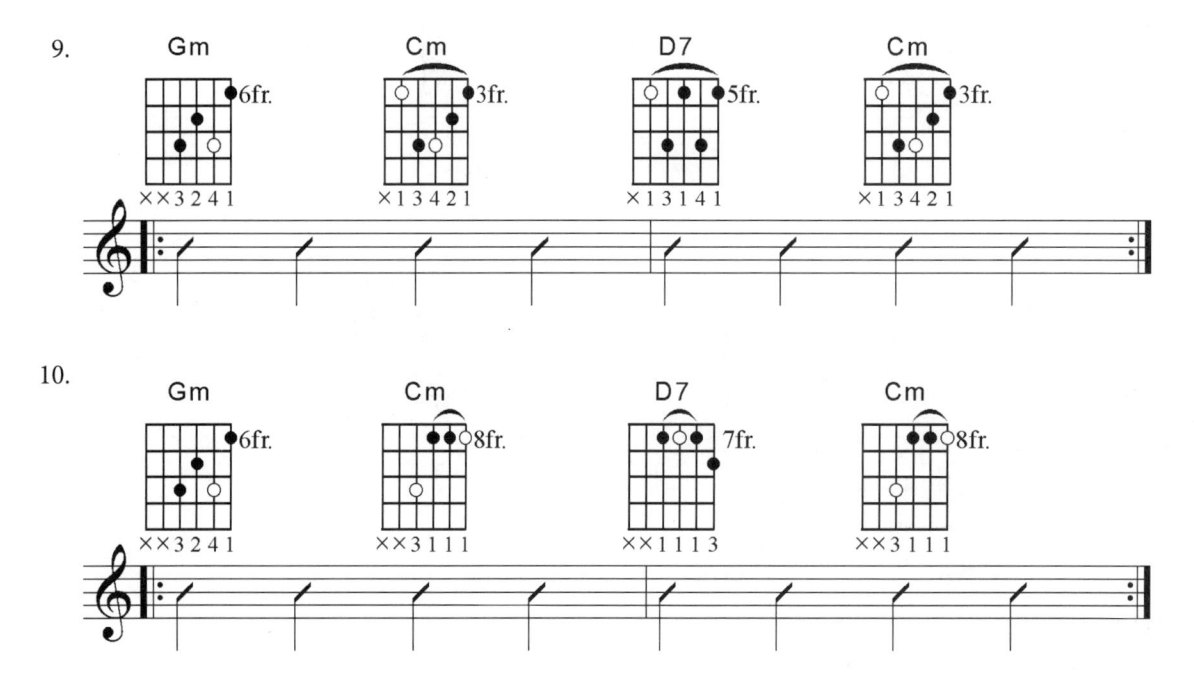

9.

10.

The next chapter looks at more complex chords and their formulas. The same ideas about finding good voicings and strong progressions will apply to those chords.

9

More Chord Formulas

As a songwriter, you don't need to know the names of chords or understand the theory behind them as long as they sound good. But this chapter may give you some ideas, some new sounds. It may also help when you're trying to communicate with other musicians.

About Chord Formulas

This chapter will give you the knowledge to find dozens of chords in many places on the neck of the guitar, but an important element is missing. That element, touched upon briefly in the preceding chapter, is good voice leading. Chords don't exist in a vacuum. You must learn how to connect them smoothly and logically. Any time you learn a new chord, you should give it a context. Find other chords that might go with it, in the harmonized scale or from the section on jazz progressions. Find chord combinations that sound logical and have fingerings to make them flow smoothly. Create exercises to utilize these chords and make them part of your working vocabulary. The following chapters will present some practical applications.

Major-Type Chord Formulas

Many years ago, the great jazz guitarist Joe Pass put out a chord book that had diagrams for dozens of chords, but no names for the chords. He just grouped them into major, minor, seventh, and a few other broad "categories of sound." He was far less concerned with the name of a chord than how it sounded, how the chords fit together.

Many chords can be fit into the broad category of major-type chords. You can try substituting them for each other in jazz tunes or other pieces with sophisticated harmonies. For example, in place of a C6 chord, try a CMaj7, CMaj9, or C6/9.

Table 9.1 shows many types of major chords and how they are constructed. It would be well worth it for you to spell the chords out in every key.

Guitar for Songwriters

Table 9.1 Major-Type Chords

Chord Type	Example	Alternate Names	Spelling	Example
Major	C	CMaj	R 3 5	C E G
6th or major 6th	C6	CMaj6, CM6	R 3 5 6	C E G A
6/9	C6/9	CMaj 6/9	R 3 5 6 9	C E G A D
Major 7th	CMaj7	CM7	R 3 5 7	C E G B
Major 9th	CMaj9	CM9	R 3 5 7 9	C E G B D
Major 13th	CMaj13	CM13	R 3 5 7 9 13	C E G B D A
Major 7th(♯11)	CMaj7(♯11)	CMaj 7(+11)	R 3 5 7 ♯11	C E G B F♯
Major 9th(♯11)	CMaj9(♯11)	CMaj 9(+11)	R 3 5 7 9 ♯11	C E G B D F♯
Add 9	C(add 9)	C(add 2)	R 3 5 9	C E G D

There are several things to be aware of. First of all, "major" can be indicated several ways, sometimes written maj, or M (capital M, as opposed to lowercase m for minor), or even with a triangle. CΔ7 means CMaj7. And + means sharp or augmented, while - means flat.

In a major 13th chord, the 11th is usually omitted.

The ninth is the same as the second, the eleventh is the same as the fourth, and the thirteenth is the same as the sixth. Why not say second, fourth, or sixth instead of ninth, eleventh, or thirteenth? Listing the ninth indicates that the root, third, fifth, and seventh are all present. The eleventh suggests presence of the root, third, fifth, seventh, and ninth (although the third is often omitted). Use of "add" means that particular chord tone is added to the basic chord—C add 2 would suggest a C major chord plus a D.

These are not the only types of major chords. Rarely, you might come across something like CMaj7(♯5). You should be able to figure these out by comparing them to other chord formulas.

Many rock songs use chords listed with a five: C5, G5, and so on. This means a root and a fifth. This type of chord is not included in Table 9.1 because without a third or flat third, it could be either major or minor.

Major-Type Chords

Many voicings of the straight major chords, with root, third, and fifth, were covered in Chapter 8. The following sections show some possible ways to hold the other main types of major chords. Try coming up with others on your own.

Chapter 9 More Chord Formulas

Major 6th (R,3,5,6)

Here are a few of the many possible voicings of a major 6th chord. Try using one in place of a major 7th or major 9th.

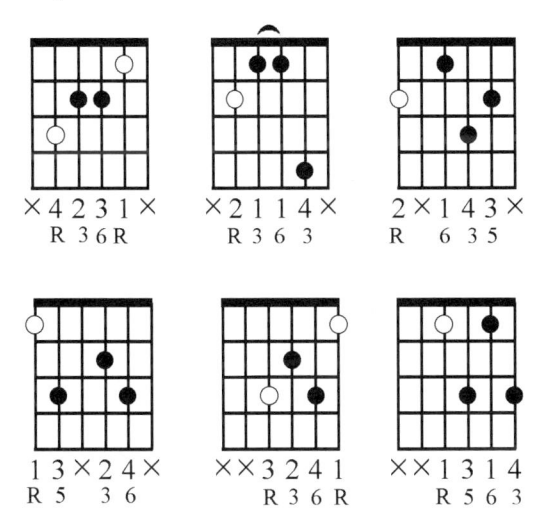

```
× 4 2 3 1 ×      × 2 1 1 4 ×      2 × 1 4 3 ×
R   3 6 R        R 3 6 3          R   6 3 5

1 3 × 2 4 ×      × × 3 2 4 1      × × 1 3 1 4
R 5   3 6        R 3 6 R          R 5 6 3
```

Major 7th (R,3,5,7)

Major 7ths are good major-type chords that can usually work in place of a major 6th, major 9th, or 6/9. If you play them in place of a major chord, they add a richer, jazzier sound.

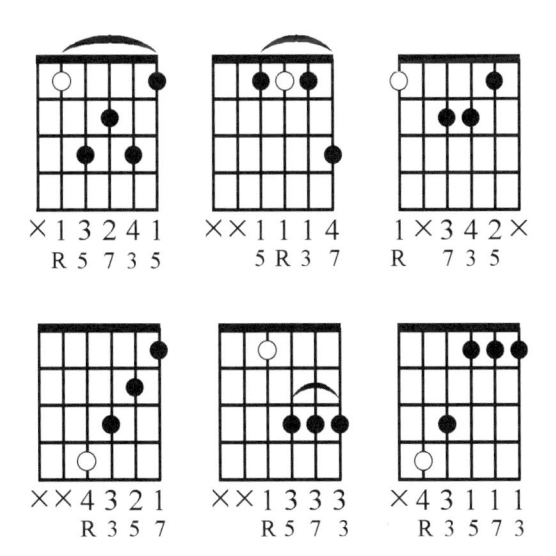

```
× 1 3 2 4 1      × × 1 1 1 4      1 × 3 4 2 ×
R 5 7 3 5        5 R 3 7          R   7 3 5

× × 4 3 2 1      × × 1 3 3 3      × 4 3 1 1 1
R 3 5 7          R 5 7 3          R 3 5 7 3
```

Major 9th (R,3,5,7,9)

The voicing of this chord on the far right has no root. It has the major 7th, 3rd, 5th, and 9th. You must imagine the root on the first or sixth string at the first fret, or the fourth string at the third fret (where the "×" is on the

117

Guitar for Songwriters

fretboard). This chord can still work if the tonic has been played recently and is still in the ear or if a bass player is sounding the root.

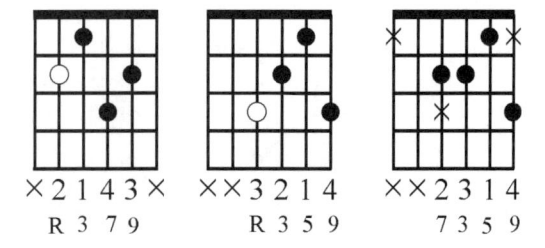

```
× 2 1 4 3 ×        × × 3 2 1 4        × × 2 3 1 4
R  3  7 9           R  3 5 9            7 3 5 9
```

6/9 (R,3,5,6,9)

These are interesting voicings because they are built almost entirely in fourths. Playing the notes in the chord one at a time gives a very modern sound.

The example on the right has the third in the bass. It would sound stronger with a bass player sounding the root.

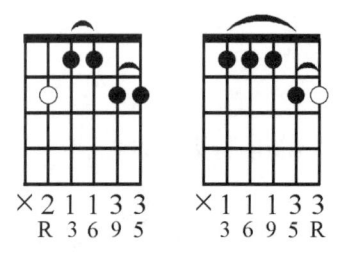

```
× 2 1 1 3 3        × 1 1 1 3 3
R  3 6 9 5          3 6 9 5 R
```

Major 13th (R,3,5,7,9,13)

With a root, third, fifth, seventh, ninth, and thirteenth, it's difficult holding all the notes of a major 13th chord on the six strings of the guitar. The fifth is often omitted, and the major 7th, 9th, or root could also be left out. Omitting the seventh turns the chord into a 6/9 chord, since the 13th is the same as a sixth. The third would never be omitted, since that is the note that makes the difference between major and minor.

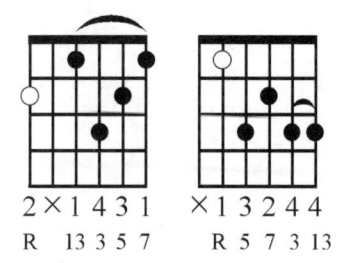

```
2 × 1 4 3 1        × 1 3 2 4 4
R   13 3 5 7        R  5 7 3 13
```

Major 7th(♯11) (R,3,5,7,♯11)

The ♯11 is the same note as the ♭5th but indicates that it is acceptable to include the 5th as well. (On a ♭5 chord, you would not include the natural 5th.) It is a more modern-sounding chord and would not always work as a substitution for a 6th, Maj 7th, or Maj 9th.

Chapter 9 More Chord Formulas

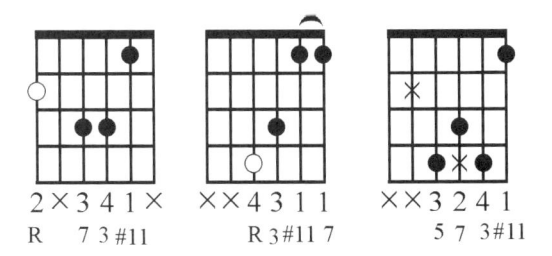

```
2 × 3 4 1 ×        × × 4 3 1 1        × × 3 2 4 1
R    7 3 #11       R 3 #11 7           5 7  3#11
```

Major 9th(♯11) (R,3,5,7,9,♯11)

Once again, this is a chord with too many notes to offer many options on the guitar. It is closely related to the M7(♯11), and the two are often used interchangeably.

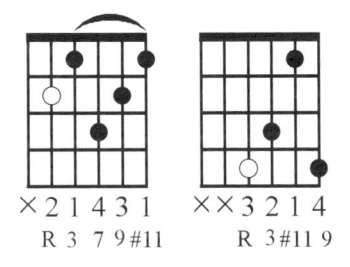

```
× 2 1 4 3 1        × × 3 2 1 4
R 3  7 9 #11       R 3 #11 9
```

Add 9 (or Add 2) (R,3,5,9)

Often called add 2, this is simply a major chord with a second added. It could be used for a major 9th, but it is often just a major chord where one note has been added. Look at the context of the song to determine whether a major 9th could be used. If most of the other chords are major or minor triads, a major 9th might stand out by sounding too complicated in relation to the other chords.

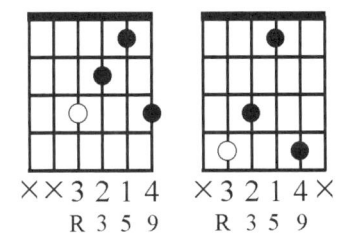

```
× × 3 2 1 4        × 3 2 1 4 ×
R 3 5 9            R 3 5 9
```

Minor-Type Chord Formulas

Table 9.2 shows many possible variations on a minor chord. Note the difference between a minor 7th chord and a minor (major 7th). The minor 7th has a flat 7th, while the minor (major 7th) has the major 7th, the seventh note as it normally appears in the major scale.

The m7(♭5) form is most often used as the II chord in songs in minor keys.

119

Guitar for Songwriters

Table 9.2 Minor-Type Chords

Chord Type	Example	Alternate Names	Spelling	Example
Minor	Cm	Cmin, C-	R b3 5	C Eb G
Minor 6	Cm6	Cmin6, C-6	R b3 5 6	C Eb G A
Minor 6/9	Cm6/9	Cmin6/9, C-6/9	R b3 5 6 9	C Eb G A D
Minor 6(major 7)	Cm6(maj7)	Cmin6(maj7)	R b3 5 6 7	C Eb G A B
Minor 7	Cm7	Cmin7, C-7	R b3 5 b7	C Eb G Bb
Minor 7(b 5)	Cm7(b5)	Cmin7-5, Cø	R b3 b5 b7	C Eb Gb Bb
Minor 7(add 11)	Cm7(add 11)	C-7(add 11)	R b3 5 b7 11	C Eb G Bb F
Minor(major 7)	Cm(maj7)	Cmin(maj7)	R b3 5 7	C Eb G B
Minor 9	Cm9	Cmin9, C-9	R b3 5 b7 9	C Eb G Bb D
Minor 9(major 7)	Cm9(maj7)	Cmin9(maj7)	R b3 5 7 9	C Eb G B D
Minor 11	Cm11	Cmin11, C-11	R b3 5 b7 9 11	C Eb G Bb D F

Minor-Type Chords

Many voicings for the basic minor chord (root, b3rd, 5th) are in Chapter 8. The following sections contain voicings for other minor chords.

Minor 7th (R, b3, 5, b7)

The minor 7th chord is much more common than the minor 6th. The next three show some of the possible voicings. The versions with notes only on the fourth string or above work better when playing with a bass player or when a fuller version of the chord has already been played and has established the tonality.

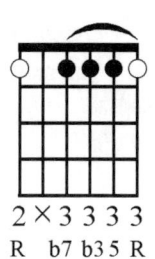

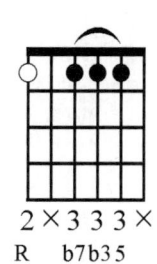

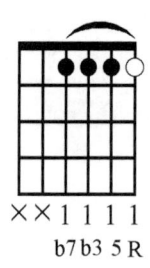

```
2 × 3 3 3 3        2 × 3 3 3 ×        × × 1 1 1 1
R   b7 b3 5 R      R    b7 b3 5              b7 b3 5 R
```

Chapter 9 More Chord Formulas

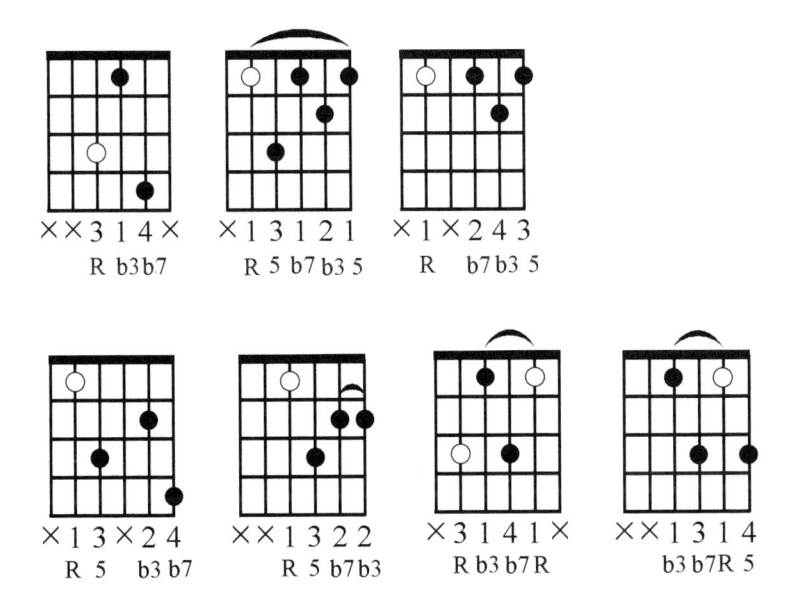

× × 3 1 4 ×
R b3 b7

× 1 3 1 2 1
R 5 b7 b3 5

× 1 × 2 4 3
R   b7 b3 5

× 1 3 × 2 4
R 5   b3 b7

× × 1 3 2 2
R 5 b7 b3

× 3 1 4 1 ×
R b3 b7 R

× × 1 3 1 4
b3 b7 R 5

The section on II-V-I chord progressions later in this book demonstrates how some of these voicings move to dominant 7th chords.

Minor 6th (R,b3,5,6)

The minor 6th chord sometimes substitutes for the dominant 9th chord a fourth higher. For instance, a Gm6 is very close to a C9. The minor 6th is also seen frequently as the IVm chord when playing in a major key. An example would be CMaj7-C7-FMaj7-Fm6.

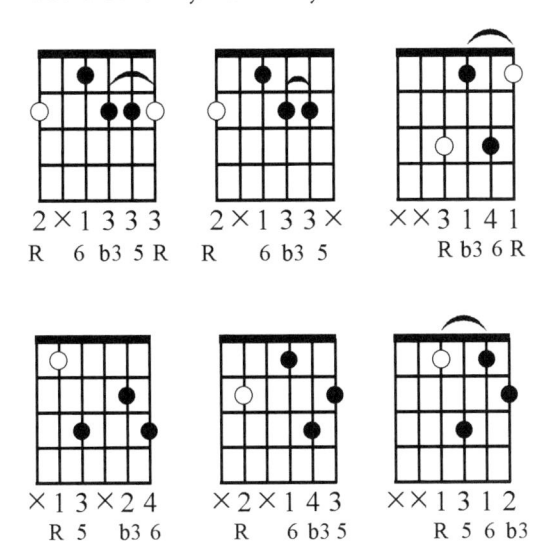

2 × 1 3 3 3
R   6 b3 5 R

2 × 1 3 3 ×
R   6 b3 5

× × 3 1 4 1
R b3 6 R

× 1 3 × 2 4
R 5   b3 6

× 2 × 1 4 3
R   6 b3 5

× × 1 3 1 2
R 5 6 b3

121

Guitar for Songwriters

Minor 6/9 (R,♭3,5,6,9)

This is a fancier version of a minor 6th. It often sounds good in passages that stay on a minor chord for a long time, alternating with a minor 7th or minor 9th.

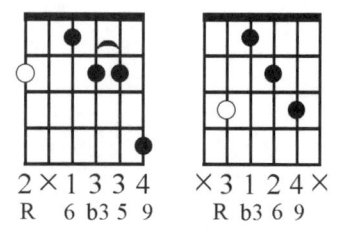

```
2 × 1 3 3 4      × 3 1 2 4 ×
R   6 ♭3 5 9     R ♭3 6 9
```

Minor 9th (R,♭3,5,♭7,9)

The minor 9th chord can add spice replacing a minor 7th.

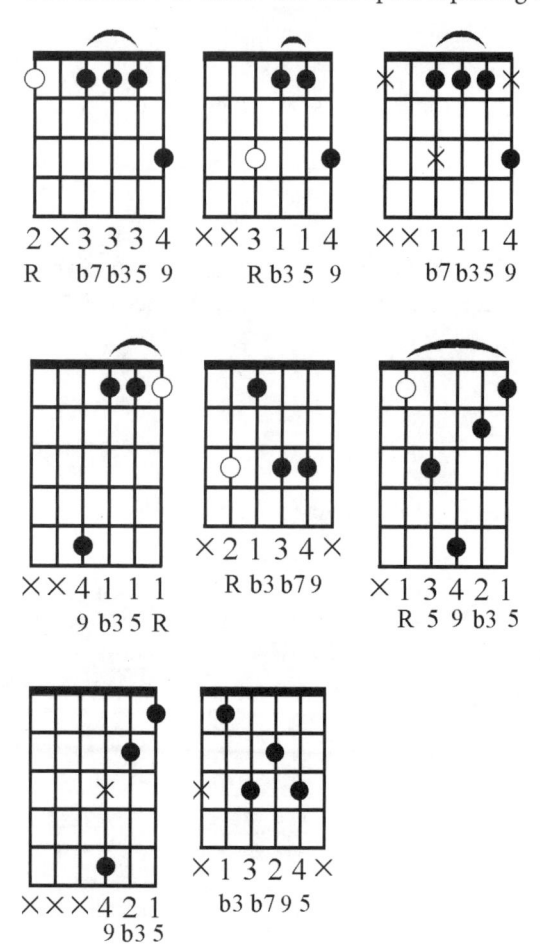

```
2 × 3 3 3 4      × × 3 1 1 4      × × 1 1 1 4
R   ♭7 ♭3 5 9    R ♭3 5 9         ♭7 ♭3 5 9

× × 4 1 1 1      × 2 1 3 4 ×      × 1 3 4 2 1
9 ♭3 5 R         R ♭3 ♭7 9        R 5 9 ♭3 5

× × × 4 2 1      × 1 3 2 4 ×
9 ♭3 5           ♭3 ♭7 9 5
```

Several examples on these pages omit the root. As mentioned earlier, the intended root is indicated by the "×" in the fretboard diagram.

Some of these fingerings involve considerable stretches. They are much easier farther up the neck.

Chapter 9 More Chord Formulas

Minor 7th (♭5) (R,♭3,♭5,♭7)

The minor 7th (♭5) chord can also be called a *half-diminished chord*, using the symbol ø. It is most often seen as the II chord in a minor key. Uses of this chord are demonstrated in the section on jazz progressions, IIm7(♭5)-V7-Im7.

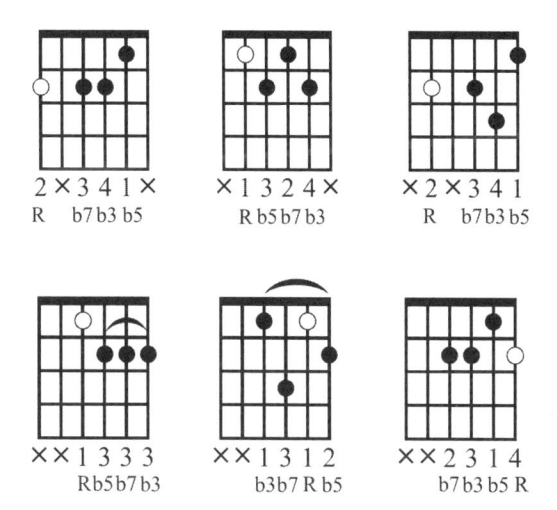

```
2 × 3 4 1 ×         × 1 3 2 4 ×         × 2 3 4 1
R    ♭7♭3 ♭5        R ♭5♭7♭3            R    ♭7♭3 ♭5

× × 1 3 3 3         × × 1 3 1 2         × × 2 3 1 4
R♭5♭7♭3             ♭3♭7 R ♭5           ♭7♭3 ♭5 R
```

Minor 11th (R,♭3,5,♭7,9,11)

To be a minor 11th, a chord must contain the flat third. Otherwise, it would be a suspended chord.

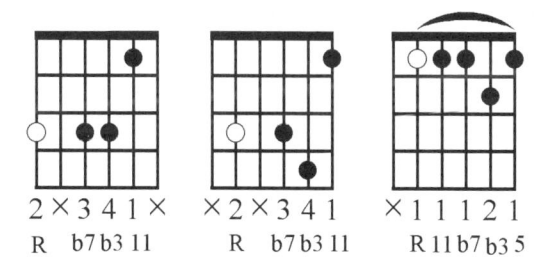

```
2 × 3 4 1 ×         × 2 3 4 1           × 1 1 1 2 1
R    ♭7♭3 11        R   ♭7♭3 11         R 11♭7♭3 5
```

Minor (Major 7th) (R,♭3,5,7)

When the root is omitted, this chord is identical to an augmented chord and is often mislabeled as one. It is written m(maj 7).

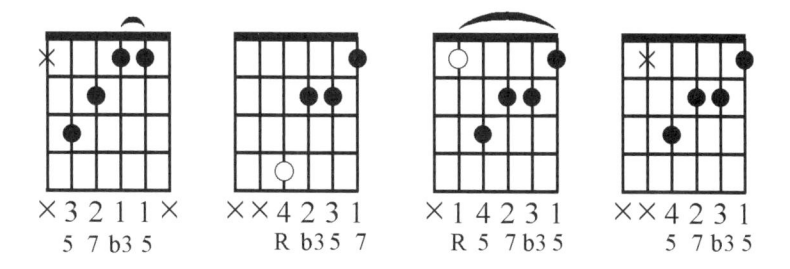

```
× 3 2 1 1 ×         × × 4 2 3 1         × 1 4 2 3 1         × × 4 2 3 1
 5  7 ♭3 5          R ♭3 5  7           R  5  7 ♭3 5         5  7 ♭3 5
```

Minor 6th (Major 7th) (R,♭3,5,6,7)

This is a variation on the minor (major 7th) chord, written m6(maj7).

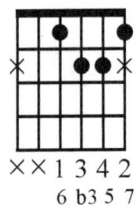

```
× × 1 3 4 2
  6 ♭3 5 7
```

Minor 9th (Major 7th) (R,♭3,5,7,9)

This variation is easier to hold on the guitar and can usually substitute for minor (major 7th) or minor 6 (major 7th).

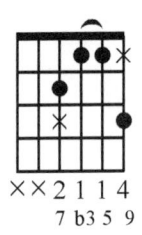

```
× × 2 1 1 4
  7 ♭3 5 9
```

Dominant Chord Formulas

There are so many variations of the dominant 7th chord and its spellings that it would be difficult to list them all. Table 9.3 is a start, though.

Table 9.3 Dominant-Type Chords

Chord Type	Example	Alternate Names	Spelling	Example
Dominant 7th	C7		R 3 5 ♭7	C E G B♭
Dominant 9th	C9		R 3 5 ♭7 9	C E G B♭ D
11th	C11	C9sus4, C9sus	R 5 ♭7 9 11	C G B♭ D F
Dominant 13th	C13		R 3 5 ♭7 9 13	C E G B♭ D A
7 (♭5)	C7(♭5)	C7(-5)	R 3 ♭5 ♭7	C E G♭ B♭
9 (♭5)	C9(♭5)	C9(-5)	R 3 ♭5 ♭7 9	C E G♭ B♭ D
7 (♯5)	C7(♯5)	C7(+5), C7+, C7aug	R 3 ♯5 ♭7	C E G♯ B♭
9 (♯5)	C9(♯5)	C9(+5), C9+, C9aug	R 3 ♯5 ♭7 9	C E G♯ B♭ D
7 (♭9)	C7(♭9)	C7(-9)	R 3 5 ♭7 ♭9	C E G B♭ D♭

Chapter 9 More Chord Formulas

Table 9.3 Dominant-Type Chords (*Continued*)

Chord Type	Example	Alternate Names	Spelling	Example
7 (♯9)	C7(♯9)	C7(+9)	R 3 5 ♭7 ♯9	C E G B♭ D♯
7 (♭5♭9)	C7(♭5♭9)	C7(-5-9)	R 3 ♭5 ♭7 ♭9	C E G♭ B♭ D♭
7 (♭5♯9)	C7(♭5♯9)	C7(-5+9)	R 3 ♭5 ♭7 ♯9	C E G♭ B♭ D♯
7 (♯5♭9)	C7(♯5♭9)	C7(+5-9)	R 3 ♯5 ♭7 ♭9	C E G♯ B♭ D♭
7 (♯5♯9)	C7(♯5♯9)	C7(+5+9)	R 3 ♯5 ♭7 ♯9	C E G♯ B♭ D♯
7 (♯11)	C7(♯11)	C7(+11), C7(+4), C7aug11	R 3 5 ♭7 ♯11	C E G B♭ F♯
9 (♯11)	C9(♯11)	C9(+11), C9(+4), C9aug11	R 3 5 ♭7 9 ♯11	C E G B♭ D F♯
7 (♭9♯11)	C7(♭9♯11)	C7(-9+11), C7(-9aug11)	R 3 5 ♭7 ♭9 ♯11	C E G B♭ D♭ F♯
7 (♯9♯11)	C7(♯9♯11)	C7(+9+11), C7(+9aug11)	R 3 5 ♭7 ♯9 ♯11	C E G B♭ D♯ F♯
13 (♭5)	C13(♭5)	C13(-5)	R 3 ♭5 ♭7 13	C E G♭ B♭ A♭
13 (♭9)	C13(♭9)	C13(-9)	R 3 5 ♭7 ♭9 13	C E G B♭ D♭ A
13 (♯11)	C13(♯11)	C13(+11), C13aug11	R 3 5 ♭7 9 ♯11 13	C E G B♭ D F♯ A
7 (♭13)	C7(♭13)	C7(-13)	R 3 5 ♭7 9 ♭13	C E G B♭ D A♭
7 sus4	C7sus4	C7sus, C7sus11	R 4 5 ♭7	C F G B♭
7 sus4 (♭9)	C7sus4(♭9)	C7sus(-9)	R 4 5 ♭7 ♭9	C F G B♭ D♭
13 sus4 (♭9)	C13sus4(♭9)	C13sus(-9)	R 4 5 ♭7 ♭9 13	C F G B♭ D♭ A
7 (alt)	C7(alt)		See below.	

Guitarists do many things in practice to suggest a chord even when several tones have been omitted. We'll examine the choices we make in the sections for each individual chord.

Chord tones above the seventh are called *extensions*. Even though you can put the notes in any order, the chord extensions—the higher notes, such as the ninth and thirteenth—are usually voiced near the top of the chord. You normally wouldn't play a 13th so that it sounds half a step below the ♭7th. You would play it an octave higher.

Chord tones requiring accidentals (going out of the basic key) are called *alterations*. They will have a sharp or flat before one or more of the chord tones (not the root). Chords like ♯5♭9 are sometimes called extensions, but they are really alterations. They can also be written one over the other rather than side by side.

Guitar for Songwriters

C7♭9♯5

C7(♭9♯5)

An "altered" chord (C7alt) means the fifth and ninth are sharp or flat. The player chooses which alterations to include.

Usually, the eleventh chord has no third in it. The augmented eleventh chords usually do contain a third.

Dominant-Type Chords

Chapter 8 has voicings for straight dominant 7th chords, with root, 3rd, 5th, and flatted 7th. The following sections contain voicings for other types of dominant chords.

9th (R,3,5,♭7,9)

The fifth is often omitted in these chords.

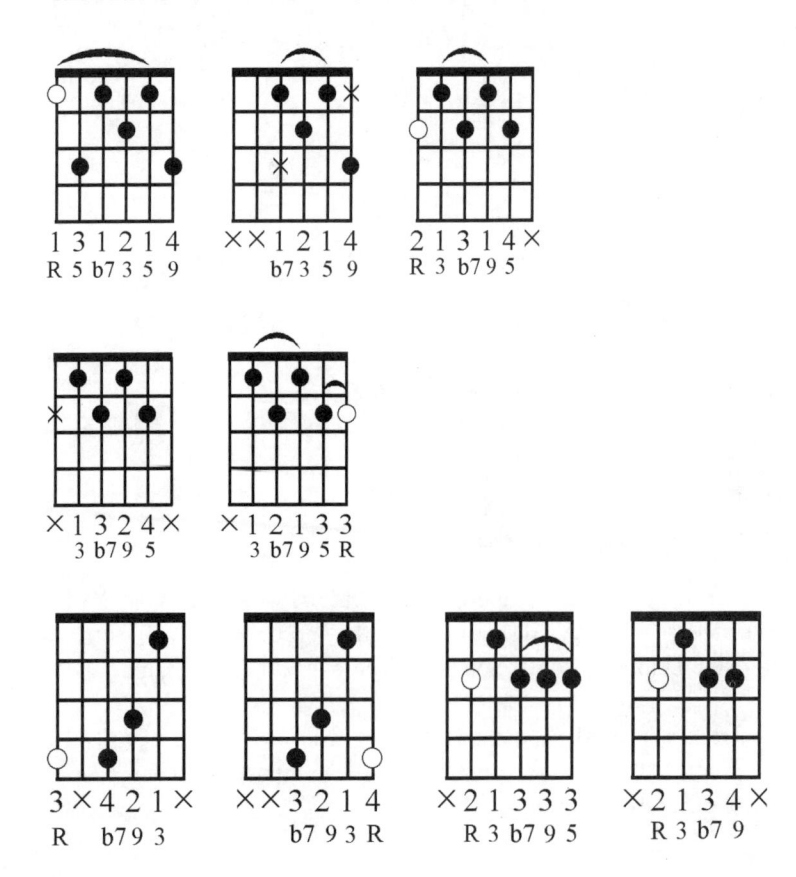

1 3 1 2 1 4
R 5 ♭7 3 5 9

× × 1 2 1 4
     ♭7 3 5 9

2 1 3 1 4 ×
R 3 ♭7 9 5

× 1 3 2 4 ×
  3 ♭7 9 5

× 1 2 1 3 3
  3 ♭7 9 5 R

3 × 4 2 1 ×
R   ♭7 9 3

× × 3 2 1 4
    ♭7 9 3 R

× 2 1 3 3 3
  R 3 ♭7 9 5

× 2 1 3 4 ×
  R 3 ♭7 9

126

Chapter 9 More Chord Formulas

11th (R,3,5,♭7,9,11)

Although, technically speaking, this chord should include the third, it is usually omitted. A common substitution for this chord is the 7sus4, which omits the 9th.

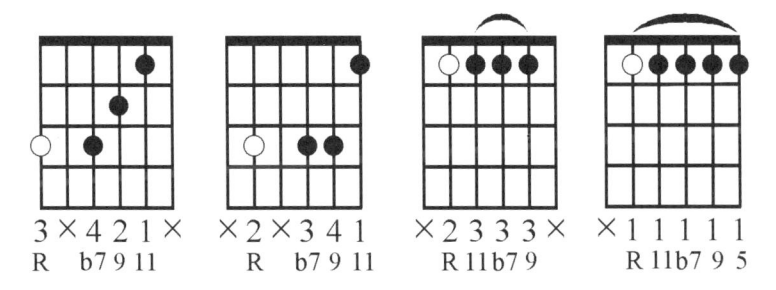

```
3 × 4 2 1 ×      × 2 × 3 4 1      × 2 3 3 3 ×      × 1 1 1 1 1
R   ♭7 9 11       R   ♭7 9 11      R 11 ♭7 9         R 11 ♭7 9 5
```

13th (R,3,5,♭7,9,13)

The 13th is the same note as the 6th, but the 13th chord includes the flatted 7th and the 9th.

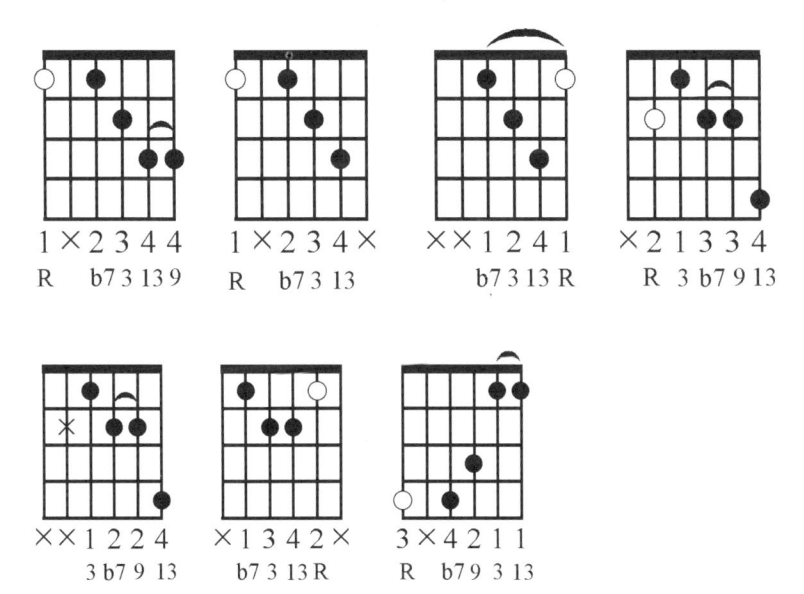

```
1 × 2 3 4 4      1 × 2 3 4 ×      × × 1 2 4 1      × 2 1 3 3 4
R   ♭7 3 13 9    R   ♭7 3 13       ♭7 3 13 R        R  3 ♭7 9 13

× × 1 2 2 4      × 1 3 4 2 ×      3 × 4 2 1 1
   3 ♭7 9 13      ♭7 3 13 R        R   ♭7 9 3 13
```

7(♭5) (R,3,♭5,♭7)

Note that the fingerings for the first two chord forms are identical, but the roots are in different locations. So the same chord could be G♭7(♭5) or C7(♭5), depending on which note is considered the root.

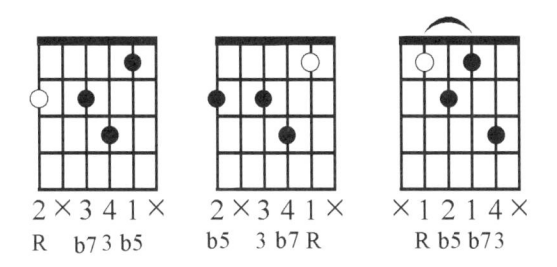

```
2 × 3 4 1 ×      2 × 3 4 1 ×      × 1 2 1 4 ×
R   ♭7 3 ♭5       ♭5   3 ♭7 R      R ♭5 ♭7 3
```

127

Guitar for Songwriters

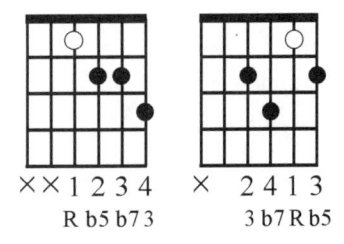

××1 2 3 4
R ♭5 ♭7 3

× 2 4 1 3
3 ♭7 R ♭5

9(♭5) (R,3,♭5,♭7,9)

This chord is very close to the 9(♯11) chord and is sometimes used in place of it.

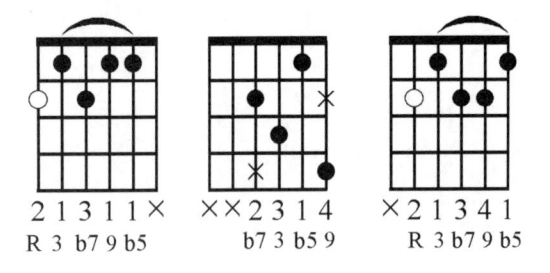

2 1 3 1 1 ×
R 3 ♭7 9 ♭5

× × 2 3 1 4
♭7 3 ♭5 9

× 2 1 3 4 1
R 3 ♭7 9 ♭5

7(♯5) (R,3,♯5,♭7)

This chord is closely related to the augmented chord, which is covered in Chapter 11.

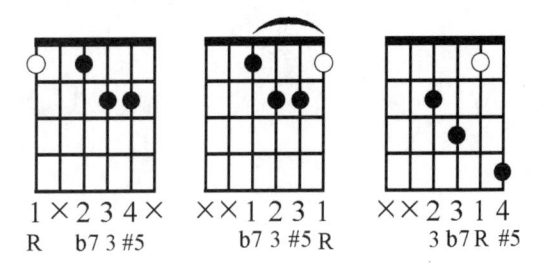

1 × 2 3 4 ×
R ♭7 3 ♯5

× × 1 2 3 1
♭7 3 ♯5 R

× × 2 3 1 4
3 ♭7 R ♯5

9(♯5) (R,3,♯5,♭7,9)

Notice how the notes on the first four strings are identical, but with a different root. The role that a note plays changes—for example, the 3rd becomes the ♭7th—but you could use the same fingers if you played just those strings.

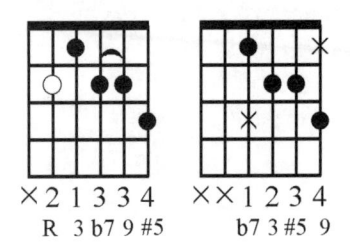

× 2 1 3 3 4
R 3 ♭7 9 ♯5

× × 1 2 3 4
♭7 3 ♯5 9

Chapter 9 More Chord Formulas

7(♭9) (R,3,5,♭7,♭9)

Diminished chords often substitute for 7(♭9). The section on diminished chords in Chapter 11 explores this more fully.

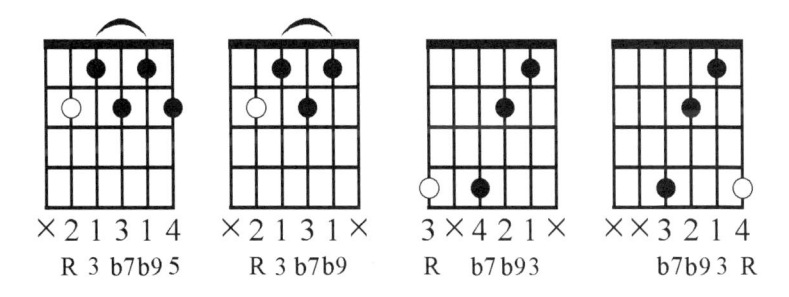

```
× 2 1 3 1 4      × 2 1 3 1 ×      3 × 4 2 1 ×      × × 3 2 1 4
R 3 ♭7♭9 5       R 3 ♭7♭9         R   ♭7♭9 3       ♭7♭9 3 R
```

These last four chords are really diminished, although they work as 7(♭9) chords with the root missing.

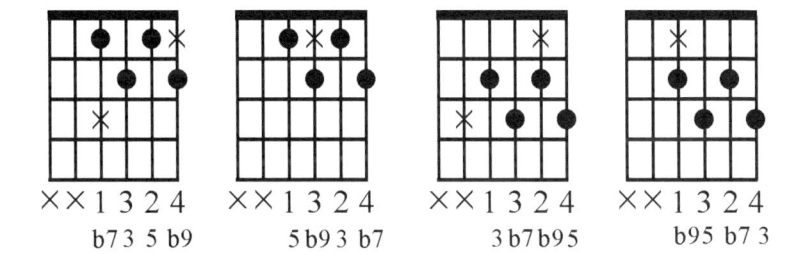

```
× × 1 3 2 4      × × 1 3 2 4      × × 1 3 2 4      × × 1 3 2 4
♭7 3 5 ♭9        5 ♭9 3 ♭7        3 ♭7 ♭9 5        ♭9 5 ♭7 3
```

7(♯9) (R,3,5,♭7,♯9)

This is the first chord in Jimi Hendrix's "Purple Haze"!

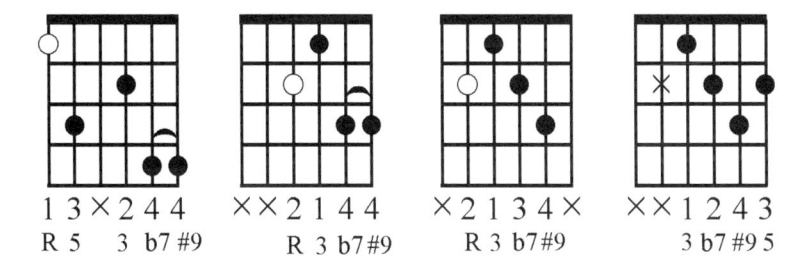

```
1 3 × 2 4 4      × × 2 1 4 4      × 2 1 3 4 ×      × × 1 2 4 3
R 5   3 ♭7 ♯9    R 3 ♭7 ♯9        R 3 ♭7 ♯9        3 ♭7 ♯9 5
```

7(♭5♭9) (R,3,♭5,♭7,♭9)

This chord may sound strange at first, but it can be beautiful when used in the right spot.

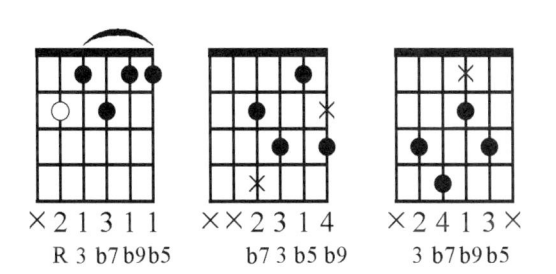

```
× 2 1 3 1 1      × × 2 3 1 4      × 2 4 1 3 ×
R 3 ♭7 ♭9 ♭5     ♭7 3 ♭5 ♭9       3 ♭7 ♭9 ♭5
```

Guitar for Songwriters

7(♭5♯9) (R,3,♭5,♭7,♯9)

Try this in place of a V7 chord going to IMaj7 or I6/9.

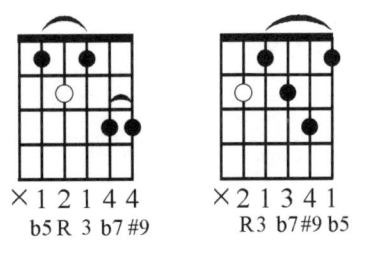

```
× 1 2 1 4 4        × 2 1 3 4 1
  ♭5 R 3 ♭7 ♯9       R 3 ♭7 ♯9 ♭5
```

7(♯5♭9) (R,3,♯5,♭7,♭9)

This chord would work well as a V7 going to Im7, but it could also go to IMaj7. Your ear might be expecting to hear it go to a minor chord, and the major chord comes as a refreshing surprise.

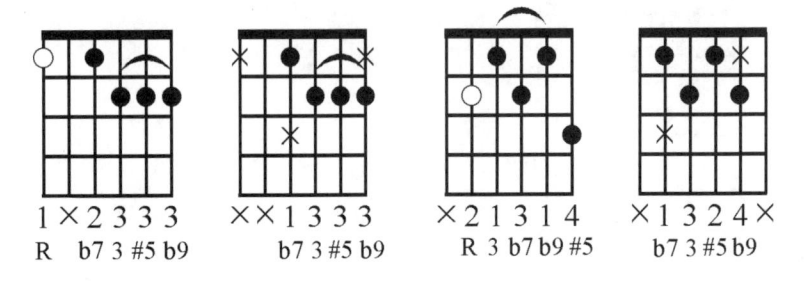

```
1 × 2 3 3 3      × × 1 3 3 3      × 2 1 3 1 4      × 1 3 2 4 ×
R  ♭7 3 ♯5 ♭9     ♭7 3 ♯5 ♭9       R 3 ♭7 ♭9 ♯5      ♭7 3 ♯5 ♭9
```

7(♯5♯9) (R,3,♯5,♭7,♯9)

Like the preceding chords, this chord implies a minor key but could also move to a major-type chord.

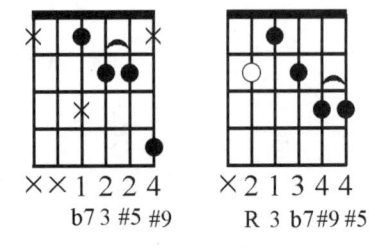

```
× × 1 2 2 4       × 2 1 3 4 4
 ♭7 3 ♯5 ♯9        R 3 ♭7 ♯9 ♯5
```

7(♯11) (R,3,5,♭7,♯11)

The ♯11 is the same note as the ♭5, but the 7(♯11) chord can also contain the regular fifth. In practice, 7(♭5) chords are generally used for 7(♯11) on the guitar. Unlike the 11th chord, the ♯11th includes the 3rd. Technically speaking, it should also contain the 9th. In practice, however, the 9(♯11) is considered a separate chord.

9(♯11) (R,3,5,♭7,9,♯11)

The 9(♭5) chord is generally used for this chord, as it is awkward to hold all six notes of this chord on the guitar. The difference is that this chord should contain both the natural 5th and the flat 5th (sharp 11th).

Chapter 9 More Chord Formulas

7(♭9♯11) (R,3,5,♭7,♭9,♯11)

This chord would normally have six notes (root, 3rd, 5th, flatted 7th, 9th, and sharp 11th). That is usually too many notes to include comfortably on the guitar, and 7(♭5♭9) is generally used in its place.

7(♯9♯11) (R,3,5,♭7,♯9,♯11)

The 7(♭5♯9) is generally used for this chord, since it is difficult to find a way to hold all six notes.

13(♭5) (R,3,♭5,♭7,9,13)

You won't be able to include all six of these notes unless you grow some extra fingers! The voicings that follow omit the ninth.

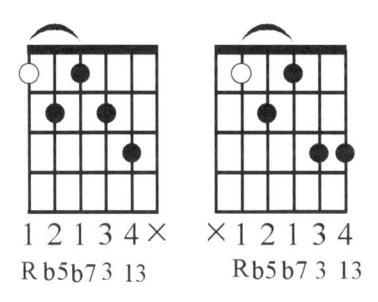

```
  1 2 3 4 ×        × 1 2 3 4
  R ♭5 ♭7 3 13     R ♭5 ♭7 3 13
```

13(♯11) (R,3,5,♭7,9,♯11,13)

13(♭5) is usually played for this chord on the guitar.

13(♭9) (R,3,5,♭7,♭9,13)

This is a beautiful chord that sounds great when progressing to an IMaj9.

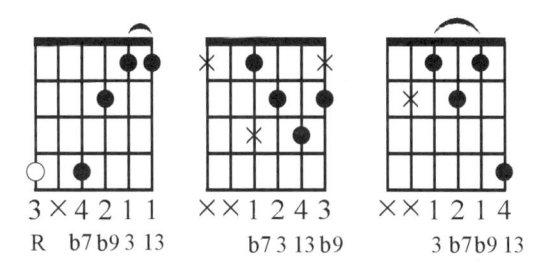

```
  3 × 4 2 1 1       × × 1 2 4 3      × × 1 2 1 4
  R    ♭7 ♭9 3 13    ♭7 3 13 ♭9       3 ♭7 ♭9 13
```

7(♭13) (R,3,5,♭7,9,♭13)

The ♭13 note is the same as a ♯5, but it implies the inclusion of the 5th and some form of 9th (natural, sharp, or flat). It often serves as a V7 going to Im. On the guitar, use a 7(♯5) chord or 7(♯5♭9) or 7(♯5♯9).

7sus4 (R,4,5,♭7)

The difference between this and the 11th chord is that the sus4 chord has no 9th. This chord is often used in place of the 11th. Note that "sus" stands for suspended, not sustained. It often resolves to the dominant 7th—for example, C7sus4 to C7—before proceeding to the next chord. (Determine the fingering of the corresponding dominant 7th chord by lowering the 4th of the chord one fret to the 3rd.)

Guitar for Songwriters

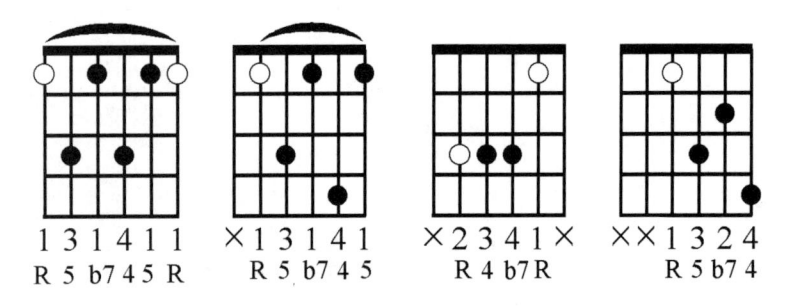

```
1 3 1 4 1 1      × 1 3 1 4 1      × 2 3 4 1 ×      × × 1 3 2 4
R 5 b7 4 5 R     R 5 b7 4 5       R 4 b7 R         R 5 b7 4
```

7sus4(♭9) (R,4,5,♭7,♭9)

This chord is basically IVm6 with V in the bass. In the key of C, for example, it would be Fm6/G.

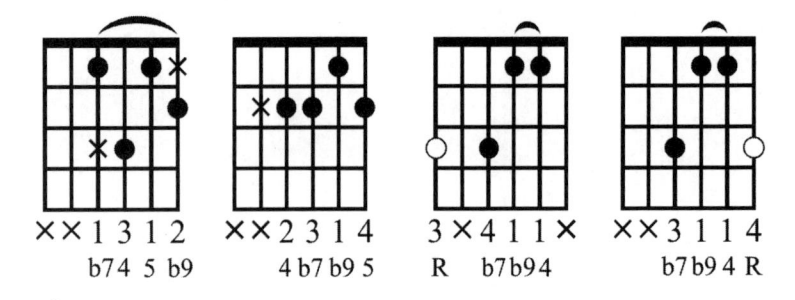

```
× × 1 3 1 2      × × 2 3 1 4      3 × 4 1 1 ×      × × 3 1 1 4
b7 4 5 b9        4 b7 b9 5        R   b7 b9 4      b7 b9 4 R
```

13sus4(♭9) (R,4,5,♭7,♭9,13)

This voicing omits the root and the fifth. If the bass player covers the root, it would work well.

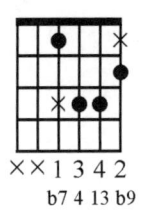

```
× × 1 3 4 2
b7 4 13 b9
```

7(alt) (R,3,♭5 or ♯5,♭7,♭9 or ♯9)

The altered chord gives the player the option of choosing between 7(♭5♭9), 7(♯5♭9), 7(♭5♯9), and 7(♯5♯9). Raise or lower the fifth and ninth at your own discretion.

In the next chapter, we'll apply many of these chords in dozens of variations on common jazz progressions.

Jazz Chords and Progressions: Adding Some Spice

It's time to put these chords together. Jazz chords—major sevenths, minor sevenths, ninths, thirteenths, and beyond—add a new level of richness to the sound of chord progressions.

II-V-I

In blues, folk, and country music, the I, IV, and V7 are the most common chords. In jazz and much music with more sophisticated harmony, the II-V-I progression is a cornerstone.

In the harmonized scale, chords are derived by adding two notes, each a third apart, to each note of a major scale. Adding one more note a third higher to each of these chords gives so-called "jazz" chords—major 7ths and minor 7ths.

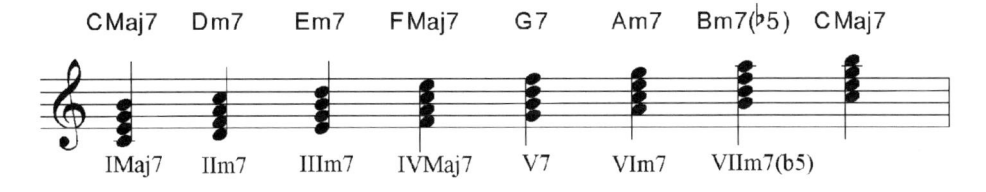

CMaj7   Dm7   Em7   FMaj7   G7   Am7   Bm7(♭5)   CMaj7

IMaj7   IIm7   IIIm7   IVMaj7   V7   VIm7   VIIm7(♭5)

In music with these types of chords, the II-V-I progression is very common. It would be more accurate to say IIm7-V7-IMaj7, but it is usually shortened to "two-five-one." In the key of C, that would be Dm7-G7-CMaj7.

The Circle of Fifths

Where does this pattern come from? The II-V-I progression follows the pattern of strong root movement described by the circle of fifths. Movement of a fifth is considered the strongest progression in music, and the circle of fifths illustrates that movement in all keys. Strong root progression goes counterclockwise in the circle. C is the 5th of F. (Count up the F scale five notes: F G A B♭ C.) The C chord wants to move to F. F is the 5th note in the key of B♭,

Guitar for Songwriters

and the F chord wants strongly to move to B♭. B♭ is the 5th of E♭, E♭ is the 5th of A♭, and so on, continuing around the circle. Pick any note on the circle, and that chord wants to move counterclockwise to the next chord.

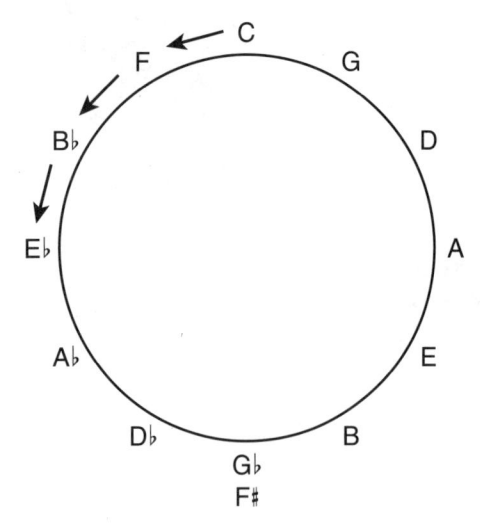

The circle of fifths: The strongest progressions follow the direction of the arrows.

One advantage of using a circle is that it has no beginning or end. Start anywhere and play chords progressing along the circle. You can do this with any type of chord or any combination of chord types (major, minor, 7th, and beyond).

Looking at the following circle, the chords in the II-V-I progression in any key can be found by starting two positions clockwise from the desired key. To find II-V-I in the key of G, count over two notes to A. Make that the IIm7 chord. Then progress one note counterclockwise to D and make that the V7. Move one more to get to your starting point, the IMaj7. The II-V-I progression in the key of G would be Am7-D7-GMaj7.

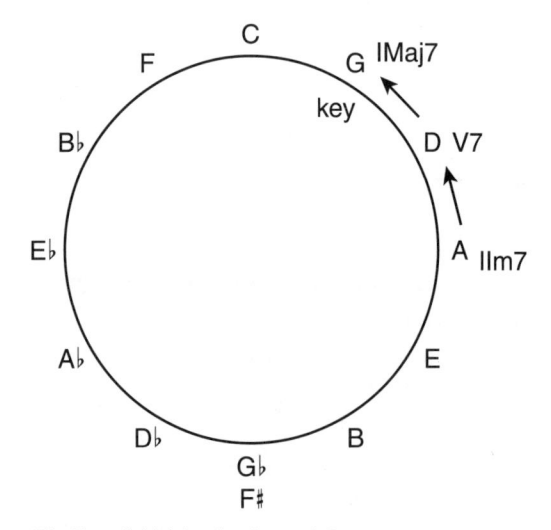

Finding II-V-I in the key of G.

In the key of D, II-V-I would be Em7-A7-DMaj7.

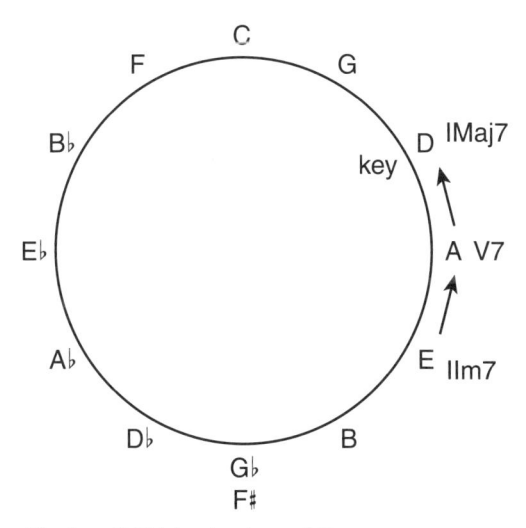

Chapter 10 Jazz Chords and Progressions: Adding Some Spice

Finding II-V-I in the key of D.

Songs often include many instances of the II-V-I progression and in many keys other than the tonic. It can indicate a temporary modulation (change of key) or just a strong movement to a certain chord. For instance, Vm7-I7 may be used when going to the IV chord, as in the following example in the key of C. The Gm7-C7-FMaj7 is really II-V-I in the key of F.

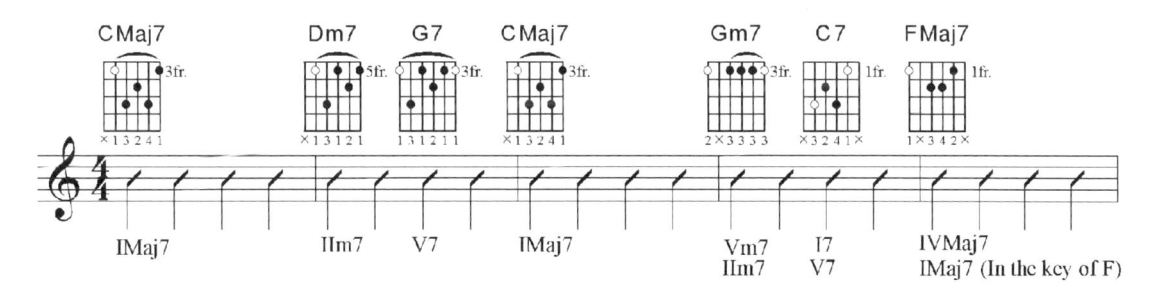

You may also encounter the II-V progression without a resolution to a tonic (I) chord. In the key of C, the progression Em7-A7-Dm7-G7-CMaj7 could be thought of as II-V, II-V-I, with the II-V progressions being in two different keys. (It is actually III-VI-II-V-I, itself a very common progression.)

The point is that the IIm7 to V7 progression is very common. Practice variations on this pattern in all keys and be alert for it when playing.

Patterns especially worth practicing are:

▷ IIm7-V7-IMaj7 in all keys
▷ IIm7-V7 in all keys
▷ IIm7(b5)-V7-Im7 in all keys (the minor key version of II-V-I)

There are many variations on the II-V-I progression, such as IIm9-V7-I6 or IIm7-V9-I6/9. These are discussed more fully in the section on II-V-I substitutions later in this chapter.

135

Guitar for Songwriters

Patterns Especially Worth Practicing:

- IIm7-V7-IMaj7 in all keys
- IIm7-V7 in all keys
- IIm7(b5)-V7-Im7 in all keys (the minor key version of II-V-I)

Table 10.1 IIm7-V7-IMaj7 in All Keys

Key	IIm7	V7	IMaj7
C	Dm7	G7	CMaj7
C♯	D♯m7	G♯7	C♯Maj7
D♭	E♭m7	A♭7	D♭Maj7
D	Em7	A7	DMaj7
E♭	Fm7	B♭7	E♭Maj7
E	F♯m7	B7	EMaj7
F	Gm7	C7	FMaj7
F♯	G♯m7	C♯7	F♯Maj7
G♭	A♭m7	D♭7	G♭Maj7
G	Am7	D7	GMaj7
A♭	B♭m7	E♭7	A♭Maj7
A	Bm7	E7	AMaj7
B♭	Cm7	F7	B♭Maj7
B	C♯m7	F♯7	BMaj7
C♭	D♭m7	G♭7	C♭Maj7

Chapter 10 Jazz Chords and Progressions: Adding Some Spice

IIm7-V7 Progressions

Each of these progressions represents a pair of chords that go together well in playing IIm7-V7. The first eight exercises are in the key of C, and the others are in F. Be sure to transpose them to other keys.

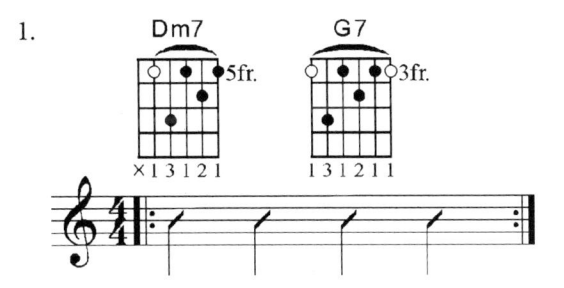

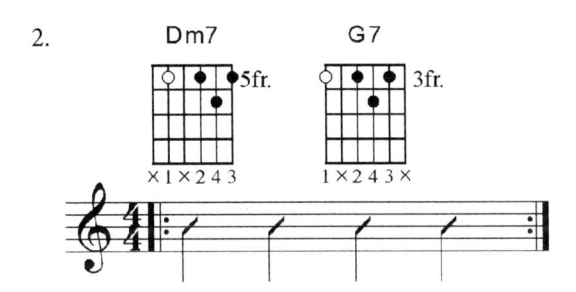

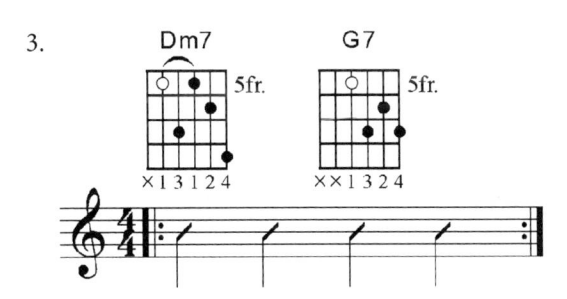

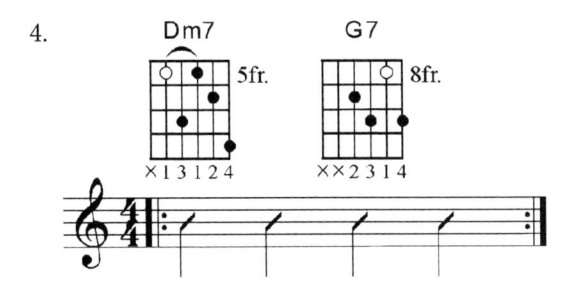

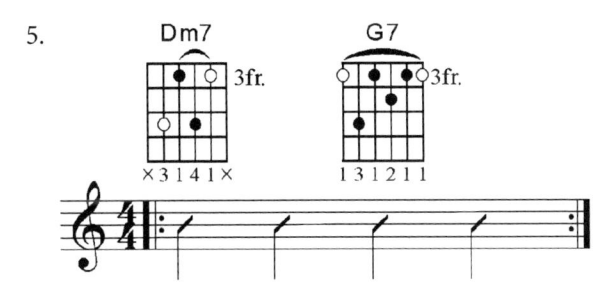

Guitar for Songwriters

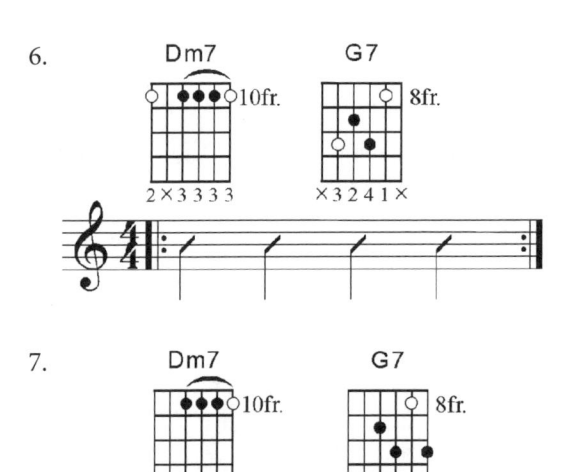

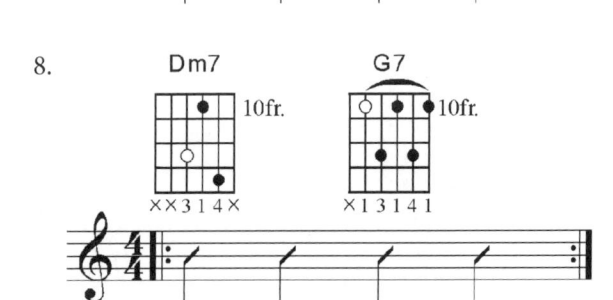

6. Dm7 (10fr, 2×3333) G7 (8fr, ×3241×)

7. Dm7 (10fr, ××1111) G7 (8fr, ××2314)

8. Dm7 (10fr, ××314×) G7 (10fr, ×13141)

The following progressions are in the key of F, since they would be too high up the neck to play comfortably in C.

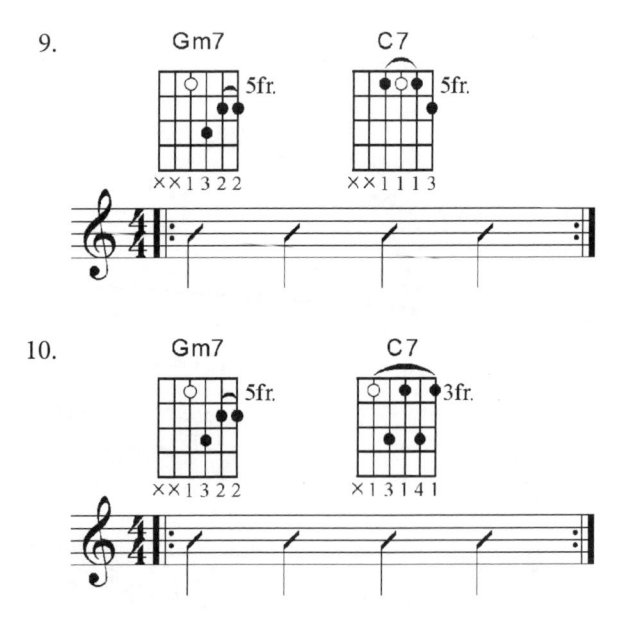

9. Gm7 (5fr, ××1322) C7 (5fr, ××1113)

10. Gm7 (5fr, ××1322) C7 (3fr, ×13141)

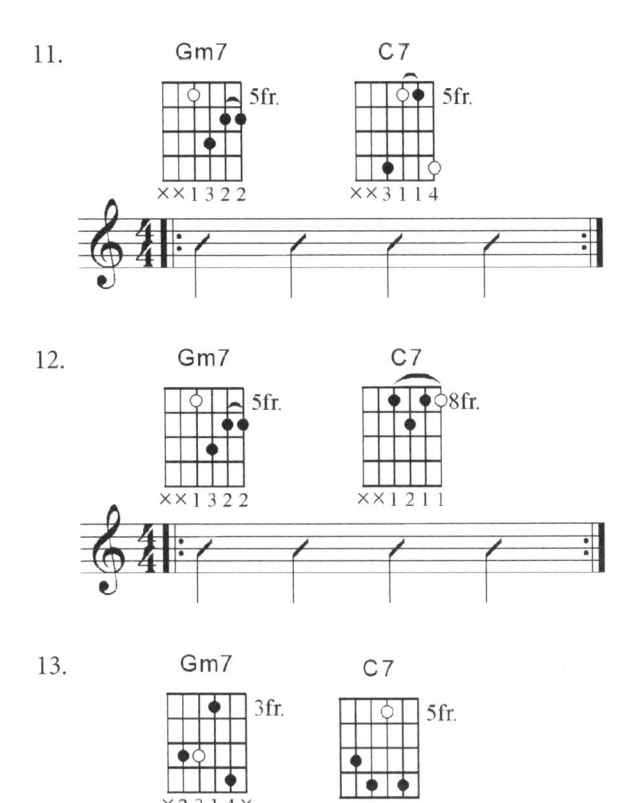

Chapter 10 Jazz Chords and Progressions: Adding Some Spice

11. Gm7 — C7

12. Gm7 — C7

13. Gm7 — C7

IIm7-V7-IMaj7 Exercises

Certain chord voicings go together very well in playing II-V-I progressions.

Practice these patterns to get comfortable with the fingerings. Find major 7th chords that complete the II-V progressions on the previous pages.

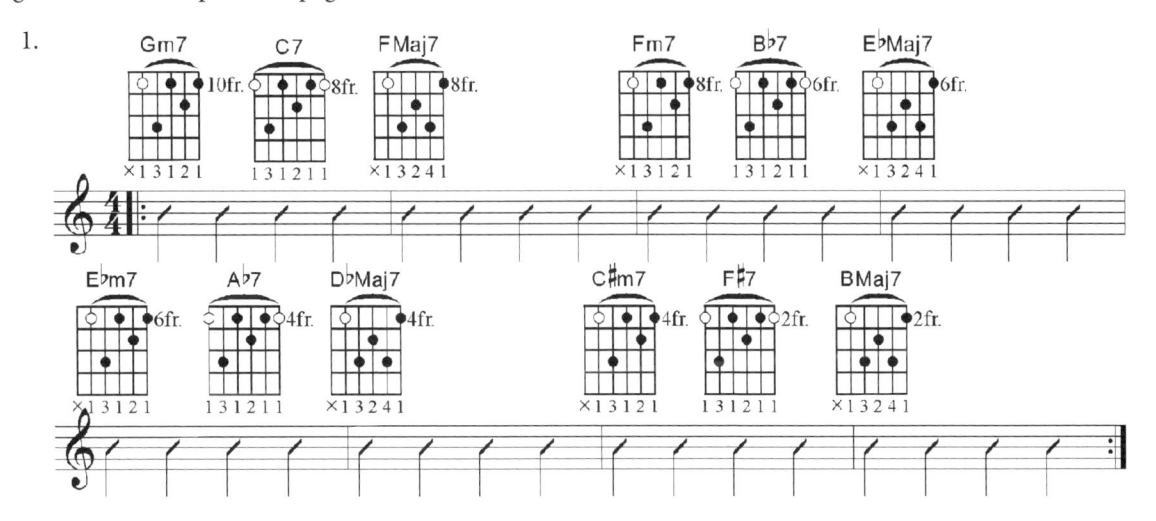

1. Gm7 — C7 — FMaj7 — Fm7 — B♭7 — E♭Maj7

  E♭m7 — A♭7 — D♭Maj7 — C♯m7 — F♯7 — BMaj7

139

Guitar for Songwriters

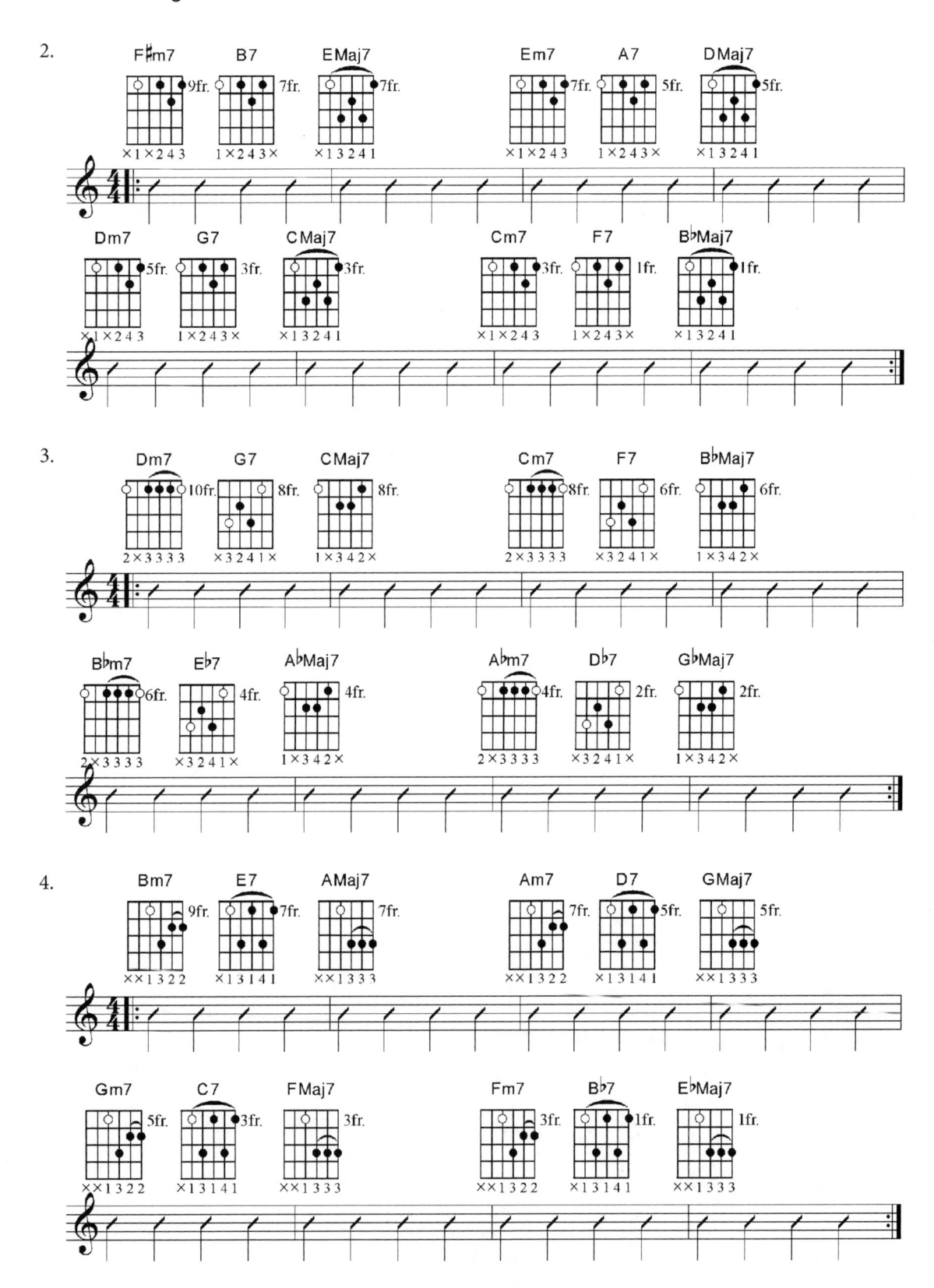

Chapter 10 Jazz Chords and Progressions: Adding Some Spice

Embellishing and Substituting Chords

Here is where it can really get fun. The ideas in this section can free you up to find new sounds and to put a lot of variety into your playing. It may take some time to get comfortable with this, but it will be well worth your time.

Sometimes chords just don't have the pizzazz you want. They are a little too "vanilla," or they don't change often enough. Rather than simplify, you may want to make them fancier. There are two main ways to do this: to embellish and to substitute.

To *embellish* a chord means to retain the basic chord type but make it a little fancier. Instead of a basic C major chord, you could try a C6 or CMaj7. An Am might become an Am7 or Am9. A dominant 7th chord could become a 9th or 13th. Retain the basic type of chord—major, minor, or dominant 7th—and add notes.

> *To embellish a chord means to retain the basic chord type but make it fancier by adding notes.*

Don't be intimidated by this idea. If you hold a chord and add or remove a finger, listen to the sound. If it sounds good, use it! You have successfully embellished a chord.

> *If it sounds good, use it!*

Many examples in the various sections of this book show different versions of the blues and the II-V-I progression. When you do this, you are adding notes, and it doesn't always work. A major or minor chord contains three different notes. A major 7th has four, a major 9th five. So you are going from a basic harmony to a more sophisticated level. To your "vanilla" chord you are now adding sprinkles, chocolate syrup, and nuts. It won't always be appropriate to a song or to your tastes.

To *substitute* means to replace a chord with one that has a different root. For G7, you might try Dm7-G7. This is arrived at by thinking of G7 as a V7 chord and then changing that into a IIm7-V7 progression. These are demonstrated in the section on II-V-I. Another possibility is to play bII7-I in place of a V7-IMaj7 progression. In place of G7-CMaj7, try Db7-CMaj7. You could think of this as approaching a chord from a half step above (Db7) rather than from the V7 chord (G7). The sound is quite a bit different, more "in your face," but it can be very striking. (This is sometimes called the *b5 substitution*, since Db is the flatted 5th of G.)

> *To substitute means to replace a chord with one that has a different root.*

Substitution is a more complicated topic than embellishment. The first requirement is a familiarity with basic chord progressions and the circle of fifths. Study the different ways the blues and rhythm changes are played and how the chords are varied. Try applying these ideas to other tunes.

Chapter 12 looks at several ways to play a very common progression. Compare the different versions to see what substitutions have been made.

After you play a lot of songs, you will start observing patterns. Perhaps one song starts with a familiar pattern and then deviates. Observation and experimentation are keys to learning to substitute. Compare how Bill Evans or other great jazz artists might reharmonize a tune, and then try applying that to other songs on your own.

Guitar for Songwriters

IIm7-V7-IMaj7 Substitutions

Here are some substitutions and embellishments that a jazz guitarist might use in place of IIm7-V7-IMaj7. Numbers 1–15 are in the key of C; the rest are in the key of F. Transpose these exercises to as many keys as are practical. Try them in place of IIm-V7-IMaj7 in songs you're playing.

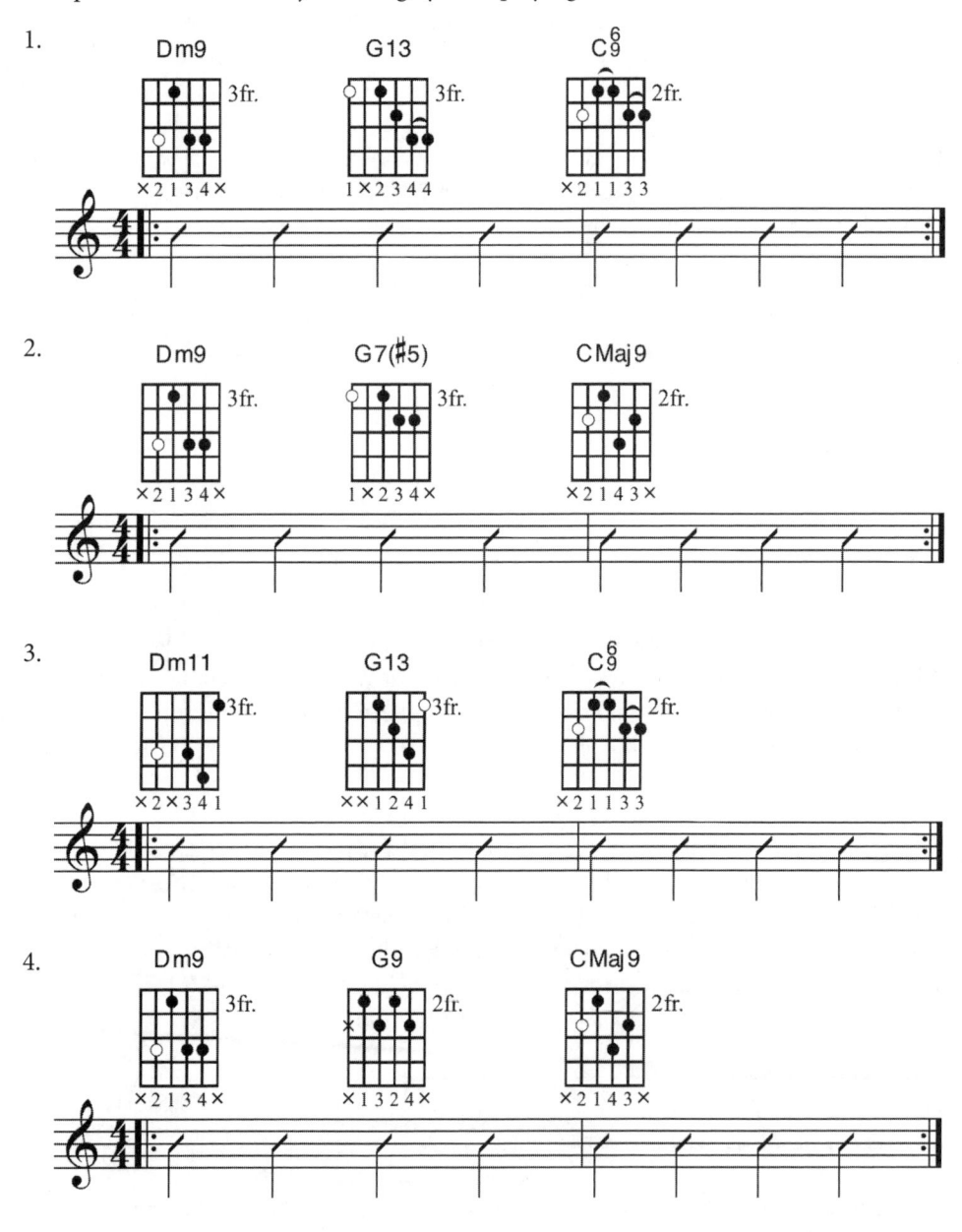

1. Dm9 — G13 — C6/9

2. Dm9 — G7(♯5) — CMaj9

3. Dm11 — G13 — C6/9

4. Dm9 — G9 — CMaj9

Chapter 10 Jazz Chords and Progressions: Adding Some Spice

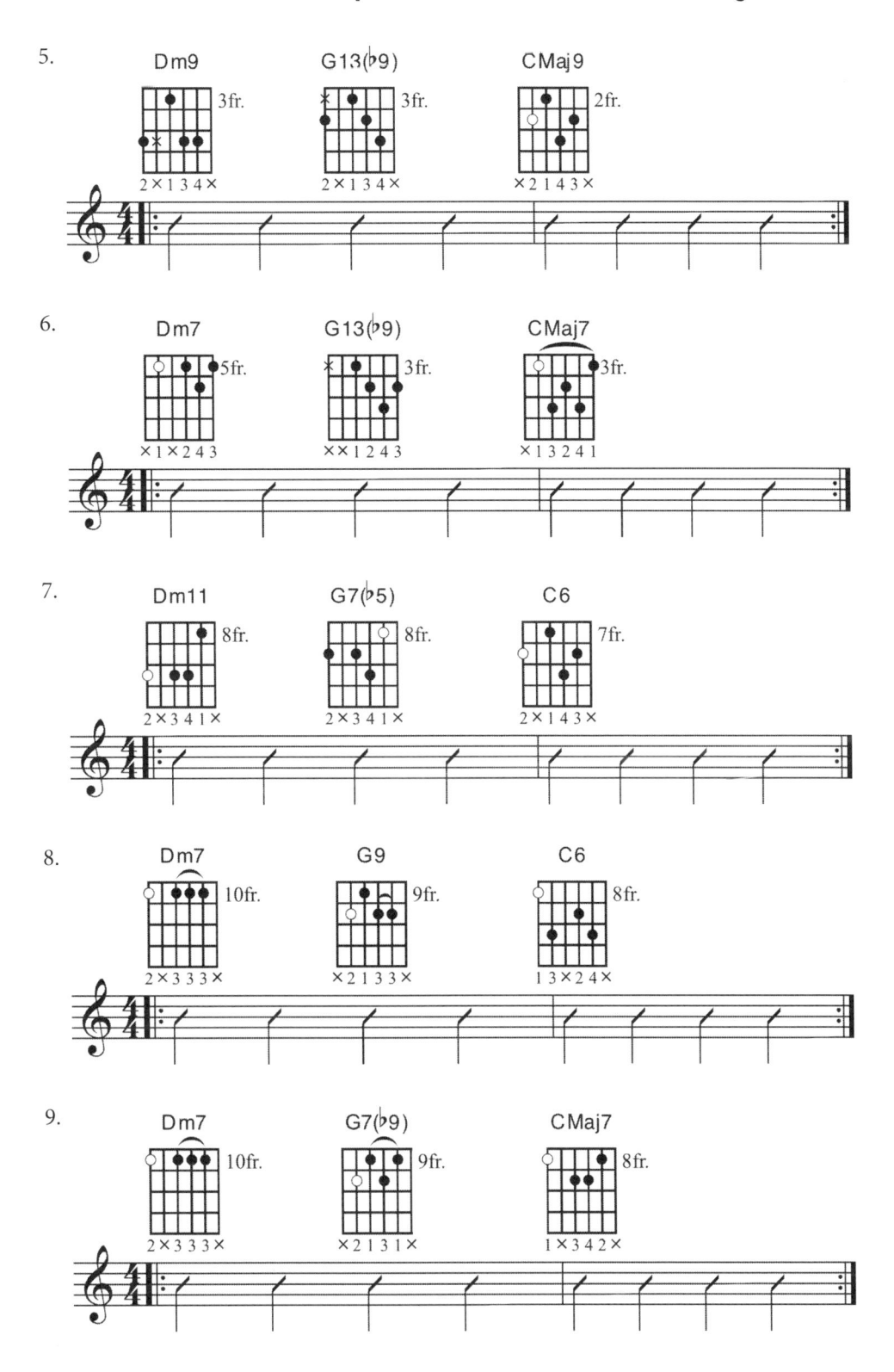

5. Dm9 — G13(♭9) — CMaj9

6. Dm7 — G13(♭9) — CMaj7

7. Dm11 — G7(♭5) — C6

8. Dm7 — G9 — C6

9. Dm7 — G7(♭9) — CMaj7

143

Guitar for Songwriters

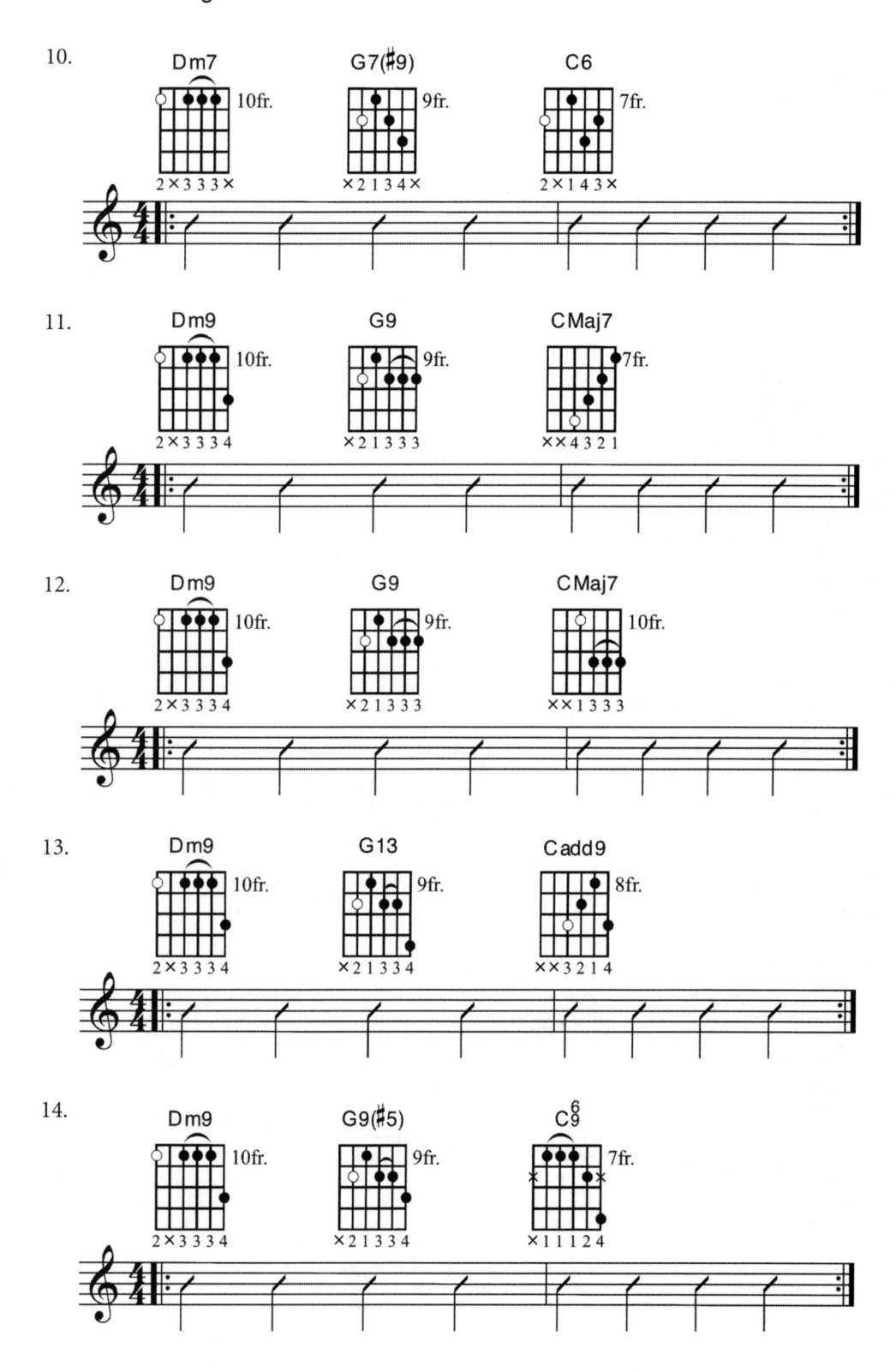

10. Dm7 (10fr.) — G7(#9) (9fr.) — C6 (7fr.)

11. Dm9 (10fr.) — G9 (9fr.) — CMaj7 (7fr.)

12. Dm9 (10fr.) — G9 (9fr.) — CMaj7 (10fr.)

13. Dm9 (10fr.) — G13 (9fr.) — Cadd9 (8fr.)

14. Dm9 (10fr.) — G9(#5) (9fr.) — C6/9 (7fr.)

Chapter 10 Jazz Chords and Progressions: Adding Some Spice

15. "T" stands for thumb.

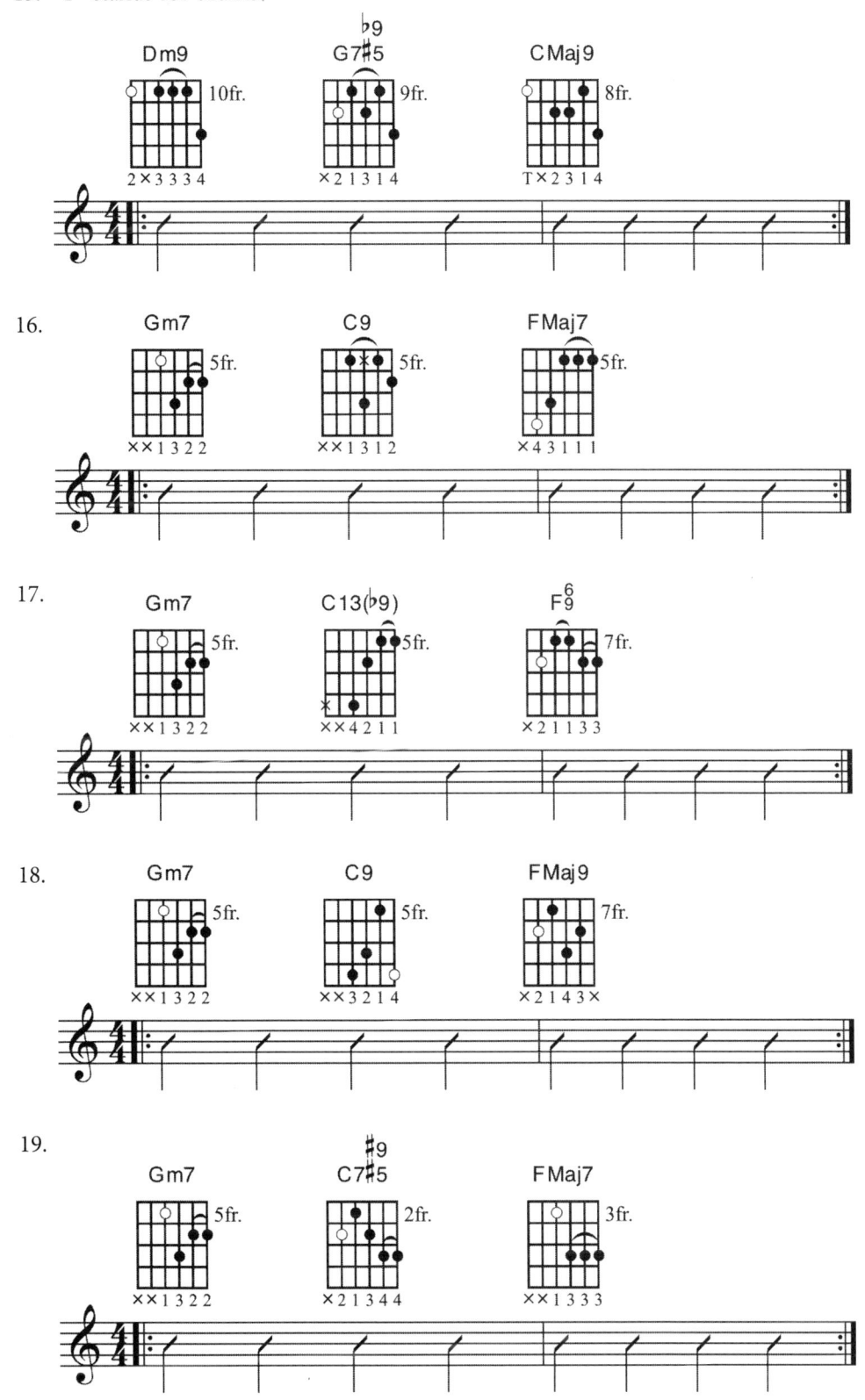

16.

17.

18.

19.

Guitar for Songwriters

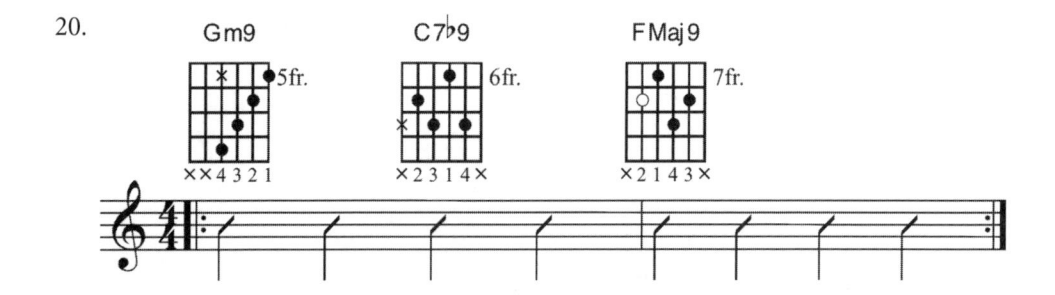

20.

Gm9 — 5fr. ××4321
C7♭9 — 6fr. ×2314×
FMaj9 — 7fr. ×2143×

II-V-I in Minor Keys

The minor key equivalent of II-V-I is IIm7(♭5)-V7-Im7. In the key of Am, the chord built on the second note of the scale would be B-D-F-A, or Bm7(♭5). This is sometimes called B half-diminished and can be written Bø. The notes in this chord are the same as in Dm6 (D-F-A-B), and you sometimes see the minor key progression of IVm6-V7-Im7. The IVm6 is really equivalent to IIm7(♭5), and Dm6-E7-Am7 is equivalent to Bm7(♭5)-E7-Am7.

Table 10.2 IIm7(♭5)-V7-Im7 in All Keys

Key	IIm7(♭5)	V7	Im7
Cm	Dm7(♭5)	G7	Cm7
C♯m	D♯m7(♭5)	G♯7	C♯m7
D♭m	E♭m7(♭5)	A♭7	D♭m7
Dm	Em7(♭5)	A7	Dm7
E♭m	Fm7(♭5)	B♭7	E♭m7
Em	F♯m7(♭5)	B7	Em7
Fm	Gm7(♭5)	C7	Fm7
F♯m	G♯m7(♭5)	C♯7	F♯m7
G♭m	A♭m7(♭5)	D♭7	G♭m7
Gm	Am7(♭5)	D7	Gm7
G♯m	A♯m7(♭5)	D♯7	G♯m7
A♭m	B♭m7(♭5)	E♭7	A♭m7
Am	Bm7(♭5)	E7	Am7
B♭m	Cm7(♭5)	F7	B♭m7
Bm	C♯m7(♭5)	F♯7	Bm7

Chapter 10 Jazz Chords and Progressions: Adding Some Spice

IIm7(♭5)-V7-Im7 Progressions and Substitutions

Practice these patterns to get comfortable playing in minor keys. Exercises 1–12 are in the key of Cm. The rest are in Fm. Transpose them into as many keys as are practical. Apply them to songs you're playing.

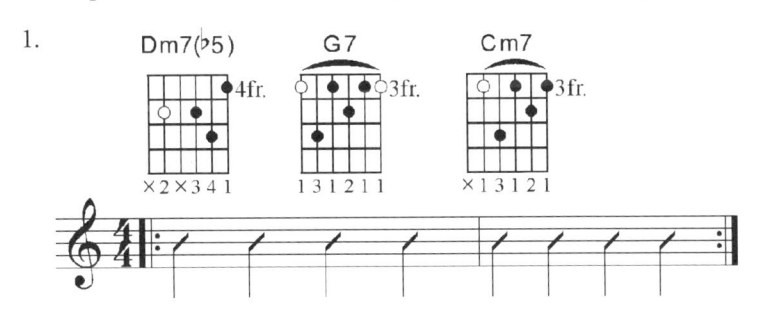

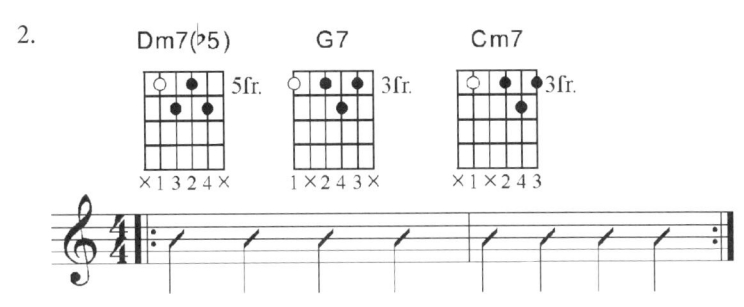

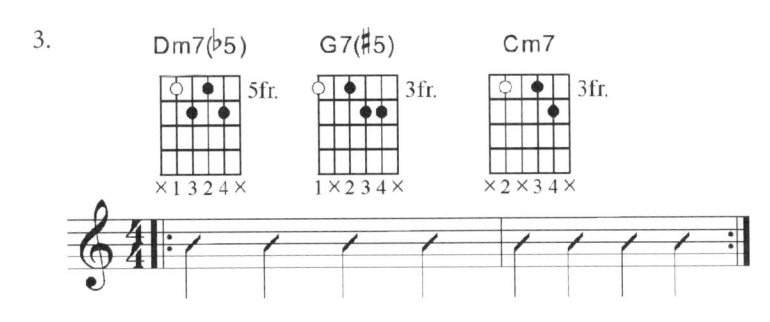

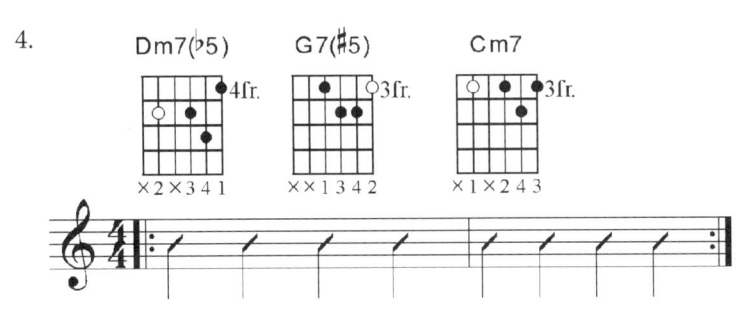

1. Dm7(♭5) G7 Cm7

2. Dm7(♭5) G7 Cm7

3. Dm7(♭5) G7(♯5) Cm7

4. Dm7(♭5) G7(♯5) Cm7

147

Guitar for Songwriters

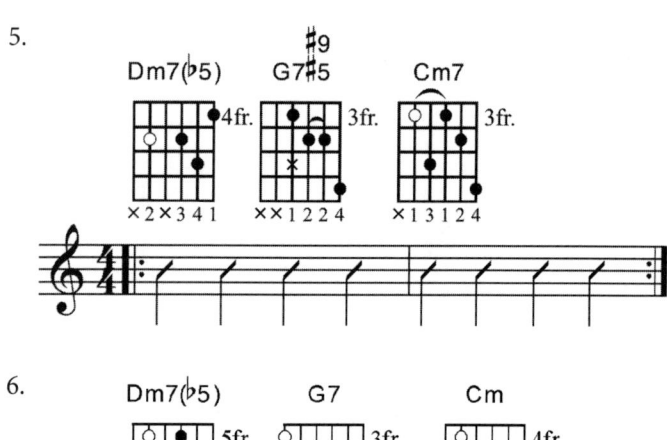

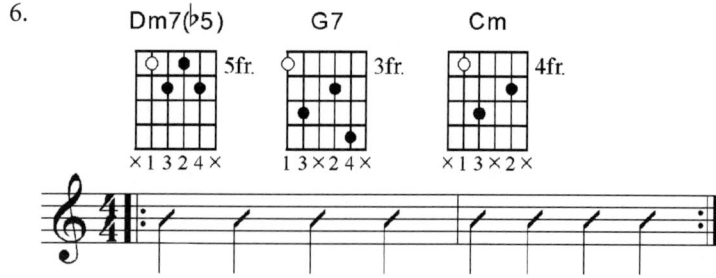

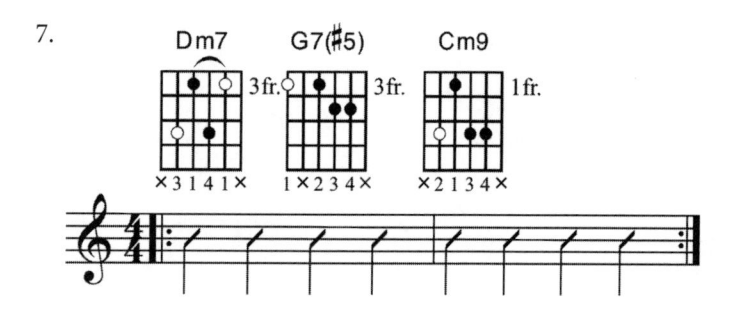

5.

6.

7.

8. Fm6/A♭ is equivalent to Dm7(♭5). Both chords contain the same notes.

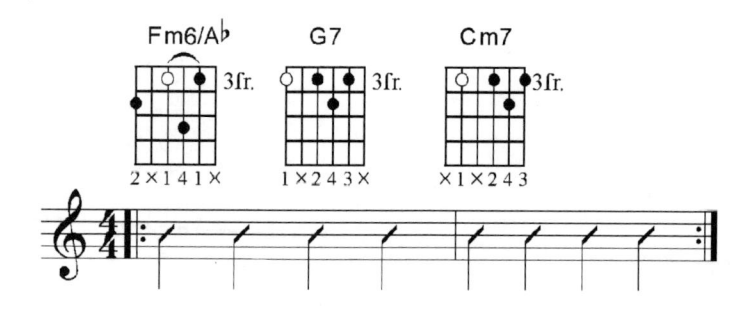

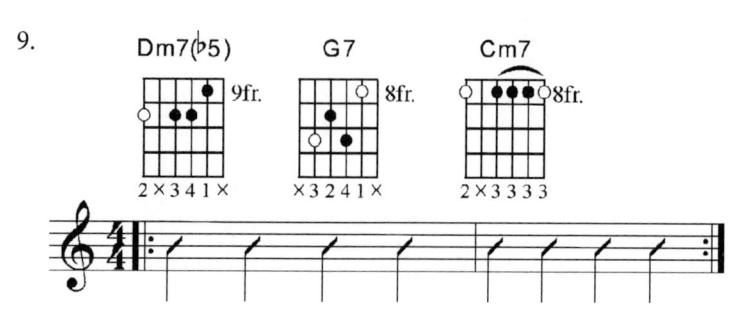

9.

Chapter 10 Jazz Chords and Progressions: Adding Some Spice

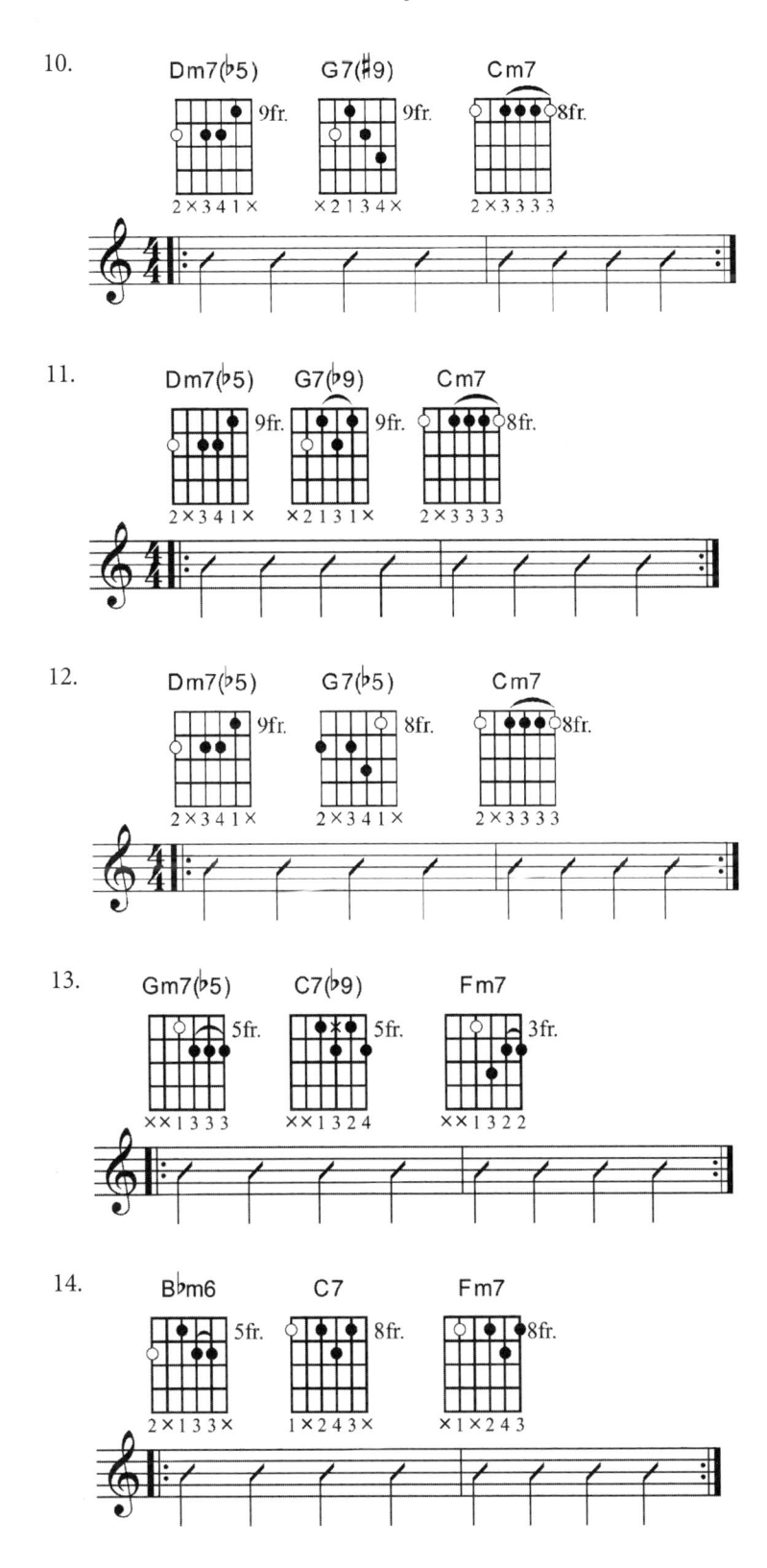

Guitar for Songwriters

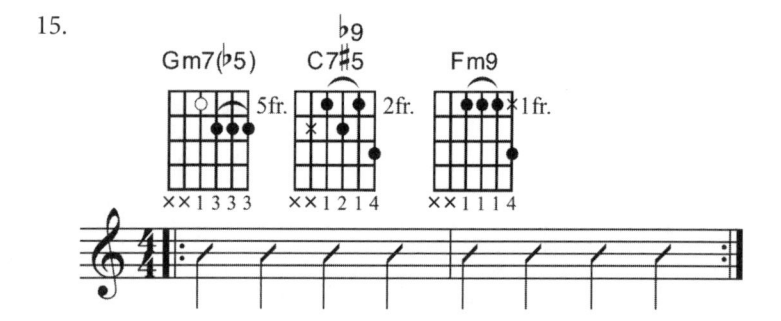

15.

16. Notice that the first two chords have the same fingering at different positions on the neck.

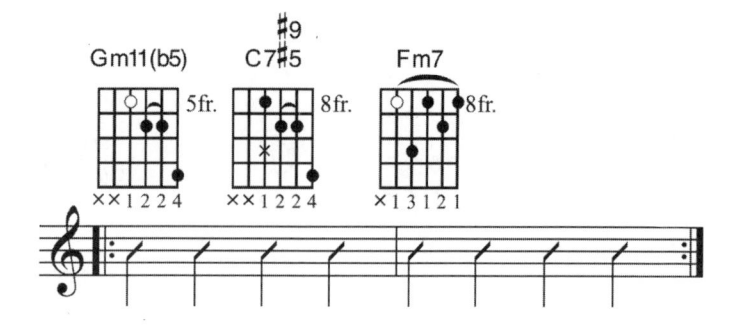

In the next chapter, we'll look at diminished and augmented chords, more ways to simplify or embellish chords, and moving voices within chords.

11

More Chords, Progressions, and Ideas

IN THIS CHAPTER, WE WILL STRIP THE MYSTERY FROM DIMINISHED AND AUGMENTED CHORDS. We will look at ways to embellish chords or to simplify them. And we will learn some examples of moving voices within chords.

Diminished Chords

Diminished chords are definitely worth a close look. An understanding of how they work can open up a lot of possibilities for colorful chord progressions.

A basic diminished chord uses the formula root, flat 3rd, and flat 5th. The symbol can be either "dim" or "°" (the degree sign). A C diminished chord would be written Cdim or C°.

The diminished 7th chord is the root, flat 3rd, flat 5th, and double-flatted 7th (which is the same as the 6th). Most people mean diminished 7th when they say "diminished."

Table 11.1 shows examples of diminished 7th chords.

Table 11.1 Diminished Chords

Chord	R	♭3	♭5	♭♭7
C°7	C	E♭	G♭	B♭♭
C♯°7	C♯	E	G	B♭
D°7	D	F	A♭	C♭
E♭°7	E♭	G♭	B♭♭	D♭♭
E°7	E	G	B♭	D♭
F°7	F	A♭	C♭	E♭♭
F♯°7	F♯	A	C	E♭
G♭°7	G♭	B♭♭	D♭♭	F♭♭

(Continued)

Guitar for Songwriters

Table 11.1 Diminished Chords (*Continued*)

Chord	R	b3	b5	bb7
G°7	G	Bb	Db	Fb
G#°7	G#	B	D	F
Ab°7	Ab	Cb	Ebb	Gbb
A°7	A	C	Eb	Gb
Bb°7	Bb	Db	Fb	Abb
B°7	B	D	F	Ab

Now look at an enharmonic spelling of these chords, shown in Table 11.2. (That means using A instead of Bbb, for example. It's not correct in terms of the theory, but it makes the notes a little easier to find.)

Table 11.2 Diminished Chords Spelled Enharmonically

Chord	R	b3	b5	bb7
C°7	C	Eb	Gb	A
C#°7	C#	E	G	Bb
D°7	D	F	Ab	B
Eb°7	Eb	Gb	A	C
E°7	E	G	Bb	Db
F°7	F	Ab	B	D
F#°7	F#	A	C	Eb
Gb°7	Gb	A	C	Eb
G°7	G	Bb	Db	E
Ab°7	Ab	Cb	D	F
G#°7	G#	B	D	F
A°7	A	C	Eb	Gb
Bb°7	Bb	Db	E	G
B°7	B	D	F	Ab

Chapter 11 More Chords, Progressions, and Ideas

Compare the C°7 with the E♭°7 and the G♭°7. They have the same notes in a different order. This is because the notes in a diminished chord are all a minor third apart (three frets). Spell out the notes in a major or minor chord on the guitar, starting on an open string, and you'll find different intervals between the notes. For instance, if you wanted to spell an E7 starting on open E, you would go up four frets to G♯, then three frets to B, three more frets to D, and two frets to the next E. But if you spell an E°7 chord, you would go up three frets to G, three more frets to B♭, three more to D♭, and three more to the next E. The next chord tone is always three frets away.

This is highly significant. It means that all the notes are equal, since no notes are closer to or farther from the other notes. There is no "weight," no tendency to focus on one note more than the others. It means there really is no root or, more accurately, that any note in the diminished chord can be considered the root. That C°7 could also be considered an E♭°7, a G♭°7, or an A°7. They all have the same notes. An E♭°7 could be considered a G♭°7, an A°7, or a C°7.

> **NOTE:** The notes in a diminished 7th chord are all three frets apart. The chord repeats every three frets.

On the guitar, this means that diminished chords repeat every three frets. If you find a C°7 at the first fret, you can slide that chord to the fourth, seventh, tenth, and thirteenth frets, and they will all be C°7 chords.

Here are the three most common diminished forms on the guitar. Any note can be considered the root.

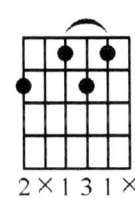

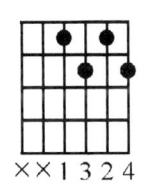

× 2 3 1 4 ×   2 × 1 3 1 ×   × × 1 3 2 4

A question arises: How do you know where to hold a diminished chord when there are so many options? Some composers, but not all, name the chord after the note they want in the bass. For instance, they might write CMaj7 C♯°7 Dm7, and you get a nice progression in the bass. If you don't see that type of progression, try putting other notes of the chord in the bass and see whether that gives you better results. In other words, if you see CMaj7 G°7 Dm7, try B♭°7, C♯°7, or E°7 instead of the G°7, and you may assemble a progression that fits together better.

> **NOTE:** When are diminished chords used? There are three primary uses:
> ▶ As passing chords
> ▶ After the IV chord in a blues piece
> ▶ In place of a 7(♭9) chord

153

Guitar for Songwriters

Diminished Chords as Passing Chords

Diminished chords are often used to connect chords. Below are some examples, along with good voicings of the chords to make smooth progressions.

1. IMaj7 ♯1°7 IIm7 ♯II°7 IIIm7. This common progression is shown here in the key of C.

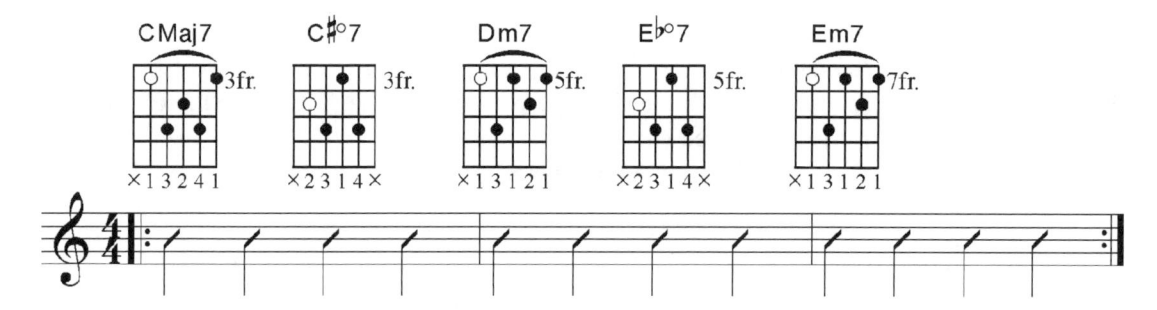

2. IMaj7 ♯1°7 IIm7 V7, in the key of A♭.

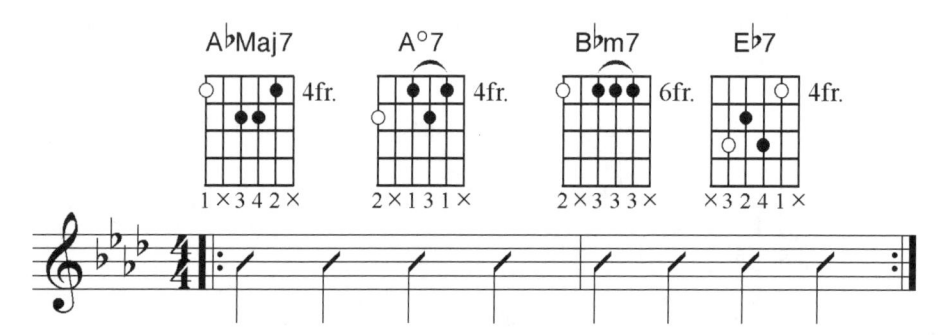

3. I6/9 ♯1°7 IIm11 V7(♭9). This example is actually just a fancier version of the previous example, in the key of G.

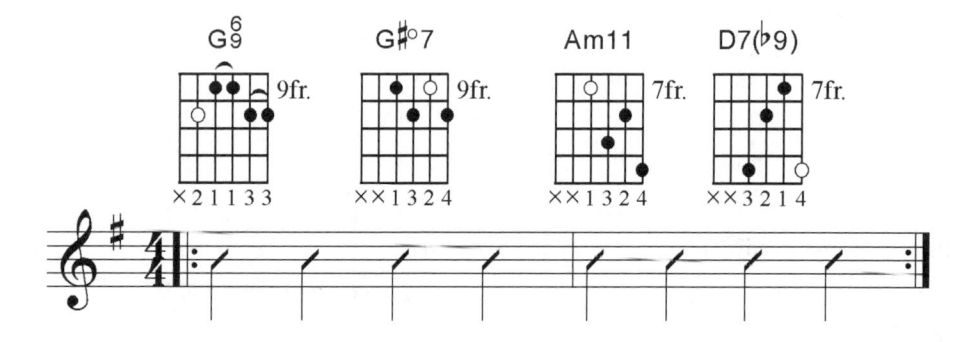

4. I6 1°7 I6. Sometimes the diminished chord adds a little interest by moving away from a chord and then returning to it, as in this example in the key of B♭.

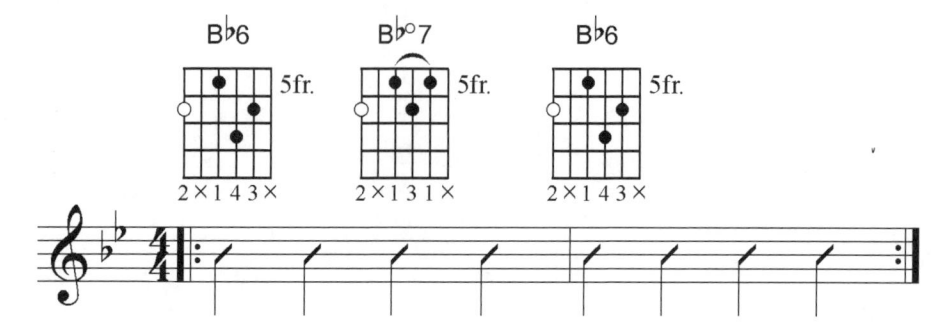

Chapter 11 More Chords, Progressions, and Ideas

5. I I° V7sus4 I°. Here is an example moving in and out of E♭. Each chord has E♭ on the second string as the top note.

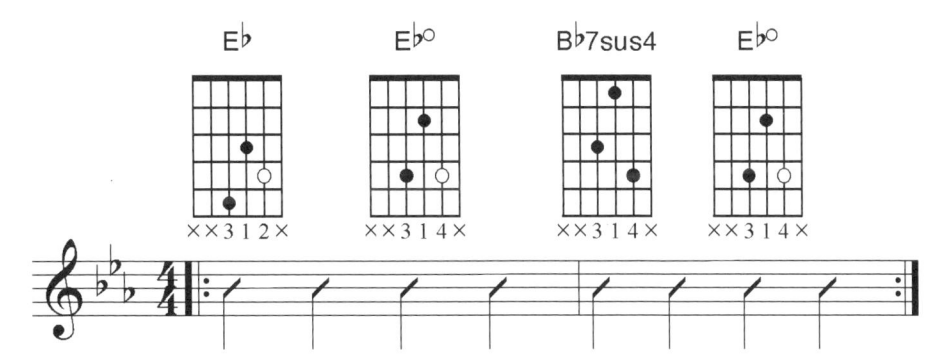

The ♯IV Diminished Chord

In playing a blues song or many other tunes using jazz changes, the ♯IV diminished chord is often used after the IV chord. In the key of C, the IV chord is F. Making it a little bluesier, it might be F7—F A C E♭. The ♯IV diminished is F♯°7—F♯ A C E♭. The only difference is between the F and the F♯. The diminished chord is like an F7 with the root raised a half-step. This might then continue back to the tonic, a C or C7. Sometimes people continue the bass progression by going to C with G in the bass, so the bass line will go F-F♯-G.

Here are a few examples of the ♯IV diminished chord.

1. IMaj7 I7 IVMaj7 ♯IV°. This example is in D.

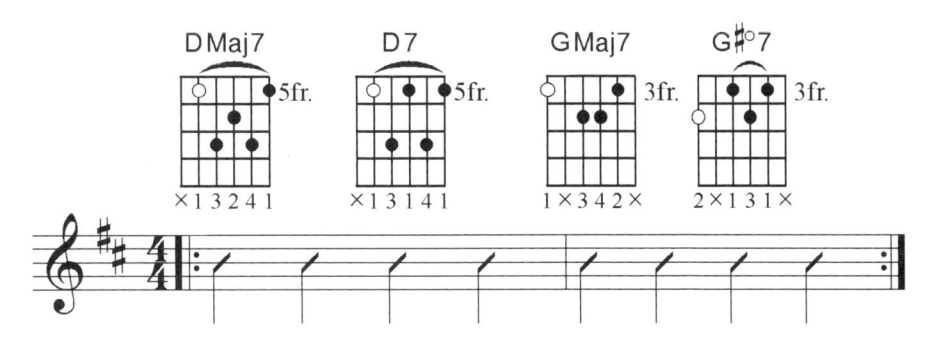

2. IMaj7 I7 IVMaj7 ♯IV°, in the key of A.

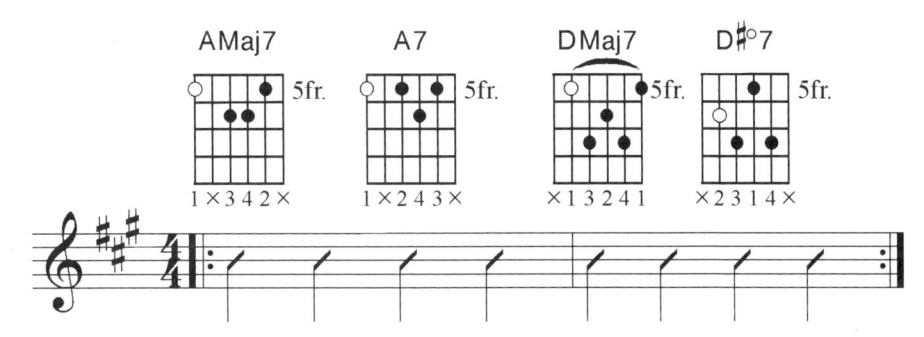

155

The Diminished Chord in Place of 7(♭9)

Look at the notes in a G7(♭9): G B D F A♭. Now look at A♭°7: A♭ B D F. It has the same notes, except the G is missing, so it could serve in place of G7(♭9). So could B°7, D°7, or F°7.

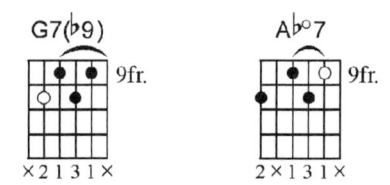

In fact, you could build a diminished chord on any chord tone except the root of a dominant 7th chord, and you would essentially have a chord that can serve as the 7(♭9) of that dominant 7th chord. For example, in place of a C7, you could play E°7, G°7, or B♭°7 (built on the 3rd, 5th, or ♭7th of a C7) to suggest C7(♭9). (Notice that these three diminished chords are really the same thing anyway, since they are each a minor third [three frets] from each other. What other diminished chord would work as well? D♭°7—which is built on the ♭9, and which is a minor third from the other chords.)

The sound of the diminished chord usually works here because we hear the root being played by the bass player or because good voice leading of the chord forms can create a logical progression even without the root.

Just as the 7(♭9) chord might not always work in place of a dominant 7th chord, the diminished chord might not always give you the sound you want, either. But try it for a while in place of 7(♭9) chords to get used to the sound.

Following are examples of chord progressions with 7(♭9) chords, followed by diminished chord substitutions.

The first example is a common progression in the key of G, followed by diminished substitutes for the E7 and D7 chords.

1. IMaj7-VI7(♭9)-IIm7-V7(♭9) in the key of G.

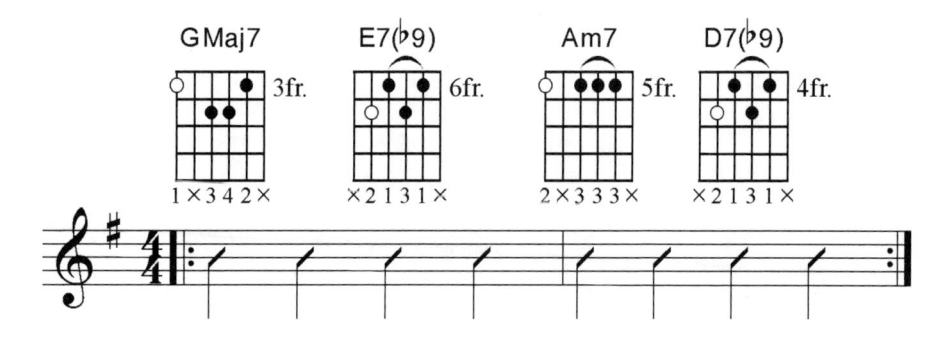

2. B°7 and A°7 in place of E7(♭9) and D7(♭9).

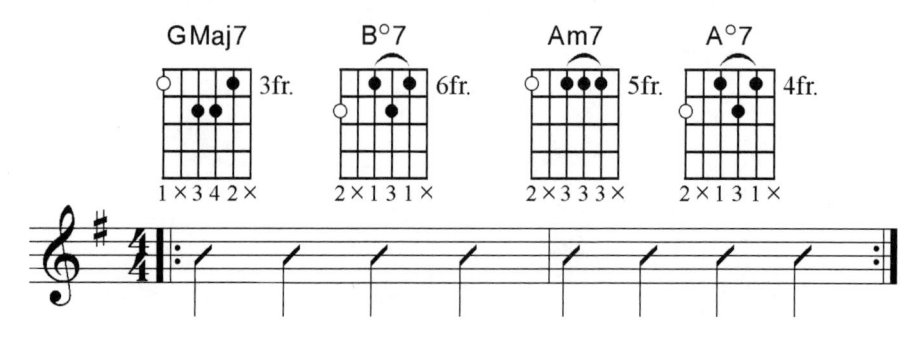

Chapter 11 More Chords, Progressions, and Ideas

The following example is very similar, except it is in the key of C. Notice that the chord for G7(♭9) lacks an F, the 7th. The F was just heard in the Dm7 chord, so our minds will retain the sound. (If there is a bass player, it might be a little stronger to omit the G in favor of an F and assume the bass will play the root.)

3. IMaj7-VI7(♭9)-IIm7-V7(♭9) in the key of C.

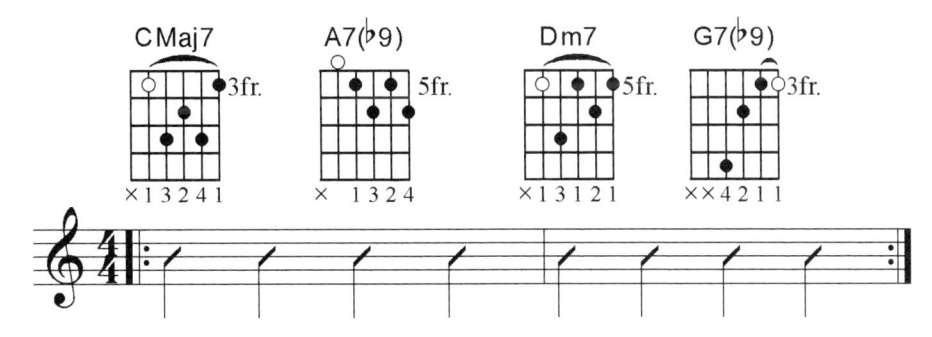

4. C♯°7 and D°7 in place of A7(♭9) and G7(♭9).

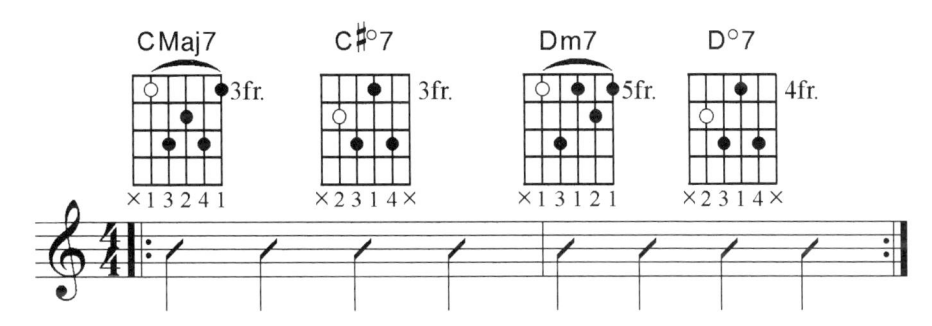

5. Here is a minor-key equivalent pattern, with E°7 used in place of A7, the V chord in D minor.

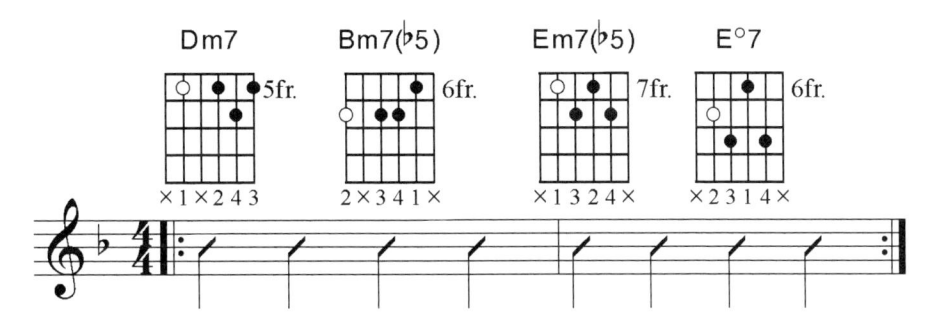

6. This last example is a variation of this progression in G minor. The A°7 substitutes for a D7(♭9).

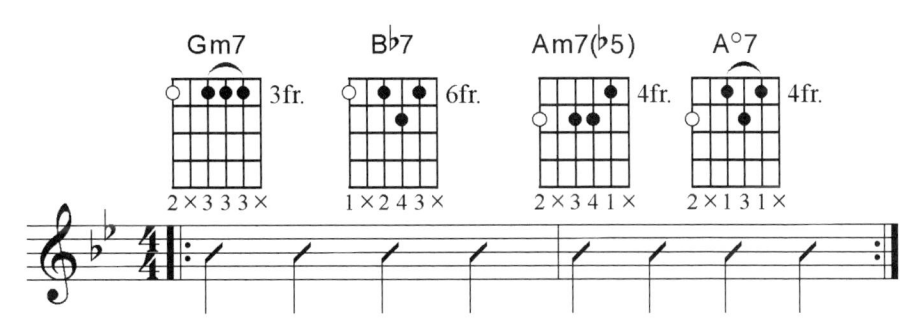

Guitar for Songwriters

Augmented Chords

The augmented chord is indicated with "aug" or with a "+" sign, as in C+. It means the fifth of the chord is sharp. A C+ has the notes C, E, and G♯, as opposed to C, E, and G in a regular C chord.

The distance between each of the chord tones is two whole steps, or four frets. As in diminished chords, this means that all notes are equal, but this time they are four frets apart. No notes are closer to or farther from the other notes. Any note in an augmented chord can be considered the root. The C+ could also be considered an E+ or G♯+. (E+ has E, G♯, and B♯ or C. G♯+ has G♯, B♯, or C, and D 𝄪 [double sharp], which is E.)

This means that, on the guitar, augmented chords repeat every four frets. You could play C+ at the first fret and slide it to the fifth fret or ninth fret and it could still be called C+.

> **NOTE:** Augmented chords repeat every four frets.

Here are the two most common augmented chords on the guitar. Any note can be considered the root.

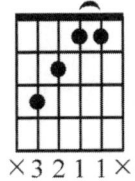

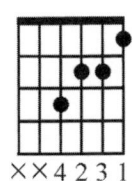

A dominant 7th chord with a sharp fifth, such as G7+ or G7(♯5), is an augmented chord with a flat 7th added. These are often used interchangeably, although the 7(♯5) doesn't repeat every four frets.

> **NOTE:** There are two main uses for augmented chords. They are often used for the dominant 7th chord in a minor key, or they can be used as passing chords.

Augmented Chords as Dominant Seventh Chords in a Minor Key

In the key of C minor, a G+ or G7(♯5) will strongly imply a return to a Cm chord, because the D♯ in the G+ is the same as the minor third (the E♭) in the Cm chord. Here are some examples of these chords in minor keys.

1. The key of Cm.

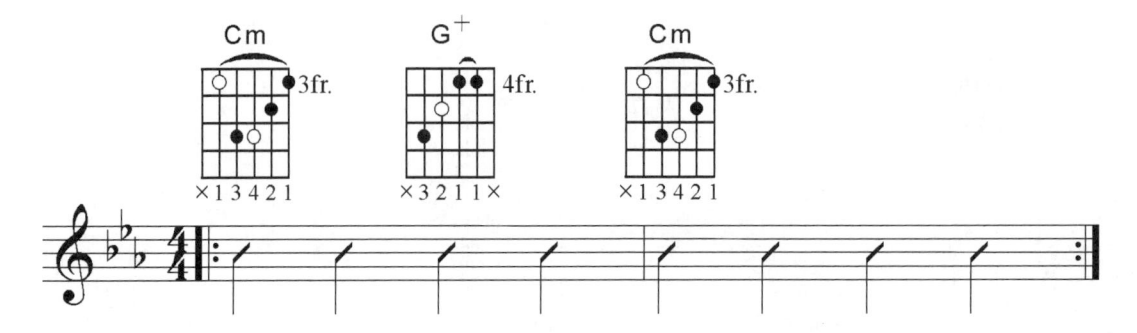

Chapter 11 More Chords, Progressions, and Ideas

2. The key of Cm.

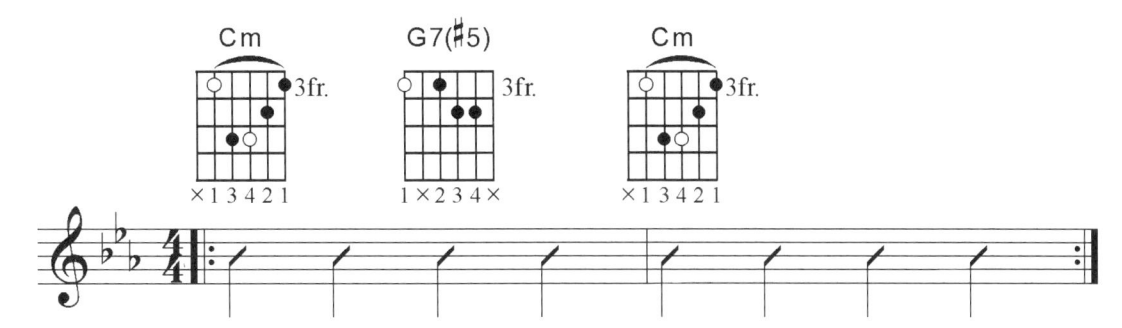

3. The key of Gm.

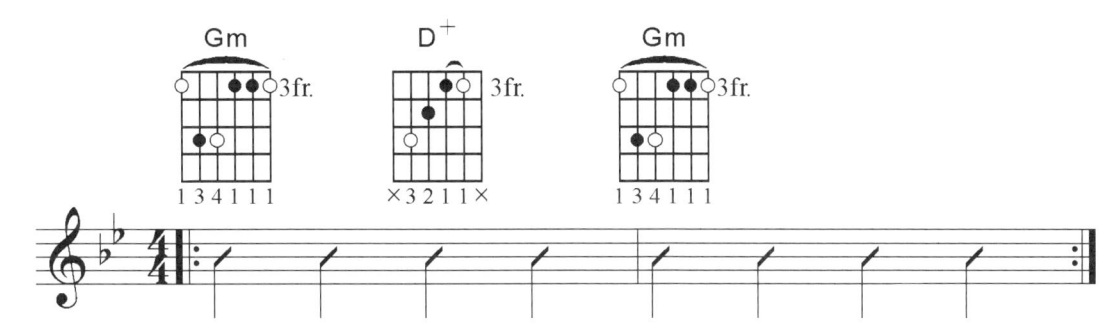

4. The key of Am.

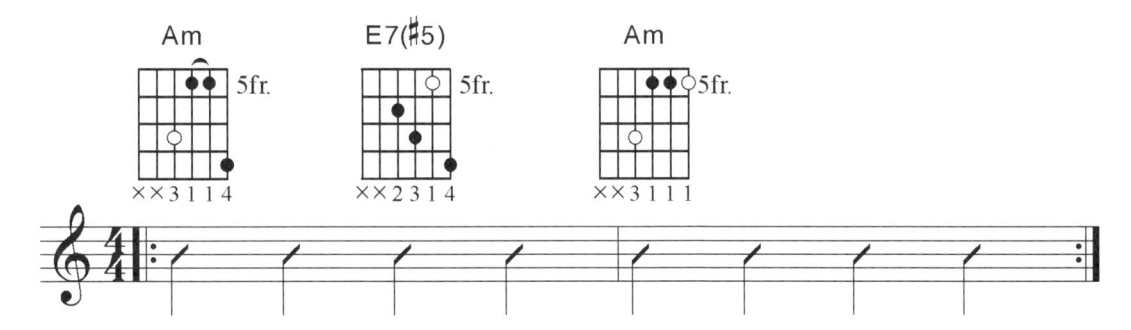

Augmented Chords as Passing Chords

Sometimes augmented chords are used to move from one chord to the next or to momentarily leave a chord and then return to it. Here are some examples of these uses.

1. The key of B.

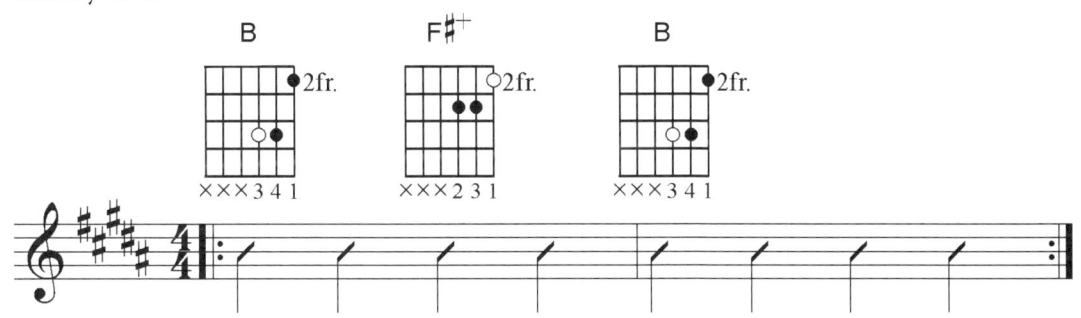

Guitar for Songwriters

2. The key of D.

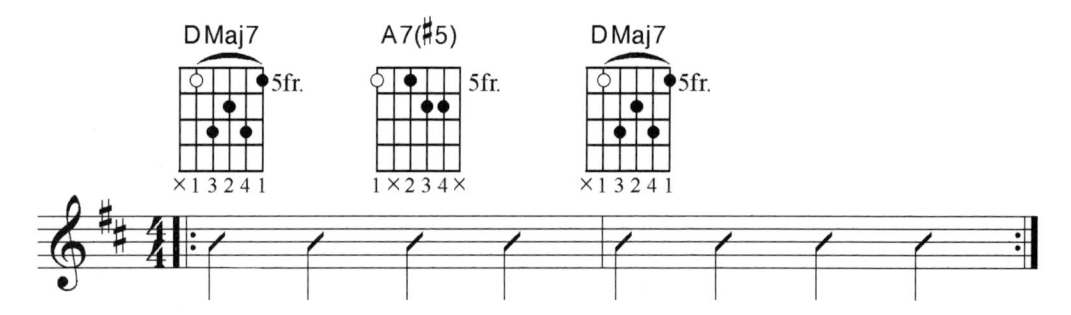

[Chord diagrams: DMaj7 (5fr, ×1 3 2 4 1), A7(♯5) (5fr, 1 ×2 3 4 ×), DMaj7 (5fr, ×1 3 2 4 1)]

[Notation in key of D, 4/4, slash rhythm for two measures with repeat.]

3. The key of A♭.

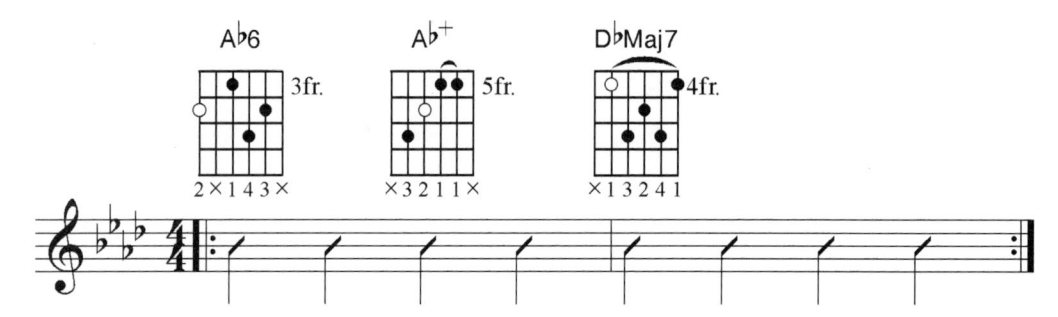

[Chord diagrams: A♭6 (3fr, 2 ×1 4 3 ×), A♭+ (5fr, ×3 2 1 1 ×), D♭Maj7 (4fr, ×1 3 2 4 1)]

[Notation in key of A♭, 4/4, slash rhythm for two measures with repeat.]

Embellishing or Simplifying

Sometimes chords sound too simple, and you want to embellish them—add some notes to the chord to get a richer sound. At other times, you may want to do the opposite. I was once asked to take part of a song and make it playable for a young girl who knew a little guitar and was acting in a musical. Although the song was originally arranged for a large orchestra and had frequent chord changes, I was able to simplify the section to just a few chords. I then gave her versions of the chords with only a few strings. The "cute" factor was incredible when the orchestra stopped and this child came out with her guitar to play and sing.

When You Don't Know That Chord, Simplify

There are times when a piece of music calls for a chord that you just don't know. It often makes sense to simplify that chord. If you play a C chord in place of a CMaj7, you will not be playing any wrong notes. Instead, you will be playing one note less. (A C chord contains the notes C, E, and G, while CMaj7 has C, E, G, and B.) If you aren't sure how to hold a certain chord, you can always lower or remove a number. For example, a G13 could be simplified to a G9, a G7, or even a G. The chord will be a little simpler and perhaps not as rich sounding, but it will have no wrong notes.

> *If you aren't sure how to hold a certain chord, you can always lower or remove a number. G9 becomes G7 or G.*

The main types of chords are major, minor, and dominant 7th. You can't change a minor to a major, or vice versa, but you can simplify within the basic chord type. Cm9 can be simplified to Cm, but not to C.

> *You can't change a minor to a major, or vice versa, but you can simplify within the basic chord type. Cm9 can be simplified to Cm, but not to C.*

Chapter 11 More Chords, Progressions, and Ideas

Major-Type Chords

Here are some examples, moving from complicated to simple. You can simplify by lowering the number (from CMaj9 to CMaj7, for example) or removing it altogether (from CMaj7 to C).

CMaj9(#11)

CMaj9

CMaj7

C

Minor-Type Chords

Here are more examples moving from complicated to simple, with minor-type chords. Any simpler version of a chord could be played in place of the more complicated one.

Cm11

Cm9

Cm7

Cm

Dominant Seventh-Type Chords

Again, move from complicated to simple.

C13

C9

C7

Similarly, a C7(♭9) could be simplified to a C7.

Chords with ♯5 or ♭5

Sometimes it won't work to omit a ♯5 or ♭5. For instance, a C7 might not be a good substitute for a C7(♭5). It depends on the context. Those alterations may reflect the melody or may be significant colors that are important elements in that particular song. Study of music theory can help clarify these cases, but often your ear can give you a good answer. Experiment with different chords. If they sound all right to you, they're probably fine.

> *Learn to trust your ear. If it sounds all right, use it.*

Suspended Chords (7sus4)

Most suspended chords usually resolve to the dominant 7th chord. A C7sus4 may move to C7, for instance. Try just playing the C7. Again, let your ear tell you whether that works.

m7(♭5)

These chords are also called half-diminished and can be indicated with the ø symbol. It's usually not a good idea to play a regular fifth in place of the ♭5.

Guitar for Songwriters

Extensions and Alterations

Chords in a song often have extensions or alterations to reflect the melody. An extension is a chord tone beyond the seventh, such as a 9 or 13. It extends the harmony of the chord. An alteration makes a chord tone sharp or flat, such as ♯5 or ♭9. These notes can often be found in the melody. The measure containing a G7(♭9), for example, frequently will have an A♭ in the melody.

Even though these notes are present in the melody, that doesn't mean they have to be present in the chord. If you play a G7 chord and the melody is an A♭, the combined result is G7(♭9). That chord is the result regardless of whether you hold the ♭9 in the chord.

Too Many Changes

Some songs have chord changes on practically every beat. Often, most of these chords are simply embellishments—making the chord a little fancier. A measure like this example can usually be played as just a GMaj7 or G6. Figure out what the basic chord type is and work from there. In this case, the chords are all G major–type chords. Even if there are other chords in the measure, try using the chord type that appears the most. Let your ear help you find a solution.

You can simplify a passage like this by just playing G6 or GMaj7 for the entire measure.

Moving Voices within Chords

It's not unusual to see a chord progression where the root stays the same while the chord changes slightly, such as G-GMaj7-G6-GMaj7. In such cases, analyze the chords to see which notes change and which ones remain the same. There is often a melodic line that should be emphasized.

1. In this example with the G chords, all three chords have the notes G-B-D, while the G6 also has an E, and the GMaj7 also has an F♯. A nice line could be created by going between the notes G, F♯, E, and F♯ as the chords progress. Try to bring out the top note of the chords.

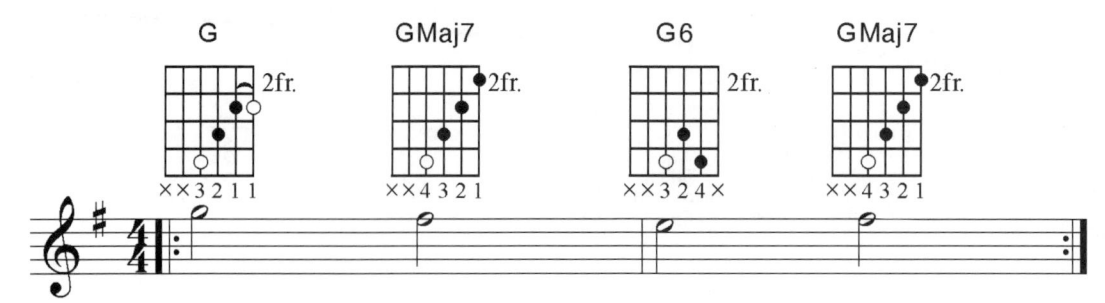

Chapter 11 More Chords, Progressions, and Ideas

2. Here is another way to play the same progression, with the moving line in the middle of the chord instead of on top.

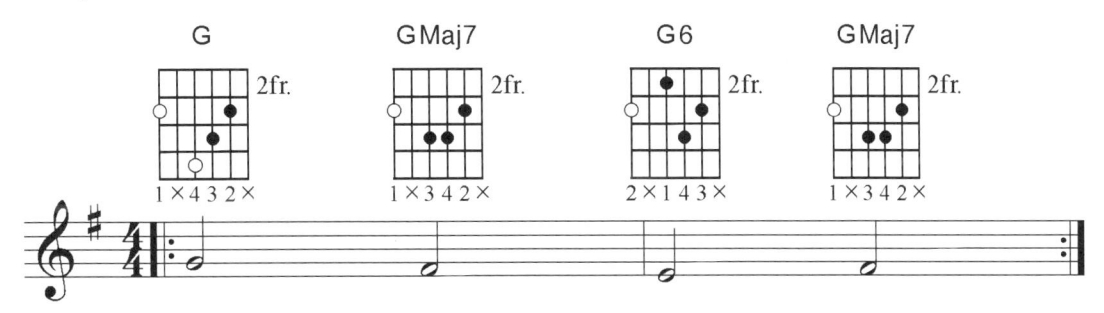

3. This is the equivalent progression in the key of E♭, based on Form 3 chords.

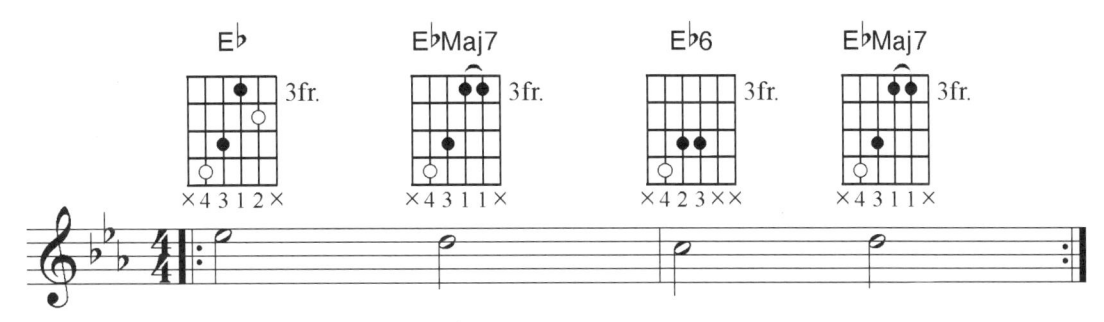

4. In this example in the key of A♭, there is an ascending chromatic line on the second string, in the middle of the chord.

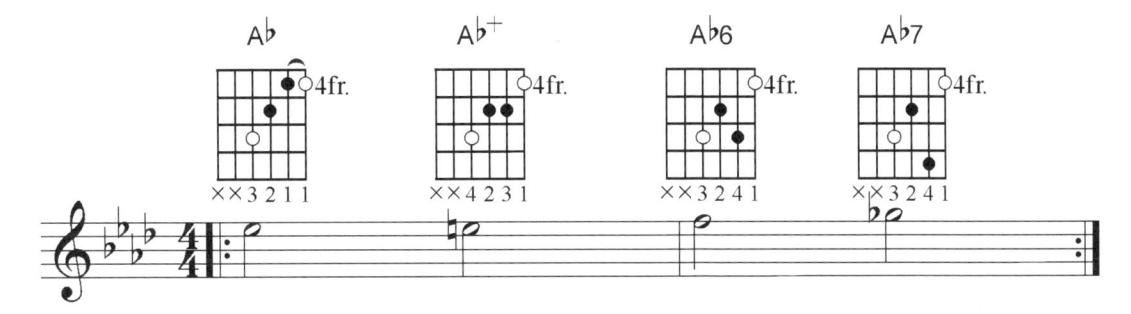

Minor Chords with Moving Voices

It's fairly common in many styles of music to see a minor chord where one note descends within the chord, but it's often difficult to recognize the pattern at first.

1. Play this example of an Am chord with a descending line. (Bring out the descending bass line in this progression.)

163

Guitar for Songwriters

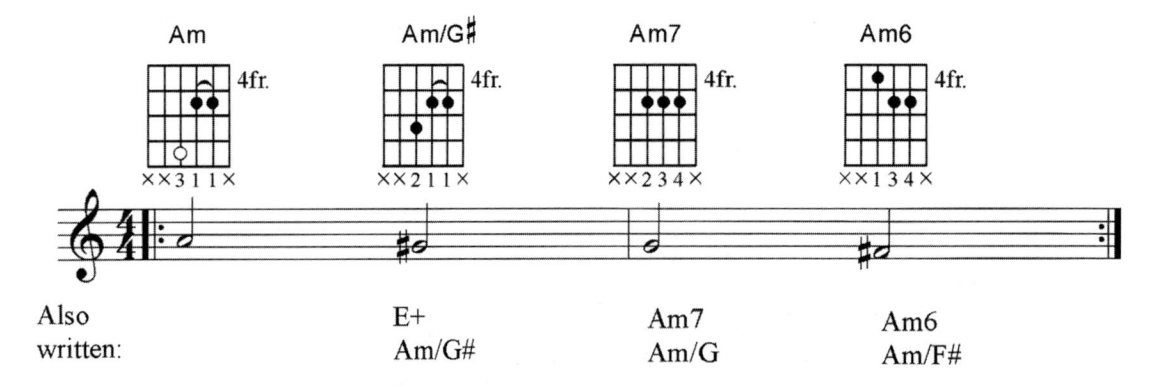

Am	Am/G♯	Am7	Am6

Also written: E+ / Am/G#   Am7 / Am/G   Am6 / Am/F#

Some of the chords could have different names. The second chord is often labeled as an augmented chord, but it is really the minor chord with a major 7th in the bass. The Am7 could also be called a C6. This progression could also be written with slash chords, as Am, Am/G♯, Am/G, Am/F♯.

How would you know to bring out the descending line if the chords were written as Am-E+-Am7-Am6? Whenever there is an augmented chord immediately after a minor chord, there is usually a one-note difference that might be signaling the start of this pattern. See whether that is the case between the first two chords, as would be true in moving from Am to E+ or to Am/G♯. Another tip-off to the use of a descending line is the move from minor 7th to minor 6th. There is a one-note difference between these chords. Try to take advantage of the one-note difference to create a progression with nice voice leading.

2. It is much clearer to call the second chord in this progression Cm/B than to call it G+.

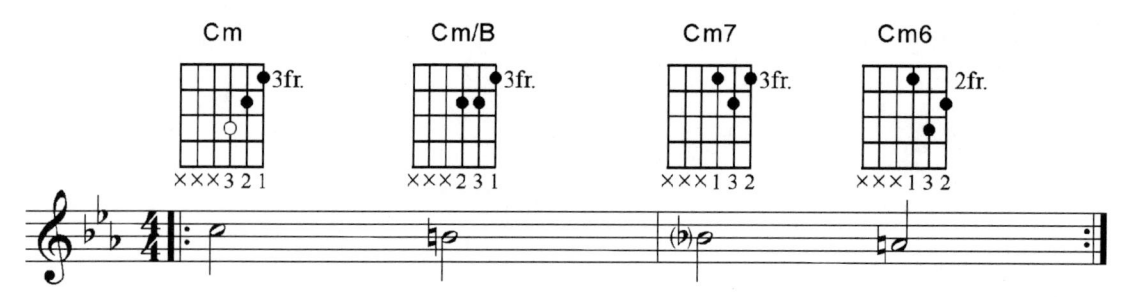

Cm	Cm/B	Cm7	Cm6

3. Here is an example of a descending line as the upper voice in an Fm chord. The F root is not present after the first chord, but our ears retain the sound in this context.

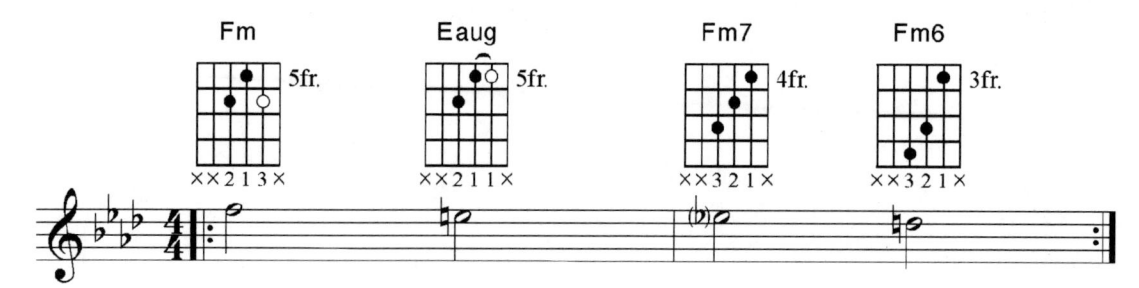

Fm	Eaug	Fm7	Fm6

Chapter 11 More Chords, Progressions, and Ideas

4. Going from minor 7th to minor 6th is quite common, and you should become familiar with many ways to play this in all keys.

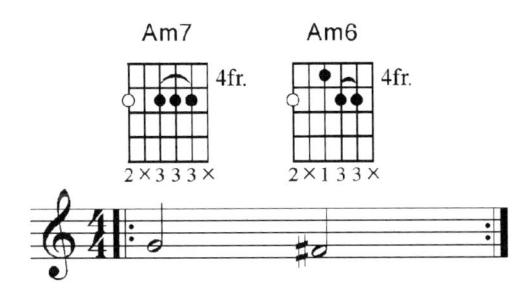

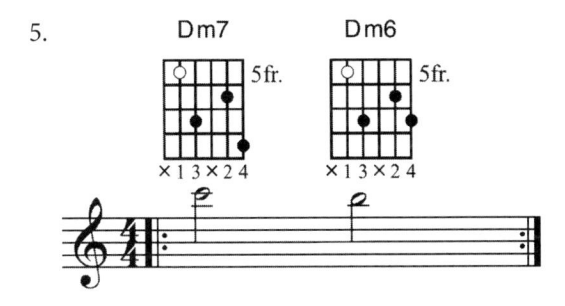

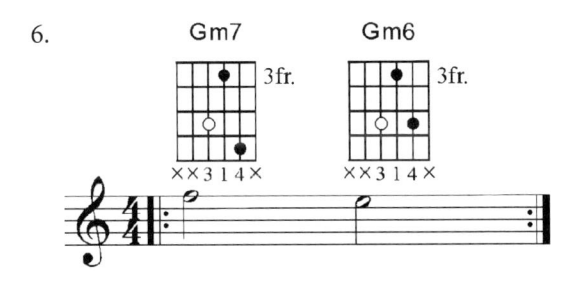

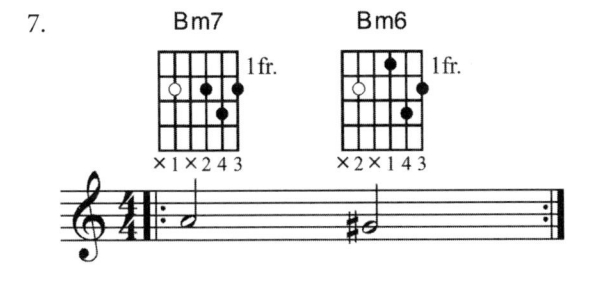

5.

6.

7.

8. The old spy-movie themes often used minor chords with ascending lines to create tension. As was the case with the descending lines, these patterns are not always apparent when they appear in sheet music. The Gm(♯5) in this example (with notes G, B♭, and D♯) could also be interpreted as an E♭/G chord (the notes E♭, G, and B♭, with the G in the bass).

Guitar for Songwriters

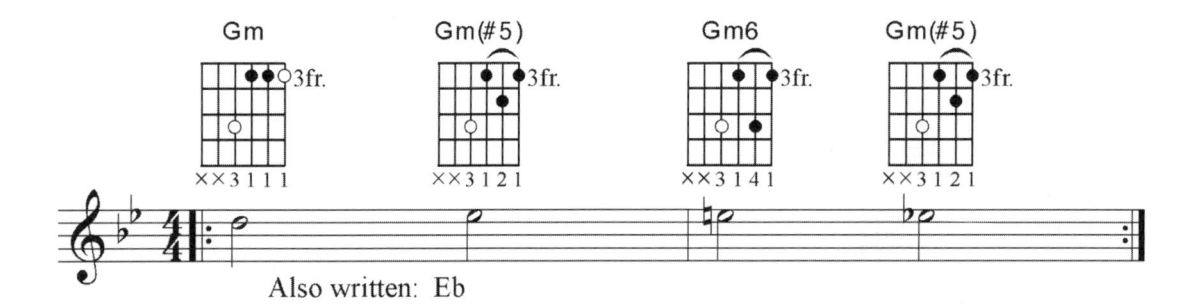

Also written: Eb

9. Here is a similar pattern in B minor, with the moving line on the first string. Bm(♯5) could also be called G/B, but it's easier in this case to think of these all as Bm chords with a moving voice.

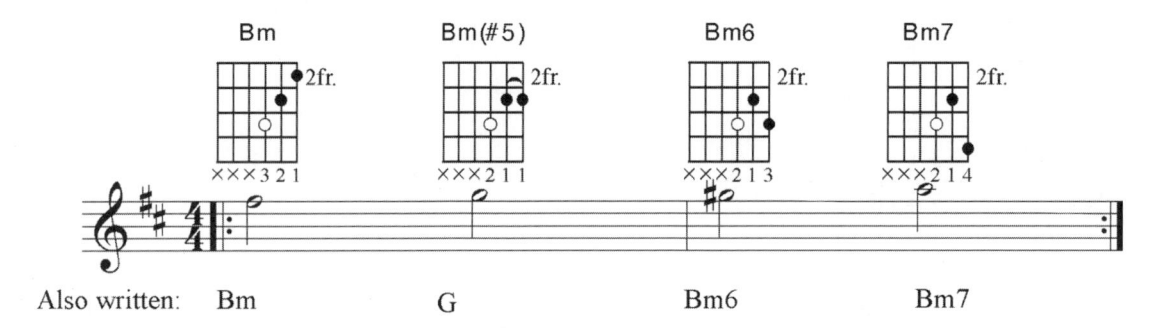

Also written: Bm   G   Bm6   Bm7

The final chapter looks at the classic American form, the blues, and some of the many ways it can be played. When we look at options available in a blues, we can see many of the possibilities open to us in songwriting and guitar playing.

The Blues

YOU'RE TRYING TO DEVELOP YOUR OWN VOICE AS A SONGWRITER. You don't want to sound like everyone else. So why study the blues, a form that has been used by thousands of people for more than a century?

Over the course of this book, we've looked at chords and accompaniment styles going from very basic to quite advanced. We've applied them to chord progressions in all keys, all over the neck. If we apply these ideas to a classic form like the blues, we can see the possibilities for many types of songs. The blues can be played in a very gritty, rocking fashion, as a country song, as a sophisticated jazz tune, or as anything in between. It's hard to play guitar for long without gaining some familiarity with the blues. Learning the blues can be a key to learning music, period.

Although there is a standard structure, there are so many variations that you seldom hear a blues piece played the same way twice. It is a form that has been used by musicians from the most down-home, self-taught country boy to the most sophisticated of jazz musicians. B.B. King, Johnny Cash, Miles Davis, the Rolling Stones, Willie Nelson, John Lee Hooker, Duke Ellington, Little Richard, the Beatles—they all used the blues in their music. This chapter will look at 20 variations on the blues.

The Basic Blues Progression

The most basic form of the blues is called the *12-bar blues*, because the chord pattern is 12 measures long. In its most elementary form, it looks like this:

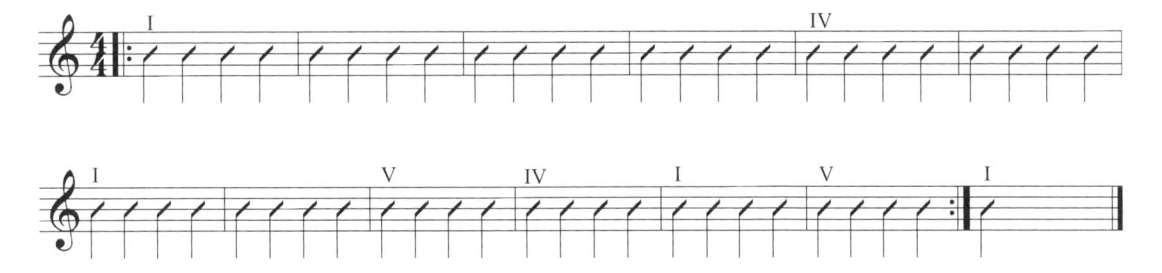

Notice that it uses only three chords—the I, IV, and V chords discussed already. The V chord in bar 12 is a "turnaround" chord—it prepares you to return to the beginning. To finish a blues song, you would continue on to the tonic (the I chord) to end the piece.

Guitar for Songwriters

Blues #1, Using Form 1 Bar Chords

In the key of C, the blues could be played as follows. In this example, only the Form 1 bar chord is used, moving to different areas of the neck.

> You can hear this example in the Example42 audio file at http://cengageptr.com/guitarforsongwriters.

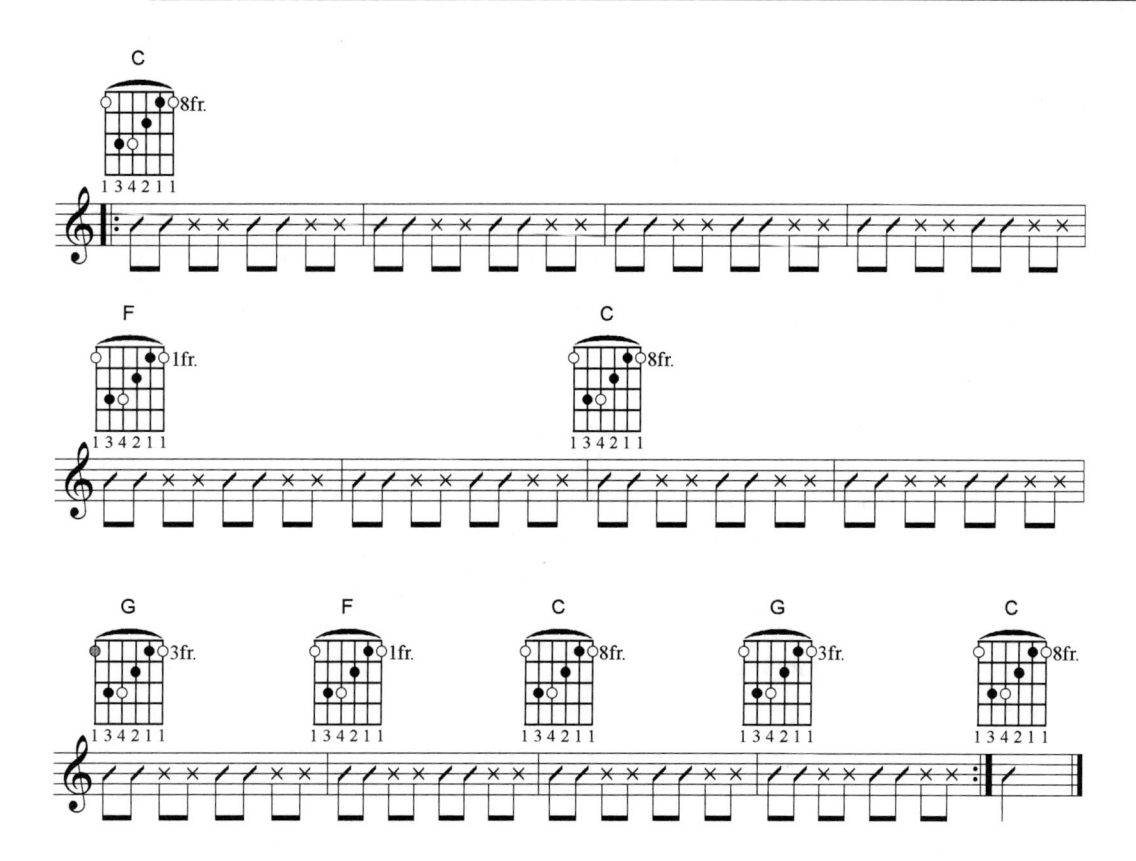

Chapter 12 The Blues

Blues #2, Using Form 1 and 2 Bar Chords

Here is another example of the 12-bar blues, using Form 1 and 2 bar chords that stay in the same area of the neck. The chord progression is the same as the previous blues example, except it is now in the key of G.

You can hear this example in the Example43 audio file at http://cengageptr.com/ guitarforsongwriters.

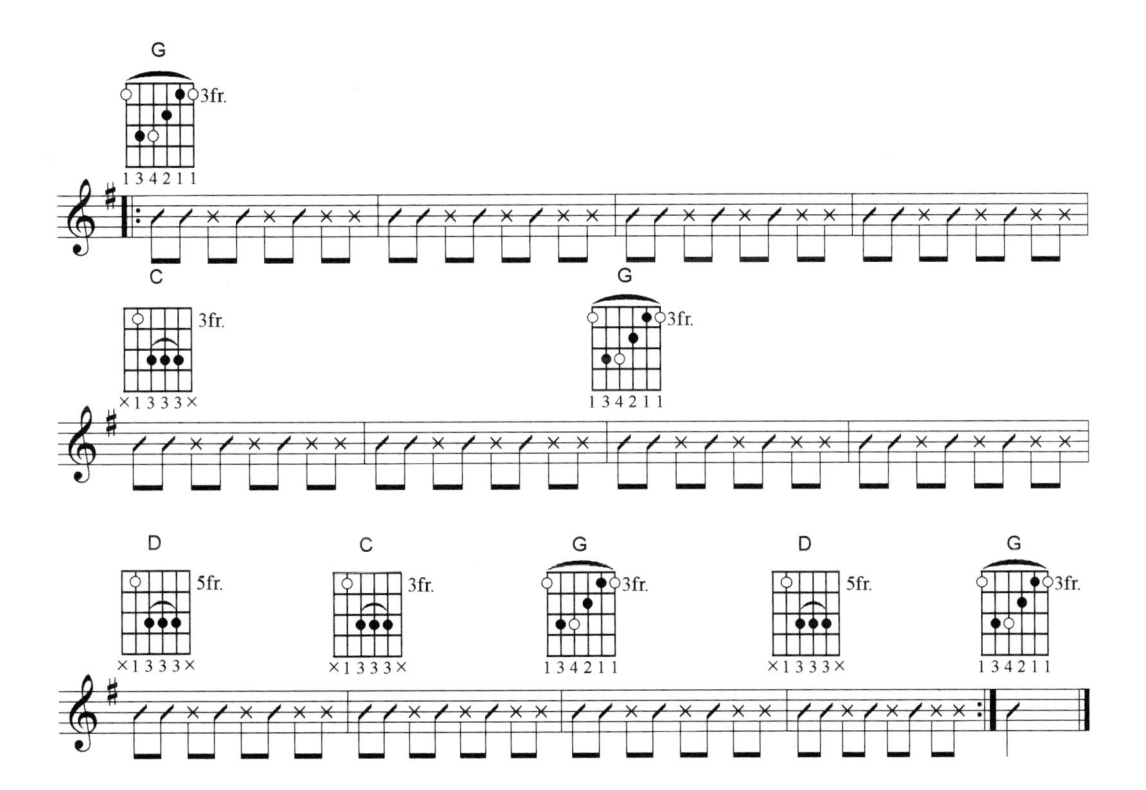

Guitar for Songwriters

Blues #3, with a Triplet Feel

The blues are often played with a "shuffle" rhythm, using triplets (three strums per beat). The next example is in the key of E♭. It starts with the Form 2 bar chord and mostly stays in the sixth position. Notice that the last two strums in each measure are often muted. Experiment with muting on different beats.

You can hear this example in the Example44 audio file at http://cengageptr.com/guitarforsongwriters.

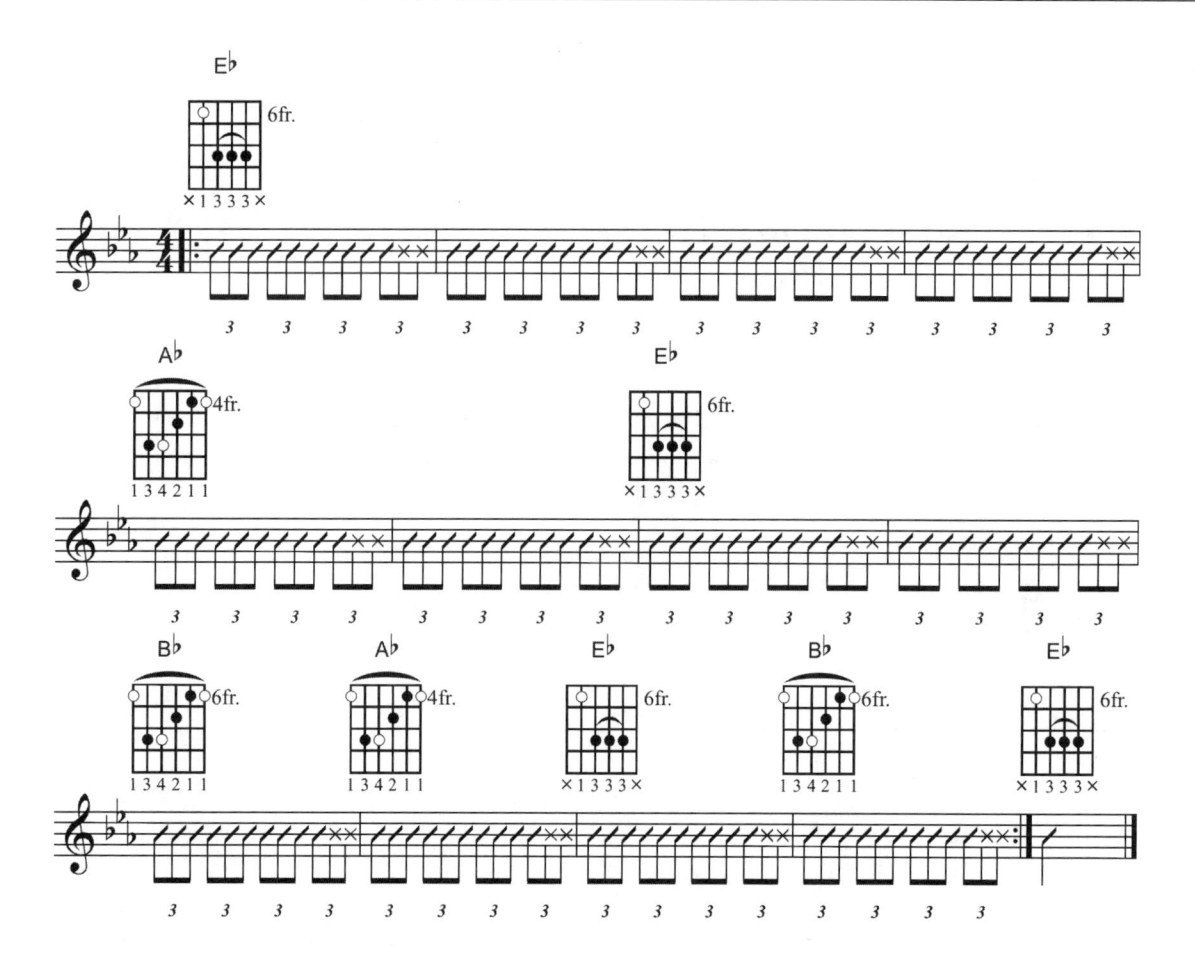

Chapter 12 The Blues

Blues #4, with Power Chords

Next is that same blues progression using power chords, in the key of A. To add some spice, we start each measure a step below the target chord. Rather than play just an A5 chord, we start with G5 and then go to A5.

> You can hear this example in the Example45 audio file at http://cengageptr.com/guitarforsongwriters.

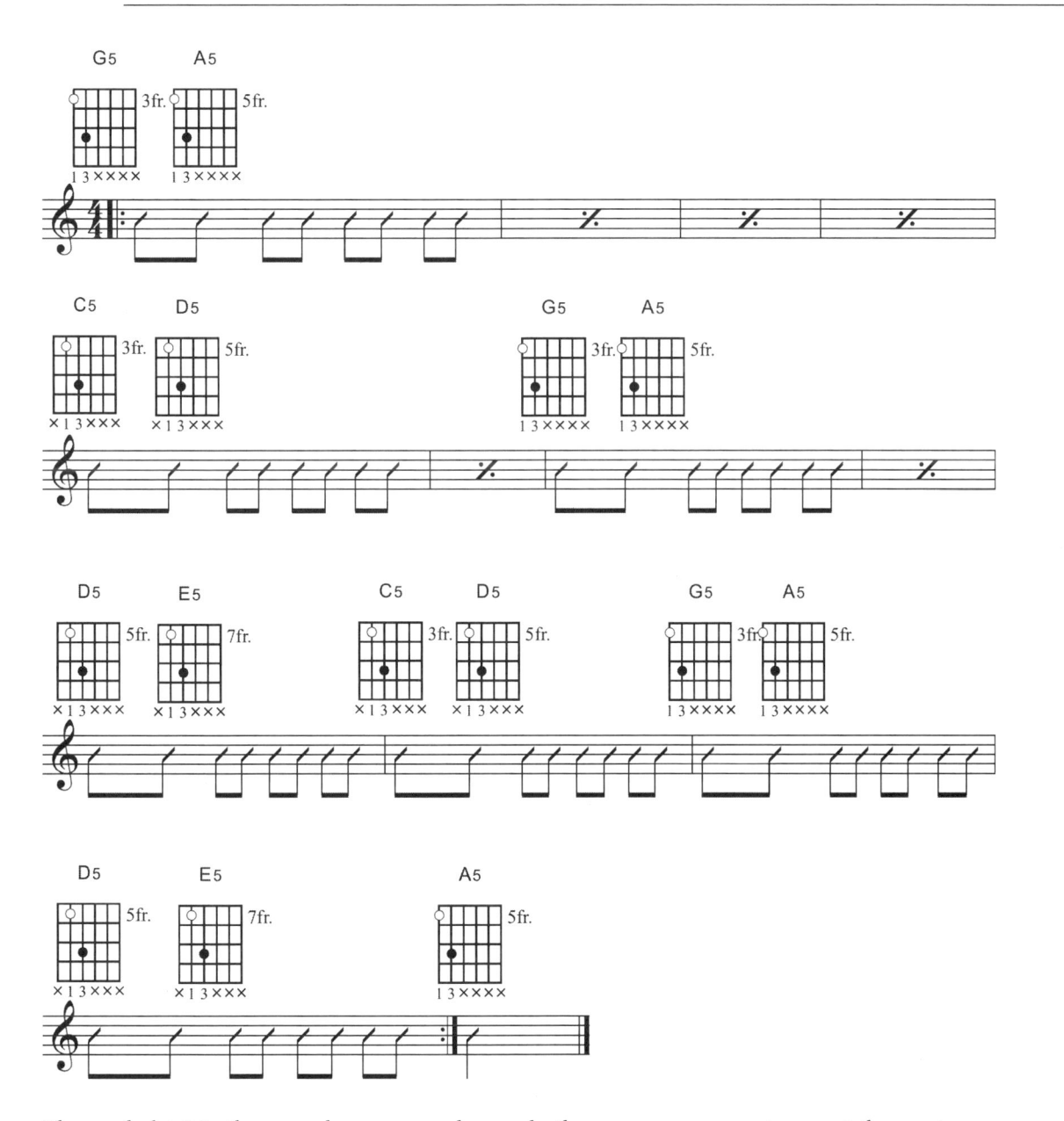

The symbol ✗ in the second measure and several other measures means to repeat the previous measure.

171

Guitar for Songwriters

A Blues Progression with More Changes

There are many variations in the basic 12-bar chord pattern for the blues. One common version involves playing the IV chord at the second bar. In the following example, the turnaround is also different. The twelfth bar usually ends with the V chord, to bring you back to the beginning, but there are many different ways to get to that V chord.

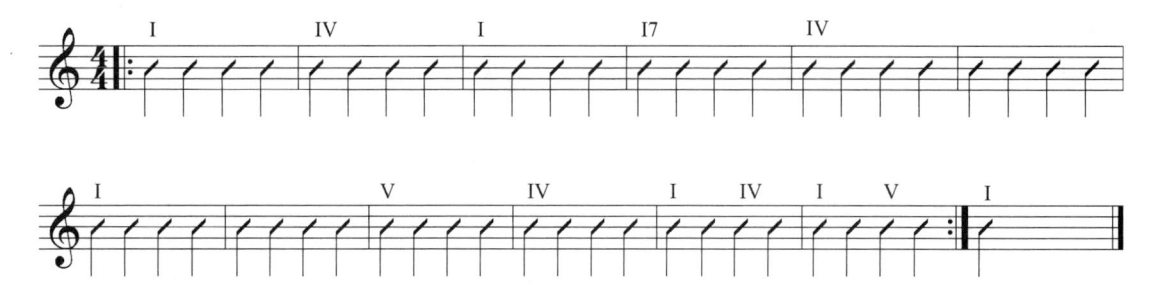

Blues #5, with More Chords

Here is a way to play that pattern in the key of G, with a shuffle rhythm.

You can hear this example in the Example46 audio file at http://cengageptr.com/guitarforsongwriters.

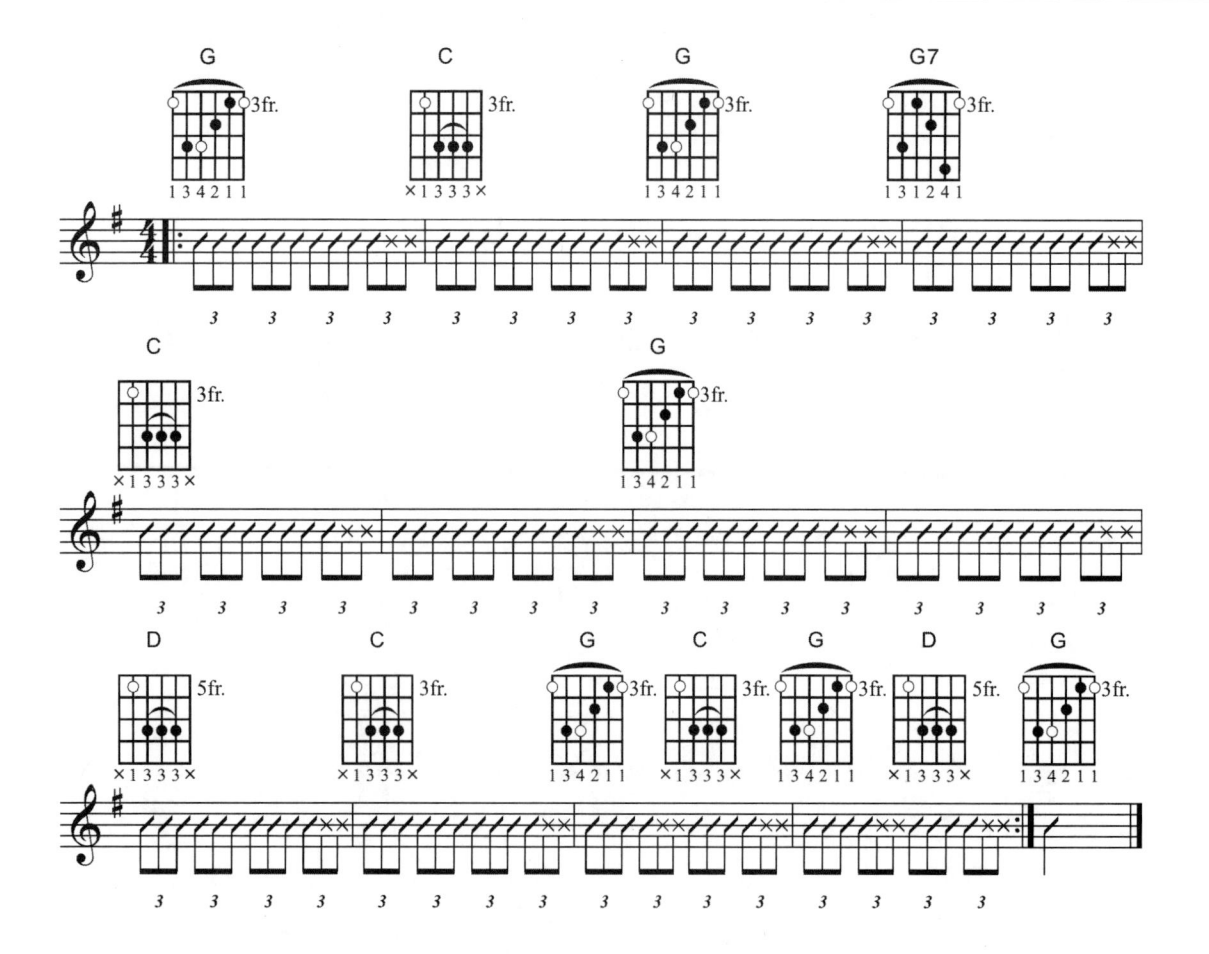

172

Chapter 12 The Blues

Blues #6, with the Form 3 F Chord

Here is a blues in the key of F, starting with the Form 3 major chord.

> You can hear this example in the Example47 audio file at http://cengageptr.com/guitarforsongwriters.

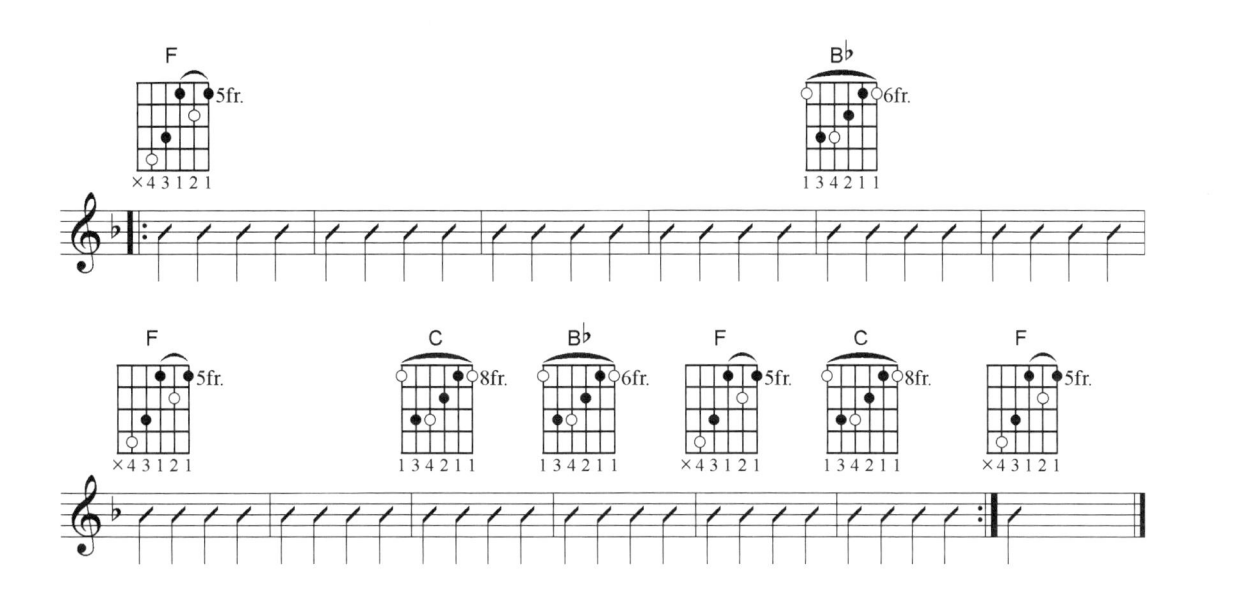

The Blues with Dominant Seventh Chords

The blues can be played using all dominant 7th chords, giving a bluesier sound.

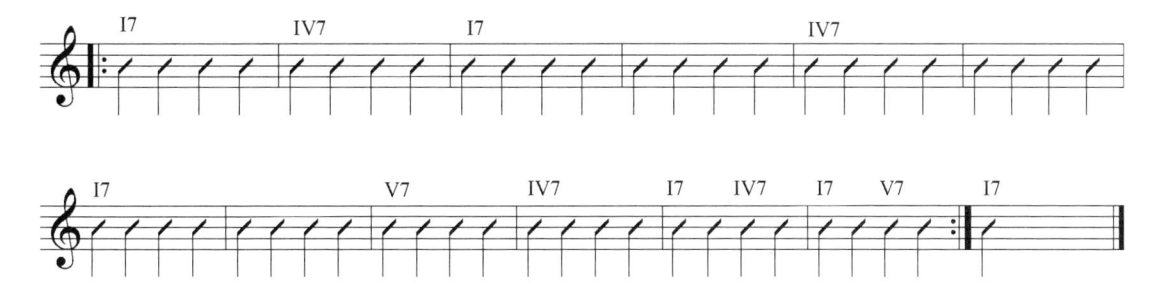

173

Guitar for Songwriters

Blues #7, with Seventh Chords

In this example in the key of F, the right hand should give a strong accent to beats two and four, marked with >.

> You can hear this example in the Example48 audio file at http://cengageptr.com/guitarforsongwriters.

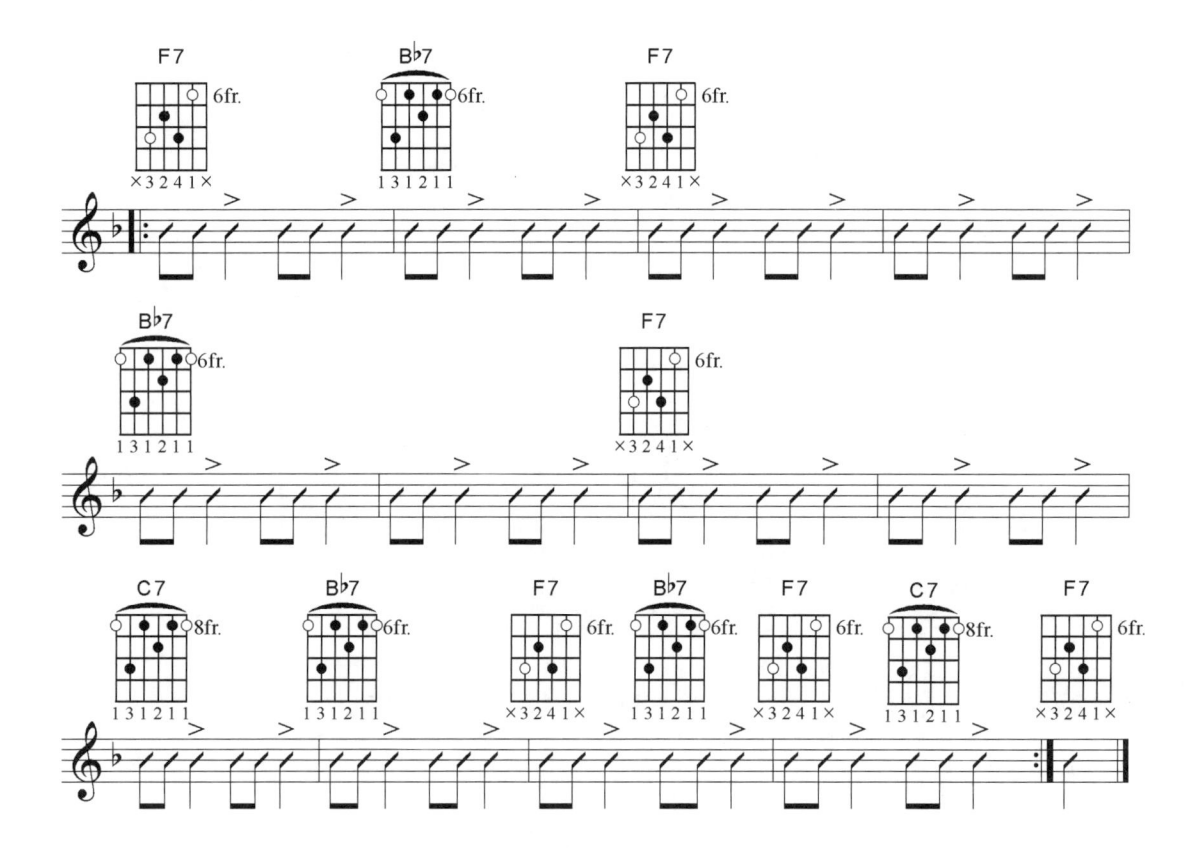

The following blues in the key of A uses a slight variation of the Form 1 seventh chord. The little finger is on the second string, and the first and fourth strings are muted by leaning the third and fourth fingers slightly. The first finger does not need to bar in this chord.

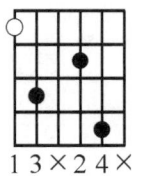

Chapter 12 The Blues

Blues #8, with Bass Notes

This example has a bass note on the first beat of each measure, a strong accent on the second beat and on the "and" of beat three, and some strums on muted strings. The rhythm for the turnaround is different from the other measures.

> You can hear this example in the Example49 audio file at http://cengageptr.com/guitarforsongwriters.

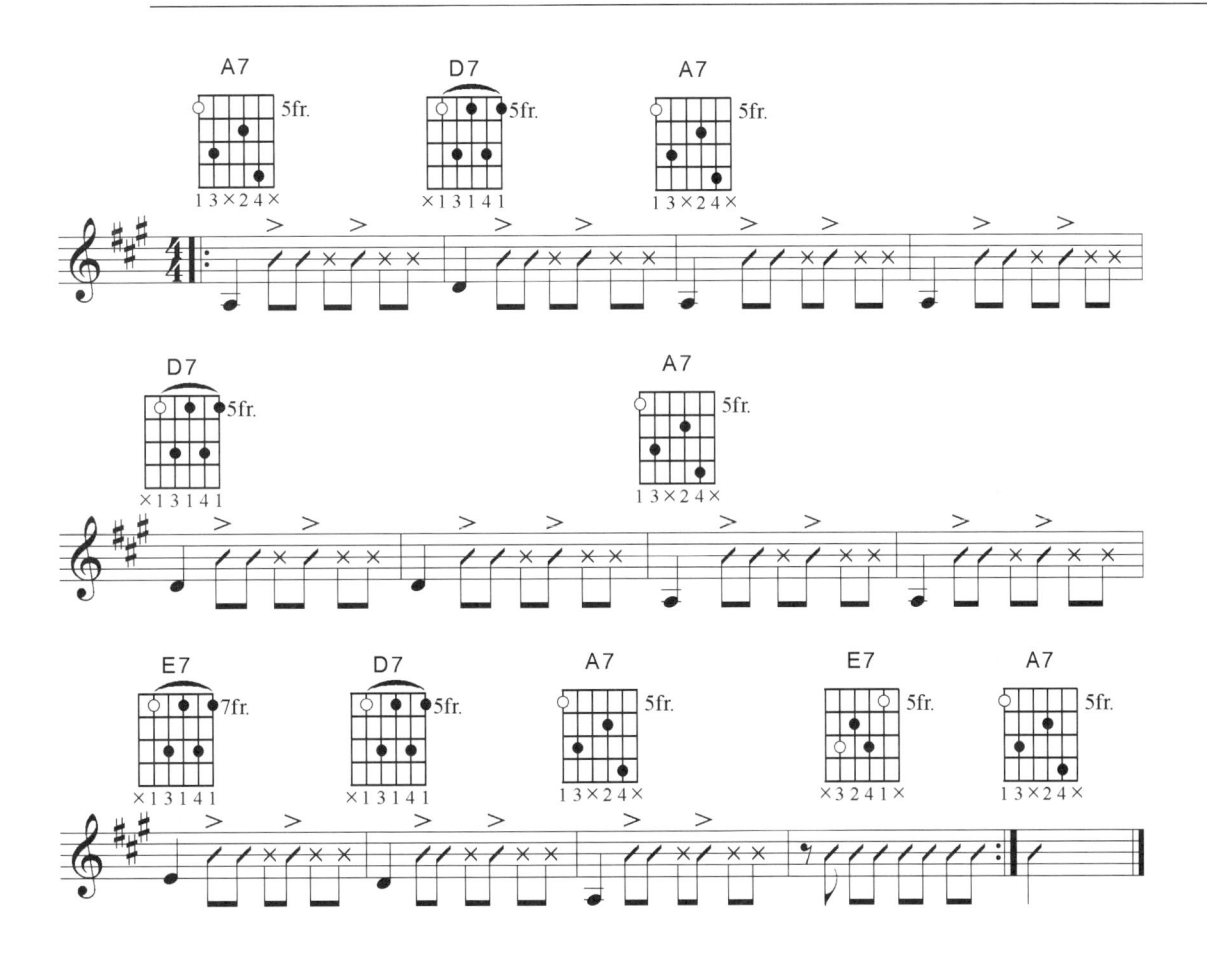

The Blues in Minor Keys

The 12-bar blues can be played in minor keys as well as major keys, with only slight differences. The I and IV chords are usually minor, but the V chord remains a dominant 7th. Sometimes a ♭VI chord is included, and there are different ways of playing the turnaround.

Here is a basic minor blues, followed by a way it might be played in the key of Am.

175

Guitar for Songwriters

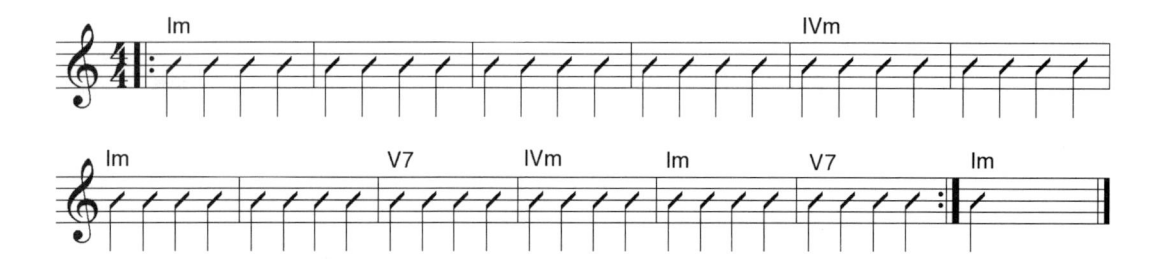

Blues #9, in A Minor

The second and fourth beats of each measure are accented and cut off. A dot above a note means staccato—cut off.

> You can hear this example in the Example50 audio file at http://cengageptr.com/guitarforsongwriters.

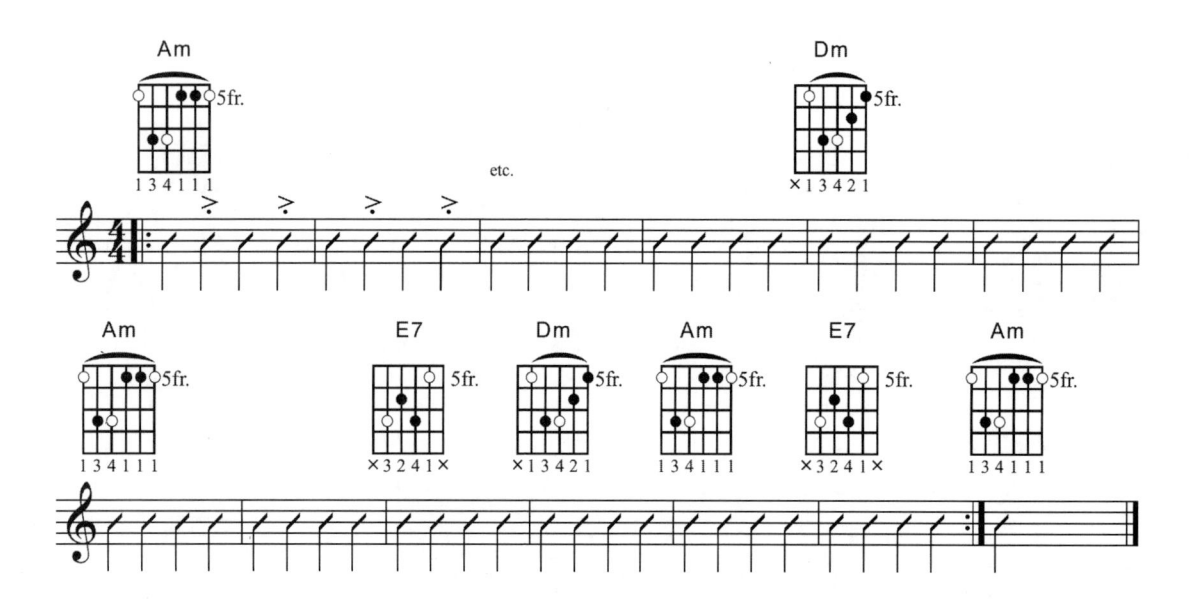

The Minor Blues with More Changes

Here is another way to play a minor blues, adding a IVm chord at the second measure and a ♭VI7 chord in bars 10 and 11.

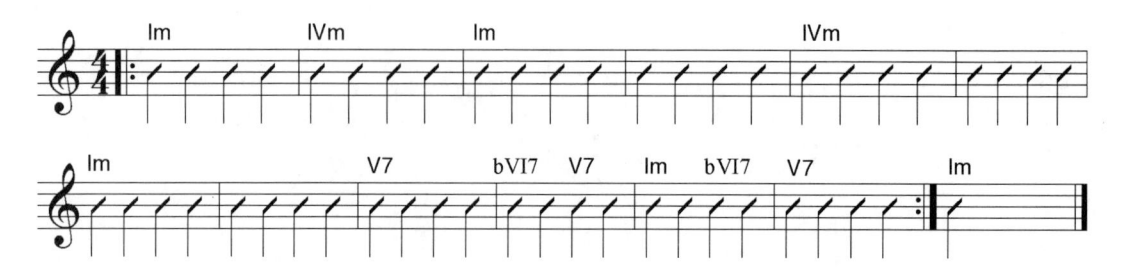

Chapter 12 The Blues

Blues #10, in D Minor

This D minor blues is typical of a slow minor blues, with a triplet feel (three strums per beat) and strong accents on 2 and 4.

> You can hear this example in the Example51 audio file at http://cengageptr.com/guitarforsongwriters.

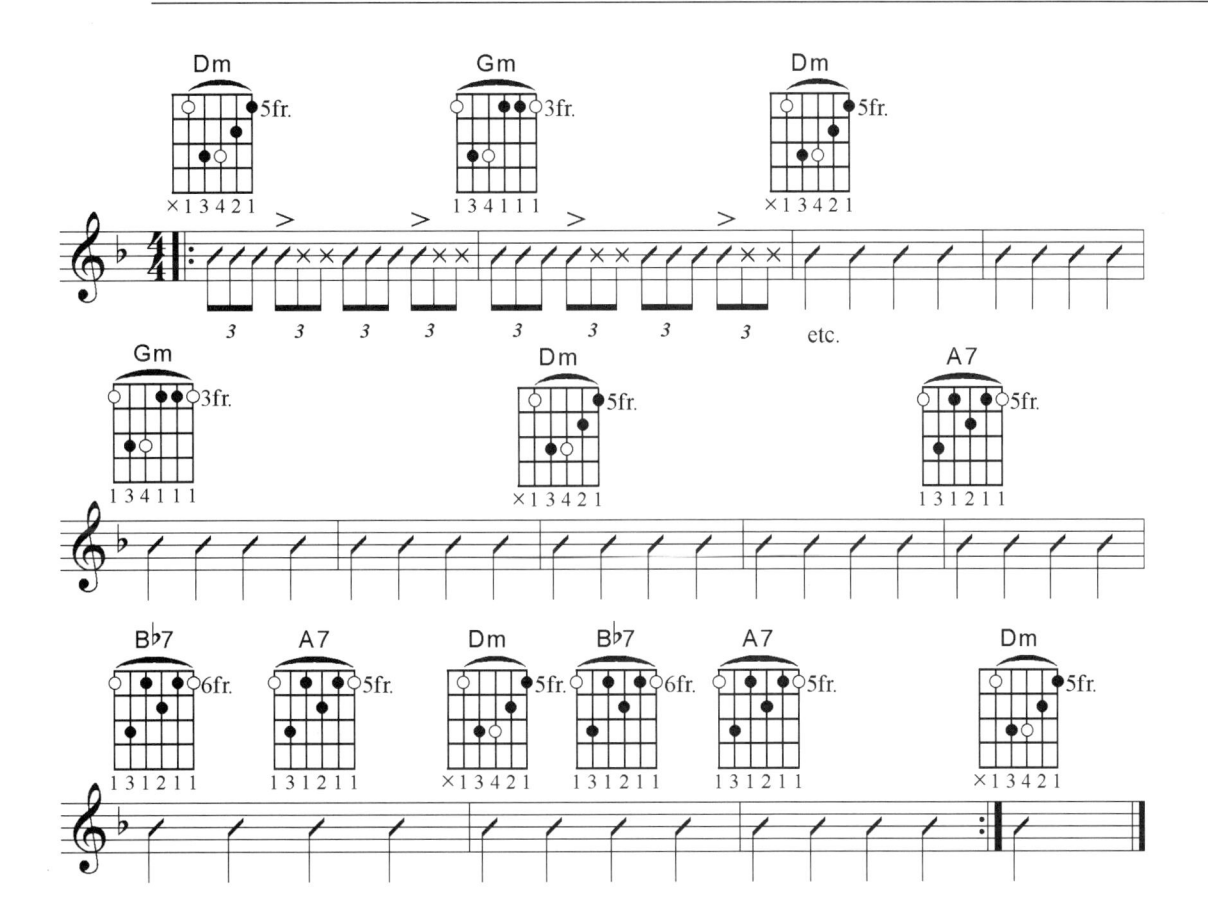

Another Version of the Minor Blues

The Im chord is sometimes changed to a I7 chord in the fourth measure, to move more strongly to the IVm chord at bar 5.

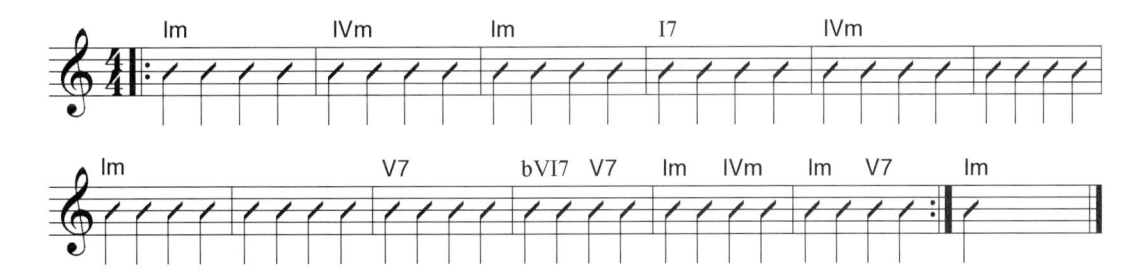

177

Guitar for Songwriters

Blues #11, in F Minor

In the key of F minor, this means bar 4 will be an F7. The fourth beat of each measure receives a strong accent on muted strings in this example.

> You can hear this example in the Example52 audio file at http://cengageptr.com/guitarforsongwriters.

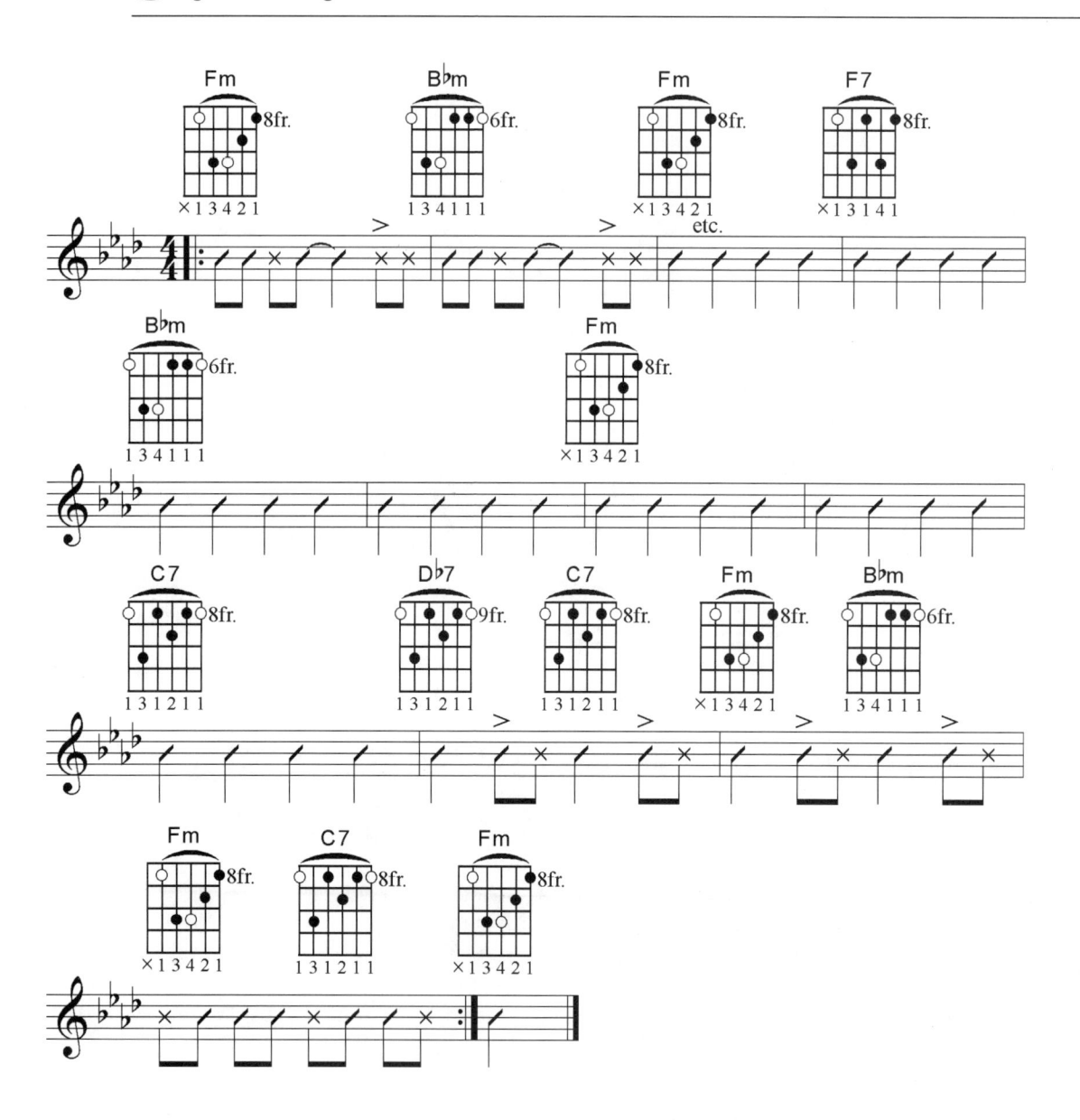

Chapter 12 The Blues

Playing the Blues with Three- and Four-String Chords

Playing fewer strings of a chord often can be quite effective. A chord played on the first three or four strings has a bright sound that can cut through and be heard easily, without interfering with the bass player. And with fewer strings, they can be much easier to hold than a six-string bar chord.

As said before, a chord needs to have certain notes in it, but they can be in any order. The voicings given in the following sections are stripped-down versions of the chords—very few notes are repeated. Many of these chords do not have the root in the bass, so they may not be as strong when played unaccompanied.

Blues #12, with Smaller Chords

This example of a blues in the key of C stays around the eighth position. The C chord is a shortened version of the Form 1 bar chord. The F is barred with the third finger, an easy transition from the C chord.

You can hear this example in the Example53 audio file at http://cengageptr.com/guitarforsongwriters.

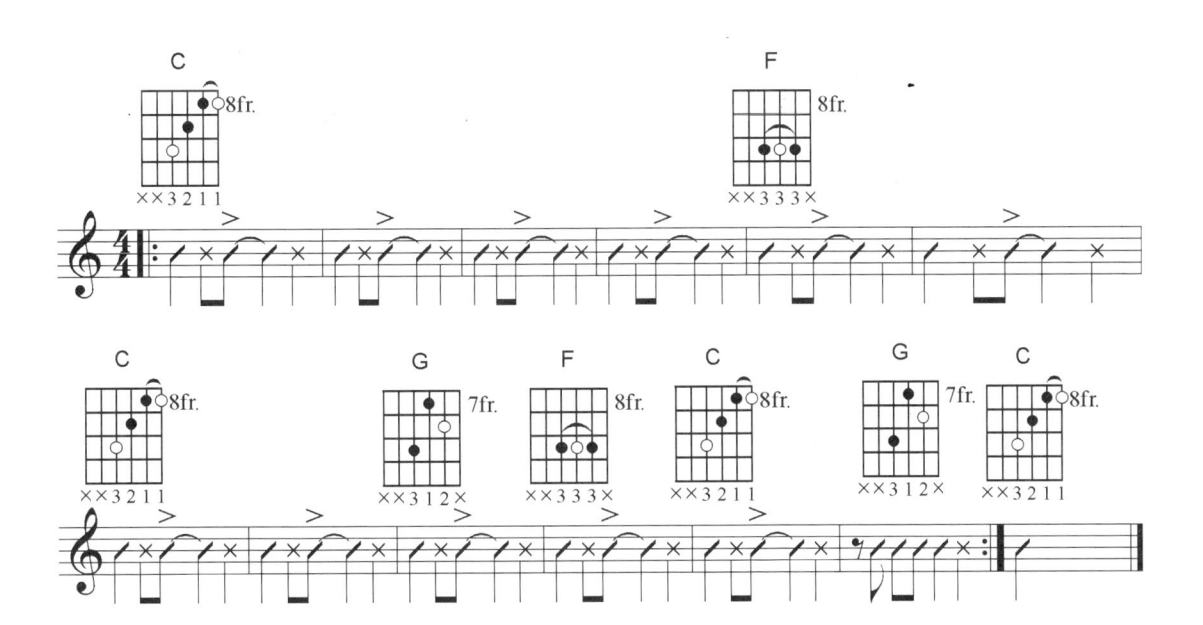

Blues #13, with Three-String Chords

Here is another example in the key of C, centered around the fifth position. The C chord, although equivalent to the F chord in the previous example (barring the second, third, and fourth strings), is now held with the first finger. It is related to the Form 2 bar chord.

You can hear this example in the Example54 audio file at http://cengageptr.com/guitarforsongwriters.

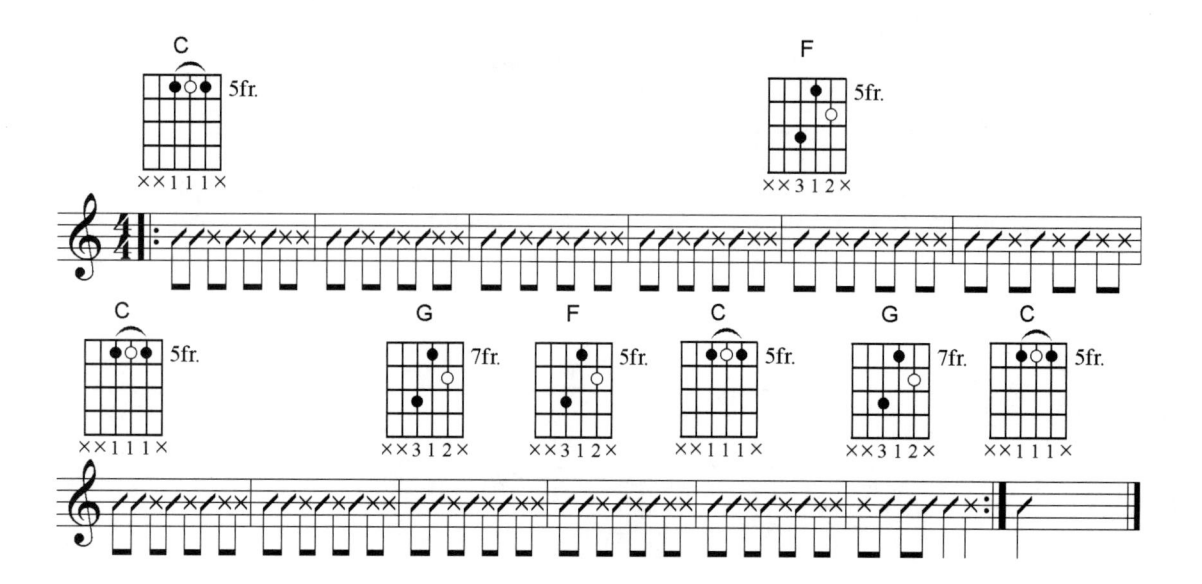

Chapter 12 The Blues

Blues #14, with Four-String Chords

The next example is in the key of F. The first chord is a shortened version of the Form 3 major chord. The beat is the Bo Diddley strum given earlier in the section on muting.

🎸 You can hear this example in the Example55 audio file at http://cengageptr.com/guitarforsongwriters.

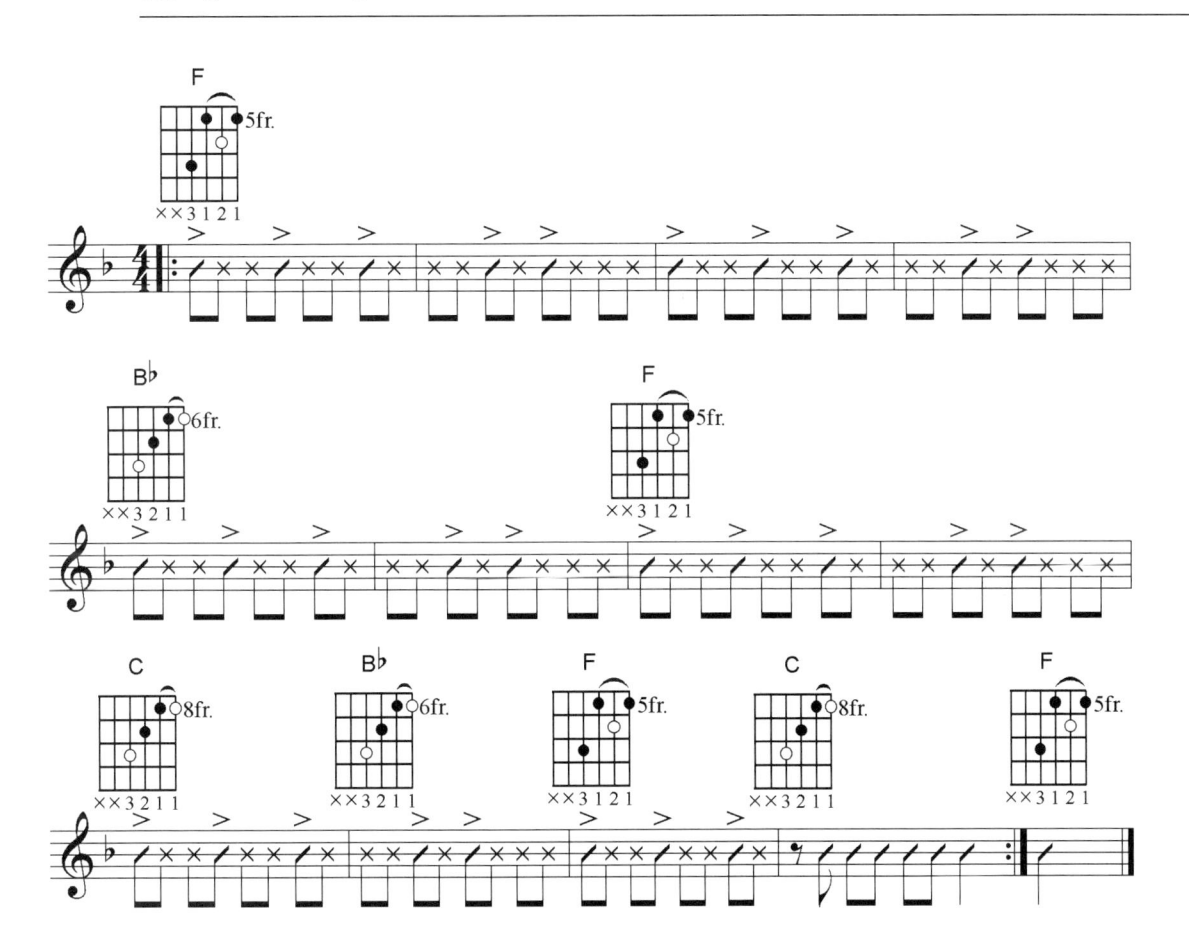

181

Guitar for Songwriters

Blues #15, with Two-String Chords

Here is a way to play chords to a blues using only two strings. With a bass player covering the root of each chord, you can play the thirds and sevenths and never move more than two frets. The audio track on the website includes guitar on one channel and bass on the other.

> You can hear this example in the Example56 audio file at http://cengageptr.com/guitarforsongwriters.

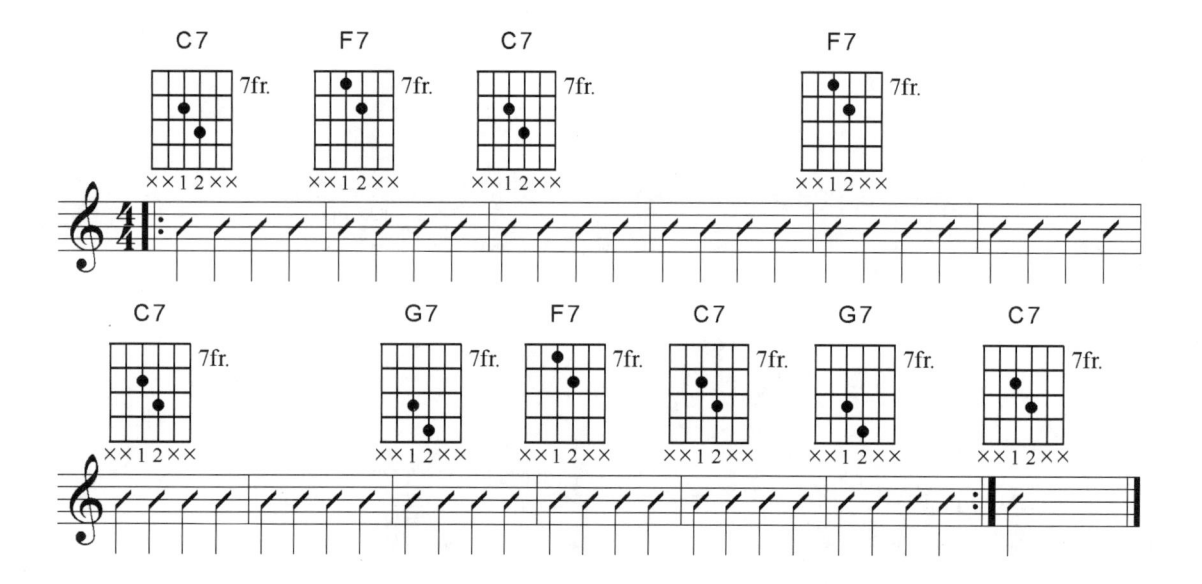

Chapter 12 The Blues

Blues #16, with Sliding, Muting, and Bass Notes

Here is a 12-bar blues in the key of C, incorporating many of the ideas covered so far. It uses three-string chords, with bass notes, sliding, and muting. If the chord diagram is not shown, use the same voicing as earlier.

You can hear this example in the Example57 audio file at http://cengageptr.com/guitarforsongwriters.

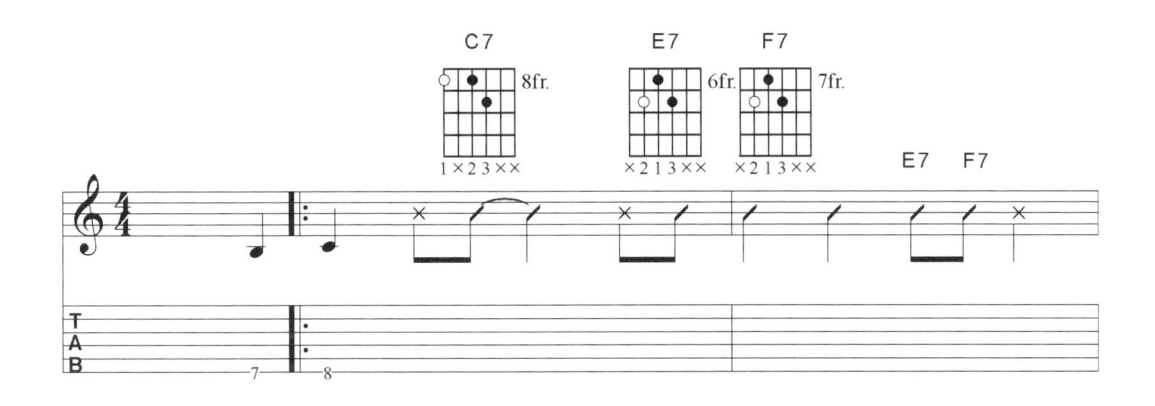

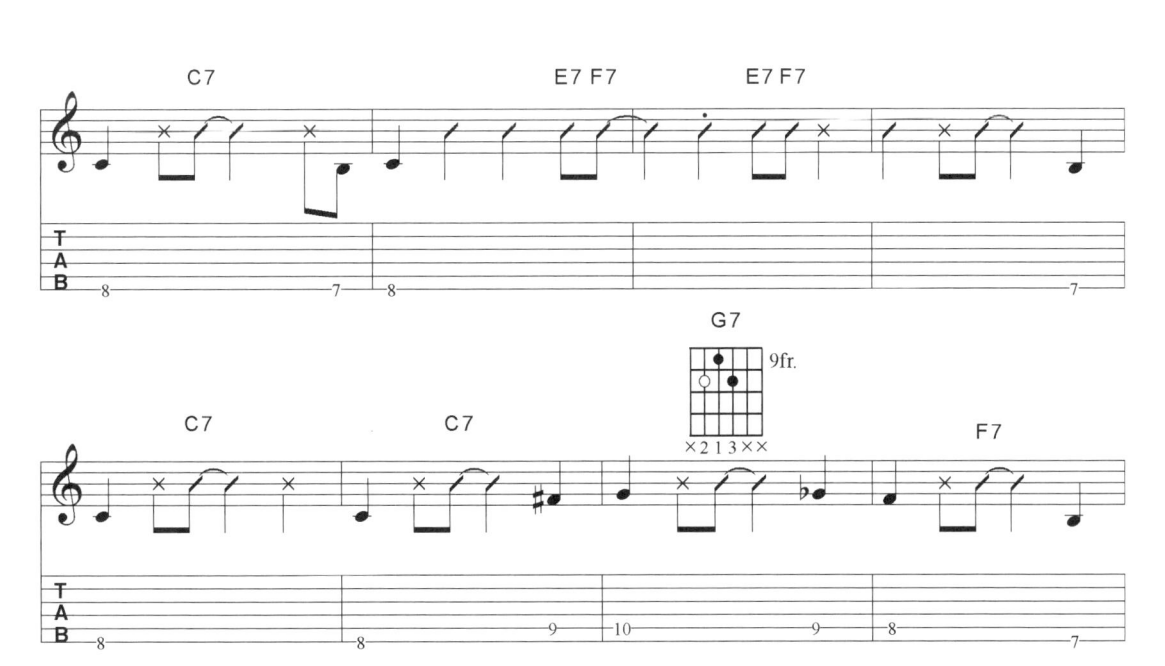

Guitar for Songwriters

The Blues and Tenth Chords

Count Basie's longtime guitarist Freddie Green was renowned for setting the groove that helped make Basie famous. Playing an unamplified guitar, he provided a rhythmic and harmonic underpinning that had to compete with saxes, trombones, and trumpets. And most of the chords he played had only three strings.

Tenth chords are the voicings favored by Green and others seeking a chord that can cut through while playing acoustically without sounding muddy. A full bar chord would not sound so clear in this setting, and it would be much more tiring to play.

This type of chord is called a *tenth chord* because the interval between the highest and lowest notes is a tenth (an octave and a third). They are generally open voicings, meaning that the notes are not arranged in their closest possible order, but have opened up the spacing by raising the second note an octave.

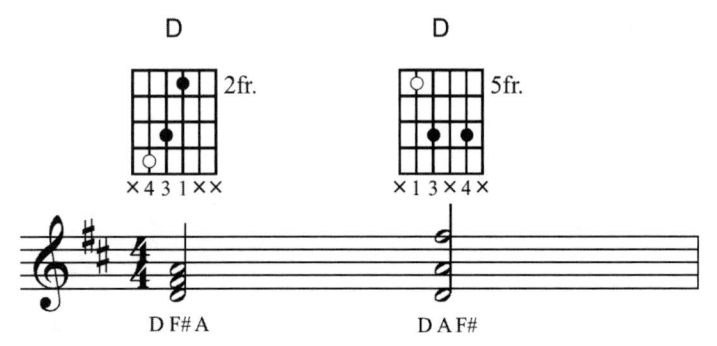

The chord on the left has the notes as close together as possible. The version on the right opens up that voicing, with the interval of a tenth between the highest and lowest notes.

Compare the D chord, with the notes D, F♯, and A in that order, with the tenth chord voicing obtained by raising the F♯ an octave. Hit them both equally hard, and you will hear how the tenth chord projects better while defining all the notes clearly. (You can lean your fingers slightly to mute the first and third strings on the tenth chord.)

The blues played using tenth chords is a great exercise in voice leading and in embellishing and substituting chords. Compare it to the jazz changes for a blues. In the tenth-chord example, there is a new chord on practically every beat. The first measure is a good example of what to play if you are on a major chord (in this case, F) and want to add a little movement. The basic chord for this measure is F, even though there are some passing chords in the middle. The last two bars demonstrate a way to play a turnaround in the key of F. Compare the whole blues to the more standard blues changes, and you will find some substitutions you may be able to apply elsewhere. (Notice that this is still only 12 bars long, but there is a lot going on.)

When is the proper time to use tenth chords? Most often, when you are playing primarily acoustic-based music, often with a swing beat. It can be a refreshing change in the middle of an extended blues or jazz standard to switch to tenth chords for a chorus or two. To bring out that swing feel, strike the strings more firmly on the second and fourth beats of each measure.

Another time to try tenth chords is when you are playing acoustically and are having a hard time finding enough volume for the situation. These chords often project better than chords using more strings.

Chapter 12 The Blues

Blues #17, with Tenth Chords

This blues has a different chord on almost every beat! This sounds very different from the other blues in the chapter, but a distinctive sound can be very refreshing.

You can hear this example in the Example58 audio file at http://cengageptr.com/guitarforsongwriters.

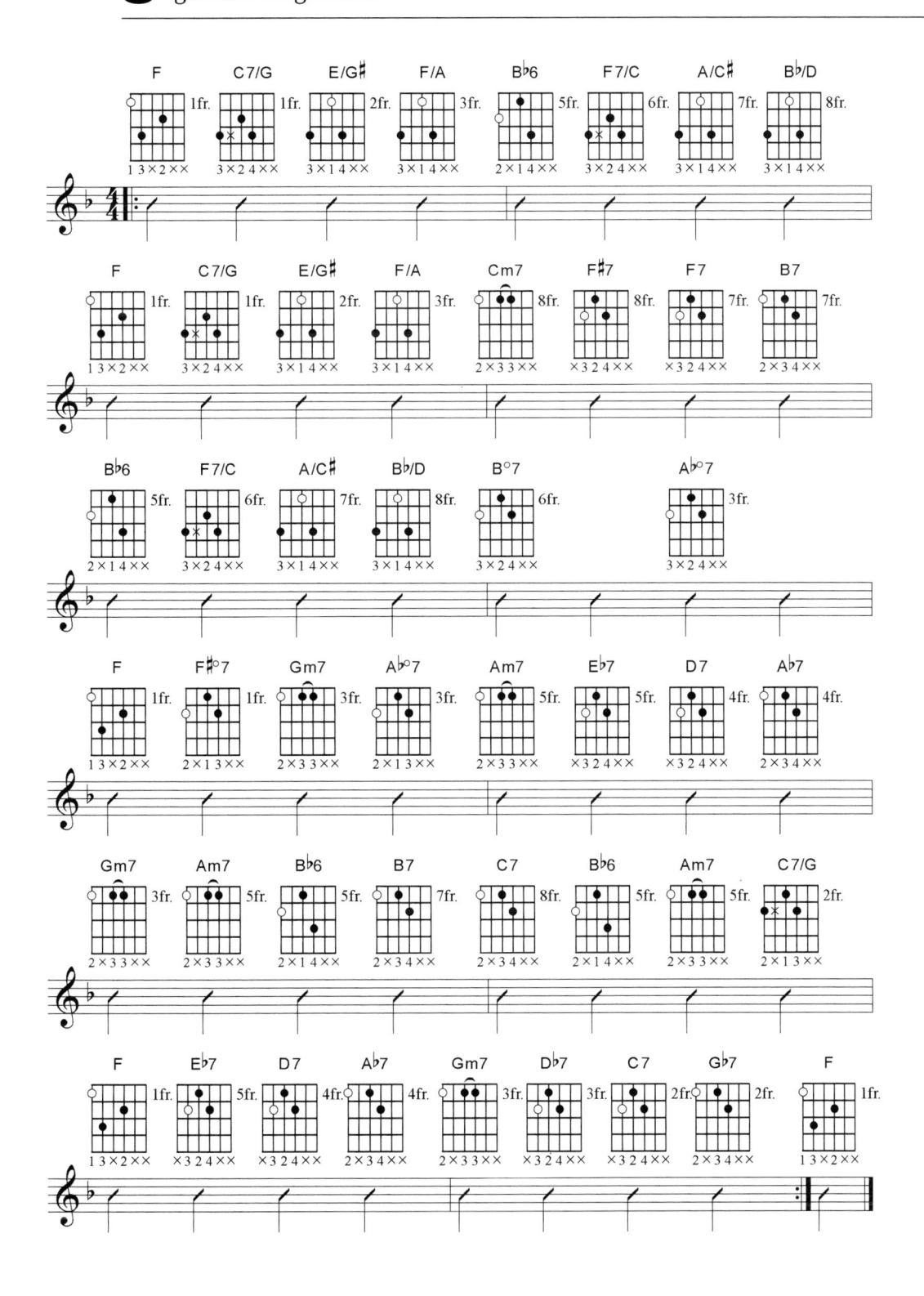

Guitar for Songwriters

Jazz Changes for the Blues

Jazz musicians play the 12-bar blues frequently, but they often use substitute changes. Here is one of many ways the blues might be played in jazz.

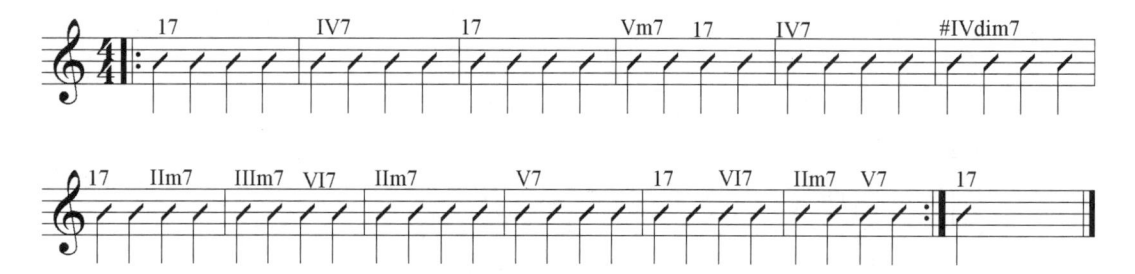

Blues #18, with Jazz Changes

This is a basic outline that can be altered in many ways. Jazz musicians like to embellish chords with extra notes. Ninths and thirteenths are sometimes played for 7th chords. Ninths may be sharped or flatted on occasion, and fifths are also altered. It takes a lot of experience and experimentation to determine when chords can be embellished or altered.

You can hear this example in the Example59 audio file at http://cengageptr.com/guitarforsongwriters.

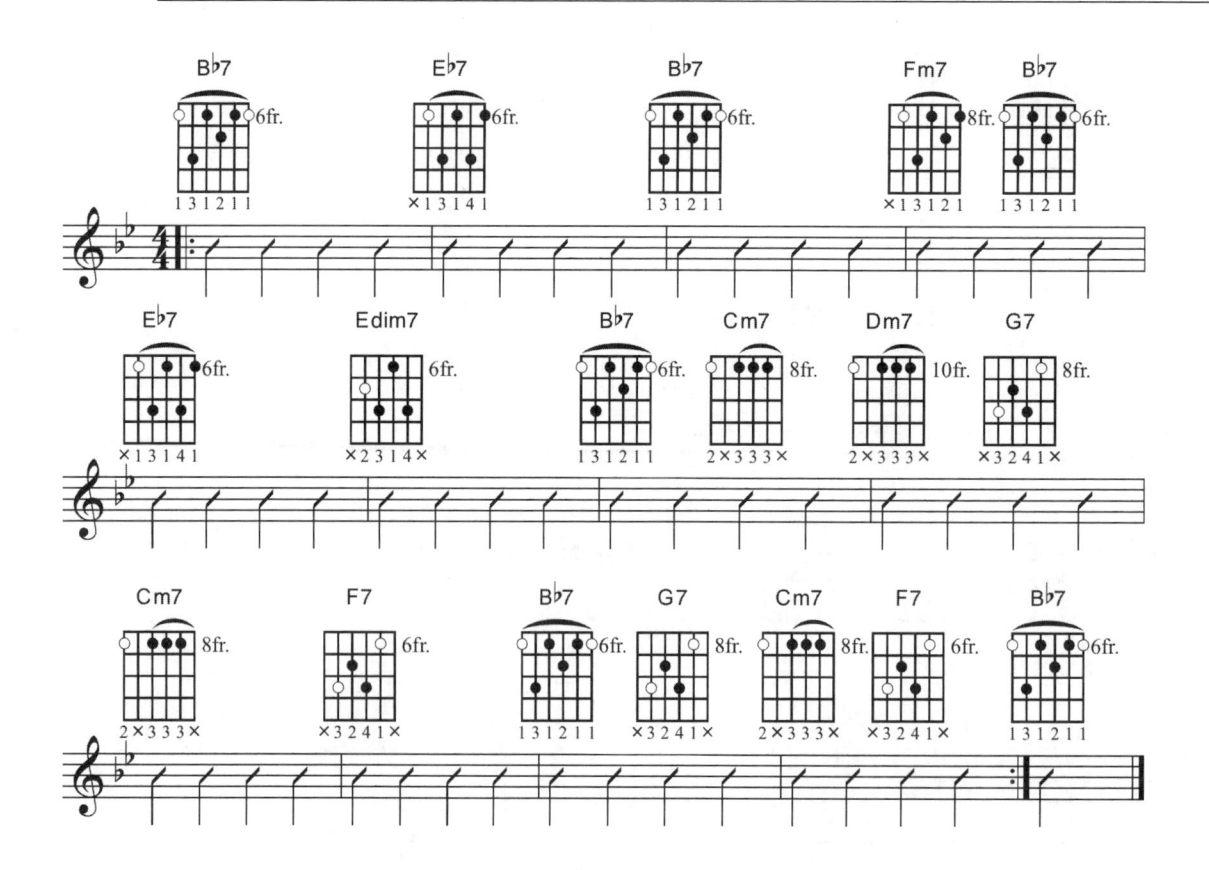

Chapter 12 The Blues

The jazz changes make frequent use of the IIm7-V7 progressions, which are examined in depth elsewhere in this book. The Vm7-I7 change in measure 4 approaches the IV chord by a IIm7-V7 progression. For example, for a blues in C, bars 4 and 5 would be Gm7-C7-F7. In the key of F, IIm7-V7-I would be the same progression, Gm7-C7-F. In bar 8, the IIIm7-VI7 progression is IIm7-V7 into the IIm7 chord. Instead of V7 to IV in bars 9 and 10, the jazz version often uses IIm7 to V7.

Instead of two measures of the IV chord at bars 5 and 6, there is only one measure, followed by a ♯IV diminished chord. This is really only one note different from the IV7 chord. (Read the section on diminished chords for more details.)

Another aspect of playing the jazzy version of the blues is the use of *anticipations*. Many chords are actually played a half-beat early—on the "and" of beat four, rather than right on the first beat of the measure.

You can hear this example in the Example60 audio file at http://cengageptr.com/guitarforsongwriters.

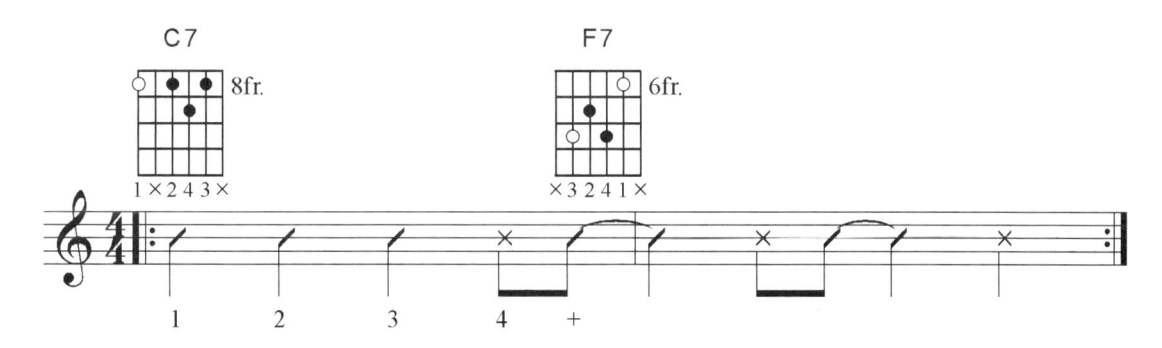

Chords are sometimes approached from a half-step above or below, as in the example below. Again, this is something best learned by experimenting.

You can hear this example in the Example61 audio file at http://cengageptr.com/guitarforsongwriters.

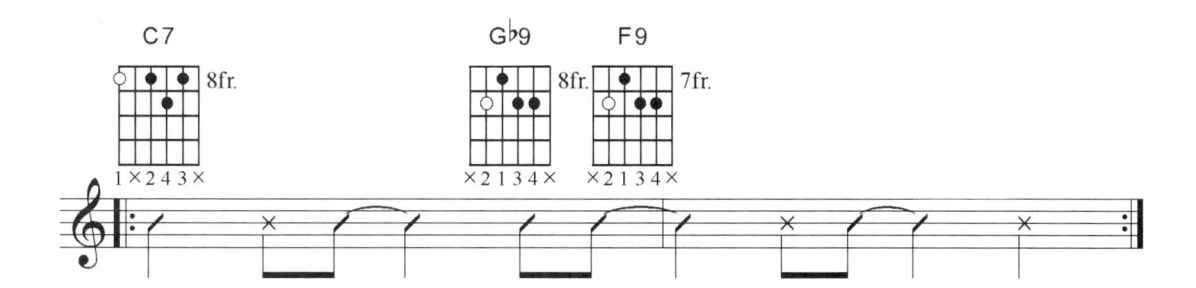

Guitar for Songwriters

Blues #19, with Anticipations

The following set of jazz changes for the blues is in the key of G. The chords have only three or four strings, making them easy to grab quickly. Use a light touch and try to swing. Transpose this into as many keys as are practical.

> You can hear this example in the Example62 audio file at http://cengageptr.com/guitarforsongwriters.

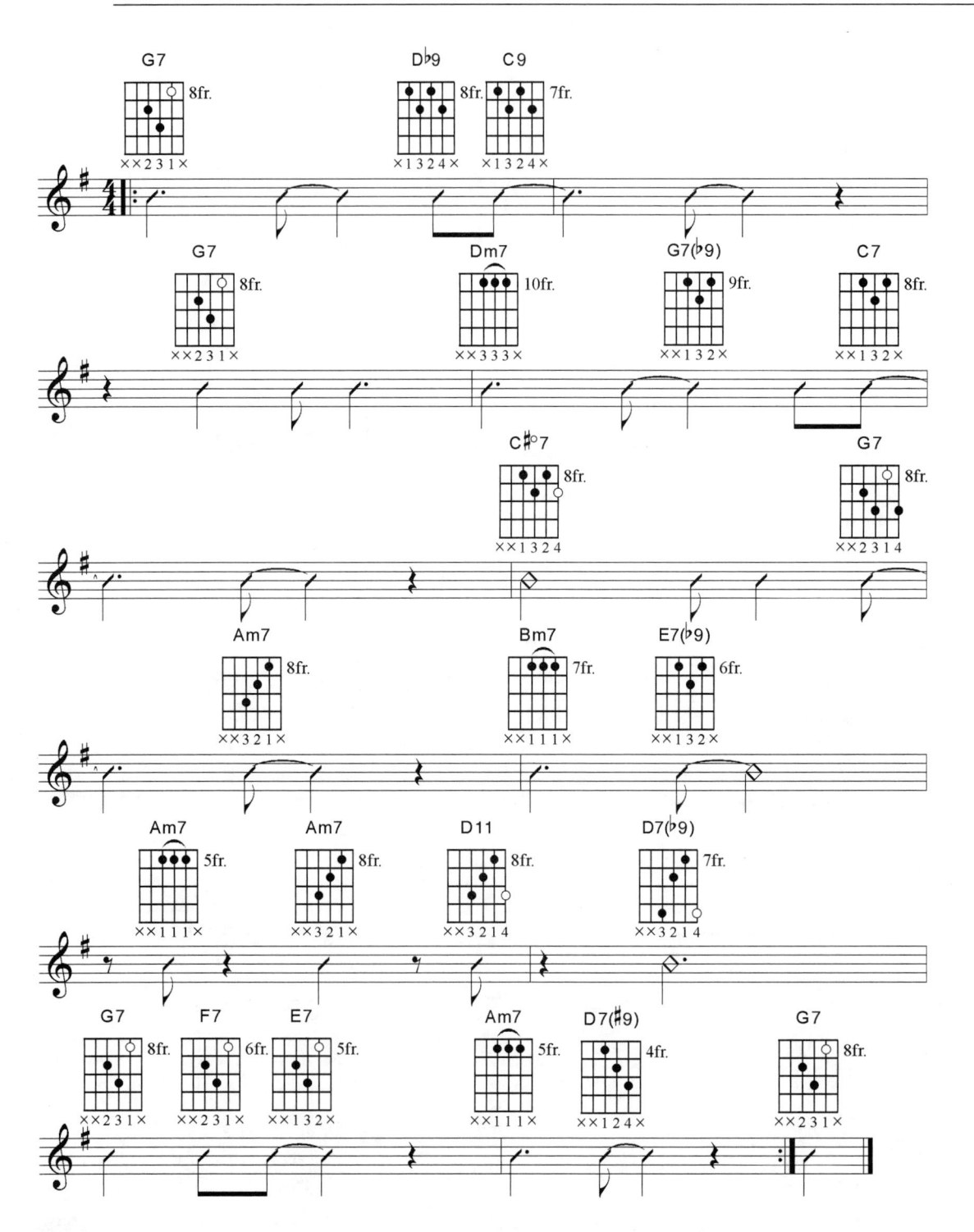

Chapter 12 The Blues

Another Set of Jazz Changes for the Blues

Here is another way a jazz musician might play the blues. Try this in different keys, and try switching around the 7th, 9th, and 13th chords. Take a few measures from the earlier example and see whether they will fit in this version.

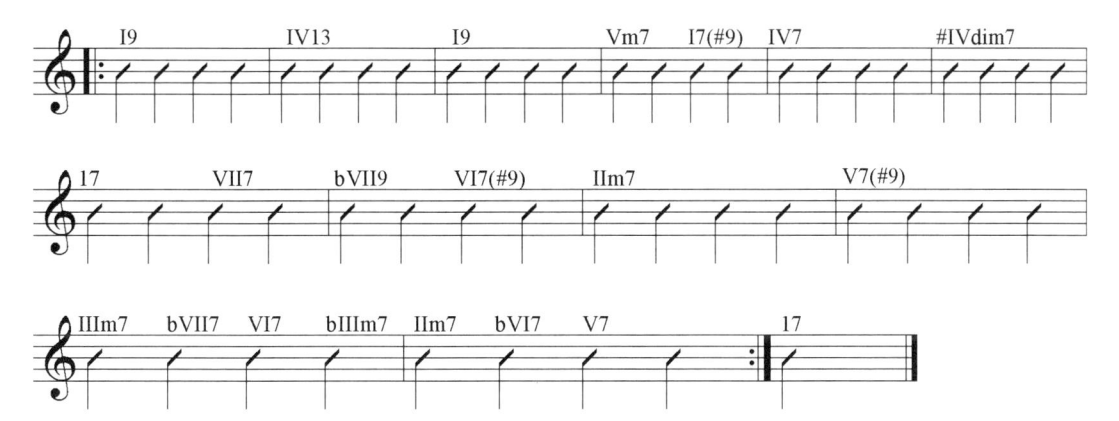

I9	IV13	I9	Vm7 I7(#9)	IV7 #IVdim7

I7	VII7 bVII9	VI7(#9) IIm7	V7(#9)

IIIm7 bVII7 VI7 bIIIm7	IIm7 bVI7 V7	I7

The next page gives you the last of 20 versions of the blues. They have been in various keys, with different chord voicings and with different beats and feels. Use them as inspiration for your own songwriting, as starting points for your own creation. Let them help you break out of old habits and step out of your comfort zone. And don't forget to have fun!

Guitar for Songwriters

Blues #20, with More Jazz Changes

In the key of G, this could be played as in the following example.

You can hear this example in the Example63 audio file at http://cengageptr.com/guitarforsongwriters.

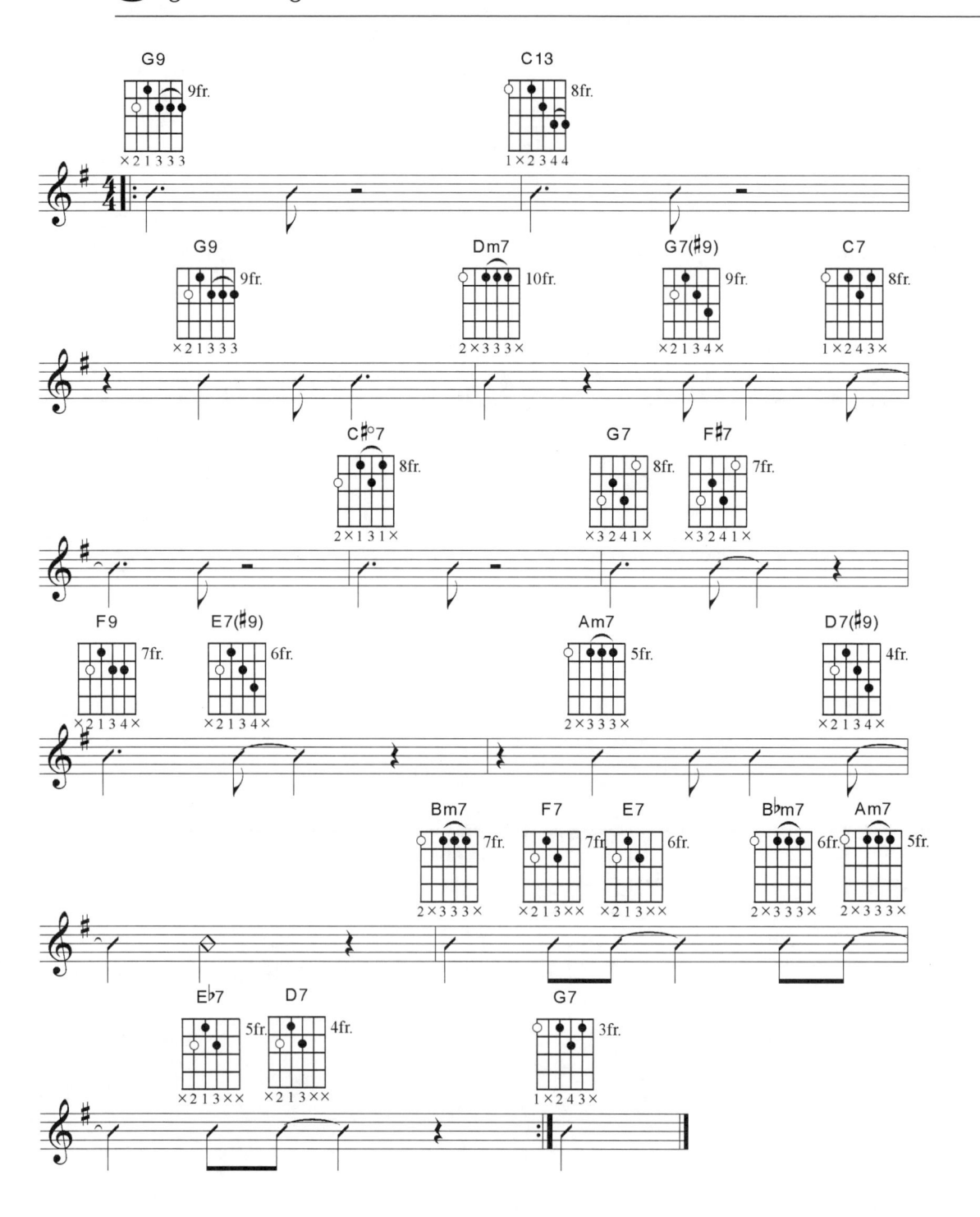

Index

Numerics

6/9 chord formula, 118
7(♯5) chord formula, 128
7(♯5♯9) chord formula, 130
7(♯5♭9) chord formula, 130
7(♯9) chord formula, 129
7(♯9♯11) chord formula, 131
7(♯11) chord formula, 130
7(♭) chord formula, 127–128
7(♭5♯9) chord formula, 130
7(♭5♭9) chord formula, 129
7(♭9) chord, 129, 156–157
7(♭9♯11) chord formula, 131
7(♭13) chord formula, 131
7sus4 chord formula, 131
7sus4(♭9) chord formula, 132
9(♯5) chord formula, 128
9(♯11) chord formula, 130
9(♭) chord formula, 128
9th chord formula, 126
11th chord formula, 127
12-bar blues, 167–169
13(♯11) chord formula, 131
13(♭5) chord formula, 131
13(♭9) chord formula, 131
13sus4(♭9) chord formula, 132
13th chord formula, 127

A

A key
  harmonized scale, 27
  I, IV, and V, 12
  I, IV, and V bar chords, 89
  IIm7-V7-IMaj7 pattern, 136
A minor, blues progression, 176
A♭ key
  harmonized scale, 27
  I, IV, and V bar chords, 89
  IIm7-V7-IMaj7 pattern, 136
A♭m key
  harmonized minor scale, 33
  II-V-I progression, 146
accents and muting, 44–45
accidentals, 125
accompaniment styles
  bass notes, 46–47
  blues, 57
  country, 57
  descending bass lines, 47–48
  fingerpicking, 48–55
  Latin, 57
  muting and accents, 44–45
  reggae/ska, 56–57
  rock, 56
  strumming chords, 43–44
  swing, 56
"All I Have to Do Is Dream," 29–30
alterations, 125, 162
Am key
  harmonized minor scale, 33
  II-V-I progression, 146
augmented chords
  as dominant 7th chord in minor key, 158–159
  most common, 158
  as passing chords, 159–160

B

B key
  harmonized scale, 27
  I, IV, and V bar chords, 89
  IIm7-V7-IMaj7 pattern, 136
backbeat, 56
bar (barre), 59
bar chords
  all forms, 82–85
  basic, 59
  exercise, 64–67
  F♯, 60
  F major chord with no open strings, 60
  finding I, IV, and V quickly with, 87–88
  Form 1, 60–66, 82
  Form 2, 68–74, 82
  Form 3, 74–80, 82
  G major, 60
  harmonized scale progressions, 85–87
  I-IV-I-V7 pattern, 90–91
  I-IV-V7-IV pattern, 89–90
  I-V7-IV-V7 pattern, 91–92
  muting, 67–68
  with root on fifth and second string, 74–75
  with root on fifth string, 68–74
  with root on sixth, fourth, and first strings, 62
  with root on sixth string, 60–61
  tips and techniques, 63–64
  to transpose, 82–83
basic bar chords, 59
basic major chords, 2–4
basic minor chords, 4–6
basic seventh chords, 6–7
bass notes, 46–47, 175, 183
B♭ key
  harmonized scale, 27
  I, IV, and V bar chords, 89
  IIm7-V7-IMaj7 pattern, 136
B♭m key
  harmonized minor scale, 33
  II-V-I progression, 146
blues style, 57
  12-bar blues, 167–169
  basic progression, 167
  with bass notes, 175
  in D minor, 177
  with dominant 7th chords, 173–175
  in F minor, 178
  Form 1 bar chords, 168–169
  Form 2 bar chords, 169

Index

blues style (*Continued*)
Form 3 bar chords, 173
four-string chords, 181
jazz changes for, 186–190
in A minor, 176
in minor keys, 175–176
with power chords, 171
with shuffle rhythm, 171
with sliding, muting, and bass notes, 183
and tenth chords, 184–185
three-string chords, 180
triplet feel, 170
two-string chords, 182
"bluesy" sound, 6
bm key
harmonized minor scale, 33
II-V-I progression, 146
bossa nova, 57
"Brown-Eyed Girl," 14

C

C key
harmonized scale, 27
I, IV, and V, 12
I, IV, and V bar chords, 88
IIM7-V7-IMaj7 pattern, 136
C♯ key
harmonized scale, 27
IIm7-V7-IMaj7 pattern, 136
C♭ key
harmonized scale, 27
IIm7-V7-IMaj7 pattern, 136
chord construction
dominant 7th chord, 99–100
how chords are built, 93–94
I-IV-V7-IV up the neck, 106–109
Im-IVm-V7-IVm up the neck, 112–114
major chords, 94–95
minor chords, 97–98
notes to omit, 103
chord diagrams, 1
chord formulas
basic description, 115
dominant 7th chord, 124–132
major chord, 115–119
minor chord, 119–124
chords
augmented, 158–160
diminished, 151–157
embellishing, 141
half-diminished, 123
inversions, 102
moving voices within, 162–163
related pairs of, 103
simplifying, 160–161

substitution, 141–146
suspended, 131
"chunk-chuck" sound, 96
circle of fifths, 133–135
close voicing, 102
Cm key
harmonized minor scale, 33
II-V-I progression, 146
C♯m key
harmonized minor scale, 33
II-V-I progression, 146
country style, 57
"Crimson and Clover," 15–16

D

D key
harmonized scale, 27
I, IV, and V, 12
I, IV, and V bar chords, 88
IIm7-V7-IMaj 7 pattern, 136
D minor, blues progression, 177
D♭ key
harmonized scale, 27
I, IV, and V bar chords, 88
IIm7-V7-IMaj7 pattern, 136
D♭m key, 146
descending bass lines, 47–48
diminished chords
examples and list of, 151–153
♯IV, 155
as passing chords, 154–155
in place of 7(♭9) chords, 156–157
primary uses, 153
Dm key, harmonized minor scale, 33
dominant 7th chord, 124–132. *See also* seventh chord
augmented chords as, 158–159
bar chords with root on fifth and second strings, 76
bar chords with root on fifth string, 70
bar chords with root on sixth and first strings, 63
blues progression, 173–175
chord construction, 99–100
Form 1, 2, and 3, 82
simplifying, 161
voicing, 100–102
dominant chord, 11
down strum, 43–44

E

E key
harmonized scale, 27
I, IV, and V, 12
I, IV, and V bar chords, 88
IIm7-V7-IMaj7 pattern, 136

E♭ key
harmonized scale, 27
I, IV, and V bar chords, 88
IIm7-V7-IMaj7 pattern, 136
E♭m key
harmonized minor scale, 33
II-V-I progression, 146
eighth notes, 43
Em key, II-V-I progression, 146
extensions, 125, 162

F

F♯ bar chord, 60, 89
F key
harmonized scale, 27
I, IV, and V bar chords, 89
IIm7-V7-IMaj7 pattern, 136
F♯ key
harmonized scale, 27
IIm7-V7-IMaj7 pattern, 136
F minor, blues progression, 178
fifth string, bar chords with root on, 68, 70–74, 90
fingerpicking
all fingers playing on first beat, 55
eighth notes with bass note on beats one and three, 53–54
right-hand fingers, 48
ring and middle fingers playing at same time, 50–51
three-four time, 55
thumb, middle, and ring fingers playing in sequence, 48–50
thumb only on first beat of measure, 52–54
two notes being played at once, 54
first inversion, 102
Fm key
harmonized minor scale, 33
II-V-I progression, 146
F♯m key
harmonized minor scale, 33
II-V-I progression, 146
Form 1 bar chords, 60–66, 82, 168–169
Form 2 bar chords, 68–74, 169
Form 3 bar chords, 74–80, 82, 173
four-string chords, blues style, 181
fourth and fifth strings, power chords on, 39–41

G

G key
harmonized scale, 27
I, IV, and V, 12
IIM7-V7-IMaj7 pattern, 136

Index

G♭ key
  harmonized scale, 27
  I, IV, and V bar chords, 89
  IIm7-V7-IMaj7 pattern, 136
G♭m key, II-V-I progression, 146
Gm key
  harmonized minor scale, 33
  II-V-I progression, 146
G♯m key
  harmonized minor scale, 33
  II-V-I progression, 146

H
half-step, 61
half-diminished chords, 123
harmonized scale
  in all keys, 27
  common progressions in minor key, 34–36
  Form 1 and 2 bar chords, 85–87
  minor keys, 33–36
  Roman numeral representation, 25–26
"Hey Jude," 4

I
I, IV, and V chords
  with bar chords, 87–88
  key of B, 12
  key of C, 11
  key of D, 11
  key of F, 12
  major chords, 13–16
  minor chords, 16–19
  in minor keys, 109–112
  with mixed chords, 22–23
  progression of keys, 12
  Roman number representation, 11
  with seventh chords, 19–22
IIm7-V7 progressions, 137–138
IIm7-V7-Im7 progressions and substitutions, 147–150
IIm7-V7-IMaj7 exercises, 139–140
IIm7-V7-IMaj7 pattern, 136
IIm7-V7-IMaj7 substitutions, 141–146
II-V-I progression
  circle of fifths, 133–135
  jazz chords, 133
  in minor keys, 146
Im-IVm examples, 109–112
inversions, 102
I-V-IV-V chord progression, 15–16

J
jazz chords
  circle of fifths, 133–135
  embellishing chords, 141
  IIm7-V7 progressions, 137–138
  IIm7-V7-IMaj7 exercises, 139–140
  II-V-I progression, 133–136
  jazz changes for blues style, 186–190
  substituting chords, 141–146

L
latin style, 57
"Like a Rolling Stone," 28
"Louie, Louie," 13

M
major 6th chord formula, 117
major 7th chord formula, 117–119
major 9th chord formula, 117–119
major 13th chord formula, 118
major chords
  bar chords with root on fifth and second strings, 76
  bar chords with root on fifth and third strings, 70
  bar chords with root on sixth, fourth, and first strings, 62
  basic, 2–4
  chord construction, 94–95
  chord formulas, 115–119
  description of, 1
  Form 1, 2, and 3, 82
  I, IV, and V, 13–16
  mixing with minor and seventh chords, 8–10
  notes in, 95
  simplifying, 161
  voicing, 95–97
mambo, 57
minor 6/9 chord formula, 122
minor 6th chord formula, 121
minor 6th (major 7th) chord formula, 124
minor 7th chord formula, 120–121, 123
minor 9th chord formula, 122
minor 9th (major 7th) chord formula, 124
minor 11th chord formula, 123
minor chords
  bar chords with root on fifth and third strings, 70
  bar chords with root on second string, 76
  bar chords with root on sixth, fourth, and first strings, 62
  basic, 4–6
  blues progression, 175–176
  chord construction, 97–98
  chord formulas, 119–124
  description of, 1
  Form 1, 2, and 3, 82
  harmonized scale, 33–36
  I, IV, and V in, 16–19
  II-V-I progression, 146
  mixing with major and seventh chords, 8–10
  with moving voices, 163–166
  simplifying, 161
  voicing, 98–99
minor (major 7th) chord formula, 123
mixed chords, 22–23
moving voices
  within chords, 162–163
  minor chords with, 163–166
muting, 44–45
  bar chords, 67–68
  blues style with, 183

N
notes, in major chords, 95

O
open voicing, 96, 102

P
Pass, Joe (guitarist), 115
passing chords
  augmented chords as, 159–160
  diminished chords as, 154–155
power chords, 41–42
  blues progression, 171
  first and fifth notes in C major scale, 37
  first and fifth notes in D major scale, 37
  on fourth and fifth strings, 39–41
  three-string, 38

R
reggae/ska style, 56–57
rhumba, 57
right hand fingerpicking, 48
rock style, 56
Roman number representation
  harmonized scale, 25–26
  I, IV, and V chords, 11
roots
  bar chords with root on fifth string, 68–69
  bar chords with root on sixth string, 60–61

Index

S
salsa, 57
samba, 57
second inversion, 102
seventh chords. *See also* dominant 7th chord
    basic, 6–7
    description of, 1
    I, IV, and V with, 19–22
    mixing with minor and major chords, 8–10
shuffle rhythm, 171
simplifying chords, 160–161
sixth string, bar chords with root on, 60–61
slash chords, 47–48
sliding, blues style with, 183
staccato, 44
strong backbeat, 56
strumming chords, 43–44
subdominant chord, 11
substitution, chord, 141–146
suspended chords, 131, 161
swing style, 56
syncopation, 57

T
tablature notation, 49
tenth chord, 96, 184–185
three-sting power chord, 38
three-string chords, blues style, 180
tonic chord, 11
transpose, using bar chords to, 82–83
transposing instruments, 26
triplets, 170
two-string chords, blues style, 182

U
up strum, 43–44

V
V chords. *See also* I, IV, and V chords
♯V diminished chord, 155
voice leading, 102
voicing
    basic description, 94
    chord construction, 102–103
    close, 102
    dominant 7th chord, 100–102
    I-IV examples with, 103–106
    major chords, 95–97
    minor chords, 98–99
    open, 96, 102

W
"Walk Don't Run," 35–36
whole step, 61
"Wild Thing," 13

AUG 1 8 2016

HEWLETT-WOODMERE PUBLIC LIBRARY
3 1327 00619 7966

28 DAY LOAN
Hewlett-Woodmere Public Library
Hewlett, New York 11557

Business Phone 516-374-1967
Recorded Announcements 516-374-1667
Website www.hwpl.org